FRENCH-ENGLISH
ENGLISH-FRENCH
DICTIONARY

FRENCH-ENGLISH
ENGLISH-FRENCH
DICTIONARY

TOPHI BOOKS

Unit 5A, 202–208 New North Road,
London N1 7BJ, England

ENGLISH-FRENCH

DICTIONARY

ABBREVIATIONS

adj. adjective	*pron*. pronoun
adv. adverb	*qch*. quelque chose
art. article	*qn*. qulqu'un
conj. conjunction	*rel*. relative
dem. demonstrative	*s*. substantive
f. feminine	*sing*. singular
fig. figurative	*s.o.* someone
impers. impersonal	*sth*. something
inf. infinitive	*v.a.* active verb
int. interjection	*v.a. & n.* active and neuter
m. masculine	verb
pers. person	*v. aux.* auxiliary verb
pl. plural	*v.n.* neuter verb
poss. possessive	* irregular verb
pp. past participle	*prep*. preposition

Pronunciation

We give below a short, simple guide to French pronunciation, giving the French sounds and their description. Vowels or consonants that are equivalent to the English ones are not indicated in this list.

Letters	French key word	Description
a, à, â	la, là, bâtir	between *bag* and *bug*
ai, aî	chaise, maîtr	resembles *ai* in *chair*
an	dans	between the vowels of *ah* and *oh* with *n* nasalised
au	pause	as in *oh* but with no final *u*
c	a) café	before *a, o, u* pronounced as *k*
	b) ici	before *e, i, y* pronounced *s* as in *say*
ç	français	as *s* in *say*
ch	chambre	as *sh* in *she*
e	a) le, petit	as the unstressed vowel of *the, standard*
	b) derriere, m	(in a closed syllable) as *e i deck*
é	été	as in *day* but with no final *i*

è, ê	père, fête	resembles the vowels in *pear* or *mare* without diphthongization
eau	eau	as in *oh* but with no final *u*
en	enfant	between *ah* and *oh* with *n* nasalized
er	donner	as in *day* but with no final
eu	jeudi, leur	closer than *earth* or *sir* pronounced with the lips pouted
g	a) rouge	before *e, i, y* pronounced as *s* in *measure, usual*
	b) grand	as *g* in *grand, good*
gn	signe	as in *new* or *lenient*
h	homme	it is never pronounced in French
i	a) ici	tenser than English short *i*
	b) mise	as *ee* in *meet*
î	île	as *ee* in *meet*
ille	fille	as in *key* with *y* at the end
in	vin	resembles the sound in *tan* pronounced through the nose
o	jour	as *s* in *usual*
jô	mot, côte	as in *oh* but with no final *u*
œ	œil	closer than *earth* pronounced with the lips pouted
oi	moi	as in *memoir* (memwaa[1])
on	non, son	between *ah* and *oh* with *n* nasalized
ou, oû	rouge, goûter	short or long *oo* as in *foot* or
qu	quand, question	as *k* in English
r	rare	as a slightly rolled English *r*
s	a) son	usually *s* as in *say*
	b) maison	(between two vowels) *z* as in *zero*
th	thé	as *t* in English
tion	nation	always *sio* + nasal *n*
u, û	sur, sûr	no equivalent in English: round lips for *oo* and try to pronounce *ee*
un	brun	the vowel of *her, earth* with a nasal *n*
w	wagon	as *v* in English
x	a) deuxième	as *z* in *zero*
	b) six	as *s* in *say*
y	y	as short *i* in English

FRENCH GRAMMAR

L i a i s o n.—Final consonants are not usually pronounced, but in most cases, when a word begins with a vowel (or the mute *h*), it is linked with the last consonant of the preceding word. In such cases final *c* and *g* are pronounced as *k*, final *s* and *x* as *z*, e.g. les‿Anglais (lezangle).

S t r e s s.—In polysyllabic words stress usually falls on the last pronounced syllable, e.g. plusieurs, le docteur, la société.

The Article

The definite article is *le* (m.), *la* (f.), *les* (m. f. pl.). *Le*, *la* are shortened to *l'* before a vowel or mute *h*.

The indefinite article is *un* (m.), *une* (f.).

The Noun

The p l u r a l is generally formed in *s*. Nouns in *s*, *x*, and *z* do not change in the plural. Nouns in *au* and *eu* form their plurals in *x*, e.g. *joyau*, *joyaux*, *jeu*, *jeux*. Nouns in *al*, form their plurals in *aux*, e.g. *cheval*, *chevaux*.

There are two *genders* in French. Nearly all nouns ending in *e* mute are feminine, except those in *isme*, *age* and *iste*. Nearly all nouns ending in a consonant or a vowel other than *e* mute are masculine, except nouns in *tion* and *té*. Nouns in *er* form their f. in *ère* e.g. *laitier*, *laitière*. Nouns in *en*, *on* form their f. in *enne*, *onne*, e.g. *chien*, *chienne*, *lion*, *lionne*. Nouns in *eur* form their 'f. in *euse* except those in *ateur* which have *atrice*, e.g. *admirateur*, *admiratrice*.

The Adjective

The p l u r a l is generally formed in *s*. Adjectives in *s* or *x* do not change. Those in *al* usually form their plurals in *aux*, e.g. *principal*, *principaux*.

The f e m i n i n e is generally formed by adding *e* to the masculine form, e.g. *élégant*, *élégante*. Adjectives in *f* change *f* into *ve*, e.g. *vif*, *vive*. Those in *x* change *x* into *se*, e.g. *heureux*, *heureuse*. Adj. in *er* form their f. in *ère*, e.g. *amer*, *amère*. Those in *el*, *eil*, *en*, *et*, *on* double the final consonant before adding *e*, e.g. *bel*, *belle*, *bon*, *bonne*.

C o m p a r a t i v e.—'more ... than' or '... er than' is to be translated by 'plus ... que'; 'less ... than' by 'moins ... que'.

S u p e r l a t i v e.—'the most ...' or 'the ... st' is to be translated by 'le plus ...', 'la plus ...' or 'les plus ...'

The Pronoun

P e r s o n a l p r o n o u n s: je, tu, il, elle; nous, vous, ils, elles.—*Accusative:* me, te, le, la; nous, vous, les. *Dative:* me, te, lui; nous, vous, leur.—

After prep.. moi, toi, lui, elle; nous, vous, eux, elles.

Reflexive pronouns: me, te, se; nous, vous, se.

Possessive pronouns: le mien (la mienne, les miens, les miennes), le tien (la tienne, les tiens, les tiennes), le sien (la sienne, les siens, les siennes); le nôtre (la nôtre, les nôtres), le vôtre (la vôtre, les vôtres), le leur (la leur, les leurs).

Relative pronouns: who = qui, whom = que, whose = dont, which = qui or que, to whom = a qui.

Interrogative pronoun: who, whom = qui; what = que.

The Adverb

Most French adverbs are formed by adding *ment*, to the feminine form of the corresponding adjective, e.g. *facile, facile+ment, heureux, heureuse + ment*. Those in *ant* and *ent* form their adverbs in *amment* and *emment*, respectively, e.g. *patient — patiemment*.

The Verb

We give here the conjugation of the two auxilliaries (*avoir, être*) and of the verbs in -**er**, -**ir**, and -**re**, giving only the principal simple forms:

avoir *Pres. Ind.* j'ai, tu as, il a, nous avons, vous avez, ils ont; *Impf.* j'avais, tu avais, il avait, nous avions, vous aviez, ils avaient; *Fut.* j'aurai, tu auras, il aura, nous aurons, vous aurez, ils auront; *Cond.* j'aurais, tu aurais, il aurait, nous aurions, vous auriez, ils auraient; *Pres. Subj.* que j'aie, que tu aies, qu'il ait, que nous ayons, que vous ayez, qu'ils aient; *Imp.* aie, ayons, ayez; *Pres. Part.* ayant; *Past.Part.* eu.

être *Pres. Ind.* je suis, tu es, il est, nous sommes, vous êtes, ils sont; *Impf.* j'étais, tu étais, il était, nous étions, vous étiez, ils étaient; *Fut.* je serai, tu seras, il sera, nous serons, vous serez, ils seront; *Cond.* je serais, tu serais, il serait, nous serions, vous seriez, ils seraient; *Pres. Subj.* que je sois, que tu sois, qu'il soit, que nous soyons, que vous soyez, qu'il soient; *Imp.* sois, soyons, soyez; *Pres. Part.* étant; *Past. Part.* été.

donner *Pres. Ind.* je donne, tu donnes, il donne, nous donnons, vous donnez, ils donnent; *Impf.* je donnais, tu donnais, il donnait, nous donnions, vous donniez, ils donnaient; *Fut.* je donnerai, tu donneras, il donnera, nous donnerons, vous donnerez, ils donneront; *Cond.* je donnerais, tu donnerais, il donnerait, nous donnerions, vous donneriez, ils donneraient; *Pres. Subj.* que je donne, que tu donnes, qu'il donne, que nous donnions, que vous donniez, qu'ils donnent; *Imp.* donne, donnons, donnez; *Pres. Part.* donnant; *Past. Part.* donné.

finir *Pres. Ind.* je finis, tu finis, il finit, nous finissons,

vous finnissez, ils finissent;
finis, il finit, nous finissons,
vous finissez, ils finissent;
Impf. je finissais, tu finissais, il finissait, nous finissions, vous finissiez, ils
finissaient; *Fut.* je finirai,
tu finiras, il finira, nous
finirons, vous finirez, ils
finiront; *Cond.* je finirais, tu
finirais, il finirait, nous
finirions, vous finiriez, ils
finiraient; *Pres. Subj.* que je
finisse, que tu finisses, qu'il
finisse, que nous finissions,
que vous finissiez, qu'ils
finissent; *Imp.* finis, finissons, finissez; *Pres. Part.*
finissant; *Past Part.* fini.

rendre *Pres. Ind.* je rends, tu
rends, il rend, nous rendons,
vous rendez, ils rendent;
Impf. je rendais, tu rendais,
il rendait, nous rendions,
vous rendiez, ils rendaient;
Fut. je rendrai, tu rendras,
il rendra, nous rendrons,
vous rendrez, ils rendront;
Cond. je rendrais, tu rendrais, il rendrait, nous rendr-
ions, vous rendriez, ils
rendraient; *Pres. Subj.* que
je rende, que tu rendes, qu'il
rende, que nous rendions,
que vous rendiez, qu'ils
rendent; *Imp.* rends, rendons, rendez; *Pres. Part.*
rendant; *Past. Part.* rendu.

Irregular Verbs
Verbs in *-ger* add *e* before
endings in *a* and *o*. Verbs in
-eler, -eter double the *l* or *t*
before a mute *e*. Verbs having
an acute *é* in the last syllable
but one change for a grave *e*
when the ending begins with a
mute *e*. Verbs in *-yer* change *y*
into *i* before a mute *e*.

In the following list of the
most frequent French irregular verbs (the root verbs only)
the numbers indicate the principal tenses and forms in a
fixed order: 1. Present Indica-
tive; 2. Imperfect; 3. Future;
4. Present Subjunctive; 5. Imperative; 6. Present Participle; 7. Past Participle. (+
être, if *être* is used to form
the past tenses e.g. je suis
allé.)

absoudre 1. j'absous, tu
absous, il absout, nous ab-
solvons, vous absolvez, ils
absolvent; **2.** j'absolvais;
3. j'absoudrai; **4.** que
j'absolve; **5.** absous, absol-
vons, absolvez; **6.** absol-
vant; **7.** absous, absoute.

acquérir 1. j'acquiers, tu acquiers, il acquiert, nous
acquérons, vous acquérez,
ils acquièrent; **2.** j'acquér-
ais; **3.** j'acquerrai; **4.** que
j'acquière; **5.** acquiers, acquérons, acquérez; **6.** ac-
quérant; **7.** acquis.

aller 1. je vais, tu vas, il va,
nous allons, vous allez, ils
vont; **2.** j'allais; **3.** j'irai;
4. que j'aille, que nous all-
ions, qu'ils aillent; **5.** va,
allons, allez; **6.** allant; **7.**
allé (être).

assaillir 1. j'assaille, tu
assailles, il assaille, nous
assaillons, vous assaillez, ils
assaillent; **2.** j'assaillais;
3. j'assaillerai; **4.** que
j'assaille; **5.** assaille, assaillons, assaillez; **6.** assaillant;
7. assailli.

asseoir 1. j'assieds, tu assieds, il assied, nous asseyons, vous asseyez, ils asseyent *or* j'assois, tu assois, il assoit, nous assoyons, vous assoyez, ils assoient; 2. j'assayais *or* j'assoyais; 3. j'assiérai *or* j'assoierai; 4. que j'asseye *or* que j'assoie; 5. assieds, asseyons *or* assoyons, asseyez *or* assoyez; 6. asseyant *or* assoyant; 7. assis.

atteindre *as* **peindre.**

battre 1. je bats, tu bats, il bat, nous battons, vous battez, ils battent; 2. je battais; 3. je battrai; 4. que je batte; 5. bats, battons, battez; 6. battant; 7. battu.

boire 1. je bois, tu bois, il boit, nous buvons, vous buvez, ils boivent; 2. je buvais; 3. je boirai; 4. que je boive; 5. bois, buvons, buvez; 6. buvant; 7. bu.

bouillir 1. je bous, tu bous, il bout, nous bouillons, vous bouillez, ils bouillent; 2. je bouillais; 3. je bouillirai; 4. que je bouille; 5. bous, bouillons, bouillez; 6. bouillant; 7. bouilli.

clore 1. je clos, tu clos, il clôt; 3. je clorai; 4. que je close; 7. clos.

concevoir 1. je conçois, tu conçois, il conçoit, nous concevons, vous concevez, ils conçoivent; 2. je concevais; 3. je concevrai; 4. que je conçoive; 5. conçois, concevons, concevez; 6. concevant; 7. conçu.

conclure 1. je conclus, tu conclus, il conclut, nous concluons, vous concluez, ils concluent; 2. je concluais; 3. je conclurai; 4. que je conclue; 5. conclus, concluons, concluez; 6. concluant; 7. conclu.

conduire 1. je conduis, tu conduis, il conduit, nous conduisons, vous conduisez, ils conduisent; 2. je conduisais; 3. je conduirai; 4. que je conduise; 5. conduis, conduisons, conduisez; 6. conduisant; 7. conduit.

connaître 1. je connais, tu connais, il connaît, nous connaissons, vous connaissez, ils connaissent; 2. je connaissais; 3. je connaîtrai; 4. que je connaisse; 5. connais, connaissons, connaissez; 6. connaissant; 7. connu.

conquérir *as* **acquérir.**

construire *as* **conduire.**

contraindre 1. je contrains, tu contrains, il contraint, nous contraignons, vous contraignez, ils contraignent; 2. je contraignais; 3. je contraindrai; 4. que je contraigne; 5. contrains, contraignons, contraignez; 6. contraignant; 7. contraint.

coudre 1. je couds, tu couds, il coud, nous cousons, vous cousez, ils cousent; 2. je cousais; 3. je coudrai; 4. que je couse; 5. couds, cousons, cousez; 6. cousant; 7. cousu.

courir 1. je cours, tu cours, il court, nous courons, vous courez, ils courent; 2. je courais; 3. je courrai; 4. que je coure; 5. cours, courons, courez; **6.** courant; **7.** couru.

couvrir *as* **ouvrir.**

croire 1. je crois, tu crois, il croit, nous croyons, vous croyez, ils croient; **2.** je croyais; **3.** je croirai; **4.** que je croie; **5.** crois, croyons, croyez; **6.** croyant; **7.** cru.

croître 1. je crois, tu crois, il croit, nous croissons, vous croissez, ils croissent; **2.** je croissais; **3.** je croîtrai; **4.** que je croisse; **5.** crois, croissons, croissez; **6.** croissant; **7.** crû, crue.

cueillir 1. je cueille, tu cueilles, il cueille, nous cueillons, vous cueillez, ils cueillent; **2.** je cueillais; **3.** je cueillerai; **4.** que je cueille; **6.** cueillant; **7.** cueilli.

cuire 1. je cuis, tu cuis, il cuit, nous cuisons, vous cuisez, ils cuisent; **2.** je cuisais; **3.** je cuirai; **4.** que je cuise; **5.** cuis, cuisons, cuisez; **6.** cuisant; **7.** cuit.

déchoir 1. je déchois, tu déchois, il déchoit, nous déchoyons, vous déchoyez, ils déchoient; **2.** je déchoyais; **3.** je décherrai; **4.** que je déchoie; **7.** déchu.

déconfire *as* **confire.**

découvrir *as* **ouvrir.**

déduire, détruire *as* **conduire.**

devoir 1. je dois, tu dois, il doit, nous devons, vous devez, ils doivent; **2.** je devais; **3.** je devrai; **4.** que je doive; **5.** dois, devons, devez; **6.** devant; **7. du, due.**

dire 1. je dis, tu dis, il dit, nous disons, vous dites, ils disent; **2.** je disais; **3.** je

dirai; **4.** que je dise; **5.** dis, disons, dites; **6.** disant **7.** dit.

dissoudre 1. je dissous, tu dissous, il dissout, nous dissolvons, vous dissolvez, ils dissolvent; **2.** je dissolvais; **3.** je dissoudrai; **4.** que je dissolve; **5.** dissous, dissolvons, dissolvez; **6.** dissolvant; **7.** dissous, dissoute.

dormir 1. je dors, tu dors, il dort, nous dormons, vous dormez, ils dorment; **2.** je dormais; **3.** je dormirai; **4.** que je dorme; **5.** dors dormons, dormez; **6.** dormant; **7.** dormi.

échoir *or* **écheoir 1.** il échoit *or* il échet, ils échoient; **2.** il échoyait; **3.** il écherra, ils écherront; **4.** qu'il échoie; **6.** échéant; **7.** échu.

écrire 1. j'écris, tu écris, il écrit, nous écrivons, vous écrivez, ils écrivent; **2.** j'écrivais; **3.** j'écrirai; **4.** que j'écrive; **5.** écris, écrivons, écrivez; **6.** écrivant; **7.** écrit.

envoyer 1. j'envoie, tu envoies, il envoie, nous envoyons, vous envoyez, ils envoient; **2.** j'envoyais; **3.** j'enverrai; **4.** que j'envoie; **5.** envoie, envoyons, envoyez; **6.** envoyant; **7.** envoyé.

éteindre *as* **peindre.**

étreindre *as* **peindre.**

exclure *as* **conclure.**

faire 1. je fais, tu fais, il fait, nous faisons, vous faites, ils font; **2.** je faisais; **3.** je ferai; **4.** que je fasse; **5.** fais, faisons, faites; **6.** faisant; **7.** fait.

falloir 1. il faut; 2. il fallait; 3. il faudra; 4. qu'il faille; 7. fallu.

feindre as **peindre.**

frire 1. je fris, tu fris, il frit; 3. je frirai; 5. fris; 7. frit.

fuir 1. je fuis, tu fuis, il fuit, nous fuyons, vous fuyez, ils fuient; 2. je fuyais; 3. je fuirai; 4. que je fuie; 5. fuis, fuyons, fuyez; 6. fuyant; 7. fui.

gésir 1. il git, nous gisons, vous gisez, ils gisent; 2. je gisais; 6. gisant.

haïr 1. je hais, tu hais, il hait, nous haïssons, vous haïssez, ils haïssent; 2. je haïssais; 3. je haïrai; 4. que je haïsse; 5. hais, haïssons, haïssez; 6. haïssant, 7. haï.

instruire as **conduire.**

joindre 1. je joins, tu joins, il joint, nous joignons, vous joignez, ils joignent; 2. je joignais; 3. je joindrai; 4. que je joigne; 5. joins, joignons, joignez; 6. joignant; 7. joint.

lire 1. je lis, tu lis, il lit, nous lisons, vous lisez, ils lisent; 2. je lisais; 3. je lirai; 4. que je lise; 5. lis, lisons, lisez; 6. lisant; 7. lu.

luire as **nuire.**

maudire 1. je maudis, tu maudis, il maudit, nous maudissons, vous maudissez, ils maudissent; 2. je maudissais; 3. je maudirai; 4. que je maudisse; 5. maudis, maudissons, maudissez; 6. maudissant; 7. maudit.

mentir as **sentir.**

mettre 1. je mets, tu mets, il met, nous mettons, vous mettez, ils mettent; 2. je mettais; 3. je mettrai; 4. que je mette; 5. mets, mettons, mettez; 6. mettant; 7. mis.

moudre 1. je mouds, tu mouds, il moud, nous moulons, vous moulez, ils moulent; 2. je moulais; 3. je moudrai; 4. que je moule; 5. mouds, moulons, moulons; 6. moulant; 7. moulu.

mourir 1. je meurs, tu meurs, il meurt, nous mourons, vous mourez, ils meurent; 2. je mourais; 3. je mourrai; 4. que je meure; 5. meurs, mourons, mourez; 6. mourant; 7. mort (être.)

mouvoir 1. je meus, tu meus, il meut, nous mouvons, vous mouvez, ils meuvent; 2. je mouvais; 3. je mouvrai; 4. que je meuve; 5. meus, mouvons, mouvez; 6. mouvant; 7. mû, mue.

naître 1. je nais, tu nais, il nait, nous naissons, vous naissez, ils naissent; 2. je naissais; 3. je naîtrai; 4. que je naisse; 5. nais, naissons, naissez; 6. naissant; 7. né, née (être.)

nuire 1. je nuis, tu nuis, il nuit, nous nouisons, vous nuisez, ils nuisent; 2. je nuisais; 3. je nuirai; 4. que je nuise; 5. nuis, nuisons, nuisez; 6. nuisant; 7. nui.

offrir as **ouvrir.**

ouvrir 1. j'ouvre, tu ouvres, il ouvre, nous ouvrons, vous ouvrez, ils ouvrent; 2. j'ouvrais; 3. j'ouvrirai; 4. que j'ouvre; 5. ouvre, ouvrons, ouvrez; 6. ouvrant; 7. ouvert.

paître 1. je pais, tu pais, il paît, nous paissons, vous paissez, ils paissent; 2. je paissais; 3. je paîtrai; 4. que je paisse; 5. pais, paissons, paissez; 6. paissant.

paraître 1. je parais, tu parais, il paraît, nous paraissons, vous paraissez, ils paraissent; 2. je paraissais; 3. je paraîtrai; 4. que je paraisse; 5. parais, paraissons, paraissez; 6. paraissant; 7. paru.

partir 1. je pars, tu pars, il part, nous partons, vous partez, ils partent; 2. je partais; 3. je partirai; 4. que je parte; 5. pars, partons, partez; 6. partant; 7. parti (être.)

peindre 1. je peins, tu peins, il peint, nous peignons, vous peignez, ils peignent; 2. je peignais; 3. je peindrai; 4. que je peigne; 5. peins, peignons, peignez; 6. peignant; 7. peint.

plaire 1. je plais, tu plais, il plaît, nous plaisons, vous plaisez, ils plaisent; 2. je plaisais; 3. je plairai; 4. que je plaise; 5. plais, plaisons, plaisez; 6. plaisant; 7. plu.

pouvoir 1. je peux *or* je puis, tu peux, il peut, nous pouvons, vous pouvez, ils peuvent; 2. je pouvais; 3. je pourrai; 4. que je puisse; 6. pouvant; 7. pu.

prendre 1. je prends, tu prends, il prend, nous prenons, vous prenez, ils prennent; 2. je prenais; 3. je prendrai; 4. que je prenne; 5. prends, prenons, prenez; 6. prenant; 7. pris.

prescrire *as* **écrire.**
produire *as* **conduire.**
proscrire *as* **écrire.**
recevoir *as* **concevoir.**
reconstruire *as* **conduire.**
réduire *as* **conduire.**
repartir *as* **partir.**
reproduire *as* **conduire.**

resoudre 1. je résous, tu résous, il résout, nous résolvons, vous résolvez, ils résolvent; 2. je résolvais; 3. je résoudrai; 4. que je résolve; 5. résous, résolvons, résolvez; 6. résolvant; 7. résolu.

restreindre *as* **peindre.**

rire 1. je ris, tu ris, il rit, nous rions, vous riez, ils rient; 2. je riais; 3. je rirai; 4. que je rie; 5. ris, rions, riez; 6. riant; 7. ri.

savoir 1. je sais, tu sais, il sait, nous savons, vous savez, ils savent; 2. je savais; 3. je saurai; 4. que je sache; 5. sais, sachons, sachez; 6. sachant; 7. sus.

sentir 1. je sens, tu sens, il sent, nous sentons, vous sentez, ils sentent; 2. je sentais; 3. je sentirai; 4. que je sente; 5. sens, sentons, sentez; 6. sentant; 7. senti.

servir 1. je sers, tu sers, ils sert, nous servons, vous servez, ils servent; 2. je servais; 3. je servirai; 4. que je serve; 5. sers, servons, servez; 6. servant; 7. servi.

sortir 1. je sors, tu sors, il sort, nous sortons, vous sortez, ils sortent; 2. je sortais;

3. je sortirai; **4.** que je sorte; **5.** sors, sortons, sortez; **6.** sortant; **7.** sorti (être).

souffrir as **ouvrir.**

se souvenir as **venir.**

suffire 1. je suffis, tu suffis, il suffit, nous suffisons, vous suffisez, ils suffisent; **2.** je suffisais; **3.** je suffirai; **4.** que je suffise; **5.** suffis, suffisons, suffisez; **6.** suffisant; **7.** suffi.

suivre 1. je suis, tu suis, il suit, nous suivons, vous suivez, ils suivent; **2.** je suivais; **3.** je suivrai; **4.** que je suive; **5.** suis, suivons, suivez; **6.** suivant; **7.** suivi.

surseoir 1. je sursois, tu sursois, il sursoit, nous sursoyons, vous sursoyez, ils sursoient; **2.** je sursoyais; **3.** je surseoirai; **4.** que je sursoie; **5.** sursois, sursoyons, sursoyez; **6.** sursoyant; **7.** sursis.

taire as **plaire.**

teindre as **peindre.**

tenir 1. je tiens, tu tiens, il tient, nous tenons, vous tenez, ils tiennent; **2.** je tenais; **3.** je tiendrai; **4.** que je tienne; **5.** tiens, tenons, tenez; **6.** tenant; **7.** tenu.

traduire as **conduire.**

traire 1. je trais, tu trais, il trait, nous trayons, vous trayez, ils traient; **2.** je trayais; **3.** je trairai; **4.** que je traie; **5.** trais, trayons, trayez; **6.** trayant; **7.** trait.

vaincre 1. je vaincs, tu vaincs, il vainc, nous vainquons, vous vainquez, ils vainquent; **2.** je vainquais: **3.** je vaincrai; **4.** que je vainque; **5.** vaincs, vainquons, vainquez; **6.** vainquant; **7.** vaincu.

valoir 1. je vaux, tu vaux, il vaut, nous valons, vous valez, ils valent; **2.** je valais, **3.** je vaudrai; **4.** que je vaille; **6.** valant; **7.** valu.

venir 1. je viens, tu viens, il vient, nous venons, vous venez, ils viennent; **2.** je venais; **3.** je viendrai; **4.** que je vienne; **5.** viens, venons, venez; **6.** venant; **7.** venu (être.)

vêtir 1. je vêts, tu vêts, il vêt, nous vêtons, vous vêtez, ils vêtent; **2.** je vêtais; **3.** je vêtirai; **4.** que je vête; **5.** vêts, vêtons, vêtez; **6.** vêtant; **7.** vêtu.

vivre 1. je vis, tu vis, il vit, nous vivons, vous vivez, ils vivent; **2.** je vivais; **3.** je vivrai; **4.** que je vive; **5.** vis, vivons, vivez; **6.** vivant; **7.** vécu.

voir 1. je vois, tu vois, il voit, nous voyons, vous voyez, ils voient; **2.** je voyais; **3.** je verrai; **4.** que je voie; **5.** vois, voyons, voyez; **6.** voyant; **7.** vu.

vouloir 1. je veux, tu veux, il veut, nous voulons, vous voulez, ils veulent; **2.** je voulais; **3.** je voudrai; **4.** que je veuille, que nous voulions; **5.** veuille, veuillions, veuillez *or* voulez; **6.** voulant; **7.** voulu.

PHRASES

Good morning. Good evening. Good-bye.	Bonjour. Bonsoir. Au revoir.
I beg your pardon. Excuse me.	Je vous demande pardon. Pardon.
How are you? Very well — and you?	Comment allez-vous? Très bien — et vous?
How do you do (delighted to meet you).	Enchanté (de faire votre connaissance) monsieur (madame, mademoiselle).
Allow me! You are very kind.	Permettez-moi ! Vous êtes très gentil.
It's all the same to me.	Cela m'est égal.
Your good health.	A votre santé.
Allow me to introduce you to...	Permettez-moi de vous présenter à...
It is fine (bad) weather.	Il fait beau (mauvais) temps.
You are right. You are wrong.	Vous avez raison. Vous avez tort.
It is not my fault.	Ce n'est pas ma faute.
To do one's best.	Faire son possible.
It is very annoying.	C'est très ennuyeux.
You're pulling my leg.	Vous vous moquez de moi.
So much the better (worse).	Tant mieux (pis).
He's a jolly nice fellow.	C'est un chic type.
To put one's foot in it.	Mettre les pieds dans le plat.
Things are going badly.	Rien ne va bien. Tout va mal.
I am an Englishmen (Englishwoman).	Je suis anglais (anglaise).
I cannot speak French.	Je ne parle pas français.
I am looking for...	Je cherche...
I don't understand you.	Je ne vous comprends pas.
Please speak slowly!	Parlez lentement, s'il vous plaît!
Is there anyone here who speaks English?	Y-a-t-il quelque'un qui parle anglais?
Where is the British Consulate?	Où est le consulat britannique?
It is wonderful, splendid !	C'est épatant, formidable !
No ... Trespassers will be prosecuted.	Défense de ... sous peine d'amende.

No entry.	Entrée interdite.
Lavatory.	Les toilettes, les lavabos, les cabinets.
What time is it?	Quelle heure est-il?
It is five past one.	Il est une heure cinq.
We are in a hurry.	Nous sommes pressés.
How long does it take to...?	Combien de temps faut-il pour...?
This evening, tonight. Last night.	Ce soir. Hier soir.
How long have you been here?	Depuis quand êtes-vous ici?
I have been here a month.	Je suis ici depuis un mois.
Can we lunch (dine) here?	Est-ce qu'on peut déjeuner (dîner) ici?
There are four of us.	Nous sommes quatre.
We only want a snack.	Nous voudrions seulement un casse-croûte.
Please give us the menu.	Voulez-vous nous donner le menu, s'il vous plaît.
Bring us the wine list, please.	Apportez-nous la carte des vins, s'il vous plaît.
We would like black coffee (white coffee).	Nous voudrions du café noir (café au lait).
The bill, please.	L'addition, s'il vous plaît.
I want some petrol (oil, water).	Je voudrais de l'essence (de l'huile, de l'eau).
I have had a breakdown.	Je suis en panne.
My car is on the road two kilometres from here.	Mon auto est sur la route à deux kilomètres d'ici.
Do you know the road to...?	Connaissez-vous la route de...?
Is the post office (bank) near here?	Y a-t-il un bureau de poste (bureau de change) près d'ici?
Are there any letters for me?	Y a-t-il des lettres pour moi?
Do you sell...?	Est-ce que vous vendez...?
You have given me the wrong change.	Vous vous êtes trompé en me rendant la monnaie.
Have you anything to declare?	Avez-vous quelque chose à déclarer?
I cannot find my ticket.	Je ne peux pas trouver mon billet.
I have left something in the train.	J'ai laissé quelque chose dans le train.
I have a train to catch.	J'ai un train à prendre.
What time is the first (last) train for...?	A quelle heure est le premier (dernier) train pour...?

From which platform?	Sur quel quai?
Where do I change for ...?	Où est-ce que je change pour ...?
Is there a hotel where I can stay the night?	Est-ce qu'il y a un hôtel où je peux passer la nuit?
The last train has gone	Le dernier train est parti.
I do not feel well.	Je ne me sens pas bien.
I want to get off at ...	Je veux descendre à ...
Do you go near ...?	Allez-vous près de ...?
Can I have a room for the night?	Puis-je avoir une chambre pour la nuit?
I am only staying for two or three days.	Je reste deux ou trois jours seulement.
I want a room with a double bed.	Je désire une chambre avec un grand lit.
Can you put me up for the night?	Pouvez-vous me donnez une chambre pour la nuit?
I shall be back at three.	Je serai de retour à trois heures.
Have you any English newspapers?	Avez-vous des journaux anglais?
What does it cost to send a letter to ...?	Combien met-on sur une lettre pour ...?
Where can I buy ...?	Où puis-je acheter ...?
Will you reserve this place for me?	Voulez-vous me reserver cette place?
Will you take a traveller's cheque?	Acceptez-vous un cheque de voyage?
Will you have letters sent on to this address?	Voulez-vous faire suivre mon courrier à cette adresse?
I need a guide who speaks English.	J'ai besoin d'un guide qui parle anglais.
Is this the right road for ...?	Est-ce bien la route pour ...?
How far is it from here to ...?	Combien de kilomètres d'ici à ...?
Have you any post-cards?	Avez-vous des cartes postales?
Have you a map (plan)?	Avez-vous une carte (un plan)?
Do you know what is on at the cinema (theatre)?	Savez-vous ce qu'on donne au cinéma (Théatre)?
Where does this road lead?	Ce chemin, ou mène-t-il?

Can you recommend a cheap restaurant?	Pouvez-vous recommander un restaurant pas trop cher?
It is too dear. Have you anything cheaper?	C'est trop cher. Avez-vous quelque chose de meilleur marché?
We are lost.	Nous sommes perdus.
Have you any identification papers?	Avez-vous une pièce d'identite?
Have you a carrier bag?	Avez-vous un sac en papier?
Here is my address.	Voici mon adresse.
That's all right.	Je vous en prie.
Don't mention it.	Il n'y a pas de quoi.
Take my seat, madame.	Prenez ma place, madame.
Can I help you?	Puis-je vous aider?
Am I disturbing you?	Est-ce que je vous dérange?
I am terribly sorry.	Je suis navré (désolé).
Thank you for your hospitality.	Je vous remercie de votre hospitalité.
We had a very good time.	Nous nous sommes bien amusés.
It's too much. It's too dear.	C'est trop. C'est trop cher.
Look out!	Attention!
You are right. You are wrong.	Vous avez raison. Vous avez tort.
Listen. Look.	Ecoutez. Regardez.
What is the matter?	Qu'est-ce qu-il y a?
Please speak slowly.	Parlez lentement, s'il vous plaît.
Wait, I am looking for the phrase in this book.	Attendez, je cherche la phrase dans ce livre.
I have already paid you.	Je vous ai déjà payé.
It's terribly funny.	C'est tordant, c'est rigolo.
You don't say!	Sans blague!
You are joking. Joking apart.	Vous plaisantez. Blague à part.
Agreed. O.K.	Entendu. D'accord.
What a pity!	Quel dommage!
Do not touch.	Ne pas toucher.
Wet paint.	Prenez garde à la peinture.
You have plenty of time.	Vous avez tout le temps.
I have no time.	Je n'ai pas le temps.
The day before yesterday.	Avant-hier.
The day after tomorrow.	Après-demain.

Waiter, bring us some bread, please.	Garçon apportez-nous du pain, s'il vous plaît.
A little more ...	Encore un peu de ...
What would you like to drink?	Que désirez-vous boire (comme boisson)?
Is the service (the cover charge) included?	Le service (le couvert), est-il compris?
Keep the change.	Vous pouvez garder la monnaie.
There is a mistake in the bill.	Il y a une erreur dans l'addition.
Please don't mention it.	Je vous en prie.
Is the garage open all night?	Est-ce que le garage est ouvert la nuit?
I want to leave early tomorrow.	Je veux partir demain de bonne heure.
How long shall I have to wait?	Combien de temps faut-il attendre?
Can you lend me ... ?	Pouvez-vous me prêter ...?
How much do I owe you?	Combien est-ce que je vous dois?
I have two first class (second class) seats reserved.	J'ai deux places réservées en première (en seconde).
Excuse me, sir, that seat is mine.	Pardon monsieur, cette place est à moi.
Porter I want to put this luggage in the cloakroom (left-luggage office).	Porteur, je veux mettre ces bagages à la consigne.
I am coming with you.	Je vous suis.
Is there a porter from the ... Hotel here?	Est-ce qu'il y a un porter de l'hôtel ... ici?
Where is the enquiry office?	Où est le bureau de renseignements?
When do we get to ... ?	A quelle heure arrive-t-on à ...?
How long does the train stop here?	Combien de temps le train s'arrête-t-il ici?
The plane for ... is twenty minutes late already.	L'avion pour ... a déjà vingt minutes de retard.
The ... plane is announced.	L'avion de ... est signalé.
Where is the Airline Office?	Où est le bureau de la compagnie aérienne?
I want to reserve a seat on the plane leaving tomorrow for ..	Je voudrais réserver une place dans l'avion qui part demain pour ..

English	French
Is there a plane for . . . today?	Est-ce qu'il y a un avion pour . . . audjourd'hui?
I do not feel well.	Je ne me sens pas bien.
Bring me some coffee (brandy, a glass of water), please.	Apportez-moi du café (cognac, un verre d'eau), s'il vous plait.
Put out your cigarettes and fasten your seat-belts, please.	Eteignez vos cigarettes et attachez vos ceintures, s'il vous plaît.
Call me a taxi.	Appelez-moi un taxi.
Go quickly, I am in a great hurry.	Dépêchez-vous, je suis très pressé.
Please wait here for a few minutes.	Attendez-moi ici quelques minutes, s'il vous plaît.
Where is the office?	Où est le bureau?
Have you a room with a private bathroom?	Avez-vous une chambre avec salle de bains?
What is the price of a room per night?	Quel est le prix d'une chambre par nuit?
I am expecting a gentleman (a lady, a young lady).	J'attends un monsieur (une dame, une demoiselle).
Give me two 25 centime stamps and two at 15 centimes.	Donnez-moi deux timbres de vingt-cinq centimes et deux de quinze.
I want to send a telegram.	Je voudrais envoyer une dépêche.
Have you the time-table of trains for . . . ?	Avez-vous l'horaire des trains pour . . . ?
Can we have an English breakfast?	Peut-on avoir un petit déjeuner anglais?
Order a taxi for 9.30, please.	Commandez un taxi pour neuf heures et demie, s'il vous plaît.
Please have my bill made out.	Préparez la note, s'il vous plaît.
We want to be together.	Nous voudrions être ensemble.
How far it to . . . ?	Quelle distance d'ici à . . . ?
What is the name of this town (village)?	Quel est le nom de cette ville (ce village)?
Where is the market place?	Où est le marché?
Weather permitting, we hope to leave at dawn.	Si le temps le permet, nous comptons partir à l'aube.
Get me Molitor 44—94,	Voulez-vous me demander

please.

Molitor quarante-quatre, quatre-vingt quatorze, s'il vous plaît.

How much do I owe you for the call?

Combien vous dois-je pour la communication?

Can I make an appointment?

Puis-je prendre un rendezvous?

Can I have something to read?

Puis-je avoir de la lecture?

Can you make up this prescription, please?

Pouvez-vous faire cette ordonnance, s'il vous plaît?

Can you give me something for insect (ant, mosquito) bites?

Pouvez-vous me donner quelque chose pour les piqûres d'insects (de fourmis, de moustiques)?

My skin is smarting; have you anything to soothe it?

La peau me cuit; avez-vous quelque-chose de calmant?

For external use.

Pour l'usage externe.

I want a reversal (negative) colour film.

Je voudrais un film en couleur inversible (negatif).

Do you sell...?

Est-ce que vous vendez ...?

Have you anything cheaper (better)?

Avez-vous quelque chose de moins cher (de meilleure qualité)?

I want something like this (that).

Je voudrais quelque chose comme ceci (cela).

Can you order it for me?

Pouvez-vous le (la) commander?

Will you send it to this address?

Voulez-vous l'envoyer à cette adresse?

That's exactly what I want.

Voilà ce qu'il me faut.

You have given me the wrong change.

Vous vous êtes trompé en me rendant la monnaie.

Can you change it?

Pouvez-vous le changer?

Do you sell English cigarettes (tobacco)?

Est-ce que vous vendez des cigarettes anglaises (du tabac anglais)?

There has been an accident.

Il y a eu un accident.

Is there a doctor near here?

Y a-t-il un médecin près d'ici?

Welcome to England (France).

Je vous souhaite la bienvenue en Angleterre

(France).

Avez-vous fait un bon voyage?	Did you have a good journey?
A quelle heure est le petit déjeuner (le déjeuner, le goûter, le dîner)?	What time is breakfast (lunch, tea, dinner)?

NUMBERS

1 one, un.	1st first, premier.
2 two, deux.	2nd second, deuxième.
3 three, trois.	3rd third, troisième.
4 four, quatre.	4th fourth, quatrième.
5 five, cinq.	5th fifth, cinquième.
6 six, six.	6th sixth, sixième.
7 seven, sept.	7th seventh, septième.
8 eight, huit.	8th eighth, huitième.
9 nine, neuf.	9th ninth, neuvième.
10 ten, dix.	10th tenth, dixième.
11 eleven, onze.	11th eleventh, onzième.
12 twelve, douze.	12th twelfth, douzième.
13 thirteen, treize.	13th thirteenth, treizième.
14 fourteen, quatorze.	14th fourteenth, quatorzième.
15 fifteen, quinze.	15th fifteenth, quinzième.
16 sixteen, seize.	16th sixteenth, seizième.

A

a, an, *art.* un, -e.
abandon, *v. a.* abandonner.
abate, *v. a. & n.* diminuer; se calmer, s'apaiser.
abbey, *s.* abbaye *f.*
abbot, *s.* abbé *m.*
abbreviate, *v. a.* abréger.
abbreviation, *s.* abréviation *f.*
abdicate, *v.a. & n.* abdiquer.
abdomen, *s.* abdomen *m.*
abhor, *v. a.* détester, abhorrer.
ability, *s.* capacité *J.*, habilité *f.*
able, *adj.* capable.
aboard, *adv.* à bord.
abode, *s.* demeure *f.*
abolish, *v.a.* abolir; supprimer.
abominable, *adj.* abominable.
abound, *v.n.* abonder (de).
about, *adv. & prep.* autour (de); environ, presque; au sujet de.
above, *adv. & prep.* au-dessus (de); *(in book)* ci-dessus.
abroad, *adv.* à l'étranger.
absence, *s.* absence *f.*, éloignement *m.*
absent, *adj.* absent.
absolute, *adj.* absolu.
absolve, *v.a.* absoudre; relever de; remettre, pardonner.
absorb, *v. a.* absorber.
abstain, *v.n.* s'abstenir de.
abstract, *adj.* abstrait.
abstraction, *s.* abstraction *f.*
absurd, *adj.* absurde; ridicule.
abundance, *s.* abondance *f.*

abundant, *adj.* abondant.
abusive, *adj.* abusif; injurieux; offensant.
academic, *adj.* académique.
academy, *s.* académie *f.*
accelerate, *v.a.* accélérer; *v.n.* s'accélérer.
accent, *s.* accent *m.*
accept, *v.a.* accepter
access, *s.* accès *m.*
accessible, *adj.* accessible.
accessory, *s. & adj.* accessoire *(m.).*
accident, *s.* accident *m.*
accidental, *s.* accidentel.
accommodate, *v. a.* accommoder; loger; ~ *oneself to* s'accommoder à.
accommodation, *s.* ajustement *m.*, adaptation *f.;* commodité *f.;* logement *m.*
accompany, *v.a.* accompagner.
accomplish, *v.a.* accomplir, achever.
accomplishment, *s.* accomplissement *m.;* talent *m.*
accord, *s.* accord *m.*, consentement *m.*
according: ~ *to* selon, d'après.
accordingly, *adv.* donc; en conséquence.

account, *s.* compte *m.;* *(narration)* récit *m.;* *on* ~ *of* à cause de; *on no* ~ dans aucun cas; *take into* ~ tenir compte de; — *v.n.* ~ *for* expliquer; rendre compte de.
accuracy, *s.* exactitude *f.*
accusation, *s.* accusation *f.*
accuse, *v.a.* accuser; in-

criminer.

accustom, *v.a.* accoutumer (à).

ache, *s.* douleur *f.*

achieve, *v.a.* accomplir, achever; atteindre.

acknowledge, *v.a.* reconnaître; accuser réception de.

acquaint, *v.a.* informer (de); faire part à.

acquaintance, *s.* connaissance *f.*

acquire, *v.a.* acquérir.

acre, *s.* arpent *m.*

across, *prep.* à travers; en croix.

act, *s.* action *f.*; *(law)* loi *f.*; *(theatre)* acte *m.*; — *v.n.* agir; *v.a.* jouer.

action, *s.* action *f.*; acte *m.*; *(war)* combat *m.*

active, *adj.* actif.

activity, *s.* activité *f.*

actor, *s.* acteur *m.*

actress, *s.* actrice *f.*

actual, *adj.* réel.

actually, *adv.* en fait.

adapt, *v.a.* adapter.

add, *v.a.* ajouter; additionner.

addition, *s.* addition *f.*; *in ~ to* en plus de.

additional, *adj.* additionnel; supplémentaire.

address, *s.* adresse *f.*; — *v.a.* adresser.

adequate, *adj.* suffisant.

adjust, *v.a.* ajuster, régler.

administer, *v.a. & n.* administrer.

administration, *s.* administration *f.*

admirable, *adj.* admirable.

admiral, *s.* amiral *m.*

admiration, *s.* admiration *f.*

admire, *v.a.* admirer.

admission, *s.* admission *f.*; entrée *f.*

admit, *v.a.* admettre; laisser entrer.

adopt, *v.a.* adopter.

adoption, *s.* adoption *f.*

adore, *v.a.* adorer.

adult, *adj. & s.* adulte *(m.f.)*

advance, *v. n.* avancer; — *s.* avance *f.*; progrès *m.*

advantage, *s.* avantage *m.*

adventure, *s.* aventure *f.*

adversary, *s.* adversaire *m.*

adverse, *adj.* adverse.

adversity, *s.* adversité *f.*

advertise, *v.a.* annoncer; faire de la réclame (pour).

advertisement, *s.* annonce *f.*; réclame *f.*

advice, conseil *m.*; avis *m.*

advise, *v.a.* conseiller.

aerial, *s.* antenne *f.*

aerodrome, *s.* aérodrome *m.*

aeroplane, *s.* avion *m.*

affair, *s.* affaire *f.*

affect, *v.a.* affecter.

affection, *s.* affection *f.*

affectionate, *adj.* affectueux.

affirmative, *adj.* affirmatif; — *s.* affirmative *f.*

afford, *v.a.* donner, fournir, accorder; *can ~* avoir les moyens de.

afraid, *adj.* effrayé; *be ~ of* avoir peur de.

African, *adj.* africain; — *s.* Africain, -e.

after, *prep. & adj.* après.

afternoon, *s.* après-midi *m.* or *f.*

afterwards, *adv.* après, ensuite.

again, *adv.* encore une fois, de nouveau.

against, *prep.* contre.

age, *s.* âge *m.*

agency, s. agence f.

agent, s. agent m.

aggression, s. agression f.

ago, adv. il y a.

agony, s. agonie f.

agree, v.n. s'accorder, être d'accord; ~ (up-) on convenir sur; ~ to consentir à; ~ with entrer dans les idées de.

agreeable, adj. agréable.

agreement, s. accord m.

agricultural, adj. agricole.

agriculture, s. agriculture f.

ahead, adv. en avant.

aid, s. aide f.; — v.a. aider, assister.

aim, s. but m.; objectif m.; visée f.; — v.a. & n. viser.

air. s. air m.

air-conditioning, s. conditionnement d'air m.; climatisation f.

aircraft, s. avion m.

air-line, s. ligne f. aérienne.

air-mail s. poste aérienne; by ~ par avion.

airport, s. aéroport m.,

alarm, v.a. alarmer; —s. alarme f.

alcoholic, adj. alcoolique.

ale, s. bière (f.) anglaise.

alike, adj. semblable; — adv. également.

alive, adj. vivant.

all, pron. s., adv. & adj. tout; not at ~ pas du tout.

allege, v.a. alléguer.

alley, s. ruelle f.

allow, v.a. permettre; laisser; admettre.

allude, v.n. faire allusion.

ally, v.a. allier; v.n.

s'allier; — s. allié, -e.

almost, adv. presque; à peu près.

alone, adj. & adv. seul.

along, prep. le long de.

aloud, adv. à haute voix.

already, adv. déjà.

also, adv. aussi.

altar, s. autel m.

alter, v.a.&n. changer.

alternate, adj. alternatif; — v.n. alterner.

although, conj. quoique; bien que.

altitude, s. altitude f., élévation f.

altogether, adv. tout à fait; entièrement.

always, adv. toujours.

amaze, v.a. frapper d'étonnement, frapper de stupeur.

amazing, adj. étonnant.

ambassador, s. ambassadeur m.

ambassadress, s. ambassadrice f.

ambition, s ambition f.

ambitious, adj. ambitieux.

ambulance, s. ambulance (automobile) f.

amend, v.a. amender.

amends: make ~ for dédommager de.

American, adj. américain; — s. Américain, -e.

among, prep. parmi; chez.

amount, s. somme f.; (total) montant m.; — v.n. ~ to monter à.

ample, adj. ample.

amplifier, s. amplificateur m.

amuse, v.a. amuser; divertir.

amusement, s. amusement m.; divertissement m.

an see a.

analogy, s. analogie f.

analyse, *v.a.* analyser.
analysis, analyse *f.*
anarchy, *s.* anarchie *f.*
anatomy, *s.* anatomie *f.*
ancestor, *s.* ancêtre *m. f.*
anchor, *s.* ancre *f.*
ancient, *adj.* ancien; antique.
and, *conj.* et.
anecdote, *s.* anecdote *f.*
angel, *s.* ange *m.*
anger, *s.* colère, *f.*
angle, *s.* angle *m.*
angler, *s.* pêcheur *m.*

Anglican, *adj.* anglican.
angry, *adj.* fâché, irrité.
animal, *s.* animal *m.* *(pl.* -aux).
ankle, *s.* cheville *f.*
anniversary, *s.* anniversaire *m.*
announce, *v.a.* annoncer.
announcement, *s.* annonce.
announcer, *s.* speaker *m.*
annoy, *v.a.* ennuyer; contrarier; gêner.
annoying, *adj.* contrariant; ennuyeux.
annual, *adj.* annuel.
annul, *v.a.* annuler.
another, *pron. & adj.* un autre, une autre.
answer, *s.* réponse *f.;* — *v.a.&n.* répondre.
ant, *s.* fourmi *f.*
antelope, *s.* antilope *f.*
antibiotic, *s.* antibiotique *m.*
anticipate, *v.a.* anticiper.
antipathy, *s.* antipathie *f.*
antiquated, *adj.* vieilli.
antiquity, *s.* antiquité *f.*
anvil, *s.* enclume *f.*
anxiety, *s.* anxiété *f.*
anxious, *adj.* inquiet; désireux; *be ~ to* désirer faire qch.
any, *adj. & pron.* quelque; *(at all)* n'importe quoi/qui/quel; *(some, in*

question) du, de la; *have you ~?* en avez vous; *not ~* ne ... pas de; *~ more* encore du.
anybody, *pron.* quelqu'un; *(at all)* n'importe qui.
anyhow, *adv.* n'importe comment.
anyone *see* anybody.
anything, *pron.* quelque chose; *(at all)* n'importe quoi.
anyway, *see* anyhow.
anywhere, *adv.* n'importe où.
apart, *adv.* à part; de côté; *~ from* en dehors de.
apartment, *s.* logement *m.;* appartement *m.*
apologize, *v.n.* faire des excuses, s'excuser.
apology, *s.* excuse *f.*
apostle, *s.* apôtre *m.*
appalling, *adj.* épouvantable.
apparatus, *s.* appareil *m.*
apparent, *adj.* manifeste.
appeal, *s.* appel *m.;* — *v.n.* en appeler (à).
appear, *v.n.* (ap)paraître; *(seem)* sembler.
appearance, *s.* apparition *f.; (look)* air *m.*
appendicitis, *s.* appendicite *f.*
appendix, *s.* appendice *m.*
appetite, *s.* appétit *m.*
applaud, *v.n.* applaudir.
applause, *s.* applaudissement *m.*
apple, *s.* pomme *f.*
appliance, *s.* appareil *m.*
applicant, *s.* postulant, -e.
application, *s.* demande *f.; (use)* application *f.*
apply, *v.a.* appliquer; — *v.n.* avoir rapport à; *~ for* solliciter.
appoint, *v.a.* nommer; désigner.

appointment, s. nomination f.; emploi m.; rendez-vous m.

appreciate, v.a. apprécier.

appreciation, s. appréciation f.

apprehend, v.a. appréhender; (understand) comprendre.

apprentice, s. apprenti m.

approach, s. approche f.; — v. a. & n. (s')approcher (de).

appropriate, adj. approprié, convenable.

approval, s. approbation f.

approve, v.a. & n. a- prouver.

approximate, adj. approximatif.

approximation, approximation f.

apricot, s. abricot m.

April, s. avril m.

apron, s. tablier m.

aptitude, s. aptitude f.

Arab, s. Arabe m.

Arabian, adj. arabe.

arbitrary, adj. arbitraire.

arcade, s. arcade f.

arch, s. arche f.; arc m.

archaeology, s. archéologie f.

archbishop, s. archevêque m.

architect, s. architecte m.

architecture, s. architecture f.

area, s. surface f.; aire f.

Argentine, adj. argentine.

argue, v.n. argumenter; v.a. discuter.

argument, s. argument m.; discussion f.

arise, v. n. se lever; (emerge) surgir; (come from) résulter de.

aristocratic, adj. aristocratique.

arm[1], s. bras m.

arm[2], s.(pl). arme(s) f.

armament, s. armement m.

armchair, s. fauteuil m.

armour, s. armure f.

army, s. armée f.

around, adv. & prep. autour (de).

arouse, v.a. réveiller.

arrange, v.a. arranger.

arrangement, s. arrangement m.; ~s mesures f. pl.

array, s. ordre m.

arrears, s. pl. arriéré m.

arrest, v.a. arrêter; — s. arrestation f.

arrival, s. arrivée f.

arrive, v.n. arriver.

arrow, s. flèche f.

art, s. art m.

artery, s. artère f.

article, s. article m.

artificial, adj. artificiel.

artillery, s. artillerie f.

artist, s. artiste m.

artistic, adj. artistique.

as, adv. & conj. comme; (like a) en; (when) comme; ~ ... ~ aussi ... que.

ascend, v.n. monter.

ash(es), s. (pl.) cendre f.

ashamed, adj. honteux; be ~ of avoir honte de.

ashore, adv. à terre.

ash-tray, s. cendrier m.

Asiatic, adj. asiatique.

aside, adv. de côté.

ask, v. a. demander (à + qn., de + inf.); ~ about se renseigner sur; ~ for demander.

asleep, adj. endormi; fall ~ s'endormir.

aspect, s. aspect m.; (look) air m.

aspire, v.n. aspirer à.

ass, s. âne m.
assail, v. a. assaillir.
assault, s. assaut m.
assemble, v. a. assembler;
v.n. s'assembler.
assembly, s. assemblée f.;
~ hall halle f. de
montage; ~ line chaîne
f. de montage.
assert, v.a. affirmer.
assess, v.a. cotiser.
assets, s. pl. actif m.
assign, v. a. assigner;
céder.
assignment, s. cession f.
assist, v.a. aider.
assistance, s. aide f.
associate, v.a. associer;
— s. associé, -e m. f.
association, s. association
f.
assume, v.a. prendre;
assumer; supposer.
assumption, s. supposi-
tion f.
assurance, s. assurance f.
assure, v.a. assurer.
astonish, v. a. étonner.
astonishment, s. étonne-
ment m.
astronomy, s. astronomie
f.
at, prep. (place, time) à;
(house, shop) chez.
athletic, adj. athlétique.
athletics, s. athlétisme m.
at-home, s. réception f.
atlas, s. atlas m.
atmosphere, s. atmos-
phère f.
atom, s. atome m.
atomic, adj. atomique; ~

bomb bombe f. atomi-
que; ~ energy énergie
f. atomique.
attach, v.a. attacher.
attaché, s. attaché m.;
~ case petite valise f.
attachment, s. attache-
ment m.
attack, v.a. attaquer; —

s. attaque f.
attain, v.a. atteindre.
attainment, s. réalisa-
tion f.; connaissances
f. pl.
attempt, s. tentative f.;
— v.a. tenter; entre-
prendre.
attend, v.a. suivre; (look
after) soigner; — v.i.
faire attention à; as-
sister.
attendance, s. présence f.;
(persons present) as-
sistance f.
attendant, s. serviteur m.;
employé m.; ouvreuse
f.
attention, s. attention f.
attitude, s. attitude f.
attorney, s. avoué m.
attract, v.a. attirer.
attraction, s. attraction f.
attractive, adj. attrayant.
attribute, v.a. attribuer.
auction, s. vente f.
audience, s. auditoire m.
audio-visual, adj. audio-
visuel.
auditorium, s. salle f. (de
cours).
August, s. août m.
aunt, s. tante f.
Australian, adj. australien
— s. Australien, -ne m.
f.
Austrian, adj. autrichien;

— s. Autrichien, -enne
m. f.
authentic, adj. authen-
tique.
author, s. auteur m.
authority, s. autorité f.
authorize, v.a. autoriser·
automatic, adj. automa-
tique.
autonomy, s. autonomie
f.
autumn, s. automne m.
avail, s. be of no ~ ne
servir à rien; — v.a.

~ *oneself of* profiter de.

available, *adj.* disponible; sous la main.

avalanche, *s.* avalanche *f.*

avenge, *v.a.* venger.

avenue, *s.* avenue *f.*

average, *s.* moyenne *f.;* — *adj.* moyen.

aversion, *s.* aversion *f.*

avoid, *v.a.* éviter.

await, *v.a.* attendre.

awake, *v. a.* éveiller; *v. n.* s'éveiller; — *adj.* éveillé.

awaken, *v.a.* éveiller.

award, *v.a.* accorder.

aware, *adj. be ~ of* avoir conscience de, savoir bien.

away, *adv.* (au) loin; *carry ~* enlever; *go ~* partir.

awful, *adj.* terrible.

awhile, *adv.* pendant quelque temps, un moment.

awkward, *adj.* *(pers.)* gauche; maladroit; *(things)* gênant, embarrassant.

axe, *s.* hache *f.*

axis, *s.* axe *m.*

axle, *s.* essieu *m.*

B

babble, *s.* babil *m.;* — *v.n.* babiller.

baby, *s.* bébé *m.*

baby-sitter, *s.* garde-bébé *m.*

bachelor, *s.* célibataire; *(arts)* licencié *m.*

back, *s.* dos *m.;* *(hand)* revers *m.;* *(football)* arrière *m.;* — *adj.* de derrière; arriéré; — *adv.* en arrière; *be ~* être de retour; — *v.a.* soutenir, seconder; *(bet)* parier pour; *v.n.*

reculer.

background, *s.* fond *m.;* arrière-plan *m.*

backstairs, *s. pl.* escalier *m.* de service.

backward, *adj.* arriéré.

backwards, *adv.* en arrière; à reculons.

bacon, *s.* lard *m.*

bad, *adj.* mauvais.

badge, *s.* insigne *m.*

badger, *s.* blaireau *m.*

badly, *adv.* mal.

bag, *s.* sac *m.;* *(large)* valise *f.*

baggage, *s.* bagage *m.*

bait, *s.* amorce *f.*

bake, *v.a.* cuire; faire cuire.

baker, *s.* boulanger *m.*

bakery, *s.* boulangerie *f.*

balance, *s.* *(weighing, account)* balance *f.;* *(bank)* solde *m.;* *(equilibrium)* équilibre *m.;* — *v.a.* balancer; *v.n.* se balancer.

balcony, *s.* balcon *m.*

bald, *adj.* chauve; plat.

ball, *s.* *(games)* balle *f.* ballon *m.;* *(bowl)* boule *f.;* *(dance)* bal *m.*

ball-bearings, *s. pl.* roulement *m.* à billes.

ballet, *s.* ballet *m.*

balloon, *s.* ballon *m.*

ball(-point) pen, *s.* stylo *m.* à bille.

bamboo, *s.* bambou *m.*

banana, *s.* banane *f.*

band, *s.* *(people)* troupe *f.;* bande *f.;* orchestre *m.;* *(ribbon, tie)* ruban *m.;* lien *m.*

bandage, *s.* bandage *m.*

bandit, *s.* bandit *m.*

bang, *s.* coup *m.;* claquement *m.*

banish, *v.a.* bannir.

banister, rampe *f.*

bank¹, *s.* *(river)* rive *f.;*

(earth) talus *m.*

bank³, *s.* banque *f.*

bank-holiday, *s.* (jour *m.* de) fête *f.* légale.

banknote, *s.* billet *m.* (de banque).

bankruptcy, *s.* banqueroute *f.;* faillite *f.*

banner, *s.* bannière *f.*

banquet, *s.* banquet *m.*

baptism, *s.* baptême *m.*

baptize, *v.a.* baptiser.

bar, *s. (iron, tribunal, music)* barre *f.; (railway)* barrière *f.; (obstacle)* obstacle *m.; (lawyers)* barreau *m.; (counter place for drink)* comptoir *m.,* débit *m.* (de boissons), bar *m.*

barber, *s.* coiffeur *m.*

bare, *adj.* nu; *(mere)* seul.

barefoot, *adj.* nu-pieds.

barely, *adv.* à peine.

bargain, *s.* marché *m.;* — *v.n.* marchander.

bark, *s.* aboiement *m.;* — *v.n.* aboyer.

barley, *s.* orge *f.*

barmaid, *s.* demoiselle *f.* de comptoir, barmaid *f.*

barman, *s.* garçon *m.* de comptoir, barman *m.*

barn, *s.* grange *f.*

barometer, *s.* baromètre *m.*

baron, *s.* baron *m.*

baroness, *s.* baronne *f.*

barracks, *s. pl.* caserne *f.*

barrel, *s.* tonneau *m.*

barren, *adj.* stérile.

barrier, *s.* barrière *f.*

barrister, *s.* avocat *m.*

bartender *see* **barman.**

barter, *s.* échange *m.;* — *v.a.* échanger.

base, *s.* fondement *m.;* base *f.*

basement, *s.* sous-sol *m.*

bashful, *adj.* timide.

basic, *adj.* fondamental; basique.

basin, *s.* bassin *m.;* cuvette *f.*

basis, *s.* base *f.*

basket, *s.* panier *m.*

basket-ball, *s.* basket-ball *m.*

bass, *s.* basse *f.*

bat¹, *s.* chauve-souris *f.*

bat², *s.* batte *f.*

bath, *s.* bain *m.; (tub)* baignoire *f.*

bathe, *v.n.* se baigner; *v.a.* baigner.

bathing-costume, *s.* costume *m.* de bain(s).

bathroom, *s.* salle *f.* de bain.

battery, *s. (military)* batterie *f.; (electr.)* pile *f.*

battle, *s.* bataille *f.*

bay, *s.* baie *f.*

be, *v. n.* être; *(be situated)* se trouver; *there is* il y a.

beach, *s.* plage *f.*

bead, *s. (string of)* collier *m.*

beak, *s.* bec *m.*

beam, *s. (timber)* poutre *f.; (light)* rayon *m.*

bean, *s.* fève *f.*

bear¹, *s.* ours *m.*

bear², *v.a.* porter; soutenir; supporter.

beard, *s.* barbe *f.*

bearing, *s.* rapport *m.*

beast, *s.* bête *f.*

beat, *v.a.* battre; frapper; — *s.* battement *m.*

beautiful, *adj.* beau, bel, belle.

beauty, *s.* beauté *f.*

beaver, *s.* castor *m.*

because, *conj.* parce que; ~ *of* à cause de.

beckon, *v.n.* faire signe (à).

become, *v. n.* devenir.

bed, *s.* lit *m.*

bed-clothes, *s. pl.* cou-

vertures *f. pl.*
bedroom, *s.* chambre *f.* à
coucher.
bee, *s.* abeille *f.*
beech, *s.* hêtre *m.*
beef, *s.* bœuf *m.*
beef-steak, *s.* bifteck *m.*
beer, *s.* bière *f.*
beetle, *s.* scarabée *m.*
beetroot, *s.* betterave *f.*
before, *prep.(time)* avant;
(space) devant; — *adv.*
avant; *(in front)* en
avant.
beforehand, *adv.* d'avance; en avance.
beg, *v.a.* demander,
prier; *v. n.* mendier;
I ∼ *your pardon!* excusez-moi!; pardon!
beget, *v.a.* engendrer.
beggar, *s.* mendiant, -e.
begin, *v. a. & n.* commencer.
beginner, *s.* commençant,
-e *m. f.*
beginning, *s.* commencement *m.*
behalf, *s. on* ∼ *of* de la
part de; *in* ∼ *of* en
faveur de.
behave, *v.n.* se conduire.
behaviour, *s.* conduite *f.*
behind, *prep.* derrière.
Belgian, *adj.* belge; — *s.*
Belge *m. f.*
belief, *s.* croyance *f.*
believe, *v.a. & n.* croire.
bell, *s.* cloche *f.*
belly, *s.* ventre *m.*
belong, *v.n.* ∼ *to* appartenir à.
belongings, *s. pl.* effets
m.; biens *m.*
below, *adv.* au-dessous; en
bas; — *prep.* au-des-
sous de.
belt, *s.* ceinture *f.*
bench, *s.* banc *m.; (work-
ing)* établi *m.*
bend, *v. a.* courber; tendre

fléchir; *v.n.* se cour-
ber; — *s.* courbure *f.;
(road)* tournant *m.*
beneath *see* below.
benefit, *s.* bienfait *m.;
(gain)* bénéfice *m.*
bent, *s.* penchant *m.*
berry, *s.* baie *f.; (coffee)*
grain *m.*
berth, *s.* couchette *f.;
(for ship)* mouillage *m.*
beseech, *v. a.* supplier.
beside, *prep.* auprès de,
à côté de.
besides, *adv.* en outre.
best, *adj.* le meilleur; *do
one's* ∼ faire tout son
possible (pour).
bestow, *v. a.* conférer (à).
bet, *v.a.* parier.
betray, *v. a.* trahir.
better, *adj.* meilleur;
adv. mieux.
between, *prep* entre.
beyond, *prep.* au delà de.
bias, *s.* biais *m.; (fig.)*
préjugé *m.*
Bible, *s.* bible *f.*
bibliography, *s.* biblio-
graphie *f.*
bicycle, *s.* bicyclette *f.*
big, *adj.* grand; gros.
bill, *s. (hotel)* note *f.;
(restaurant)* addition
f.; (invoice) facture *f.;
(of exchange)* lettre *f.*
de change; *(of fare)*
carte *f.,* menu *m.;
(poster)* affiche *f.;(parliament)* projet *m.* de
loi.
bin, *s.* huche *f.,* coffre *m.*
bind, *v.a.* lier; *(book)*
relier.
biological, *adj.* biologique.
biology, *f.* biologie *f.*
birch, *s.* bouleau *m.*
bird, *s.* oiseau *m.*
birth, *s.* naissance *f.*
birthday, *s.* anniversaire
m.

birth-place, s. lieu m. de naissance.
biscuit, s. biscuit m.
bishop, s. évêque m.
bit[1], s. morceau m.; (drill) mèche f.; a ~ un peu (de).
bit[2], s. (horse) mors m.
bite, v. a. & n. mordre.
bitter, adj. amer; mordant; (cold) âpre.
bitterness, s. amertume f.
black, adj. noir.
blackbird, s. merle m.
blackmail, s. chantage m.
blacksmith, s. forgeron m.
bladder, s. vessie f.
blade, s. lame f.
blame, s. blâme m.; — v. a. blâmer, accuser qn.
blameless, adj. innocent.
blank, adj. blanc; nu; — s. blanc m.
blanket, s. couverture f.
blast, s. rafale f.; coup m. de vent; souffle m.; — v.a. faire sauter; détruire.
blaze, s. flamme f.; — v.n. flamber.
bleak, adj. lugubre.
bleed, v.a. & n. saigner.
blend, s. mélange m.; — v.a. fondre; mêler.
bless, v.a. bénir.
blessing, s. bénédiction f.
blind[1], adj. aveugle.
blind[2], s. store m.
blindness, s. cécité f.
blink, v. n. clignoter.
bliss, s. félicité f.
blister, s. ampoule f.
block, s. bloc m.; (wood) billot m.; (buildings) pâté m.; (traffic) encombrement m.
blond adj. blond.
blood, s. sang m.
bloody, adj. sanglant.
bloom, s. fleur f.; — v. n. fleurir.
blossom, s. fleur f.
blot, s. tache f.; pâté m.
blouse, s. blouse f.
blow[1], v. a. (trumpet) sonner; (glass) souffler; ~ out éteindre; ~ up faire sauter; v.n. (wind) souffler.
blow[2], s. coup m.
blue, adj. bleu.
blunder, s. bévue f.; — v. n. faire une bévue
blunt, adj. émoussé; (person) brusque.
blush, v.n. rougir.
board, s. planche f.; (meals) pension f.; (council) conseil m.; (paper) carton m.; (theatre) ~s planches; ~ and lodging pension f. et chambre(s); on ~ (ship) à bord d'un navire; — v.n. prendre pension chez; v.a. monter à bord de.
boarder, s. pensionnaire m. f.
boarding-house, s. pension f.
boarding-school, s. pensionnat m.
boast, s. vanterie f.; — v. n. se vanter (de).
boat, s. bateau m.
body, s. corps m.
bog, s. marécage m.
boil[1], v.a. faire bouillir; (cook) faire cuire; v. n. bouillir.
boil[2], s. furoncle m.
boiler, s. chaudière f.
bold, adj. hardi; effronté.
boldness, s. hardiesse f.; effronterie f.
bolt, s. verrou m.; — v. a. verrouiller; v. n. filer.
bomb, s. bombe f.
bond, s. lien m.
bone, s. os m.; (fish)

arête *f.*

bonnet, *s.* chapeau *m.;* bonnet *m.; (motor)* capot *m.*

bony, *adj.* osseux; maigre.

book, *s.* livre *m.;* — *v.a* prendre (un billet); retenir.

bockcase, *s.* bibliothèque *f.*

booking-office, *s.* guichet *m.*

book-keeper, *s.* teneur *m.* de livres.

book-keeping, *s.* compatibilité *f.*

booklet, *s.* livret *m.*

bookseller, *s.* libraire *m.*

bookshelf, *s.* rayon *m.*

bookshop, *s.* librairie *f.*

book-stall, *s.* bibliothèque (de gare) *f.*

boot, *s.* bottine *f.;* brodequin *m.*

booth, *s.* baraque *f.*

booty, *s.* butin *m.*

border, *s.* bord *m.;* frontiere *f.*

bore, *v. a.* ennuyer, raser; — *s.* raseur *m.*

boring, *adj.* ennuyeux, assomment.

born, *pp.* né; *be* ~ naître.

borrow, *v. a.* emprunter.

bosom, *s.* sein *m.*

boss, *s.* patron *m.*

botanical, *adj.* botanique.

botany, *s.* botanique *m.*

both, *pron. & adj.* l'un(e) et l'autre; tous (les) deux; ~ ... *and* et ... et ...

bother, *v.a.* tracasser.

bottle, *s.* bouteille *f.*

bottom, *s.* bas *m.;* fond *m.;* derrière *m.*

bough, *s.* rameau *m.*

bound, *pp.* ~ *for* à destination de, en route pour.

boundary, *s.* borne *f.*

bounty, *s.* générosité *f.*

bouquet, *s.* bouquet *m.*

bow[1], *s.* arc *m.; (violin)* archet *m.; (knot)* nœud *m.*

bow[2], *v.a.* incliner; courber; *v.n.* s'incliner; se courber; — *s.* salut *m.; (ship)* avant *m.*

bowels, *s. pl.* entrailles *f.*

bowl, *s.* bol *m.,* jatte *f.*

box, *s.* boîte *f.,* caisse *f.; (horse)* stalle *f.; (theatre)* loge *f.; (on the ears)* soufflet *m.;* — *v. n.* boxer.

box-office, *s.* bureau *m.* de location.

boy, *s.* garçon *m.;* ~ *scout* boy-scout *m.,* éclaireur *m.*

bra, *s.* soutien-gorge *m.*

brace, *s.* couple *f.;* lien *m.;* ~*s* bretelles *f. pl.*

bracelet, *s.* bracelet *m.*

brain, *s.* cerveau *m.;* ~*s* cervelle *f.*

brainy, *adv.* intelligent.

brake, *s.* frein *m.*

branch, *s.* branche *f.*

brand, *s.* tison *m.;* marque *f.;* — *v.a.* marquer.

brandy, *s.* cognac *m.*

brass, *s.* cuivre jaune *m.*

brave, *adj.* brave.

brawl, *s.* querelle *f.*

bread, *s.* pain *m.*

breadth, *s.* largeur *f.*

break, *v.a.* briser, casser; *(law)* violer; *(promise)* manquer; *(news)* apprendre à; *v. n.* se casser; se briser; ~ *down* abattre; s'effondrer; *(motor)* avoir une panne; ~ *in* dresser; ~ *up* lever; — *s.* interruption *f.;* pause *f.*

break-down, *s. (motor)* panne *f.; (health)* débâcle; ~ *lorry* dépanneuse *f.*

breakfast, *s.* déjeuner *m.*

breast, *s.* poitrine *f.,* sein *m.*

breath, *s.* haleine *f.;* souffle *m.*

breathe, *v.a.* & *n.* respirer.

breathless, *adj.* essoufflé; sans souffle.

breeches, *s. pl.* culotte *f.*

breed, *s.* race *f.;* — *v.a.* élever.

breeze, *s.* brise *f.*

breezy, *adj.* venteux.

brew, *v.a.* brasser.

bribe, *s.* pot-de-vin *m.;* — *v.a.* corrompre.

brick, *s.* brique *f.*

bricklayer, *s.* maçon *m.*

bride, *s.* mariée *f.*

bridegroom, *s.* marié *m.*

bridge, *s.* pont *m.*

bridle, *s.* bride *f.*

brief, *adj.* bref.

briefcase, *s.* serviette *f.*

briefly, *adv.* brièvement.

briefs, *s. pl.* slip *m.*

bright, *adj.* brillant; vif; clair; éclatant.

brighten, *v.a.* faire briller; égayer.

brightness, *s.* éclat *m.*

brilliant, *s.* brillant *m.*

brim, *s.* bord *m.*

bring, *v.a.* amener; apporter; ~ *about* amener; ~ *back* rapporter; ~ *forth* produire; ~ *up* élever.

brink, *s.* bord *m.*

brisk, *adj.* vif; actif.

bristle, *s. (brush)* poil *m.*

British, *adj.* britannique.

brittle, *adj.* cassant.

broad, *adj.* large; vaste.

broadcast, *v.a.* radiodiffuser.

broadcasting, *s.* radiodiffusion *f.*

broken, *adj.* brisé.

bronze, *s.* bronze *m.*

brooch, *s.* broche *f.*

brood, *s.* couvée *f.;* — *v.n.* couver.

brook, *s.* ruisseau *m.*

broom, *s.* balai *m.*

brother, *s.* frère *m.*

brother-in-law, *s.* beau-frère *m.*

brow, *s.* sourcil *m.*

brown, *adj.* brun.

bruise, *s.* contusion *f.;* — *v.a.* meurtrir.

brush, *s.* brosse *f.;* pinceau *m.;* balai *m.;* — *v.a.* brosser; ~ *up* donner un coup de brosse à.

brutal, *adj.* brutal, cruel.

brutality, *s.* brutalité *f.*

bubble, *s.* bulle *f.;* — *v. n.* bouillonner.

buck, *s.* daim *m.*

bucket, *s.* seau *m.*

buckle, *s.* boucle *f.*

bud, *s.* bourgeon *m.*

budget, *s.* budget *m.*

buffet, *s.* soufflet *m.*

bug, *s.* punaise *f.*

build, *v.a.* bâtir; construire; sur; ~ *up* établir.

builder, *s.* entrepreneur *m.* de bâtiments; constructeur *m.*

building, *s.* bâtiment *m.*

bulb, *s.* bulbe *m.; (lamp)* ampoule *f.*

bulge, *v.n.* bomber.

bulk, *s.* masse *f.;* volume *m.*

bull, *s.* taureau *m.*

bullet, *s.* balle *f.*

bulletin, *s.* bulletin *m.*

bump, *s.* bosse *f.;* collision *f.;* coup *m.*

bumper, *s.* pare-choc *m.*

bun, *s.* brioche *f.*

bunch, *s.* bouquet *m.;* botte *f.;* grappe *f.*

bundle, *s.* botte *f.;* paquet

m.; fagot m.
bunk, s. couchette f.
buoy, s. bouée f.
burden, s. charge f.; fardeau m.
burglar, s. cambrioleur m.
burial, s. enterrement m.
burn, v.a. & n. brûler.
bursary, s. bourse f.
burst, v.n. éclater; crever; exploser; v.a. faire éclater; rompre; crever; — s. éclat m.; explosion f.
bury, v.a. enterrer.
bus, s. autobus m.
bush, s. buisson m.
business, s. affaires f. pl.;

profession f.; on ~ pour affaires; ~ hours heures (f. pl.) d'ouverture.
businessman, s. homme m. d'affaires.
bus-stop, s. arrêt m. d'autobus.
busy, adj. occupé, affairé.
but, conj. mais.
butcher, s. boucher m.; ~'s (shop) boucherie f.
butter, s. beurre m.
butterfly, s. papillon m.
buttock, s. fesse f., derrière m.
button, s. bouton m.
buy, v.a. acheter.
buyer, s. acheteur m.
by, prep. par; de; ~ Monday d'ici à lundi.
bystander, s. spectateur, -trice m. f.

C

cab, s. taxi m.; fiacre m.
cabbage, s. chou m.
cabin, s. cabane f.; (ship) cabine f.
cabinet, s. (politics) cabinet m.
cable, s. câble m.
cablegram. s. câblo-

gramme m.
café, s. café(-restaurant) m.
cage, s. cage f.
cake, s. gâteau m.
calculate, v.a.&n. calculer.
calculation, s. calcul m.
calendar, s. calendrier m.
calf, s. veau m.; (leg) mollet m.
call, v. a. & n. appeler; ~ for, réclamer; ~ on faire visite à; — s. appel m.; cri m.; (visit) visite f.
call-box, s. cabine f. téléphonique.
calm, adj. calme.
calorie, s. calorie f.
camel, s. chameau, -elle m. f.
camera, s. appareil m. (photographique).
camp, s. camp m.
campaign, s. campagne f.
camping, s. camping m.
can¹, s. broc m.; pot m.
can², v. aux. pouvoir;

savoir.
canal, s. canal m.
canary, s. canari m.
cancel, v.a. annuler.
cancer, s. cancer m.
candle, s. chandelle f.; bougie f.
cannon, s. canon m.
canoe, e s. canoë m.
canteen, s. cantine f.
canvas, s. toile f.
cap, s. bonnet m.; casquette f.
capable, adj. capable (de).
capacity, s. capacité f.
cape, s. (land) cap m.; (cloak) pèlerine f.; cape f.
capital, s. (city) capitale f.; (letter) majuscule f. (commerce) capital m;
capsule, s. capsule f.

captain, s. capitaine m.
caption, s. sous-titre m.
captivate, v.a. captiver.
capture, v.a. capturer; — s. capture f.
car, s. voiture f., auto f.
caravan, s. roulotte f. (de camping), caravane f.
carbon-paper, s. papier m. carbone.
carburetter, s. carburateur m.
card, s. carte f.
cardboard, s. carton m.
cardinal, adj. m. cardinal m.
care, s. attention f.; soin m.; souci m.; ~ of aux bons soins de; take ~ of prendre soin de; — v.n. ~ for se soucier de; ~ to aimer.
career, s. carrière f.
careful, adj. soigneux.
careless, adj. insouciant, négligent.
caress, v.a. caresser.
cargo, s. cargaison f.
caricature, s. caricature f.
carnation, s. œillet m.
carpenter, s. charpentier m.
carpet, s. tapis m.
carriage, s. voiture f.; (transport) transport m.
carriage-way, s. chaussée f.
carrier, s. voiturier m.
carrot, s. carotte f.
carry, v.a. porter; transporter; ~ on exercer; ~ out mettre à exécution.
cart, s. charrette f.
cartridge, s. cartouche f.
carve, v. a.& n. sculpter; (meat) découper.
case, s. (box) étui m., caisse f.; (instance) cas m.; cause f.
casement, s. croisée f.
cash, s. espèces f. pl.
cash-book, s. livre m. de caisse.
cashier, s. caissier, -ère m. f.
cash-register, s. caisse f. enregistreuse.
cask, s. tonneau m.
cast, v.a. jeter; (metal) fondre; — s. coup m.; (theatre) distribution f.
castle, s. château m.
casual, adj. casuel.
casualty, s. accident m.
cat, s. chat, -te m. f.
catalogue, s. catalogue m.
catastrophe, s. catastrophe f.
catch, v.a. saisir; attraper; (eye) frapper; ~ up rattraper; — s. prise f.; attrape f.
category, s. catégorie f.
cater, v.n. pourvoir à.
caterpillar, s. chenille f.
cathedral, s. cathédrale f.
catholic, adj. catholique.
catholicism, s. catholicisme m.
cattle, s. bétail m. (pl. bestiaux).
cauliflower, s. chou-fleur m.
cause, s. cause f.; motif m.; — v.a. causer.
caution, s. prudence f.
cautious, adj. prudent.
cave, s. caverne f.
cavity, s. cavité f.
cease, v.a. & n. cesser.
ceiling, s. plafond m.
celebrate, v.a. célébrer.
celebration, s. célébration f.; commémoration f.
celery, s. céleri m.
cell, s. cellule f.
cellar, s. cave f.
cello, s. violoncelle m.
cellophane, s. cellophane

f.

cement, *s.* ciment *m.;* — *v.a.* cimenter.
cemetery, *s.* cimetière *m.*
centenary, *s.* centenaire *m.*
central, *adj.* central.
centre, *s.* centre *m.*
century, *s.* siècle *m.*
cereal, *s.* céréale *f.*
ceremony, *s.* cérémonie *f.*
certain, *adj.* certain.
certainly, *adj.* certainement; sans doute
certainty, *s.* certitude *f.*
certificate, *s.* certificat *m.*
certify, *v.a.* certifier.
chain, *s.* chaîne *f.*
chair, *s.* chaise *f.;* (professorship) chaire *f.;* take the ~ présider.
chairman, *s.* président *m.*
chalk, *s.* craie *f.*
challenge, *s.* défi *m.;* — *v.a.* défier; provoquer.
chamber, *s.* chambre *f.;* ~s étude *f.;* appartement *m.*
champagne, *s.* champagne *m.*
champion, *s.* champion *m.*
championship, *s.* championnat *m.*
chance, *s.* chance *f.;* bv ~ par hasard.
chancellor, *s.* chancelier *m.*
chancery, *s.* chancellerie *f.*
change, *s.* changement *m.;* (money) monnaie *f.;* — *v.a.&n.* changer.
channel, *s.* canal *m.;* the English Channel la Manche.
chap, *s.* type *m.*
chapel, *s.* chapelle *f.*
chaplain, *s.* chapelain *m.*
chapter, *s.* chapitre *m.*
character *s.* caractère *m.;* (theatre) personnage

m.

characteristic, *adj.* caractéristique; — *s.* trait *m.* caractéristique.
charcoal, *s.* charbon *m.* de bois
charge, *s.* charge *f.;* (price) prix *m.;* (accusation) accusation *f.;* — *v.a.* charger (de); (price) demander; faire payer; (accuse) accuser (de).
charity, *s.* charité *f.*
charm, *s.* charme *m.*
charming, *adj.* charmant.
chart, *s.* carte *f.* marine.
charter, *s.* charte *f.*
charwoman, *s.* femme *f.* de ménage.
chase, *v.a.* chasser; poursuivre; — *s.* chasse *f.*
chassis, *s.* châssis *m.*
chat, *s.* causette *f.;* — *v. n.* causer.
chatter, *v.n.* babiller; (teeth) claquer.
cheap, *adj.* bon marché.
cheat, *v.a.* tromper; tricher; — *s.* tromperie *f.;* tricherie; (pers.) fourbe *m.*
check, *v.a.* contrôler, vérifier; (stop) arrêter; — *s.* vérification *f.,* contrôle *m.*
checkmate, *s.* échec et mat *m.*
check-up, *s.* examen *m.* médical.
cheek, *s.* joue *f.*
cheeky, *adj.* impertinent.
cheer, *v.a.* réjouir, encourager; acclamer; *v.n.* ~ up reprendre sa gaieté; courage!; — *s.* joie *f.;* ~s acclamations *f.*
cheerful, *adj.* joyeux.
cheese, *s.* fromage *m.*
chemical, *adj.* chimique.
chemist, *s.* chimiste *m.;*

pharmacien *m.;* ~'s
(shop) pharmacie *f.*
chemistry, *s.* chimie *f.*
cheque, *s.* chèque *m.;*
traveller's ~ chéque
m. de voyage.
cheque-book, *s.* carnet
m. de chèques.
cherish, *v. a.* soigner;
(hope) caresser.
cherry, *s.* cerise *f.*
chess, *s.* échecs *m. pl.*
chess-board, *s.* échiquier
m.
chest, *s.* coffre *m.; (part
of body)* poitrine *f.;*
~ *of drawers* commode
f.
chestnut, *s.* châtaigne *f.*
chew, *v.a.* mâcher.
chicken, *s.* poulet *m.*
chief, *adj.* principal; —
s. chef *m.*
chiefly, *adv.* principa-
lement.
child, *s.* enfant *m.f.*
childhood, *s.* enfance *f.*
childish, *adj.* enfantin.
childless, *adj.* sans enfant.
chill, *s.* coup *m.* de
froid; — *v.a.* refroi-
dir, glacer.
chilly, *adj. (weather)* frais;
(un peu) froid.
chimney, *s.* cheminée *f.*
chin, *s.* menton *m.*
china, *s.* porcelaine *f.*
Chinese, *adj.* chinois; —
s. Chinois, -e.
chip, *s.* éclat *m.;* copeau
m.; ~s frites *f. pl.*
chirp, *v.n.* gazouiller.
chisel, *s.* ciseau *m.;* —
v.a. ciseler.
chivalry, *s.* chevalerie *f.*
chocolate, *s.* chocolat *m.*
choice, *s.* choix *m.*
choir, *s.* chœur *m.*
choke, *v.a. & n.* étouffer.
choose, *v.a.* choisir.
chop, *s.* côtelette *f.*

chorus, *s.* chœur *m.*
Christian, *adj.* chrétien;
~ *name* prénom *m.*
Christianity, *s.* christianisme *m.*
Christmas, *s.* Noël *m.;*
~ *eve* veille *f.* de Noël.
chuckle, *v.n.* rire tout
bas; — *s.* rire étouffé.
church, *s.* église *f.*
churchyard, *s.* cimetière
m.
cider, *s.* cidre *m.*
cigar, *s.* cigare *m.*
cigarette, *s.* cigarette *f.*
cigarette-case, *s.* étui *m.*
à cigarettes.
cigarette-holder, *s.* porte-
cigarette *m.*
cinders, *s.pl.* cendres *f.*
cine-camera, *s.* camera *f.*
cinema, *s.* cinéma *m.*
cinerama, *s.* cinérama *m.*
circle, *s.* cercle *m.*
circuit, *s.* circuit *m.;*
détour *m.;* tournée *f.*
circular, *adj.* circulaire.
circulate, *v.n.* circuler;
v.a. faire circuler.
circulation, *s.* circulation
f.
circumstance, *s.* circonstance *f.*
circus, *s.* cirque *m.*
cistern, *s.* citerne *f.*
citation, *s.* citation *f.*
cite, *v. a.* citer.
citizen, *s.* citoyen, -ne
m. f., habitant *m.*
citizenship, *s.* droit *m.*
de cité.
city, *s.* ville *f.; the City*
Cité *f.*
civil, *adj.* civil; *(polite)*
poli; ~ *servant* fonc-
tionnaire *m.*
civilization, *s.* civilisation *f.*
civilize, *v.a.* civiliser.
claim, *s.* demande *f.,*
réclamation *f.;* droit
m.; — *v.a.* revendi-

quer, réclamer.

clamp, s. crampon m.

clang, s. bruit m. métallique; — v.n. retentir.

clap, s. battement m.; applaudissements m. pl.; — v.n. applaudir.

clash, v.a. choquer; v.n. s'entre-choquer.

clasp, s. agrafe f.; fermoir m.; — v.a. agrafer; joindre.

class, s. classe f.

classic(al), adj. classique.

classify, v.a. classifier.

class-room, s. classe f.

clatter, s. bruit m.; fracas m.; — v.n. faire du bruit.

clause, s. clause f., article m.

claw, s. griffe f.; serre f.; ongle m.

clay, s. glaise f.; argile f.

clean, adj. propre; blanc; pur; — v.a. nettoyer.

cleanse, v.a. nettoyer.

clear, adj. clair; — v.a. déblayer; éclaircir; v.n. s'éclaircir; ~ away enever; ~ out filer.

clearly, adv. clair, clairement; évidemment.

cleave, v.a. fendre; v.n. se fendre.

clergy, s. clergé m.

clergyman, s. ministre m.

clerk, s. employé m., commis m.

clever, adj. habile, adroit; intelligent.

client, s. client m.

cliff, s. falaise f.

climate, s. climat m.

climb, v.a. & n. grimper.

cling, v.n. ~ to se cramponner à.

clinic, s. clinique f.

clip, s. pince; — v.a. tondre; couper; rogner; (tickets) poinconner.

cloak, s. manteau m.

cloak-room, s. consigne f.; vestiaire m.

clock, s. horloge f.; pendule f.; it is 10 o'clock il est dix heures.

close, v.a. (shut) fermer; (end) terminer; v.n. (se) fermer; se terminer; — adj. fermé; (narrow) étroit; (relations) proche; intime; — adv. tout près; — s. enclos m.; (end) fin f.

closely, adv. de près; étroitement.

closet, s. cabinet m.; armoire f.

cloth, s. drap m.; (table) nappe f.

clothe, v.a. vêtir.

clothes, s.pl. habits m.pl.

clothing, s. vêtements m. pl.

cloud, s. nuage m.

cloudy, adj. couvert.

clover, s. trèfle m.

club, s. (stick) massue f.; (people) cercle m., club m., société f.; (cards) trèfle m.

clue, s. fil m.; (crossword) définition f.

clumsy, adj. gauche.

cluster, s. grappe f.

clutch, v.a. empoigner; m. pour empoigner; (motor) embrayage m.

coach, s. voiture f.; wagon m.; autocar m.; (sports) entraîneur m.

coal, s. charbon m.

coal-mine, s. mine f. de houille.

coarse, adj. grossier; vulgaire.

coast, s. côte f.

coat, s. (jacket) veston m.; (top) pardessus m., manteau m.

cock, s. coq m., mâle m.; (gun) chien m.; (tap) robinet m.

cocktail, s. cocktail m.

cocoa, s. cacao m.

cod, s. morue f.

code, s. code m.

coffee, s. café m.

coffee-pot, s. cafetière f.

coffin, s. cercueil m.

cog-wheel, s. roue f. dentée.

coil, s. rouleau m.; bobine f.; — v.a. lover; enrouler.

coin, s. pièce f.

coincidence, s. coïncidence f.

coke, s. coke m.

cold, adj. froid; be ~ (pers.) avoir froid; (weather) faire froid; — s. froid m.; (in the head) rhume m.; catch a ~ s'enrhumer.

collaborate, v. n. collaborer.

collaborator, s. collaborateur, -trice m.f.

collapse, v.n. s'effondrer; (pers.) s'affaisser; — s. effondrement m.; (pers.) affaissement m. subit.

collar, s. col m.; collet m.

colleague, s. collègue m. f.

collect, v.a. rassembler; recueillir.

collection, s. collection f.; collecte f.; (mail) levée f.

college, s. collège m.

collide, v.n. se heurter (contre), entrer en collision.

colliery, s. houillère f.; mine f.

collision, s. collision f.

colon, s. deux points m. pl.

colonel, s. colonel m.

colony, s. colonie f.

colour, s. couleur f.

colourful, adj. coloré.

colourless, adj. terne, pâle.

column, s. colonne f.

comb, s. peigne m.; v.a. peigner.

combat, s. combat m.

combination, s. combinaison f.

combine, v.a. combiner.

come, v.n. venir, arriver; ~ across rencontrer; ~ back revenir; ~ by obtenir; passer; ~ down descendre; ~ in entrer; ~ off avoir lieu; se détacher; ~ out sortir; ~ up monter.

comedian, s. comédien m.

comedy, s. comédie f.

comely, adj. avenant, bienséant.

comfort, s. consolation f.; bien-être m.; — v.a. consoler.

comfortable, adj. confortable; commode; be ~ être à l'aise.

comic, adj. comique.

comma, s. virgule f.

command, s. ordre m.; — v.a. commander.

commander, s. commandant m.

commandment, s. commandement m.

commemorate, v.a. commémorer.

commence, v.a.& n. commencer.

commend, v.a. recommander; louer.

comment, s. commentaire *m.;* — *v.n.* commenter.

commentary, *s.* commentaire *m.*

commerce, *s.* commerce *m.*

commercial, *adj.* commercial; ~ *traveller* voyageur *m.* de commerce.

commission, *s.* commission *f.;* commande *f.*

commissioner, *s.* commissaire *m.* ·

commit, *v.a.* commettre; confier; ~ *oneself* se compromettre.

commitment, *s.* engagement *m.*

committee, *s.* comité *m.*

commodity, *s.* marchandise *f.,* article *m.*

common, *adj.* commun.

commonwealth, *s.* *the British Commonwealth* commonwealth *m.*

communicate, *v. a. & n.* communiquer.

communication, *s.* communication *f.*

communication-cord, *s.* signal *m.* d'alarme.

communion, *s.* communion *f.*

communiqué, *s.* communiqué *m.*

community, *s.* communauté *f.*

compact, *s.* pacte *m.;* poudrier *m.;* — *adj.* compact; concis.

companion, *s.* compagnon, -agne *m. f.*

company, *s.* compagnie *f.;* société *f.*

comparatively, *adv.* comparativement.

compare, *v.a.* comparer

(to à, *with* avec).

comparison, *s.* comparaison *f.*

compartment, *s.* compartiment *m.*

compass, *s.* *(mariner's)* boussole *f.; (pair of)* ~*es* compas *m.*

compassion, *s.* compassion *f.*

compel, *v.a.* forcer.

compete, *v.n.* faire concurrence (à); concourir.

competence, *s.* compétence *f.;* capacité *f.*

competent, *adj.* capable.

competition, *s.* concurrence *f.;* concours *m.;* compétition *f.*

competitor, *s.* concurrent *m.*

compilation, *s.* compilation *f.*

compile, *v.a.* compiler.

complain, *v.n.* se plaindre

complaint, *s.* plainte *f.;* maladie *f.;* réclamation *f.*

complement, *s.* complément *m.*

complete, *v.a.* compléter, achever; — *adj.* complet.

complicated, *adj.* compliqué.

complication, *s.* complication *f.*

compliment, *s.* compliment *m.*

comply, *v.n.* ~ *with* se conformer à.

component, *adj. & s.* composant *(m.).*

compose, *v.a.* composer; *be* ~*d of* se composer de.

composer, *s.* compositeur *m.*

composition, *s.* composition *f.;* dissertation *f.*

compound, *s. & adj.* composé *(m.);* — *v.a.* composer.

comprehend, *v.a.* comprendre.

comprehension, *s.* compréhension *f.*

compress, *v.a.* comprimer.

compromise, *s.* compromis *m.; — v.a.* compromettre.

compulsory, *adj.* obligatoire.

compute, *v.a.* calculer, computer.

computer, *s.* calculateur *m.* (électronique).

comrade, *s.* camarade *m.*

conceal, *v. a.* cacher.

conceit, *s.* vanité *f.*

conceive, *v.a.* concevoir.

concept, *s.* concept *m.*

concern, *v.a.* concerner; regarder; *be ~ed (in, with)* s'intéresser (à); *(about)* s'inquiéter (de); *— s.* affaire *f.;* entreprise *f.;* anxiété *f.*

concerning, *prep.* concernant.

concert, *a.* concert *m.*

concession, *s.* concession *f.*

conciliation, *s.* réconciliation *f.*

concise, *adj.* concis.

conclude, *v.a. &n.* conclure.

conclusion, *s.* conclusion *f.; in ~* pour conclure.

concrete, *s.* béton *m.; — adj.* concret.

condemn, *v.a.* condamner.

condense, *v.a.* condenser.

condition, *s.* condition *f.;* état *m.; on ~ that* à condition que.

conduct, *s.* conduite *f.; — v. a.* conduire; diriger.

conductor, *s.* receveur *m.;* chef *m.* d'orchestre.

cone, *s.* cône *m.*

confederacy, *s.* confédération *f.*

confer, *v.a. & n.* conférer.

conference, *s.* conférence *f.*

confess, *v.a.* avouer; confesser.

confession, *s.* confession *f.*

confidence, *s.* confiance *f.*

confident, *adj.* confiant.

confidential, *adj.* confidentiel.

confine, *v.a.* confiner, enfermer; *be ~d to bed* être alité.

confirm, *v. a.* confirmer.

confirmation, *s.* confirmation *f.*

conflict, *s.* conflit *m.*

confound, *v. a.* confondre.

confront, *v.a.* être en face; confronter.

confuse, *v.a.* brouiller, mettre en désordre.

confusion, *s.* confusion *f.*

congratulate, *v.a.* féliciter (de).

congratulation, *s.* félicitations *f. pl.*

congregation, *s.* assemblée *f.,* congrégation *f.*

congress, *s.* congrès *m.*

conjunction, *s.* conjonction *f.*

connect, *v.a.* joindre, lier; associer.

connection, *s.* connexion *f.;* rapport *m.; (railw.)* correspondance *f.*

conquer, *v.a.* vaincre; conquérir.

conqueror, *s.* vainqueur *m.;* conquérant *m.*

conscience, *s.* conscience *f.*

conscious *adj. be ~ (= not fainting)* avoir connaissance; *be ~ of* avoir la conscience de.

consciousness, *s.* connaissance *f.;* conscience *f.*

conscript, *adj. & s.* conscrit *(m.).*

consent, *s.* consentement; *— v.n.* consentir.

consequence, *s.* conséquence *f.*

consequent, *adj.* conséquent.

consequently, *adv.* par conséquent.

conservation, *s.* conservation *f.*

consider, *v.a.* considérer.

considerable, *adj.* considérable.

considerate, *adj.* attentif; réfléchi.

consideration, *s.* considération *f.; (money)* rémunération *f.*

consign, *v.a.* livrer; consigner, expédier.

consignment, *s.* expédition *f.;* envoi *m.*

consist, *v. n.* ~ *of* se composer de, consister en.

consistent, *adj.* conséquent.

consolation, *s.* consolation *f.*

consonant, *s.* consonne *f.*

conspicuous, *adj.* en vue; frappant.

conspiracy, *s.* conspiration *f.*

conspire, *v. a. & n.* conspirer.

constable, *s.* agent *m.* (de police).

constant, *adj.* continuel; constant.

constipation, *s.* constipation *f.*

constitute, *v.a.* constituer.

constitution, *s.* constitution *f.*

constrain, *v.a.* contraindre (à).

constraint, *s.* contrainte *f.*

construct, *v. a.* construire.

construction, *s.* construction *f.*

consul, *s.* consul *m.*

consulate, *s.* consulat *m.*

consult, *v.a. & n.* consulter.

consultation, *s.* consultation *f.;* ~ *room* cabinet *m.* (de consultation).

consume, *v.a. (destroy)* consumer; *(use up)* consommer.

consumer, *s.* consommateur, -trice *m.f.;* ~ *goods* articles *m.* de grande consommation.

consumption, *s.* consommation *f.; (disease)* phtisie *f.*, tuberculose *f.*

contact, *s.* contact *m.;* — *v.a.* entrer en relations avec.

contain, *v.a.* contenir.

container, *s.* récipient *m.*

contemplate, *v.a.* contempler; projeter.

contemplation, *s.* contemplation *f.*

contemporary, *adj. & s.* contemporain *(m.).*

contempt, *s.* mépris *m.*

contemptuous, *adj.* méprisant.

contend, *v.n.* lutter contre (pour).

content, *s.* contentement *m.;* ~*s* contenu *m.; table of* ~*s* table *f.* des matières; — *adj.* content.

contest, *s.* lutte *f.; (sport)* rencontre *f.*, match *m.; (dispute)* contestation *f.;* — *v. a.* contester.

continent, *s.* continent *m.*

continental, *adj.* continental.

continual, *adj.* continuel.

continuation, *s.* continuation *f.;* suite *f.*

continue, *v.a. & n.* continuer.

continuous, *adj.* continu.

contract, *s.* contrat *m.;* — *v.a.* contracter.

contractor, *s.* entrepreneur *m.*

contradiction, *s.* contradiction *f.*

contrary, *adj.* contraire; — *adv.* contrairement.

contrast, *s.* contraste *m.;* — *v.a.* mettre en contraste.

contribute, *v. a. & n.* contribuer.

contribution, *s.* contribution *f.;* article *m.*

contributor, *s.* contribuant *m.;* collaborateur *m.*

contrive, *v.a.* inventer.

control, *s.* autorité *f.;* maîtrise *f.;* direction *f.,* commande *f.;* — *v.a.* gouverner, commander, maîtriser, diriger; contrôler.

controversy, *s.* polémique *f.,* controverse *f.*

convenience, *s.* commodité *f.,* convenance *f.;* public ~ cabinets *m. pl.* d'aisances.

convenient, *adj.* commode; be ~ to s.o. convenir à qn.

conversation, *s.* conversation *f.*

converse, *v.n.* converser; causer.

convert, *v.a.* convertir.

convey, *v.a.* transporter; transmettre; présenter.

conveyance, *s.* transport *m.;* voiture *f.,* véhicule *m.*

conveyer, *s.* porteur *m.;* ~ belt bande *f.* transporteuse.

convict, *s.* forçat *m.;* — *v.a.* convaincre (de), condamner.

convince, *v. a.* convaincre (de).

convoy, *s.* convoi *m.*

cook, *s.* cuisinier, -ière *m. f.; head* ~ chef *m.;*

— *v.a.* faire cuire; *v.n.* cuire.

cooking, *s.* cuisine *f.*

cool, *adj.* frais (*f.* fraîche); (*fig.*) calme; — *v.a.* rafraîchir.

co-operate, *v.n.* coopérer.

co-operation, *s.* coopération *f.*

copper, *s.* cuivre *m.*

copy, *s.* copie *f.;* exemplaire *m.;* numéro *m.* — *v. a.* copier.

copy-book, *s.* cahier *m.*

copyright, *s.* droit *m.* d'auteur.

coral, *s.* corail *m.*

cord, *s.* corde *f.*

cordial, *adj.* cordial.

cork, *s.* bouchon *m.*

corkscrew, *s.* tire-bouchon *m.*

corn, *s.* grain *m.;* grains *m. pl.;* (*wheat*) blé *m.;* (*maize*) maïs *m.*

corner, *s.* coin *m.*

corporal, *adj.* corporel; — *s.* caporal *m.*

corporation, *s.* corporation *f.*

corps, *s.* corps *m.*

corpse, *s.* cadavre *m.*

correct, *adj.* correct; exact; — *v.a.* corriger, rectifier.

correction, *s.* correction *f.;* rectification *f.*

correspond, *v.n.* correspondre; être conforme (à).

correspondence, *s.* correspondance *f.*

correspondent, *s.* correspondant *m.*

corresponding, *adj.* correspondant.

corridor, *s.* corridor *m.;* couloir *m.*

corridor-train, *s.* train *m.* à couloir.

corrupt, *adj.* corrompu

cosmetics, *s. pl.* cosmétiques *m. pl.*, produits *m.pl.* de beauté.

cosmonaut, *s.* cosmonaute *m.*

cost, *s.* coût *m.*, frais *m. pl.;* prix *m.;* ~ *of living* coût de la vie; *at the* ~ *of* au prix de; — *v.n.* coûter.

costly, *adj.* coûteux.

costume, *s.* costume *m.*

cosy, *adj.* confortable.

cottage, *s.* chaumière *f.*

cotton, *s.* coton *m.*

couch, *s.* canapé *m.*, divan *m.*

cough, *s.* toux *f.;* — *v.n.* tousser.

council, *s.* conseil *m.*

councillor, *s.* conseiller *m.*

counsel, *s.* conseil *m.;* avocat *m.*

count¹, *s.* compte *m.; (title)* comte *m.*

count², *v.a. & n.* compter.

countenance, *s.* visage *m.;* air· *m.*

counter, *s.* comptoir *m.*, guichet *m.;* jeton *m.*

counterfoil, *s.* souche *f.*

countersign, *v.a.* contresigner.

countess, *s.* comtesse *f.*

countless, *adj.* innombrable.

country, *s.* pays *m.; (not town)* campagne *f.*

countryman, *s.* campagnard *m.*

countryside, *s.* (les) campagnes *f.pl.*

countrywoman, *s.* paysanne *f.*

county, *s.* comté *m.*

couple, *s.* couple *f.*

courage, *s.* courage *m.*

courageous, *adj.* courageux.

course, *s.* cours *m.*: route *f.; (meal)* service *m.*, plat *m.;* of ~ bien entendu.

court, *s.* cour *f.;* tribunal *m.;* court *m.* (de tennis); — *v.a.* faire la cour à.

courteous, *adj.* courtois.

courtesy, *s.* courtoisie *f.*

courtship, *s.* cour *f.*

courtyard, *s.* cour *f.*

cousin, *s.* cousin, -e *m. f.*

cover, *s.* couverture *f.;* couvercle *m.; (meal)* couvert *m.; (post)* enveloppe *f.;* — *v.a.* couvrir.

cow, *s.* vache *f.*

coward, *s. & adj.* lâche *m.*

crab, *s.* crabe *m.*

crack, *s.* craquement *m.;* — *v.a.* faire craquer; *v.n.* craquer; se fêler.

cradle, *s.* berceau *m.*

craft, *s.* habileté *f.;* embarcation *f.;* métier *m.;* profession *f.*

craftsman, *s.* artisan *m.*

cram, *v.a.* fourrer; bourrer.

crane, *s.* grue *f.*

crash, *s.* fracas *m.;* débâcle; atterrissage brutal, collision; *v.n,* tomber avec fracas; s'écraser sur le sol.

crash-helmet, *s.* serretête *m.*

crave, *v.n.* ~ *for* désirer ardemment.

crawl, *v.n.* ramper; *(pers.)* se traîner.

crayon, *s.* crayon *m.*

craze, *s.* manie *f.*

crazy, *adj.* fou, toqué.

creak, *s.* cri *m.*, grincement *m.;* — *v. n.* crier, grincer.

cream, *s.* crème *f.*

crease, *s.* (faux) pli *m.*

create, *v.a.* créer.

creation, *s.* création *f.*

creature, *s.* créature *f.*

credit, *s.* crédit *m.;* mérite *m.;* honneur *m.;* on ~ à terme; *give* ~ *to* ajouter foi à; — *v.a.* ajouter foi à, créditer.

creditor, *s.* créancier *m.*

creek, *s.* crique *f.*

creep, *v.n.* ramper; se glisser.

crew, *s.* équipage *m.;* équipe *f.*

crib, *s.* mangeoire *f.;* lit *m.* d'enfant; berceau *m.*

cricket, *s. (game)* cricket *m.*

crime, *s.* crime *m.*

criminal, *adj. & s.* criminel, -elle.

cripple, *s.* estropié *m.*

crisis, *s.* crise *f.*

crisp, *adj.* croquant, croustillant; *(air)* vif.

critic, *s.* critique *m.*

critical, *adj.* critique.

criticize, *v.a.* critiquer.

critique, *s.* critique *f.*

croak, *v.n.* croasser.

crochet, *s.* crochet *m.*

crop, *s.* récolte *f.;* cueillette *f.*

cross, *s.* croix *f.;* — *v.a.* croiser, traverser.

crossing, *s.* passage *m.;* *(sea)* traversée *f.;* *level* ~ passage à niveau.

cross-question, *s.* contre-interrogatoire *m.;* — *v.a.* contre-interroger.

cross-reference, *s.* renvoi *m.*

crossroad, *s.* chemin *m.* de traverse; ~s carrefour *m.*

cross-section, *s.* coupe *f.* en travers.

cross-word (puzzle) *s.*

mots *m.pl.* croisés.

crouch, *v. n.* se blottir.

crow, *s.* corneille *f.*

crowd, *s.* foule *f.;* tas *m.*

crowded, *adj.* encombré, comble.

crown, *s.* couronne *f.;* — *v.a.* couronner.

crucial, *adj.* décisif.

crude, *adj* brut; cru; grossier.

cruel, *adj.* cruel.

cruelty, *s.* cruauté *f.*

cruet, *s.* burette *f.*

cruise, *v.n.* croiser; — *s.* voyage *m.*

cruising, *adj.* ~ *speed* vitesse *f.* de croisière.

crumb, *s.* mie *f.;* miette *f.*

crumble, *v.a.* émietter; *v.n.* s'émietter.

crusade, *s.* croisade *f.*

crush, *s.* écrasement *m.;* cohue *f.;* — *v.a.* écraser.

crust, *s.* croûte *f.*

crutch, *s.* béquille *f.*

cry, *s.* cri *m.;* — *v.a.* crier; ~ *down* décrier; *v.n.* crier; *(weep)* pleurer.

crystal, *s.* cristal *m.*

cub, *s.* petit *m.;* *(boy scout)* louveteau *m.*

cube, *s.* cube *m.*

cuckoo, *s.* coucou *m.*

cucumber, *s.* concombre *m.*

cue, *s.* réplique *f.*

cuff, *s.* poignet *m.*, manchette *f.*

cuff-links, *s. pl.* boutons *m.pl.* de manchette.

culminate, *v.n.* se terminer.

culprit, *s.* accusé, -e *m. f.*

cultivate, *v.a.* cultiver.

cultural, *adj.* cultural.

culture, *s.* culture *f.*

cunning, *s.* ruse *f.*, finesse *f.;* — *adj.* rusé.

cup, *s.* tasse *f.;* gobelet *m.*

cupboard, *s.* armoire *f.;* placard *m.*

curate, *s.* vicaire *m.*

curb, *s.* gourmetté *f.*

curd, *s.* (lait) caillé *m.*

curdle, *v.a.* čailler; *v.n.* se cailler.

cure, *s.* guérison *f.;* cure *f.;* remède *m.;* — *v.a.* guérir.

curiosity, *s.* curiosité *f.*

curious, *adj.* curieux.

curl, *s.* boucle *f.;* — *v.a.* & *n.* boucler, friser; ~ *up* s'enrouler.

curly, *adj.* bouclé, frisé.

currant, *s. black* ~ cassis *m.; red* ~ groseille *f.* rouge.

currency, *s.* circulation *f.,* cours *m.;* terme *m.* d'échéance; unité *f.* monétaire, monnaie *f.; foreign* ~ monnaie étrangère.

current, *adj.* courant, en cours; *in* ~ *use* d'usage courant; ~ *events* actualités *f.;* ~ *account* compte *m.* courant; — *s.* courant *m.;* cours *m.*

curse, *s.* malédiction *f.;* — *v.a.* maudire; *v.n.* blasphémer.

curtain, *s.* rideau *m.*

curve, *s.* courbe *f.*

cushion, *s.* coussin *m.*

custom, *s.* coutume *f.;* ~s douane *f.;* ~s *duties* droits *m.* de douane; ~s *declaration* déclaration *f.* de douane; ~s *formalities* la visite de la douane.

customary, *adj.* coutumier; accoutumé.

customer, *s.* client *m.,* acheteur *m.*

custom-house, *s.* douane *f.;* ~ *officer* douanier *m.*

cut, *v.a.* couper; trancher; tailler; hacher; ~ *down* abattre, couper; réduire; ~ *off* couper; ~ *out* tailler; ~ *up* couper, débiter; — *s. (knife)* coup *m.; (wound)* coupure *f.; (clothes)* coupe *f.; (meat)* morceau *m.; (in wages)* réduction *f.*

cutlery, *s.* coutellerie *f.*

cutlet, *s.* côtelette *f.*

cutter, *s.* tailleur *m.;* coupeur *m.*

cycle, *s.* cycle *m.;* bicyclette *f.;* — *v.n.* pédaler.

cycling, *s.* cyclisme *m.*

cylinder, *s.* cylindre *m.*

cynic, *adj.* & *s.* cynique *m.*

Czech, *adj.* tchèque; — *s.* Tchèque *m.*

D

dad, daddy, *s.* papa *m.*

dagger, *s.* poignard *m.*

daily, *adj.* journalier, quotidien; — *s.* (journal) quotidien *m.*

dainty, *adj.* friand, délicat; gentil; — *s.* friandise *f.*

dairy, *s.* laiterie *f.*

daisy, *s.* marguerite *f.*

dam, *s.* barrage *m.;* digue *f.*

damage, *s.* dommage *m.;* préjudice *m.;* ~s dommages-intérêts *m.*

damn, *v.a.* condamner; — *s.* juron *m.*

damp, *adj.* humide; — *s.* humidité *f.;* — *v. a* mouiller, humecter.

dance, *s.* danse *f.;* bal *m.; v.n.* & *a.* danser.

dancer, *s.* danseur, -euse *m. f.*

dancing-hall, s. salle f. de danse; dancing m.

dancing-shoes, s.pl. souliers m. de bal, escarpins m.

Dane, s. Danois, -e m. f.

danger, s. danger m.

dangerous, adj. dangereux.

Danish, adj. danois; — s. (language) danois m.

dare, v. aux. & v. oser.

daring, adj. audacieux.

dark, adj. obscur, sombre; (colour) foncé; (fig.) triste; be ~ faire sombre; — s. obscurité f.; in the ~ dans l'obscurité.

darken, v.a. obscurcir.

darkness, s. obscurité f.

darling, adj. & s. chéri, -e.

darn, v.a. repriser.

darning, s. reprise f.

dart, s. dard m.; ~s (game) fléchettes f.pl.

dash, v.a. lancer; flanquer (par terre); ~ to pieces briser en morceaux; v.n. ~ against se heurter contre; ~ at se précipiter sur — s. (with pen) trait m., tiret m.; (vigour) élan m., fougue f.; attaque f. soudaine.

dash-board, s. tablier m; tableau m. de bord.

data, s. pl. données f.

date¹, s. date f.; millésime m.; be up to ~ être à la page; — v.a. & n. dater.

date², s. datte f.

daughter, s. fille f.

daughter-in-law, s. belle-fille f.

dawn, s. point m. du jour; aube f.

day, s. jour m.; (whole day) journée f.

daylight, s. jour m.

daytime, s. jour m., journée. f.

daze, v.a. étourdir; éblouir.

dazzle, v.a. éblouir.

deacon, s. diacre m.

dead, adj. mort; the ~ les morts m.pl.

deadly, adj. mortel.

deaf, adj. sourd; ~ and dumb sourd-muet.

deal, v.a. ~ out distribuer; donner; v.n. ~ with traiter qn; commercer, traiter avec qn; traiter (d'un sujet); ~ in commercer de; — s. (cards) donne f.; (commerce) affaire f.; a good ~, a great ~ beaucoup (de).

dealer, s. marchand m. (in de).

dean, s. doyen m.

dear, s. & adj. cher m., chère f.

death, s. mort f.

debate, s. débat m., discussion f.; — v.a. discuter, mettre en discussion.

debt, s. dette f.

debtor, s. débiteur, -trice m. f.

decay, s. décadence f.; — v.n. tomber en décadence; pourrir.

decease, s. décès m.; — v.n. décéder.

deceit, s. déception f.; tromperie f.

deceive, v.a. tromper; décevoir.

December, s. décembre m.

decent, adj. décent; assez bon.

deception, s. déception f.

decide, v.a. décider.

decision, s. décision f.

decisive, *adj.* décisif.

deck, *s.* pont *m.*

deck-chair, *s.* transatlantique *f.*

declaration, *s.* déclaration *f.*

declare, *v.a.* déclarer.

decline, *s.* décadence *f.;* — *v.a.* décliner; *v.n.* baisser.

decorate, *v.a.* décorer (de).

decoration, *s.* décoration *f.*

decrease, *v.a. & n.* diminuer; — *s.* diminution *f.*

decree, *s.* décret *m.*

dedicate, *v.a.* dédier.

deed, *s.* action *f.;* acte *m.*

deem, *v.a.* juger.

deep, *adj.* profond; *ten feet ~* dix pieds de profondeur.

deer, *s.* cerf *m.*

deface, *v.a.* défigurer.

defeat, *s.* défaite *f.;* — *v.a.* vaincre.

defect, *s.* défaut *m.*

defence, *s.* défense *f.*

defend, *v.a.* défendre.

defender, *s.* défenseur *m.*

defer, *v.a.* retarder, ajourner; *~ to* déférer à.

defiance, *s.* défi *m.; set at ~* défier.

deficiency, *s.* manque *m.*

deficient, *adj.* insuffisant.

defile, *s.* défilé *m.;* — *v.n.* défiler; *v.a.* souiller.

define, *v.a.* définir.

definite, *adj.* déterminé, défini.

definition, *s.* définition *f.*

defy, *v.a.* défier; braver.

degrade, *v.a.* dégrader.

degree, *s.* degré *m.; (university)* grade *m.;* diplôme *m.*

delay, *s.* retard *m.,* délai *m.;* — *v.a.* retarder; différer; *v.n.* tarder.

delegate, *s.* délégué *m.*

delegation, *s.* délegation *f.*

deliberate, *adj.* délibéré; — *v.a. & n.* délibérer.

delicacy, *s.* délicatesse *f.*

delicate, *adj.* délicat.

delicious, *adj* délicieux.

delight, *v.a. be ~ed at* être enchanté de.

delightful, *adj.* délicieux.

delinquent, *s.* délinquant *m.*

deliver, *v.a. (letters)* distribuer, *(goods etc.)* livrer, *(message)* remettre; *(speech)* faire, prononcer; *(free)* délivrer; *be ~ed of* accoucher de.

delivery, *s. (letters)* distribution *f.,* *(message)* remise *f.,* *(goods)* livraison *f.;* *(speech)* prononciation *f.,* débit *m.*

delusion, *s.* illusion *f.*

demand, *s.* demande, *f.* réclamation *f.;* — *v. a.* demander, réclamer.

democracy, *s.* démocratie *f.*

democrat, *s.* démocrate *m.*

democratic, *adj.* démocratique.

demolish, *v.a.* démolir.

demonstrate, *v.a.* démontrer.

demonstration, *s.* démonstration *f.*

den, *s.* antre *m.;* repaire *m.*

denial, *s.* dénégation *f.*

denomination, *s.* dénomination *f.;* secte *f.*

denote, *v.a.* dénoter.

denounce, *v.a.* dénoncer.

dense, *adj.* dense, épais.

density, *s.* densité *f.*

dentist, *s.* dentiste *m.*

denture, *s. (artificial)* dentier *m.*

deny, *v.a.* nier.
depart, *v.n.* partir.
department, *s.* départe-
ment *m.*
departure, *s.* départ *m.*
depend, *v.n.* dépendre
(de), compter (sur).
dependence, *s.* dépendance *f.*
dependent, *adj.* dépen-
dant.
deplore, *v.a.* déplorer.
deposit, *s.* dépôt *m.;* —
v.a. déposer.
depot, *s.* dépôt *m.*
depression *s.* abattement
m.
deprive, *v.a.* priver (de).
depth, *s.* profondeur *f.*
deputy, *s.* délégué *m.;*
vice-, sous-.
derive, *v.a.* retirer (de);
be ~d from dériver de.
descend, *v.n.* descendre.
descendant, *s.* descen-
dant, -e *m. f.*
descent, *s.* descente *f.*
describe, *v.a.* décrire.
description, *s.* description *f.;* sorte *f.*
desert, *s.* désert *m.;* —
v.a. déserter.
deserve, *v.a.* mériter.
design, *s.* dessein *m.;*
projet *m.;* dessin *m.;*
— *v.a.* dessiner.
desirable, *adj.* désirable.
desire, *s.* désir *m.;* — *v.a.*
désirer.
desk, *s.* bureau *m.*
desolation, *s.* désolation *f.*
despair, *s.* désespoir *m.;*
— *v.n.* désespérer.

despatch *see* dispatch.
desperate, *adj.* désespéré.
despise, *v.a.* mépriser.
despite, *prep.* ~ (of) en
dépit de.
dessert, *s.* dessert *m.*
destination, *s.* destination *f.*

destine, *v.a.* destiner.
destiny, *s.* destin *m.*
destinée *f.*
destroy, *v.a.* détruire.
destruction, *s.* destruction
f.
detach, *v.a.* détacher.
detachment, *s.* détache-
ment *m.*
detail, *s.* détail *m.*
detain, *v.a.* retenir;
détenir.
detect, *v.a.* découvrir.
detective, *s.* détective *m.*
detention, *s.* détention *f.*
detergent, *s.* détergent *m.*
deteriorate, *v.n.* se dé-
tériorer.
determination, *s.* détermination *f.*
determine, *v.a. & n.* déterminer, décider.
detrimental, *adj.* pré-
judiciable.
develop, *v.a.* développer;
v.n. se développer.
development, *s.* développement *m.*
deviation, *s.* déviation *f.*
device, *s* expédient *m.;*
invention *f.*
devil, *s.* diable *m.*
devilish, *adj.* diabolique.
devise, *v.a.* combiner;
tramer.
devote, *v.a.* consacrer.
devoted, *adj.* dévoué.
devotion, *s.* dévotion *f.;*

dévouement *m.*
devour, *v.a.* dévorer.
dew, *s.* rosée *f.*
diagnosis, *s.* diagnostic *m.*
diagram, *s.* diagramme *m.*
dial, *s.* cadran *m.;* —
v.a. composer un
numéro.
dialogue, *s.* dialogue *m.*
diameter, *s.* diamètre *m.*
diamond, *s.* diamant *m.;*
(cards) carreau *m.*
diaper, *s.* couche *f.*

diarrhoea, *s.* diarrhée *f.*

diary, *s.* journal *m.;* agenda *m.*

dictate, *v.a.* dicter; *v.n.* ~ *to* donner des ordres à.

dictation, *s.* dictée *f.*

dictator, *s.* dictateur *m.*

dictionary, *s.* dictionnaire *m.*

die¹, *s.* dé *m.*

die², *v.n.* mourir.

Diesel engine, *s.* moteur *m.* Diesel; diesel *m.*

diet, *s.* alimentation *f.;* régime *m.*

differ, *v.n.* différer.

difference, *s.* différence *f.*

different, *adj.* différent.

difficult, *adj.* difficile.

difficulty, *s.* difficulté *f.*

diffuse, *adj.* diffus.

dig, *v.a.* bêcher.

digest, *v.a.* digérer.

digestion, *s.* digestion *f.*

dignity, *s.* dignité *f.*

diligent, *adj.* diligent.

dim, *adj.* faible, pâle, obscur.

dimension, *s.* dimension *f.*

diminish, *v. a. & n.* diminuer.

dimple, *s.* fossette *f.*

dine, *v.n.* dîner.

dining-car, *s.* wagon-restaurant *m.*

dining-hall, *s.* salle *f.* à manger; réfectoire *m.*

dining-room, *s.* salle *f.* à manger.

dinner, *s.* dîner *m.*

dinner-jacket, *s.* smoking *m.*

dip, *v.a. & n.* plonger.

diploma, *s.* diplôme *m.*

diplomacy, *s.* diplomatie *f.*

diplomat, *s.* diplomate *m.*

diplomatic, *adj.* diplomatique.

direct, *adj.* direct; — *v. a.* diriger; commander; adresser.

direction, *s.* direction *f ;* instructions *f. pl.*

directly, *adv.* directement; tout de suite.

director, *s.* directeur *m.*

directory, *s.* annuaire *m.;* Bottin *m.*

dirt, *s.* saleté *f.;* boue *f.,* crotte *f.;* crasse *f.*

dirty, *adj.* sale; crotté; crasseux.

disadvantage, *s.* désavantage *m.*

disagree, *v.n.* différer; se brouiller; ne pas convenir (à).

disagreeable, *adj.* désagréable.

disappear, *v. n.* disparaître

disappearance, *s.* disparition *f.*

disappoint, *v.a.* désappointer; tromper.

disappointment, *s.* désappointement *m.*

disapprove, *v.n.* ~ *of* désapprouver qch.

disaster, *s.* désastre *m.*

disastrous, *adj.* désastreux.

disc *see* **disk.**

discern, *v.a.* discerner.

discharge, *v. a.* décharger; *(employee)* congédier; renvoyer; *(prisoner)* élargir; *(gas)* dégager; *(debt)* liquider; *(duty)* s'acquitter de; — *s.* décharge *f.; (employee)* congé *m.; (prison)* elargissement *m.*

discipline, *s.* discipline *f.*

disclose, *v.a.* découvrir.

discontented, *adj.* mécontent (de).

discourage, *v. a.* décourager.

discouragement, *s.* décou-

ragement *m.*
discourse, *s.* discours *m.*
discover, *v.a.* découvrir.
discovery, *s.* découverte *f.*
discredit, *s.* discrédit *m.;*
— *v.a.* discréditer.
discreet, *adj.* discret.
discretion, *s.* discrétion
f.; prudence *f.*
discuss, *v.a.* discuter.
discussion, *s.* discussion *f.*
disdain, *v.a.* dédaigner;
— *s.* dédain *m.*
disease, *s.* maladie *f.*
disembark *v.a. & n.* débarquer.
disgrace, *s.* disgrâce *f.;*
— *v.a.* disgracier.
disgraceful, *adj.* honteux.
disguise, *s.* déguisement;
— *v.a.* déguiser.
disgust, *s.* dégoût *m.;*
— *v.a.* dégoûter.
disgusting, *adj.* dégoûtant
dish, *s.* plat *m.;* mets *m.;*
wash up the ~es laver la
vaisselle.
dishonest, *adj.* malhonnête.
dishonour, *s.* déshonneur
m.; — *v.a.* déshonorer
(bill) ne pas honorer.
disinfect, *v.a.* désinfecter.
disk, *s.* disque *m.*
dislike, *s.* aversion *f.,*
dégoût *m.;* — *v.a.* ne
pas aimer.
dismal, *adj.* lugubre, sombre.
dismay, *s.* consternation
f.
dismiss, *v.a.* congédier;
bannir, écarter.
disobedience, *s.* désobéissance *f.*
disobedient, *adj.* désobéissant.
disobey, *v. a.* désobéir (à).
disorder, *s.* désordre *m.*
dispatch, *s.* expédition
f.; dépêche *f.*

dispensary, *s.* pharmacie
f.
dispense, *v.a.* dispenser;
préparer; *v.n. ~ with*
se disposer de.
disperse, *v.a.* disperser.
displaced, *adj. ~ person*
personne *f.* déplacée.
displacement, *s.* déplacement *m.*
display, *v.a.* exposer;
étaler; déployer, faire
preuve de; — *s.* exposition *f.;* étalage *m.;*
parade *f.*
displease, *v.a.* déplaire à
disposal, *s. at s.o.'s ~*
à la disposition de qn.
dispose, *v.n. ~ of* disposer de; vendre.
disposition, *s.* disposition
f.
dispute, *s.* dispute *f.* discussion *f.;* — *v.a* discuter; *v. n.* se disputer.
disqualify, *v.a.* disqualifier.
dissatisfy, *v.a.* mécontenter.
dissolve, *v.a.* dissoudre;
v.n. se dissoudre.
distance, *s.* distance *f.*
distant, *adj.* lointain; éloigné.
distil, *v. a. & n.* distiller.
distinct, *adj.* distinct (de);
marqué.
distinction, *s.* distinction
f.
distinguish, *v.a.* distinguer.
distract, *v.a.* distraire.
distraction, *s.* distraction
f.; confusion *f.*
distress, *s.* détresse *f.;*
— *v.a.* affliger.
distribute, *v. a.* distribuer.
distribution, *s.* distribution *f.*
district, *s.* région *f.,*
contrée *f.;* district *m.*

disturb, *v.a.* troubler; déranger.

disturbance, *s.* trouble *m.*, dérangement *m.*

ditch, *s.* fossé *m.*

dive, *v.n.* plonger *(into* dans).

diver, *s.* plongeur *m.*, scaphandrier *m.*

divergent, *adj.* divergent.

diversion, *s.* déviation *f.*

divide, *v.a.* diviser.

dividend, *s.* dividende *m.*

divine, *adj.* divin.

divinity, *s.* théologie *f.*

division, *s.* division *f.*

divorce, *s.* divorce *m.;* — *v. a.* divorcer (d'avec).

dizzy, *adj. feel* ~ avoir le vertige.

do, *v. a.* faire; finir; ~ *away with* supprimer; ~ *up* envelopper; ~ *with* se contenter de.

dock, *s.* bassin *m.*

doctor, *s.* docteur *m.;* médecin *m.*

doctrine, *s.* doctrine *f.*

document, *s.* document *m.*

dog, *s.* chien *m.*

dogma, *s.* dogme *m.*

doll, *s.* poupée *f.*

dollar, *s.* dollar *m.*

domestic, *adj. & s.* domestique *(m. f.).*

domicile, *s.* domicile *m.*

dominate, *v.a. &. n.* dominer.

dominion, *s.* domination *f.;* ~s colonies *f.*

donkey, *s.* âne *m.*

doom, *s.* sentence *f.;* — *v.a.* condamner; ~ed *to* voué à.

door, *s.* porte *f.;* *(vehicle)* portière *f.*

dormitory, *s.* dortoir *m.*

dose, *s.* dose *f.*

dot, *s.* point *m.*

double, *adj. & s.* double *(m.).*

doubt, *s.* doute *m.; no* ~ sans doute; — *v.a. & n.* douter.

doubtful, *adj.* douteux.

doubtless, *adj.* sans doute.

dough, *s.* pâte *f.*

dove, *s.* colombe *f.*

down, *adv.* à bas, en bas, par en bas; *be* ~ *with (illness)* être au lit avec; *fall* ~ tomber à terre; *go* ~ aller en bas; — *prep.* le long de; ~ *the river* en aval; ~ *the street* plus bas dans la rue.

downhill, *s.* pente *f.;* — *adv.* en pente, en descendant.

downstairs, *adv.* en bas.

downwards, *adv.* en bas.

dozen, *s.* douzaine *f.*

draft, *s.* projet *m.; (letter)* minute *f.; (troops)* détachement *m.; (drawing)* esquisse *f.*

drag, *v.a.* traîner; tirer.

drain, *s.* égout *m.*, canal *m.;* — *v.a.* drainer; vider.

drama, *s.* drame *m.;* théâtre *m.*

dramatic, *adj.* dramatique.

draper, *s.* marchand *m.* d'étoffes, (marchand) drapier *m.;* ~'s magasin *m.* de nouveautés.

draught, *s.* tirage *m.; (drink)* trait *m.; (air)* courant *m.* d'air.

draw, *v.a. (pull)* tirer, traîner; *(tooth)* arracher; *(sketch)* dessiner; ~ *down* baisser; ~ *on* tirer; ~ *out* prolonger; — *v. n.* tirer; ~ *near* s'approcher.

drawer, s. tiroir m.

drawing, s. dessin m.

drawing-pin, s. punaise f.

drawing-room, s. salon m.

dread, v.a. redouter.

dreadful, adj. redoutable.

dream, s. rêve m.; — v.a. & n. rêver.

dress, s. habits m.pl.; robe f.; — v. a. habiller; v.n. s'habiller; ~ a wound panser.

dress-circle, s. (premier) balcon m.

dressing-gown, s. (woman) peignoir m., (man) robe f. de chambre.

dressmaker, s. couturière f.

drift, v.n. flotter; dériver; — s. dérive f.; amoncellement m.

drill, s. foret m.; (soldiers) exercice m.

drink, s. boisson f.; — v.a. boire.

drip, v.n. dégoutter.

drive, v.a. conduire; ~ in (nail) enfoncer; v.n. conduire; aller en voiture.

driver, s. (engine) mécanicien m.; (bus) conducteur m.; (car) chauffeur m.

driving, s. conduite f.; ~ licence permis m. de conduire.

drop, s. goutte f.; — v.a. laisser tomber; abandonner; v.n. (dé-)goutter; ~ in entrer en passant.

drown, v.a. noyer; v.n. se noyer.

drug, s. drogue f.

druggist, s. droguiste m.

drum, s. tambour m.

drunk, adj. ivre.

dry, adj. sec, sèche; aride; tari; — v.a. sécher.

dry-clean, v.a. nettoyer à sec.

dual, adj. double.

dub, v.a. doubler.

duchess, s. duchesse f.

duck, s. cane f.; canard m.

due, adj. (proper) dû; (owing) exigible; échéant, payable; in ~ form en bonne et due forme; in ~ time en temps voulu; ~ to causé par, par suite de; the train is ~ at le train arrive à; — s. dû m.; droit m.

duke, s. duc m.

dull, adj. borné; ennuyeux; (colour) terne; (weather, sad) triste.

dumb, adj. muet.

dummy, s. mannequin m.; (cards) mort m.

dung, s. fumier m.

dupe, s. dupe f.; — v.a. duper.

duplicate, s. duplicata m.; — adj. en double; — v.a. faire en double.

during, adv. pendant, au cours de.

dusk, s. crépuscule m.

dust, s. poussière f.

dustbin, s. poubelle f.

dusty, adj. poussiéreux, poudreux.

Dutch, adj. hollandais.

Dutchman, s. Hollandais m.

duty, s. devoir m.; (customs) droit m.; (task) tâche f., fonction(s) f.(pl.); be on ~ être de service.

duty-free, adj. exempt de droits, en franchise.

dwarf, s. nain, -e m. f.

dwell, v.n. habiter; ~ (up)on s'appesantir sur.

dwelling, s. habitation f.

dwelling-house s. maison f. d'habitation.
dwindle, v.n. diminuer.
dye, s. teinte f., teinture f.; — v.a. teindre.
dynasty, s. dynastie f.

E

each, pron. chacun, -e; ~ other l'un l'autre; — adj. chaque.
eager, adj. ardent.
eagle, s. aigle m.
ear, s. oreille f.
earl, s. comte m.
early, adv. de bonne heure — adj. précoce; premier.
earn, v. a. gagner; mériter
earnest, adj. sérieux.
earnings, s.pl. salaire m.
earth, s. terre f.
earthenware, s. poterie f.
earthquake, s. tremblement m. de terre.
ease, s. aise f.; repos m.; at one's ~ à son aise; with ~ avec facilité.
east, s. est m.; — adj. d'est, de l'est; — adv. à l'est (de).
Easter, s. Pâques m. pl.
eastern, adj. (de l')est, oriental.
eastwards, adv. vers l'est.
easy, adj. facile.
easy-chair, s. fauteuil m.
easy-going, adj. nonchalant.
eat, v.a. manger; ~ up finir; dévorer.
ebb, s. reflux m.
ecclesiastic, adj. & s. ecclésiastique (m.).
economic, adj. économique.
economical, adj. économe

economics, s. économie f. politique.
economize, v.n. faire des économes.
economy, s. économie f.
ecstasy, s. extase f.
edge, s. tranchant m., fil m.; bord m.
edition, s. édition f.
editor, s. rédacteur m.
editorial, s. article m. de fond.
educate, v.a. élever.
education, s. éducation f.
effect, s. effet m.
effective, adj. efficace; effectif.
efficiency, s. efficacité f
efficient, adj. capable.
effort, s. effort m.
egg, s. œuf m.; boiled ~ œuf à la coque; fried ~ œuf sur le plat.
Egyptian, adj. égyptien; — s. Egyptien, -enne m. f.
eight, adj. & s. huit.
eighteen, adj. & s. dix-huit.
eighteenth, adj. dix-huitième.
eighth, adj. huitième.
eighty, adj.&s. quatre-vingt(s).
either, pron. & adj. l'un ou l'autre; chacun; chaque; ~ ... or ou ... ou.
elaborate, v.a. élaborer; — adj. minutieux.
elastic, adj. élastique.
elbow, s. coude m.
elderly, adj. d'un certain âge.
elect, v.a. choisir; élire.
election, s. élection f.
electric(al), adj. électrique; ~al engineer (ingénieur) électricien m.

electricity, *s.* électricité *f.*
electron, *s.* électron *m.*
electronic, *adj.* électronique.
elegance, *s.* élégance *f.*
elegant, *adj.* élégant.
element, *s.* élément *m.*
elementary, *adj.* élémentaire.
elephant, *s.* éléphant *m.*
elevate, *v.a.* élever.
eleven, *adj.* & *s.* onze.
eleventh, *adj.* onzième.
elm, *s.* orme *m.*
else, *adj.* autre; *anything* ~, *madam?* encore quelque chose, Madame?; — *adv. or* ~ ou bien, autrement.
elsewhere, *adv.* ailleurs.
embankment, *s.* remblai *m.*
embark, *v.a.* embarquer; *v.n.* s'embarquer.
embarrass, *v.a.* embarrasser.
embassy, *s.* ambassade *f.*
embrace, *v.a.* embrasser.
embroidery, broderie *f.*
emerge, *v.n.* émerger; apparaître.
emergency, *s.* circonstance *f.* critique; *in case of* ~ en cas d'accident *or* d'urgence; ~ *exit* sortie *f.* de secours.
emigrant, *s.* émigrant, -e *m. f.*
emigrate, *v.n.* émigrer.
emigration, *s.* émigration *f.*
eminent, *adj.* éminent.
emit, *v.a.* émettre.
emotion, *s.* émotion *f.*
emphasis, *s.* accent *m.*, force *f.*; *lay* ~ *on* appuyer sur.
emphasize, *v. a.* appuyer sur.
empire, *s.* empire *m.*
employ, *v.a.* employer.

employee, *s.* employé *m.*
employer, *s.* employeur *m.*
employment, *s.* emploi *m.*
empty, *adj.* vide.
enable, *v. a.* rendre capable.
enclose, *v.a.* entourer (de); joindre (à une lettre).
encounter, *v.a.* affronter; rencontrer.
encourage, *v.a.* encourager.
encouragement, *s.* encouragement *m.*
encyclopaedia, *s.* encyclopédie *f.*
end, *s.* bout *m.; fin f.;* — *v.a.&n.* finir; ~ *in* finir en.
endeavour, *s.* effort *m.;* — *v. n.* s'efforcer (à *or* de).
ending, *s.* terminaison *f.; fin f.*
endless, *adj.* sans fin.
endorse, *v.a.* endosser.
endorsement, *s.* endossement *m.*
endow, *v.a.* doter (de).
endure, *v.a.* supporter, endurer.
enemy, *s.* ennemi, -e *m. f.*
energetic, *adj.* énergique.
energy, *s.* énergie *f.*
enforce, *v.a.* imposer; *(law)* faire exécuter.
engage, *v.a.* engager; fiancer; *be* ~*d* être occupé; être fiancé(e).
engagement, *s.* engagement *m.; fiançailles f. pl.*
engine, *s.* machine *f.*
engine-driver, *s.* mécanicien *m.*
engineer, *s.* ingénieur *m.*
English, *adj.* anglais.
Englishman, *s.* Anglais *m.*

Englishwomen, *s.* Anglaise *f.*

enjoy, *v. a.* jouir de; trouver bon; ~ *oneself* s'amuser.

enjoyment, *s.* jouissance *f.*

enlarge, *v.a.* agrandir.

enlist, *v.a.* enrôler.

enormous, *adj.* énorme.

enough, *adj.* & *adv.* assez (de).

enquire *see* **inquire.**

enrage, *v.a.* exaspérer.

enrol(l), *v.a.* enrôler.

ensign, *s. (flag)* drapeau *m.*, pavillon *m.*; *(pers.)* porte-drapeau *m.*

ensue, *v.n.* s'ensuivre.

enter, *v.a.* entrer (dans); *(in list)* inscrire.

enterprise, *s.* entreprise *f.*

entertain, *v.a.* amuser; recevoir; avoir (une opinion).

entertainment, *s.* divertissement *m.;* amusement *m.;* hospitalité *f.*

enthusiasm, *s.* enthousiasme. *m.*

enthusiastic, *adj.* enthousiaste.

entire, *adj.* entier.

entirely, *adv.* entièrement.

entitle, *v.a. be* ~*d to* avoir droit à. ,

entrance, *s.* entrée *f.;* ~ *examination* examen d'entrée *m.*

entreat, *v.a.* supplier.

entry, *s.* entrée *f.;* inscription *f.*

enumerate, *v.a.* énumérer.

envelope, *s.* enveloppe *f.*

envious, *adj.* envieux (de).

enviromment, *s.* milieu *m.*

envy, *s.* envie *f.;* — *v.a.* envier.

epidemic, *s.* épidémie *f.*

equal, *adj.* égal.

equality, *s.* égalité *f.*

equation, *s.* équation *f.*

equip, *v.a.* équiper.

equipment, *s.* équipement *m.*

erase *v.a.* effacer.

erect, *adj.* droit ; — *v.a.* dresser; ériger.

err, *v.n.* errer.

error, *s.* erreur *f.*

escalator, *s.* escalator *m.*, escalier *m.* roulant.

escape, *v. n.* (s')échapper; — *s.* fuite *f.*

escort, *s.* escorte *f.;* — *v.a.* escorter.

essay, *s.* essai *m.*, composition *f.*

essential, *adj.* essentiel.

establish, *v.a.* établir.

establishment, *s.* établissement *m.*

estate, *s.* propriété *f.;* biens *m. pl.*

esteem, *s.* estime *f.;* — *v.a.* estimer.

estimate, *s.* estimation *f.;* évaulation *f.;* — *v.a.* estimer.

eternal, *adj.* éternel.

eucharist, *s.* eucharistie *f.*

European, *adj.* européen.

evacuate, *v.a.* évacuer.

even, *adj.* uni; égal; pair; — *adv.* même; ~ *if* même si.

evening, *s.* soir *m.;* *(party)* soirée *f.*

event, *s.* événement *m.*

eventual, *adj.* éventuel.

ever, *adv.* toujours; *(any time)* jamais.

evermore, *adv.* toujours.

every, *adj. (all)* tous; *(each)* chaque; ~ *day* tous les jours.

everybody, *pron.* tout le monde.

everyday, *adj.* de tous les jours.

everyone *see* **everybody.**

everything, *pron.* tout *m.*

everywhere, *adv*. partout.
evidence, *s*. évidence *f*.
evident, *adj*. évident.
evil, *s*. mal *m*.; — *adj*. mauvais.
evolution, *s*. évolution *f*.
ewe, brebis *f*.

exact, *adj*. exact.
exactly, *adv*. exactement.
exaggerate, *v.a*. exagérer.
exaggeration. *s*. exagération *f*.
examination, *s*. examen *m*.
examine, *v.a*. examiner; vérifier; *(customs)* visiter.
example, *s*. example *m*.; *for* ~ par exemple.
excavation, *s*. fouille *f*.
exceedingly, *adv*. excessivement.
excel, *v. a*. surpasser; *v. n*. exceller à.
excellent, *adj*. excellent.
except, *v.a*. excepter; — *prep*. excepté; sauf; ~ *for* exception faite pour.
exception, *s*. exception *f*.
exceptional, *adj*. exceptionnel.
excess, *s*. excès *m*.; ~ *luggage* excédent *m*. de bagages.
excessive, *adj*. excessif.
exchange, *s*. échange *m*.; *(telephone)* bureau central *m*.; *foreign* ~ change *m*.; — *v.a*. échanger.
excite, *v.a*. exciter.
excitement, *s*. excitation *f*.
exclaim, *v.n*. s'écrier.
exclamation, *s*. exclamation *f*.
exclude, *v.a*. exclure.
exclusive, *adj*. exclusif.
excursion, *s*. excursion *f*.
excuse, *s*. excuse *f*.; — *v.a*. excuser.

execute, *v.a*. exécuter.
execution, *s*. exécution *f*.
executive, *adj. & s*. exécutif *m*.; agent *m*. d'exécution
exempt, *adj*. exempt (de); *v.a*. exempter (de).
exercise, *s*. exercice *m*.; — *v.a*. exercer.
exertion, *s*. effort *m*.
exhaust, *v.a*. épuiser.
exhaust-pipe, *s*. tuyau *m*. d'échappement.
exhibit, *v. a*. présenter, exhiber; exposer.
exhibition, *s*. exhibition *f*.; exposition *f*.
exist, *v.n*. exister.
existence, *s*. existence *f*.
exit, *s*. sortie *f*.
expand, *v.a*. étendre; dilater.
expansion, *s*. expansion *f*.
expect, *v.a*. attendre, s'attendre à; *(think)* croire.
expedient, *s*. expédient *m*.
expedition, *s*. expédition *f*.
expel, *v.a*. expulser.
expense, *s*. dépense *f*.
expensive, *adj*. coûteux, cher.
experience, *s*. expérience *f*.; — *v.a*. éprouver.
experiment, *s*. expérience *f*.; — *v.n*. faire des expériences, expérimenter.
experimental, *adj*. expérimental.
expert, *s*. expert *m*.
expire, *v.n*. expirer.
explain, *v.a*. expliquer.
explanation, *s*. explication *f*.
exploration, *s*. exploration.
explore, *v.a*. explorer.

explosion, *s*. explosion *f*.
export, *s*. exportation *f*.; ~*s* articles *m.pl*. d'ex-

portation; — *v.a.* exporter.
exporter, *s.* exportateur *m.*
expose, *v.a.* exposer.
exposure, *s.* exposition *f.*; révélation *f.*
express, *adj.* exprès; formel; exact; ~ *letter* lettre *f.* par exprès; — *s.* *(train)* express *m.*; — *v.a.* exprimer.
expression, *s.* expression *f.*
exquisite, *adj.* exquis.
extend, *v.a.* étendre; prolonger.
extension, *s.* extension *f.*; prolongation *f.*
extensive, *adj.* étendu, vaste.
extent, *s.* étendue *f.*
extinguish, *v.a.* éteindre.
extra, *adj.* supplémentaire.
extract, *s.* extrait *m.*; — *v.a.* extraire.
extraordinary, *adj.* extraordinaire.
extravagant, *adj.* extravagant.
extreme, *adj.* & *s.* extrême *(m.)*.
extremely, *adv.* extrêmement.
extremity, *s.* extrèmité *f.*
eye, *s.* œil *m.*
eyebrow, *s.* sourcil *m.*
eyelid, *s.* paupière *f.*
eyepiece, *s.* oculaire *m.*

F

fable, *s.* fable *f.*
fabric, *s.* tissu *m.*; textile *m.*
face, *s.* visage *m.*; face *f.*; figure *f.*; *in ~ of* devant; — *v.a.* affronter, faire face à, braver.
facility, *s.* facilité *f.*
fact, *s.* fait *m.*; *in ~* de fait; en effet.
factor, *s.* facteur *m.*; élément *m.*
factory, *s.* fabrique *f.*; usine *f.*
faculty, *s.* faculté *f.*
fade, *v.n.* se faner; ~ *away* s'évanouir.
fail, *v.n.* manquer (de); *(not succeed)* échouer, *(in an exam)* être refusé.
failure, *s.* insuccès *m.*
faint, *v.n.* s'évanouir.
fair, *adj.* beau; bel, belle; *(hair)* blond; *(just)* juste; *(weather)* clair; ~ *play* jeu loyal *m.*
fairly, *adv.* assez bien.
faith, *s.* foi *f.*
faithful, *adj.* fidèle.
falcon, *s.* faucon *m.*
fall, *v.n.* tomber; baisser; ~ *back on* avoir recours à; ~ *in* s'effondrer; ~ *off* se déprécier; ~ *under* être compris dans; — *s.* chute *f.*; baisse *f.*
false, *adj.* faux; artificiel.
falter, *v.n.* hésiter.
fame, *s.* réputation *f.*; renommée *f.*
familiar, *adj.* familier, intime (avec).
family, *s.* famille *f.*
famous, *adj.* célèbre, fameux.
fan¹, *s.* éventail *m.*; ventilateur *m.*
fan², *s.* passionné, -e *m. f.*, fervent *m.*
fancy, *s.* fantaisie *f.*, imagination *f.*
fantastic, *adj.* fantastique; fantasque.
far, *adv.* loin; ~ *off* au loin; *as ~ as* autant que; *by ~* de beaucoup; *how ~ is it?* à

quelle distance est-ce?;
— *adj.* lointain.

fare, *s.* prix de (la) place
m.; (taxi) prix de la
course*m.; (food)* chère*f.*

farewell, *s.* adieu *m.; bid*
~ *to* dire adieu à.

farm, *s.* ferme *f.*

farmer, *s.* fermier *m.*

farming, *s.* agriculture *f.*

farmyard, *s.* cour *f.* de
ferme.

farther, *adv.* plus loin
(que).

fashion, *s.* mode *f.;*
manière *f.*

fashionable, *adj.* élégant.

fast, *adj.* vite, rapide;
be ~ *(clock)* avancer;
— *adv.* vite.

fasten, *v.a.* attacher.

fastener, *s.* attache *f.;*
agrafe *f.; zip* ~ ferme-
ture éclair *f.*

fat, *adj.* gros, gras; — *s.*
gras *m.;* graisse *f.*

fatal, *adj.* fatal.

fate, *s.* destin *m.,* sort *m.*

father, *s.* père *m.*

father-in-law, *s.* beau-
père *m.*

fatigue, *s.* fatigue *f.*

fault, *s.* défaut *m.;* faute
f.

faultless, *adj.* sans faute.

faulty, *adj.* défectueux.

favour, *s.* faveur *f.; in* ~
of en faveur de; *do a* ~
rendre un service (à).

favourable, *adj.* favorable.

favourite, *adj.* favori.

fear, *s.* crainte *f.;* —
v.a.& n. craindre.

fearful, *adj.* affreux,
effrayant.

feast, *s.* fête *f.;* festin *m.*

feat, *s.* exploit *m.*

feather, *s.* plume *f.*

feature, *s.* trait *m.;* caractéristique *f.;* ~ *film* le

grand film.

February, *s.* février *m.*

federal, *adj.* fédéral.

federation, *s.* fédération *f.*

fee, *s.* honoraires *m. pl.;*
(school) ~*s* frais *m. pl.*

feeble, *adj.* faible.

feed, *v. a.* nourrir; paître.

feel, *v.n.&a.* (se) sentir;
éprouver, ressentir,
(with hand) toucher;
tâter; ~ *cold* avoir
froid.

feeling, *s.* sentiment *m.*

fellow, *s.* camarade *m.;*
compagnon *m.;* gar-
çon *m.; (of a society)*
membre *m., (univer-
sity)* agrégé *m.*

fellowship, *s.* camaraderie
f.; communauté *f.*

female, *adj.* féminin;
(animal) femelle; — *s.*
femme *f.;* femelle *f.*

feminine, *adj.* féminin.

fence, *s.* clôture *f.;* pa-
lissade *f.;* — *v.a.*
enclore; *v. n.* faire de
l'escrime.

fencing, *s.* escrime *f.*

fender, *s.* pare-choc(s) *m.*

ferry, *s.* (passage *m.* en)
bac *m.*

ferry-boat, *s.* bac *m.*

fertile, *adj.* fertile.

fertilize, *v.a.* fertiliser.

festival, *s.* festival *m.*

fetch, *v.a.* aller chercher;
apporter.

feudal, *adj.* féodal.

fever, *s.* fièvre *f.*

few, *pron.* & *adj.* peu
(de); *a* ~ quelques-
(-uns).

fiancé, -e, *s.* fiancé, -e
m. f.

fibre, *s.* fibre *f.*

fiction, *s.* fiction *f.;*
(novels) romans *m. pl.*

field, *s.* champ *m.;*
(sport) terrain *m.*

fierce, *adj.* cruel, violent,

féroce.

fiery, adj. de feu; ardent.

fifteen, adj. & s. quinze (m.).

fifteenth, adj. quinzième.

fifth, adj. cinquième; cinq.

fiftieth, adj. cinquantième.

fifty, adj. & s. cinquante (m.).

fig, s. figue f.

fight, s. combat m.; lutte f.

fighter, s. combattant m.; avion m. de chasse.

figure, s. figure f.; (arithm.) chiffre m.

file¹, s. (tool) lime f.; — .a. limer.

file², s. classeur m., dossier m.; liasse f.; (people) file f.; — v.a. classer; enregistrer.

filing-cabinet, s. cartonnier m., fichier m.

fill, v.a. remplir; occuper; ~ in, up remplir.

film, s. (photo) pellicule f.; (cinema) film m.

filter, s. filtre m.; — v.a. filtrer.

filthy, adj. sale; (fig.) obscène.

fin, s. nageoire f.

final, adj. final.

finally, adv. enfin.

finance, s. finance f.

financial, adj. financier.

find, v.a. trouver; ~ out inventer, découvrir.

fine¹, s. (penalty) amende f.; — v.a. mettre à l'amende.

fine², adj. fin; beau.

finger, s. doigt m.; first ~ index m.

finger-print, s. empreinte f. digitale.

finish, v. a. finir; terminer.

Finnish, adj. finlandais.

fir, s. sapin m.

fire, s. feu m.; on ~ en feu; — v.a. mettre feu à; (gun) tirer; v.n. tirer.

fire-arm, s. arme f. à feu.

fire-brigade, s. les pompiers m. pl.

fire-engine, s. pompe f. à incendie.

fire-escape, s. escalier m. de sauvetage.

fireplace, s. cheminée f.

fire-station, s. poste m. d'incendie.

fireworks, s.pl. feu m. d'artifice.

firm¹, s. maison f. (de commerce).

firm², adj. ferme.

firmament, s. firmament m.

firmness, s. fermeté f.

first, adj. premier; — adv. premièrement; d'abord; (railway) en première; at ~ d'abord.

firstly, adv. premièrement.

first-rate, adj. de premier ordre.

fish, s. poisson m.; — v. a. & n. pêcher.

fisher(man), s. pêcheur m.

fishmonger, s. poissonnier m.

fist, s. poing m.

fit¹, s. attaque f.; accès m.

fit², adj. convenable, bon, propre; en état (de), capable (de).

five, adj. & s. cinq (m.).

fix, v.a. fixer; ~ up arranger.

flag, s. drapeau m.; (navy) pavillon m.

flagrant, adj. flagrant.

flake, s. flocon m.

flame, s. flamme f.
flannel, s. flanelle f.
flap, s. coup m., tape f.
flare, v.n. flamboyer.
flash, s. éclair m.; —
v.n. jeter des éclairs,
étinceler.
flashlight, s. flash (électronique) m.
flat[1], adj. plat; insipide;
(postitive) formel, net;
— s. plat m.; (music)
bémol m.
flat[2], s. appartement m.;
étage m.
flatter, v.a. flatter.
flattery, s. flatterie f.
flavour, s. saveur f.,
goût m., arome m.
flax, s. lin m.
flea, s. puce f.
flee, v.a. & n. fuir, se
sauver.
fleece, s. toison f.
fleet, s. flotte f.
flesh, s. chair f.; viande f.
flexible, adj. flexible.
flight, s. vol m. (birds,
stairs) volée f.; (flee-
ing) fuite f.
flimsy, adj. ténu; fragile;
frivole.
fling, v.a. jeter.
flirt, s. coquette f.; —
v.n. flirter.
float, v.n. flotter; v.a.
faire flotter.
flock, s. troupeau m.,
troupe f.
flood, s. inondation f.;
(tide) flux m.; — v.a.
inonder.
flood-light, v.a. illuminer
par projecteurs.
floor, s. plancher m.,
parquet m.; (storey)
étage m.
flour, s. farine f.
flourish, v.n. fleurir;
prospérer.
flow, v.n. couler, s'écouler; — s. flux m.; cours

m.
flower, s. fleur f.
flower-bed, s. plate-bande
f.
flu, s. grippe f.
flue, s. tuyau m.
fluent, adj. facile, cou-
lant.
fluid, adj. & s. fluide (m.).
fluorescent, adj. ~ lamp
tube m. fluorescent.
flush, v.a. inonder; net-
toyer avec une chasse
d'eau; v. n. rougir.
flute, s. flûte f.
flutter, s. voltigement m.;
— v. a. agiter; v. n. voltiger.
fly[1], s. mouche f.
fly[2], v.n. voler; prendre
l'avion (pour).
foam, s. écume f.; (beer)
mousse f.
focus, s. foyer m.
fodder, s. fourrage m.
fog, s. brouillard m.
foil[1], s. feuille f.; tain m.
foil[2], s. (fencing) fleuret
m.
fold, s. pli m.; — v.a.
plier; envelopper;
(arms) croiser; ~ up
replier.
folding, adj. pliant.
foliage, s. feuillage m.
folk, s. gens m. pl.
follow, v.a. suivre; ac-
compagner; v.n. sui-
vre; s'ensuivre; as ~s
comme suit.
follower, s. suivant m.,
compagnon m., parti-
san m.
following, adj. suivant;
the ~ ce qui suit.
folly, s. sottise f.
fond, adj. be ~ of aimer.
food, s. nourriture f.,
aliments m. pl.
fool, s. sot m.
foolish, adj. sot; fou.

foot, *s.* pied *m.; on* ~ à pied.

football, *s.* football *m.;* ballon *m.*

foot-brake, *s.* frein *m.* à pied

foot-note, *s.* note *f.* (au bas de la page).

footstep, *s.* pas *m.*

for[1], *prep.* pour; *(in exchange for)* contre; *(because of)* à cause de; *(time)* pendant; *(in spite of)* malgré.

for[2], *conj.* car.

forbid, *v.a.* défendre; interdire.

force, *s.* force *f.;* violence *f.; —* *v.a.* forcer.

forearm, *s.* avant-bras *m.*

forecast, *s.* prévision *f.; — v.a.* prévoir.

forefinger, *s.* index *m.*

foreground, *s.* premier plan *m.*

forehead, *s.* front *m.*

foreign, *adj.* étranger.

foreigner, *s.* étranger, -ère *m. f.*

foremost, *adj.* premier; — *adv. first and* ~ tout d'abord.

foresee, *v.a.* prévoir.

forest, *s.* forêt *f.*

foretell, *v.a.* prédire.

foreword, *s.* avant-propos *m.*

orge, *v.a.* forger.

forgery, *s.* contrefaçon *f.;* faux *m.*

forget, *v.a.* oublier.

forgetful, *adj.* oublieux.

forgive, *v.a.* pardonner.

fork, *s.* fourchette *f.;* *(hay)* fourche *f.*

form, *s.* torme *f.;* *(bench)* banc *m.;* *(class)* classe *f.;* *(paper)* formule *f.;* ~ *of government* régime *m.; — v.a.* former.

formal, *adj.* formel.

formality, *s.* formalité *f.*

former, *pron.* le premier, la première; celui-là, celle-là; — *adj.* premier, -ère; précédent.

formerly, *adv.* autrefois.

formula, *s.* formule *f.*

forsake, *v. a.* abandonner.

fortieth, *adj.* quarantième.

fortification, *s.* fortification *f.*

fortify, *v.a.* fortifier.

fortnight, *s.* quinze jours *m. pl.*

fortress, *s.* forte sse *f.*

fortunate, *adj.* ureux.

fortunately *ad* heureusement

fortune, *s.* fortune *f*

forty, *adj. & s.* quarante *(m.).*

forward, *adv.* en avant; *go* ~ (s')avancer; — *adj.* avancé; — *v.a.* faire suivre; expédier.

forwarding, *s.* expédition *f.;* ~ *agency* entreprise *f.* de transport.

forwards, *adv.* en avant.

foul, *adj.* sale; impure; *(language)* ordurier.

found, *v. a.* fonder.

foundation, *s.* fondation *f.*

founder, *s.* fondateur *m.*

fountain, *s.* fontaine *f.*

fountain-pen, *s.* stylo-(graphe) *m.*

four, *adj. & s.* quatre *(m.).*

fourteen, *adj. & s.* quatorze *(m.).*

fourth, *adj.* quatrième; quatre.

fowl, *s.* poule *f.*

fox, *s.* renard *m.*

fraction, *s.* fraction *f.*

fracture, *s.* fracture *f.*

fragile, *adj.* fragile.

fragment, *s.* fragment *m.*

fragrant, *adj.* parfumé.

frame, *s. (picture)* cadre *m.; (structure)* charpente *f.; (window)* châssis *m.*

framework, *s.* charpente *f.*

frank, *adj.* franc.

frankness, *s.* franchise *f.*

fraud, *s.* fraude *f.*

free, *adj.* libre; ~ *of, from* exempt de.

freedom, *s.* liberté *f.*

freely, *adv.* librement; gratis.

freeze, *v.a.* geler.

freight, *s.* fret *m.*

French, *adj.* français; — *s. (language)* le français; *the* ~ les Français *m. pl.*

French-bean(s), *s. (pl.)* haricots *m.pl.* verts.

Frenchman, *s.* Français *m.*

Frenchwoman, *s.* Française *f.*

frequent, *adj.* fréquent; — *v. a.* fréquenter.

frequently, *adv.* fréquemment.

fresh, *adj.* frais, fraîche; nouveau, nouvel, -elle.

friar, *s.* moine *m.*

fricassee, *s.* fricassée *f.*

friction, *s.* friction *f.*

Friday, *s.* vendredi *m.*

fridge, *s.* frigo *m.*

friend, *s.* ami, -e *m. f.*

friendly, *adj.* aimable; ami; amical.

friendship, *s.* amitié *f.*

fright, *s.* peur *f.; take* ~ prendre peur.

frighten, *v.a.* effrayer.

frightful, *adj.* affreux; effrayant.

frock, *s.* robe *f.*

frog, *s.* grenouille *f.*

frolic, *s.* ébats *m. pl.; — v.n.* folâtrer, gambader.

from, *prep. (place)* de; *(time)* depuis; *(separation)* de, à; *(change)* de.

front, *s.* front *m.; devant m.;* façade *f.; in* ~ *of* en face de, en avant de; — *adj.* de devant.

front-door, *s.* porte *f.* d'entrée.

frontier, *s.* frontière *f.*

frost, *s.* gelée *f.*

frosty, *adj.* de gelée; *fig.* froid.

frown, *v.a. & n.* froncer les sourcils.

frozen, *adj.* gelé.

fruit, *s.* fruit *m.*

fruitful, *adj.* fructueux.

fruit-tree, *s.* arbre fruitier *m.*

frustrate, *v.a.* déjouer; décevoir; contrecarres.

fry, *v. a. & n.* (faire) frire.

frying-pan, *s.* poêle (à frire) *f.*

fuel, *s.* combustible *m.*

fulfil, *v.a.* accomplir.

full, *adj.* plein; complet; ~ *name* les nom et prénoms *m. pl.;* ~ *stop* point *m.*

full-time, *adj.* de toute la journée.

fully, *adv.* pleinement.

fume, *s.* fumée *f.*

fun, *s.* amusement *m.; for* ~ pour rire.

function, *s.* fonction *f.*

fund, *s.* fonds *m.*

fundamental, *adj.* fondamental.

funeral, *s.* funérailles *f. pl.*

funnel, *s.* entonnoir *m.; (steamer)* cheminée *f.*

funny, *adj.* drôle.

fur, *s.* fourrure *f.*

fur-coat, *s.* manteau *m.* de fourrure.

furious, *adj.* furieux.

furnace, *s.* fourneau *m.*

furnish, *v. a.* pourvoir (de), fournir; meubler (de).

furniture, *s.* meubles *m. pl.*, ameublement *m.;*

piece of ~ meuble m.
furrier, s. fourreur m.
furrow, s. sillon m.
further, adv. plus loin; (any longer) davantage; — adj. ultérieur; autre; plus lointain; supplémentaire, nouveau.
furthermore, adv. en outre, de plus.
fury, s. fureur f.; (pers.) furie f.
fuss, s. embarras m.; bruit m.; make a ~ faire des embarras; — v. n. faire des embarras; ~ about faire l'affairé.
future, s. avenir m.; (gramm.) futur m.; in the ~ à l'avenir; — adj. futur.

G

gain, s. gain m., — v.a. gagner.
gait, s. allure f.
gala, s. gala m.
gale, s. grand vent m.
gall, s. bile f.; fiel m; amertume f.
gallant, adj. brave; galant.
gallery, s. galerie f.
gallon, s. gallon m.
gallop, s. galop m.; — v.n. galoper.
gamble, v. n. jouer; — s. jeu m.
game, s. jeu m.; partie f.; (animal) gibier m.
gamekeeper, s. garde-chasse m.
gang, s. bande f.; équipe f.
gangway, s. passage m.
gaol see **jail.**
gap, s. trou m.; brèche f.; vide m.
gape, v.n. bâiller; stand gaping gober des mouches; ~ at regarder bouche bée.
garage, s. garage m.

garden, s. jardin m.
gardener, s. jardinier m.
garlic, s. ail m.
garment, s. vêtement m.
garnish, s. garniture f.; — v.a. garnir.
garter, s. jarretière f.
gas, s. gaz m.
gasp, s. soupir m.
gas-works, s. pl. usine f. à gaz.
gate, s. porte f.
gateway, s. portail m.
gather, v.a. réunir; amasser; cueillir; (understand) conclure; v.n. s'assembler.
gathering, s. rassemblement m.; abcès m.
gauge, s. jauge f.; calibre m.; indicateur m.; — v.a. jauger; calibrer.
gauze, s. gaze f.
gay, adj. gai.
gear, s. attirail m., appareil m.; (motorcar) vitesse f.
gear-box, s. boîte f. des vitesses.
gear-lever, s. levier m. des vitesses.
general, adj. général; — s. général m. (pl. généraux).
generation, s. génération f.
generator, s. générateur m.
generosity, s. générosité f.
generous, adj. généreux.
genial, adj. doux, douce; bienfaisant.
genius s. génie m.
gentle, adj. doux, douce.
gentleman, s. gentleman m.
genuine, adj. authentique; vrai.
geographical, adj. géographique.
geography, s. géographie f
geology, s. géologie f.
geometric(al), adj. géomé-

trique.

geometry, *s.* géométrie *f.*
germ, *s.* germe *m.*
German, *adj.* allemand; —
—*s.* Allemand, -e *m.f.*
gesticulate, *v.n.* gesticuler.
gesture, *s.* geste *m.*
get, *v.a.* obtenir, procurer, trouver, recevoir; — *v.n.* arriver; *(become)* devenir; ~ *at* parvenir (à); ~ *in* entrer; ~ *off* partir; ~ *on* prospérer; *(agree)* s'accorder (avec); ~ *out of* sortir (de); ~ *over* surmonter; *(illness)* se remettre; ~ *up* se lever.
geyser, *s.* chauffe-bain *m.*
ghost, *s.* esprit *m.;* revenant *m.,* fantôme *m.*
giant, *s.* géant *m.*
gift, *s.* don *m.*
gifted, *adj.* bien doué.
gills, *s. pl.* ouïes *f.*
gin, *s.* genièvre *m.;* gin *m.*
giraffe, *s.* girafe *f.*
girdle, *s.* ceinture *f.;* — *v.a.* ceinturer.
girl, *s.* jeune fille *f.*
give, *v. a.* donner; ~ *up* renoncer à; livrer; *v.n.* ~ *in* céder (à).
glacier, *s.* glacier *m.*
glad, *adj.* heureux; content; joyeux.
gladness, *s.* joie *f.*
glance, *s.* coup *m.* d'œil,; — *v. n.* ~ *at* jeter un regard sur.
glare, *s.* lumière *f.* éblouissante; clinquant *m.;* — *v.n.* briller d'un éclat éblouissant.
glass, *s.* verre *m.;* *(pane)* vitre *f.;* ~*es* lunettes *f. pl.*
glazier, *s.* vitrier *m.*
gleam, *s.* lueur *f.;* — *v. n.* luire.

glide, *v. n.* glisser; planer.
glider, *s.* planeur *m.*
glimmer, *s.* lueur *f.;* — *v.n.* jeter une lueur faible.
glimpse, *s.* coup *m.* d'œil (rapide).
glitter, *v.n.* étinceler.
globe, *s.* globe *m.*
gloomy, *adj.* sombre.
glorious, *adj.* glorieux.
glory, *s.* gloire *f.*
glove, *s.* gant *m.*
glow, *v.n.* luire rouge; *(joy)* rayonner; *(coal)* être rouge; — *s.* chaleur *f.;* lumière *f.;* *fig.* ardeur *f.*
glue, *s.* colle (forte) *f.;* — *v.a.* coller.
gnat, *s.* cousin *m.;* moustique *f.*
gnaw, *v.a. & n.* ronger.
go, *v. n.* aller; ~ *away* s'en aller; ~ *back* retourner; ~ *back on one's word* reprendre sa parole; ~ *down* descendre; baisser; ~ *in for* s'occuper de, s'adonner à, faire (de); ~ *into* entrer dans; ~ *off* s'en aller; ~ *on* continuer; *(happen)* se passer; ~ *out* sortir; ~ *over, through* traverser; *(read)* parcourir; ~*up* monter; ~ *with* accompagner; ~ *without* se passer de; *let* ~ lâcher prise.
goal, *s.* but *m.*
goalkeeper, *s.* gardien (de but) *m.*
goat, *s.* bouc *f.,* chèvre *f.*
God, *s.* Dieu *m.*
god-child, *s.* filleul, -e *m. f.*
godfather, *s.* parrain *m.*
godmother, *s.* marraine *f.*
goggles, *s. pl.* bésicles *f.*

gold, *s.* or *m.*

golden, *adj.* d'or, en **or**.

golf, *s.* golf *m.*

good, *adj.* bon; ~ *evening!* bonsoir!; ~ *morning!* bonjour!; *be so ~ as to* avoir la bonté de; *make* ~ remplir; indemniser de; — *s.* bien *m.*; ~*s* marchandise *f.*; ~*s station* gare *f.* de marchandises; ~*s train* train *m.* de marchandises.

good-bye, *int.* & *s.* adieu *(m.).*

good-looking, *adj.* de belle mine, beau.

goodness, *s.* bonté *f.*

good-tempered, *adj.* de caractère facile, de bonne humeur.

goodwill, *s.* bonne volonté *f.*

goose, *s.* oie *f.*

gooseberry, *s.* groseille *f.* à maquereau.

gospel, *s.* évangile *m.*

gossip, *s.* bavardage *m.*; racontar *m.*, cancan *m.*; *(pers.)* compère *m.*; commère *f.*; — *v.n.* bavarder.

Gothic, *adj.* gothique.

govern, *v.a.* & *n.* gouverner.

governess, *s.* gouvernante *f.*

government, *s.* gouvernement *m.*

governor, *s.* gouverneur *m.*

gown, *s.* robe *f.*

grace, *s.* grâce *f.*

graceful, *adj.* gracieux.

gracious, *adj.* gracieux.

grade, *s.* grade *m.*; classe *f.*

gradual, *adj.* graduel.

graduate, *s.* gradué, -e *m. f.*; — *v.a.* graduer;

v.n. prendre ses diplômes.

grain, *s.* grain *m.*

grammar, *s.* grammaire *f.*

grammar-school, *s.* lycée *m.*, collège *m.*

grammatical, *adj.* grammatical.

gram(me), *s.* gramme *m.*

gramophone, *s.* gramophone *m.*, phonographe *m.*

gramophone-record, *s.* disque *m.*

grand, *adj.* grand; magnifique; ~ *stand* tribune *f.*

grandchild, *s.* petit-fils *m.*, petite-fille *f.* *(pl. petits-enfants m.)*

granddaughter, *s.* petite-fille *f.*

grandfather, *s.* grand-père *m.*

grandmother, *s.* grand' mère *f.*

grandson, *s.* petit-fils *m.*

granite, *s.* granit *m.*

granny, *s.* grand'maman *f.*

grant, *v.a.* accorder, concéder; accéder; ~ *that* admettre ·que; — *s.* don *m.*, concession *f.*; subside *m.*

grape, *s.* grain *m.* de raisin; *bunch of* ~*s* grappe *f.* de raisin.

grape-fruit, *s.* pamplemousse *f.*

graph, *s.* graphique *m.*, courbe *f.*

graphic, *adj.* graphique.

grasp, *v.a.* saisir; comprendre; — *s.* prise *f.*, étreinte *f.*

grass, *s.* herbe *f.*; gazon *m.*

grasshopper, *s.* sauterelle *f.*

grate, *s.* grille *f.*; — *v.a.*

râper; faire grincer;
v.n. grincer.

grateful, *adj.* reconnaissant (à).

gratitude, *s.* reconnaissance *f.*

grave[1], *s.* tombe *f.*, tombeau *m.*

grave[2], *adj.* grave.

gravel, *s.* gravier *m.*

gravy, *s.* jus *m.*

gray, *adj.* gris.

graze, *v.n.* paître.

grease, *s.* graisse *f.*; —
v.a. graisser.

great, *adj.* grand; *a ~
many* beaucoup (de).

greatly, *adj.* très; beaucoup.

greatness, *s.* grandeur *f.*

greed, *s.* avidité *f.*

greedy, *adj.* avide.

Greek, *adj.* grec, grecque;
—*s.* Grec *m.*, Grecque *f.*

green, *adj.* vert.

greengrocer, *s.* fruitier,
-ère *m. f.*

greenhouse, *s.* serre *f.*

greet, *v.a.* saluer.

greeting, *s.* salutation *f.*

grey, *adj.* gris.

grief, *s.* chagrin *m.*

grieve, *v.a.* affliger; *v.n.*
s'affliger.

grill, *s.* gril *m.*; — *v.a.*
griller.

grim, *adj.* sévère, mena-
çant, sinistre.

grin, *v.n.* grimacer; *~ at*
faire des grimaces à; —
s. rire *m.*; grimace *f.*

grind, *v.a.* moudre.

grinder, *s.* *(tooth)* mo-
laire *f.*

grindstone, *s.* meule *f.*

grip, *s.* étreinte *f.*; prise
f.; — *v.a.* saisir,
étreindre.

groan, *v. n.* gémir; — *s.*
gémissement *m.*

grocer, *s.* épicier, -ère *m.*

f.; *~'s (shop)* épicerie *f.*

grocery, *s.* épicerie *f.*

groove, *s.* rainure *f.*

gross, *adj.* gros; grossier;
(weight) brut.

ground, *s.* terre *f.*; terrain *m.*; *(reason)* raison *f.*; *~s* jardins *m.*
pl.; — *v.a.* fonder.

group, *s.* groupe *m.*

grow, *v.a.* cultiver; *v.n.*
(pers.) grandir; *(plant)*
croître; *(become)* deve-
nir.

growl, *s.* grondement *m.*;
— *v.n.* gronder.

grown-up, *s.* grande personne *f.*

growth, *s.* croissance *f.*;
culture *f.*; récolte *f.*

grudge, *s.* rancune *f.*; —
v.a. donner à contre-
cœur à.

grumble, *v.n.* grommeler;
— *s.* grognement *m.*

grunt, *s.* grognement *m.*;
— *v.n.* grogner.

guarantee, *s.* garantie *f.*;
(pers.) garant, -e *m.*
f.; — *v.a.* garantir.

guard, *s.* garde *f.*; *(train)*
conducteur *m.*; — *v.a.*
garder; *v.n.* *~ against*
se garder.

guardian, *s.* gardien,
-enne *m. f.*

guess, *v.a. & n.* deviner;
conjecturer; — *s.* con-
jecture *f.*

guest, *s.* invité *m.*, convive *m.*; hôte, -esse *m.*
f.

guide, *s.* guide *m.*; — *v. a.*
guider.

guide-book, *s.* guide *m.*

guilt, *s.* culpabilité *f.*

guilty, *adj.* coupable (de).

guitar, *s.* guitare *f.*

gulf, *s.* golfe *m.*

gull, *s.* mouette *f.*

gullet, *s.* gosier *m.*

gum¹, s. gomme f.; —
v.a. gommer.
gum², s. *(teeth)* gencive f.
gun, s. fusil m.; canon m.
gush, v.i. jaillir; — s.
jaillissement m.
gutter, s. *(street)* ruisseau m.
gymnasium, s. gymnase
m.
gymnastics, s. gymnastique f.

H

haberdashery, s. mercerie
f.
habit, s. habitude f.
hail, s. grêle f.; — v.n.
grêler.
hair, s. *(single)* cheveu
m.; *(whole)* cheveux m.
pl.; *(animal)* poil m.
hairdresser, s. coiffeur,
-euse m. f.
half, s. moitié f.; demi m.;
— adj. demi; ~ an
hour une demi-heure f.
half-time, s. mi-temps m.
half-way, adv. à mi-che-
min; à moitié chemin;
à mi-distance.
hall, s. (grande) salle f.;
(college) réfectoire m.;
(house) vestibule m.;
(hotel) hall m.
halt, s. halte f.; v.a. faire
arrêter; v.n. faire
halte; boiter.
ham, s. jambon m.
hammer, s. marteau m.
hand, s. main f.; *(pers.)*
ouvrier m.; *(clock)*
aiguille f.; *on the one* ~
:...*on the other* d'une
part ... d'autre part.
handbag, s. sac (à main)
m.
handbook, s. manuel m.
handkerchief, s. mouchoir

m.
handle, s. manche m.,
anse f.; poignée f.; bras
m.; — v.a. manier;
traiter.
hand-made, adj. fait à la
main.
handsome, adj. joli.
handwriting, s. écriture f.
handy, adj. *(pers.)* adroit;
(thing) commode.
hang, v.a. pendre; *(with
tapestry)* tendre; ~ up
accrocher; v. n. pendre;
dépendre (de).
hanger, s. crochet m.;
cintre m.
happen, v.n. arriver; se
trouver; *I* ~ed *to be
present* je me trouvais
là par hasard.
happiness, s. bonheur m.
happy, adj. heureux.
harbour, s. port m.
hard, adj. dur; difficile;
sévère; ~ up gêné; —
adv. durement; *work* ~
travailler dur.
hardly, adv. à peine.
hardware, s. quincaillerie
f.
hare, s. lièvre m.
harm, s. mal m.; tort m.;
do ~ *to* nuire à.
harmful, adj. nuisible.
harmless, adj. inoffensif.
harmony, s. harmonie f.
harness, s. harnais m.
harp, s. harpe f.
harsh, adj. revêche;
âpre; rigoureux.
hart, s. cerf m.
harvest, s. moisson f.;
(crop) récolte f.
haste, s. hâte f.; *make* ~
se dépêcher.
hasten, v.a. hâter; v. n. se
dépêcher.
hasty, adj. précipité.
hat, s. chapeau m.
hate, v: a. haïr; — s.
haine f.

hateful, *adj.* odieux.
hatred, *s.* haine *f.*
haul, *v.a.* traîner; haler; — *s.* traction *f.*
haulage, *s.* roulage *m.*; frais *m.pl.* de roulage.
haunch, *s.* hanche *f.*
haunt, *v.a.* fréquenter; hanter.
have, *v.a.* avoir; *(food)* prendre; ~ *to* il faut que, il faut (+ *inf.*); *had rather* préférer (+ *inf.*); ~ *on (clothes)* porter.
haversack, *s.* havresac *m.*
hawk, *s.* faucon *m.*
hay, *s.* foin *m.*
hazard, *s.* hasard *m.*
hazy, *adj.* brumeux; *(fig.)* vegue.
he, *pron.* il, *(alone)* lui; ~ *who* celui qui.
head, *s.* tête *f.*; *(chief)* chef *m.*; *(river)* source *f.*; — *v.a.* être en tête de; — *adj.* principal.
headache, *s.* mal *m.* de tête.
heading, *s.* en-tête *m.*
headlight, *s.* phare *m.*, projecteur *m.*
headline, *s.* manchette *f.*
headmaster, *s.* directeur *m.*
headquarters, *s. pl.* quartier *m.* général.
heal, *v.a.* guérir; *v.n.* se guérir.
health, *s.* santé *f.*
healthy, *adj.* bien portant; sain.
heap, *s.* amas *m.*, tas *m.*; — *v.a.* ~ *up* entasser.
hear, *v.a.* entendre; *(listen to)* écouter; *v. n.* entendre; ~ *from* recevoir une lettre de; ~ *of* avoir des nouvelles de; entendre parler de.
heart, *s.* cœur *m.*; *by* ~ par cœur.

hearth, *s.* foyer *m.*
hearty, *adj.* cordial.
heat, *s.* chaleur *f.*; *(anger)* colère *f.*; — *v.a.&n.* chauffer.
heating, *s.* chauffage *m.*
heave, *v.a.* lever; pousser; jeter; *v.n.* se soulever.
heaven, *s.* ciel *m.*
heavy, *adj.* pesant; lourd.
hedge, *s.* haie *f.*
hedgehog, *s.* hérisson *m.*
heed, *s.* attention *f.*; *take* ~ *to* faire attention à.
heedless, *adj.* insouciant; inattentif.
heel, *s.* talon *m.*
height, *s.* hauteur *f.*
heir, *s.* héritier *m.*
heiress, *s.* héritière *f.*
helicopter, *s.* hélicoptère *m.*
hell, *s.* enfer *m.*
hello, *int.* allô!
helm, *s.* barre (du gouvernail) *f.*
helmet, *s.* casque *m.*
help, *v.a.* aider; secourir; ~ *oneself* se servir; — *s.* aide *f.*
helpful, *adj.* *(pers.)* serviable; *(thing)* utile.
helping, *s.* portion *f.*
helpless, *adj.* sans secours.
hem, *s.* ourlet *m.*; bord *m.*
hen, *s.* poule *f.*
hence, *adv.* *(place, time)* d'ici; *(reason)* de là.
her, *pron.* *(acc.)* la; *(dat.)* lui; *(alone)* elle.
herb, *s.* herbe *f.*
herd, *s.* troupeau *m.*
here, *adv.* ici; *from* ~ d'ici; *look* ~! dites donc!; ~ *he is!* le voici!
heritage, *s.* héritage *m.*
hermit, *s.* ermite *m.*
hero, *s.* héros *m.*
heroic, *adj.* héroïque.
heroine, *s.* héroïne *f.*

herring, *s.* hareng *m.*

hers, *pron.* à elle; le sien, la sienne, les siens, les siennes.

herself, *pron.* elle-même; *(reflex.)* se.

hesitate, *v.n.* hésiter.

hew, *v.a.* couper.

hiccough, hiccup, *s.* hoquet *m.*

hide, *v.a.* cacher; *v.n.* se cacher.

hideous, *adj.* hideux; horrible.

high, *adj.* haut; *(speed)* grand; *(price)* élevé; — *adv.* haut.

highness, *s.* altesse *f.*

highroad, highway, *s.* grande route *f.*

hike, *v.n.* faire du tourisme à pied.

hiker, *s.* touriste *f.*, randonneur, -euse (à pied) *m. f.*

hill, *s.* colline *f.*

hilly, *adj.* montueux.

him, *pron.* *(acc.)* le; *(dat.)* lui; *(alone)* lui.

himself, *pron.* lui-même; *(reflex.)* se; *by* ~ tout seul.

hinder, *v.a.* empêcher.

hindrance, *s.* empêchement *m.*

hinge, *s.* gond *m.;* charnière *f.;* — *v.n.* tourner (sur).

hint, *s.* allusion *f.;* avis *m.;* — *v.n.* ~ *at* faire allusion à.

hip, *s.* hanche *f.*

hire, *s.* louage *m.; for* ~ à louer; — *v.a. & n.* louer.

his, *pron.* son, sa; ses.

hiss, *s.* sifflement *m.;* — *v. a. & n.* siffler.

historic(al), *adj.* historique.

history, *s.* histoire *f.*

hit, *v.a.* frapper; at-

teindre; trouver; — *s.* coup *m.; succès *m.*

hitch-hike, *v.n.* faire de l'auto-stop.

hive, *s.* ruche *f.*

hoard, *s.* magot *m.*, amas *m.;* — *v. a.* thésauriser; entasser.

hoarse, *adj.* raque.

hobby, *s.* dada *m.*

hockey, *s.* hockey *m.*

hoe, *s.* houe *f.*

hog, *s.* porc *m.*

hoist, *v.a.* hisser; —*s.* monte-charge *m.*

hold, *v.a.* tenir; retenir; maintenir; contenir; *(consider)* tenir (pour); ~ *back* retenir; ~ *out* tendre; offrir; ~ *that* soutenir que; — *v.n.* tenir; *(be true)* être vrai; ~ *on* ne pas lâcher prise; ~ *out* durer.

holder, *s.* possesseur *m.*

hole, *s.* trou *m.*

holiday, *s.* fête *f.*, jour *m.* férié; *(holidays)* vacances *f. pl.*, congé *m.; be on* être en congé, en vacance(s).

hollow, *adj.* reux, -euse; *fig.* faux, fausse.

holy, *adj.* saint; bénit.

home, *s.* foyer *m.*, demeure *f.; at* ~ chez soi, à la maison; — *adv.* chez soi; *come, go* ~ rentrer; — *adj.* domestque; de l'intérieur.

homeless, *adj.* sans asile.

homely, *adj.* simple; modeste.

homesickness, *s.* mal du pays *m.*

homeward, *adv.* vers la maison; ~ *bound* en retour.

honest, *adj.* honnête.

honesty, *s.* honnêteté *f.*

honey, *s.* miel *m.*

honeymoon, s. lune f. de miel.

honour, s. honneur m.; — v.a. honorer.

hood, s. capuchon m.; capeline f.; (motor) capote f.

hoof, s. sabot m.

hook, s. crochet m., croc m.; (fishing) hameçon m.

hoop, s. cercle m.

hoot, v.a. huer; v.n. corner; — s. huée f.

hooter, s. sirène f.; corne f., trompe f.

hop, v.n. sautiller.

hope, s. espérance f.; espoir m.; — v.n. espérer.

hopeful, adj. plein d'espoir.

hopeless, adj. sans espoir

horizon, s. horizon m.

horizontal, adj. horizontal.

horn, s. corne f.; trompe f.

horrible, adj. affreux, -euse.

horse, s. cheval m. (pl. chevaux).

horseback: on ~ à cheval.

horseman, s. cavalier m.

horse-race, s. course f. de chevaux.

horseshoe, s. fer m. à cheval.

hose, s. bas m. pl.

hospitable, adj. hospitalier.

hospital, s. hôpital m.

hospitality, s. hospitalité f.

host, s. hôte m.

hostel, s. pension f. pour étudiants, hôtellerie f.

hostess, s. hôtesse f.

hostile, adj. hostile (à).

hostility, s. hostilité f.

hot, adj. chaud.

hotel, s. hôtel m.

hour, s. heure f.

house, s. maison f.; (theatre) salle f.

household, s. ménage m.

housekeeper, s. gouvernante f.

housekeeping, s. ménage m.

housewife, s. ménagère f.

housework, s. travaux (m. pl.) domestiques; do the ~ faire le ménage.

how, adv. comment; ~ many, much? combien de?; ~ long? combien de temps?; ~ are you? comment allez-vous?

however, adv. de quelque manière que...; toutefois, cependant.

howl, v. a. & n. hurler; — s. hurlement m.

hue, s. couleur f.; cri m.

hug, v.a. serrer dans les bras.

huge, adj. énorme.

hullo, int. holà; allô!

hum, v. n. bourdonner; — s. bourdonnement m.

human, adj. humain.

humanity, s. humanité f.

humble, adj. humble.

humorous, adj. amusant; humoristique; drôle.

humour, s. humour m.; be in a ~ to être d'humeur à.

hundred, s. cent m.

hundredth, adj. centième.

hundredweight, s. quintal m.

Hungarian, adj. hongrois; — s. Hongrois, -e m. f.

hunger, s. faim f.; — v.n. avoir faim.

hungry, adj. affamé; be ~ avoir faim.

hunt, v.a. & n. chasser; (with hounds) chasser à courre; — s. chasse (à courre) f.

hunter, s. chasseur m.

hurl, *v.a.* jeter; lancer.

hurry, *s.* hâte; *be in a ~ to* être pressé de; — *v.n.* se presser; *~ up!* pressez-vous!; *v.a.* presser, hâter.

hurt, *v.a.* faire mal à; blesser; *(feelings)* froisser.

husband, *s.* mari *m.*

hush, *int.* chut!; — *s.* calme *m.;* — *v.a.* calmer.

husk, *s.* cosse *f.;* glume *f.;* — *v. a.* écosser, monder.

hut, *s.* cabane *f.*

hydrogen, *s.* hydrogène *m.*

hygiene, *s.* hygiène *f.*

hymn, *s.* hymne *m.*

hyphen, *s.* trait d'union *m.*

hypnotize, *v.a.* hypnotiser.

hypocrisy, *s.* hypocrisie *f.*

hysterical, *adj.* hystérique.

I

I, *pron.* je; moi.

ice, *s.* glace *f.*

ice-cream, *s.* glace *f.*

icy, *adj.* glacial.

idea, *s.* idée *f.*

ideal, *adj. & s.* idéal *(m.).*

identical, *adj.* identique.

identity, *s.* identité *f.;* ~ *card* carte *f.* d'identité.

idle, *adj.* désœuvré;*(lazy)* paresseux; — *v.a.* ~ *away* perdre.

idleness, *s.* oisiveté *f.;* paresse *f.*

if, *conj.* si; *as ~* comme si.

ignition, *s.* ignition *f.;* *(motor)* allumage *m.*

ignorant, *adj.* ignorant; *be ~ of* ignorer.

ignore, *v.a.* refuser de connaître.

ill, *adj.* malade; *(bad)*

mauvais; *be taken ~* tomber malade; *~ luck* malheur *m.;* — *adv.* mal; — *s.* mal *m.*

illegal, *adj.* illégal.

illegitimate, *adj.* illégitime.

illicit, *adj.* illicite.

illness, *s.* maladie *f.*

illusion, *s.* illusion *f.*

illustrate, *v.a.* illustrer.

illustration, *s.* illustration *f.;* exemple *m.*

image, *s.* image *f.*

imagination, *s.* imagination *f.*

imagine, *v. a.* imaginer; se figurer.

imitate, *v.a.* imiter.

immediate, *adj.* immédiat.

immense, *adj.* immense.

immigrant, *adj. & s.* immigrant, -e *(m. f.).*

immigrate, *v. n.* immigrer

immigration, *s.* immigration *f.*

immoral, *adj.* immoral.

immortal, *adj.* immortel.

impatience, *s.* impatience *f.*

impatient, *adj.* impatient.

impediment, *s.* obstacle *m.*

impel, *v.a.* forcer; pousser.

imperfect, *adj. & s.* imparfait *(m.).*

imperial, *adj.* impérial.

impertinent, *adj.* impertinent.

implement, *s.* outil *m.,* ustensile *m.*

implication, *s.* implication *f.*

implore, *v.a.* implorer.

imply, *v.a.* impliquer; donner à entendre.

import, *v.a.* importer; *(mean)* signifier; — *s.* *(usu. pl.)* importation(s) *f.*

importance, *s.* importance *f.*

important, *adj.* important.

importer, *s.* importateur
m.

impose, *v.a.* imposer (à).

impossibility, *s.* impossibilité *f.*

impossible, *adj.* impossible.

impression, *s.* impression *f.*

imprison, *v.a.* emprisonner.

imprisonment, *s.* emprisonnement.

improbable, *adj.* improbable.

improper, *adj.* impropre;
inconvenant.

improve, *v.a.* améliorer;
perfectionner; *v.n.* s'a-
méliorer.

improvement, *s.* améliora-
tion *f.;* progrès *m.*

impulse, *s.* impulsion *f.*

in, *prep.* dans; en; à; ~
the morning le matin;
~ *the evening* le soir; ~
time à temps; ~ *spring*
au printemps.

inadequate, *adj.* insuffisant.

incapable, *adj.* incapable
(de).

incense, *s.* encens *m.*

inch, *s.* pouce *m.*

incident, *s.* incident *m.*

incidental, *adj.* fortuit;
incidental.

incline, *v. a. & n.* incliner.

include, *v.a.* comprendre;
renfermer.

inclusive, *adj.* inclusif; ~
of y compris.

income, *s.* revenu *m.*

income-tax, *s.* impôt *m.*
sur (le) revenu.

incompatible, *adj.* incompatible.

incompetent, *adj.* incom-

pétent.

inconsistent, *adj.* inconséquent.

inconvenient, *adj.* incommode, gênant.

increase, *v.a.&n.*
augmenter; — *s.* aug-
mentation *f.*

incredible, *adj.* incroyable.

incur, *v. a.* contracter; en-
courir; s'attirer.

incurable, *adj.* incurable.

indebted, *adj.* endetté.

indeed, *adv.* de fait; vraiment.

independence, *s.* indépendance *f.*

independent, *adj.* indépen-
dant.

index, *s.* index *m.; (on
dial)* aiguille *f.; (math.)*
exposant *m.; ~ finger*
index *m.*

Indian, *adj.* indien; des
Indes; ~ *corn* maïs *m.*
— *s.* Indien, -enne *m. f.*

India-rubber, *s.* gomme *f.*

indicate, *v.a.* indiquer.

indicator, *s.* indicateur *m.*

indifference, *s.* indifféren-
ce *f.*

indifferent, *adj.* indifférent (à).

indigestion, *s.* indigestion
f.

indignant, *adj.* indigné.

indirect, *adj.* indirect.

indiscreet, *adj.* indiscret.

indiscretion, *s.* indiscrétion *f.;* imprudence *f.*

indispensable, *adj.* indispensable.

individual, *adj.* individuel;
— *s.* individu *m.*

indoor, *adj.* d'intérieur.

indoors, *adv.* à la maison;
stay ~ ne pas sortir.

induce, *v.a.* persuader;
(cause) occasionner.

inducement, *s.* encouragement *m.* ~s attraits

m. pl.

indulge, *v. a.* se livrer (à); caresser; *v.n.* ~ *in* s'abandonner à; se laisser aller à.

indulgence, *s.* indulgence *f.;* laisser-aller *m.*

industrial, *adj.* industriel.

industrious, *adj.* travailleur.

industry, *s.* industrie *f.*

inefficient, *adj.* incapable; inefficace.

inestimable, *adj.* inestimable.

inevitable, *adj.* inévitable.

inexpensive, *adj.* peu coûteux, peu cher, bon marché.

inexperienced, *adj.* inexpérimenté.

inexplicable, *adj.* inexplicable.

infallible, *adj.* infaillible.

infamous, *adj.* infâme.

infant, *s.* enfant *m. f.*

infantry, *s.* infanterie *f.*

infant-school, *s.* école *f.* maternelle.

infection, *s.* infection *f.*

infer, *v.a.* conclure, déduire.

inferior, *adj.* inférieur.

infinitive, *s.* infinitif *m.*

infirm, *adj.* infirm.

infirmary, *s.* infirmerie *f.*

inflame, *v.a.* enflammer

inflammable, *adj.* inflammable.

inflate, *v.a.* gonfler.

inflexion, *s.* inflexion *f.*

inflict, *v.a.* infliger; imposer à.

influence, *s.* influence *f.;* — *v.a.* influencer.

influenza, *s.* grippe *f.*

inform, *v.a.* informer.

informal, *adj.* sans cérémonie.

information, *s.* information *f.;* renseignements

m. pl.

ingenious, *adj.* ingénieux.

ingenuity, *s.* ingéniosité *f.*

ingredient, *s.* ingrédient *m.*

inhabit, *v.a.* habiter.

inhabitant, *s.* habitant *m.*

inherit, *v.a. & n.* hériter (de).

inheritance, *s.* héritage *m.*

initial, *s.* initiale *f.*

initiative, *s.* initiative *f.*

injection, *s.* injection *f.*

injure, *v.a.* nuire à; blesser.

injury, *s.* préjudice *m.;* dommage *m.;* blessure *f.*

injustice, *s.* injustice *f.*

ink, *s.* encre *f.*

inland, *s. & adj.* intérieur *(m.).*

inn, *s.* auberge *f.;* taverne *f.*

inner, *adj.* intérieur.

innocence, *s.* innocence *f.*

innocent, *adj.* innocent.

innumerable, *adj.* innombrable.

inoculate, *v.a.* inoculer.

inquire, *v.n.* ~ *about* s'enquérir, se renseigner sur; ~ *after* demander après, demander des nouvelles de.

inquiry, *s.* demande *f.;* recherche *f.; make inquiries about* s'informer de; ~ *office* bureau *m.* des renseignements.

insane, *adj.* fou, fol, folle.

inscription, *s.* inscription *f*

insect, *s.* insecte *m.*

insecure, *adj.* peu sûr, mal assuré.

insensible, *adj.* sans connaissance; insensible.

inseparable, *adj.* inséparable.

insert, *v. a.* insérer (dans).

inside, *s. & adj.* intérieur

(m.); — adv. à l'inté-
rieur.
insignificant, *adj.* insignifiant.
insist, *v.n.* insister *(on
sur).*
insistence, *s.* insistance *f.*
inspect, *v.a.* inspecter.
inspection, *s.* inspection
f.
inspector, *s.* inspecteur *m.*
inspiration, *s.* inspiration *f.*
inspire, *v.a.* inspirer.
install, *v.a.* installer.
instalment, *s.* fraction *f.,*
acompte *m.*
instance, *s.* exemple *m.;*
cas *m.; for* ~ par
exemple.
instant, *adj.* urgent; — *s.*
instant *m.*
instead, *adv.* ~ *of* au lieu
de.
instinct, *s.* instinct *m.*
institute, *s.* institut *m.;*
— *v.a.* instituer.
institution, *s.* institution *f.*
instruct, *v. a.* instruire.
instruction, *s.* instruction *f.*
instructive, *adj.* instructif.
instrument, *s.* instrument
m.
instrumental, *adj.* instrumental.
insufficiency, *s.* insuffisance *f.*
insufficient, *adj.* insuffisant.
insult, *s.* insulte *f.;* —
v.a. insulter.
insurance, *s.* assurance *f.*
insure, *v. a.* (faire) assurer.
integral, *adj.* intégral; —
s. intégrale *f.*
integrity, *s.* intégrité *f.*
intellectual, *adj.* intéllec-
tuel.
intelligence, *s.* intelligence *f.; (information)*
renseignements *m.pl.*

intelligent, *adj.* intelligent.
intend, *v. a.* avoir l'intention de (faire qch.), se
proposer de; destiner
qn., qch. (à); vouloir
dire.
intense, *adj.* intense.
intensity, *s.* intensité *f.*
intent, *s.* intention *f.;* —
adj. ~ *on* absorbé dans.
intention, *s.* intention *f.*
intercontinental, *adj.* intercontinental.
interest, *s.* intérêt *m.;* —
v.a. intéresser.
interesting, *adj.* intéressant.
interfere, *v. n.* intervenir;
~ *with* gêner; se mêler
de.
interior, *adj. & s.* intérieur *(m.).*
intermediate, *adj.* intermédiaire.
intermission, *s.* interruption *f.,* pause *f.*
internal, *adj.* interne; intérieur.
international, *adj.* international.
interpret, *v.a.* interpréter.
interpretation, *s.* interprétation *f.*
interpreter, *s.* interprète *m.*
interrogation, *s.* interrogation *f.*
interrupt, *v.a.* interrompre.
interruption, *s.* interruption *f.*
interval, *s.* intervalle *m.*
intervention, *s.* intervention *f.*
interview, entrevue *f.;*
interview *m. f.*
intimate, *adj.* intime.
into, *prep.* dans; en.
intolerable, *adj.* intolérable.
introduce, *v.a.* introduire; *(pers.)* présenter.

introduction, s. introduction f.; (pers.) présentation f.
invade, v.a. envahir.
invalid¹, s. malade m. f.
invalid², adj. invalide.
invasion, s. invasion f.
invent, v.a. inventer.
invention, s. invention f.
inverted, adj. ~ commas guillemets m.
invest, v.a. (money) placer.
investigate, v.a. rechercher.
investigation, s. investigation f.
investment, s. placement m.
invisible, adj. invisible.
invitation, s. invitation f.
invite, v.a. inviter.
invoice, s. facture f.
involuntary, adj. involontaire.
involve, v.a. envelopper (dans); impliquer (dans); entraîner.
inward, adj. intérieur; interne.
inwards, adv. intérieurement; en dedans.
Irish, adj. irlandais
iron, s. fer m. — v.a. repasser.
ironical, adj. ironique.
ironware, s. quincaillerie f.
ironworks, s. ferronnerie f.
irony, s. ironie f.
irregular, adj. irrégulier.
irrelevant, adj. non pertinent; hors de la question; inapplicable (à).
irresolute, adj. irrésolu.
irritate, v.a. irriter.
island, s. île f.; (street) refuge m.
isle, s. île f.
isolate, v.a. isoler.

isotope, s. isotope m.
issue, s. (way out) sortie f.; (end) issue f., fin f., résultat m.; (publication) publication f., édition, (paper) numéro m., (money) émission f.; — v. a. émettre; publier.
it, pron. il, elle; (acc.) le, la; of it en; to ~ y.
Italian, adj. italien; — s. Italien, -enne m.f.
itch, s. démangeaison f.; — v.n. démanger.
itchy, adj. galeux.
item, s. article m., détail m.
its, pron. son, sa, pl. ses.
itself, pron. lui-même, elle-même; se; (emphatic) même.
ivory, s. ivoire m.
ivy, s. lierre m.

J

jack, s. (cards) valet m.; (lifting) cric m., lève-auto m.
jackal, s. chacal m.
jacket, s. veston m.
jail, s. prison f.
jam¹, s. confiture f.
jam², v.a. serrer; coincer; encombrer; — s. encombrement m.
January, s. janvier m.
Japanese, adj. japonais.
jar, s. jarre f.; bocal m.
javelin, s. javeline f.
jaw, s. mâchoire f.
jealous, adj. jaloux.
jealousy, s. jalousie f.
jelly, s. gelée f.
jerk, s. saccade f.; secousse f
jersey, s. jersey m.
jet, s. jet m.; (gas) bec m.; ~ plane avion m. à réaction.

Jew, s. Juif m.

jewel, s. bijou m.

jeweller, s. bijoutier m.;
~'s shop bijouterie f.

jewellery, s. bijouterie f.

jib, s. foc m.

job, s. tâche f.; travail m. (pl. -aux); emploi m.; odd ~s petits travaux m.

join, v.a. joindre; unir; se joindre (à); v.n. se joindre; s'unir; ~ in prendre part à.

joiner, s. menuisier m.

joint, s. joint m.; articulation f.; (meat) gros morceau m.; — adj. commun; indivis; co-; ~-stock company société f. par actions.

joke, s. plaisanterie f.

jolly, adj. joyeux; jovial.

journal, s. journal m. (pl. -aux).

journalist, s. journaliste m.

journey, s. voyage m.

joy, s. joie f.

joyful, adj. joyeux.

judge, s. juge m.; — v.a.&n. juger.

judg(e)ment, s. jugement m.

jug, s. cruche f.; pot m.

juggler, s. jongleur m.

Jugoslav, adj. yougoslave.

juice, s. jus m.

July, s. juillet m.

jump, s. saut m.; — v.n. & a. sauter.

junction, s. jonction f.; (gare f. d')embranchement. m.

June, s. juin m.

jungle, jungle f.

junior, adj. jeune.

jury, s. jury m.

juryman, s. juré m.

just, adj. juste; — adv. (exactly) juste; (barely) à peine; ~ now il n'y a qu'un instant; ~ so précisément.

justice, s. justice f.

justification, s. justification f.

justify, v.a. justifier.

jut, v.n. ~ out faire saillie.

juvenile, adj. juvénile; d'enfants.

K

kangaro, s. kangourou m.

keel, s. quille f.

keen, adj. aigu; tranchant; (mind) pénétrant; be ~ on être enthousiaste de, avoir la passion de.

keep, v.a. tenir; garder; maintenir; observer; ~ back retenir; ~ up soutenir; — v.n. rester; ~ on continuer à.

keeper, s. gardien m.

kerb, s. bordure f.

kernel, s. amande f.

kettle, s. bouilloire f.

key, s. clé f.; (piano) touche f.; (music) ton m.

keyboard, s. clavier m.

kick, v.a. donner un coup de pied (à); v.n. ruer; — s. coup m. de pied.

kid, s. chevreau m.; (child) gosse m. f.

kidney, s. rein m.; (food) rognon m.

kill, v.a. & n. tuer; abattre.

kilogram(me), s. kilogramme m.

kilometre, s. kilomètre m.

kind, adj. bon; bienveillant; aimable.

kindle, v.a. allumer; exciter; enflammer; v.n. s'enflammer.

kindly, *adj.* bon; doux.

kindness, *s.* bonté *f.;* bienveillance *f.*

kindred, *s.* parenté *f.;* parents *m.pl.*

king, *s.* roi *m.*

kingdom, *s.* royaume *m.*

kinsman, *s.* parent *m.*

kiss, *s.* baiser *m.; v.a.* embrasser; baiser.

kit, *s.* fourniment *m.*

kitchen, *s.* cuisine *f.*

kite, *s.* cerf-volant *m.*

kitten, *s.* petit chat *m.*

knapsack, *s.* havresac *m.*

knee, *s.* genou *m. (pl. -x).*

kneel, *v.n.* s'agenouiller; ~ *down* se mettre à genoux.

knife, *s.* couteau *m.*

knight, *s.* chevalier *m.; (chess)* cavalier *m.*

knit, *v. a.* tricoter; *(brow)* froncer.

knob, *s.* bosse *f.;* bouton *m.*

knock, *s.* coup *m.; — v.a. & n.* frapper; ~ *down* renverser.

knocker, *s.* marteau *m.*

knot, *s.* nœud *m.; — v.a.* nouer; *v.n.* se nouer.

know, *v.a.* savoir; connaître; reconnaître; ~*n for* connu pour; — *v.n.* savoir; ~ *of* avoir connaissance de; *let* ~ prévenir.

knowledge, *s.* connaissance *f.; (acquired)* savoir *m.*

knuckle, *s.* articulation *f.* de doigt.

L

label, *s.* étiquette *f.; — v.a.* étiqueter.

laboratory, *s.* laboratoire *m.*

labour, *s.* travail *m.;* ~ *(e)exchange* bureau *m.* de placement; — *v.n.* travailler.

labourer, *s.* travailleur *m.*

lace, *s.* dentelle *f.*

lack, *s.* manque; — *v.a. & n.* ~ *(for)* manquer (de).

lad, *s.* jeune garçon *m.*

ladder, *s.* échelle *f.*

lading, *s.* chargement *m.*

ladle, *s.* louche *f.*

lady, *s.* dame *f.; young* ~ jeune dame *f.;* demoiselle *f.,* jeune fille *f.*

lag, *v.n.* ~ *behind* rester en arrière.

lake, *s.* lac *m.*

lamb, *s.* agneau *m.*

lame, *adj.* boiteux.

lamp, *s.* lampe *f.*

lamp-shade, *s.* abat-jour *m.*

land, *s. (not sea)* terre *f.; (country)* pays *m.; — v.n. & a.* débarquer; *(plane)* atterrir.

landing, *s.* débarquement *m.; (plane)* atterrissage *m.*

landing-strip, *s.* piste *f.* d'atterrissage.

landlady, *s.* propriétaire *f.;* aubergiste *f.*

landlord, *s.* propriétaire *m.;* aubergiste *m.*

landscape, *s.* paysage *m.*

lane, *s.* ruelle *f.;* chemin *m.*

language, *s.* langue *f.; (expression)* langage *m.*

lap¹, *s.* genoux *m. pl.; (coat)* pan *m.; (sports)* tour (de piste) *m.*

lap², *v. a.* envelopper (de); laper.

lapse, *s.* faute *f.;* chute *f.;* lapsus *m.; (time)* laps *m.; — v.n.* retomber (dans); *(time)* s'écouler; *(fail)* faire un faux pas.

lard, *s.* saindoux *m.*

larder, *s.* dépense *f.*

large, *adj.* gros, grand; considérable; *at* ~ en liberté, en général.

lark, *s.* alouette *f.*

last, *adj.* dernier; — *adv.* dernièrement, en dernier lieu; — *v.n.* durer.

lasting, *adj.* durable.

latch, *s.* loquet *m.*

latch-key, *s.* clef *f.* de porte.

late, *adj.* tardif; *be* ~ être en retard; — *adv.* tard; ~*r on* par la suite; plus tard.

lately, *adv.* dernièrement, recemment.

latest, *adj.* récent, le dernier; *at (the)* ~ au plus tard.

lathe, *s.* tour *m.*

lather, *s.* mousse *f.*

Latin, *adj.* latin; — *s.* latin *m.*

latter, *adj.* dernier; *the* ~ ce dernier; celui-ci, celle-ci, ceux-ci.

laugh, *v.n.* rire *(at* de); — *s.* rire *m.*

laughter, *s.* rire *m.*

launch, *v.a.* lancer.

launching, *adj.* ~ *site* rampe *f.* à fusées.

laundry, *s.* buanderie *f.,* blanchisserie *f.*

lavatory, *s.* lavabo *m.* cabinet *m.* de toilette,

lavish, *adj.* prodigue (de). — *v.a.* prodiguer.

law, *s.* loi *f.; droit *m.*

law-court, *s.* cour *f.* de justice, tribunal *m.*

lawful, *adj.* légal; permis; légitime.

lawn, *s.* pelouse *f.*

lawn-mower, *s.* tondeuse *f.*

lawsuit, *s.* procès *m.*

lawyer, *s.* homme *m.* de loi avoué *m.; avocat *m.*

lay, *v.a.* coucher, poser, étendre; ~ *aside, by* mettre de côté; *(money)* réserver; ~ *down* poser; ~ *on* appliquer; *be laid up* être allté.

lay-by, *s.* refuge *m.,* garage *m.*

layer, *s.* couche *f.*

lazy, *adj.* paresseux.

lead¹, *s. (metal)* plomb *m.*

lead², *v.a. & n.* mener, conduire; ~ *the way* montrer le chemin.

leader, *s.* conducteur *m.; (newspaper)* éditorial *m.*

leadership, *s.* conduite *f.;* direction *f.*

leaf, *s.* feuille *f.; (book)* feuillet *m.;* page *f.*

leak, *s.* fuite *f.;* voie d'eau *f.;* — *v.n.* fuir.

lean, *adj.* maigre.

leap, *v. n. & a.* sauter; — *s.* saut *m.*

learn, *v.a. & n.* apprendre.

learning, *s.* savoir *m.,* science *f.*

leash, *s.* laisse *f.*

least, *adj.* le plus petit; le moindre; — *adv.* le moins; — *s.* moins *m.; at* ~ au moins, à tout le moins; *not in the* ~ pas le moins du monde.

leather, *s.* cuir *m.*

leave, *v. a.* laisser; quitter; *be left* rester; — *s.* permission *f.;* congé *m.; on* ~ en congé.

lecture, *s.* conférence *f. (on* sur); — *v.n.* faire des conférences.

lecturer, *s.* conférencier

m.; (univ.) professeur *m.* (de faculté).

left, *adj. & s.* gauche *(f.).*

left-luggage office, *s.* consigne *f.*

leg, *s.* jambe *f.;* patte *f.*

legal, *adj.* légal.

legislature, *s.* législature *f.*

legitimate, *adj.* légitime.

leisure, *s.* loisir *m.; be at ~* être de loisir.

lemon, *s.* citron *m.*

lemonade, *s.* limonade *f.*

lend, *v.a.* prêter.

length, *s.* longueur *f.; (time)* durée *f.*

lengthen, *v.a.* allonger; prolonger.

lens, *s.* lentille *f.*

leopard, *s.* léopard *m.*

less, *adj.* moindre; moins de; — *adv.* moins; *~ than* moins de.

lessen, *v. a. & n.* diminuer.

lesson, *s.* leçon *f.*

lest, *conj.* de peur que.

let, *v.a.* laisser, permettre à; *(house)* louer; *~ me go* laisse-moi aller; *~ down* laisser tomber (à); *~ in* laisser entrer.

letter, *s.* lettre *f.; ~s* belles-lettres *f. pl.*

lettuce, *s.* laitue *f.*

level, *s.* niveau *m.; — adj.* uni; plat; horizontal; — *v.a.* niveler; pointer.

lever, *s.* levier *m.*

levy, *s.* levée *f.; — v.a.* lever.

lexicon, *s.* lexique *m.*

liability, *s.* responsabilité *f.; liabilities* passif *m.*

liable, *adj.* responsable (de); sujet (à).

liar, *s.* menteur, *m.*

liberal, *adj.* libéral; généreux.

liberty, *s.* liberté *f.*

librarian, *s.* bibliothécaire *m. f.*

library, *s.* bibliothèque *f.*

licence, *s.* permission *f.;* permis *m.,* patente *f.; (excess of liberty)* licence *f.*

license, *v.a.* accorder un permis (à).

lick, *v.a.* lécher.

lid, *s.* couvercle *m.*

lie¹, *s.* mensonge *m.; — v.n.&a.* mentir.

lie², *v.n.* être couché; *(dead)* reposer; *(be situated)* se trouver; *~ down* se coucher; *it ~s with you* cela dépend de vous.

lieutenant, *s.* lieutenant *m.*

life, *s.* vie *f.*

life-insurance, *s.* assurance *f.* sur la vie.

lifeless, *adj.* inanimé.

lift, *v.a.* lever; *fig.* élever; *~ up* soulever; — *s. (apparatus)* ascenseur *m.; give s. o. a ~* faire monter qn (dans sa voiture).

light¹, *s.* lumière *f.;* éclairage *f.;* jour *m.;* lampe *f.; (fire)* feu *m.; come to ~* se révéler; — *v. a.* allumer; éclairer; *v.n.* s'éclairer; — *adj.* clair; éclairé.

light², *adj.* léger; *make ~ of* faire peu de cas de.

lighten¹, *v.a.* éclairer; *v.n.* faire des éclairs.

lighten², *v.a.* alléger.

lighter, *s.* briquet *m.*

lighthouse, *s.* phare *m.*

lighting, *s.* éclairage *m.*

lightning, *s.* éclair *m.*

like¹, *adj.* semblable, pareil, ressemblant; — *prep.* comme.

like², *v.a.* aimer; *I should ~ to* je voudrais + *inf.*

likely, *adv.* probable.

likeness, *s.* ressemblance *f.;* portrait *m.*

lily, *s.* lis *m.*

limb, *s.* membre *m.*

limit, *s.* limite *f.;* *v.a.* limiter.

limited, *adj.* ~ *liability company* société anonyme *f.*

line, *s.* ligne *f.;* *(poetry)* vers *m.;* *(railw.)* voie *f.;* — *v.a.* *(garment)* doubler; *v.n.* ~ *up* s'aligner; faire la queue.

linen, *s.* toile *f.;* ligne *m.*

lining, *s.* doublure *f.*

link, *s.* chaînon *m.*, *fig.* lien *m.;* — *v.a.* lier; unir.

lion, *s* lion *m.*

lip, *s.* lèvre *f.*

lipstick, *s.* rouge *m.* à lèvres.

liquid, *adj..* & *s.* liquide *(m.).*

list, *s.* liste *f.;* — *v.a.* enregistrer.

listen, *v.n.* (also ~ *in)* écouter.

listener, *s.* auditeur, -trice *m. f.*

literary, *adj.* littéraire.

literature, *s.* littérature *f.*

litter, *s.* litière *f.*

little, *adj.* petit; peu de.

live, *v.n.* vivre; *(reside)* habiter, demeurer; ~ *on* vivre de.

lively, *adv.* vivant, gai.

liver, *s.* foie *m.*

living-room, *s.* salle *f.* de séjour.

load, *s.* charge *f.;* fardeau *m.;* — *v.a.* charger.

loaf, *s.* pain *m.*

loan, *s.* prêt *m.;* emprunt *m.*

loathe, *v.a.* détester.

lobby, *s.* couloir *m.*, vestibule *m.*

lobster, *s.* homard *m.*

local, *adj.* local.

location, *s.* emplacement *m.;* situation *f.*

lock[1], *s.* serrure *f.*

lock[2], *s.* *(hair)* boucle *f.*

locksmith, *s.* serrurier *m.*

lodger, *s.* locataire *m. f.*

lodging, *s.* logement *m.* *furnished* ~s garni *m.*

log, *s.* bûche *f.;* bille *f.*

logical, *adj.* logique.

loin, *s.* *(pork)* longe *f.;* *(beef)* aloyau *m.;* rein *m.*

lonely, *adj.* solitaire.

long[1], *adj.* long; *a* ~ *time (since)* depuis longtemps; *be* ~ *in* être long à; — *adv.* longtemps; *how* ~? combien de temps?; ~ *ago* il y a longtemps.

long[2], *v.n.* ~ *for* désirer qch., soupirer après.

long-distance, *adj.* à (longue) distance.

long-play(ing), *adj.* ~ *record* microsillon *m.*

look, *v. n.* & *a.* regarder; ~ *after* soigner; ~ *at* regarder; ~ *back* regarder en arrière; ~ *for* chercher; ~ *into* examiner; ~ *out* être sur ses gardes, *int.* gare!; ~ *over* parcourir; ~ *up* chercher; — *s.* regard *m.;* air *m.;* aspect *m.*

looking-glass, *s.* miroir *m.*

loom, *s.* métier *m.* de tisserand

loop, *s.* boucle .

loose, *adj.* lâche; délié, détaché; vague.

loosen, *v.a.* desserrer.

lord, *s.* maître *m.;* seigneur *m.*

lorry, *s.* camion *m.*

lose, *v.a.* & *n.* perdre.

loss, s. perte f.
lot, s. sort m.; (portion) partage m.; a ~ of beaucoup de.
lottery, s. loterie f.
loud, adj. fort; bruyant.
loud-speaker, s. haut-parleur m.
lounge, s. (grand) vesti-bule m.; foyer m., hall m.; — v.n. flâner.
lounge-suit, s. complet veston m.
love, s. amour m.; — v.a. aimer.
lovely, adj. beau, bel, belle; charmant.
lover, s. amoureux m.; amant m.
low, adj. & adv. bas.
lower, adj. inférieur; (deck) premier (pont); — v.a. baisser; (flags, sails) amener.
loyal, adj. loyal; fidèle.
loyalty, s. loyauté f.
lubricate, v.a. lubrifier.
luck, s. chance f.; bad ~ malchance f.
lucky, adj. heureux.
luggage, s. bagages m. pl.
luggage-van, s. fourgon m. (aux bagages).
lump, s. morceau m.
lunch, s. déjeuner m.; — v.n. déjeuner.
lung, s. poumon m.
lute, s. luth m.
luxurious, adj. luxueux.
luxury, s. luxe m.
lyre, s. lyre f.
lyric, adj. lyrique.

M

machine, s. machine f.
machinery, s. machines f.pl.; fig. mécanisme m.

mackintosh, s. imperméa-ble m.
mad, adj. fou, fol, folle.
madam, s. madame f.
magazine, s. revue f.; (rifle) magasin m.
magic, adj. magique.
magistrate, s. magistrat m.
magnet, s. aimant m.
magnetic, adj. magné-tique.
magnificent, adj. mag-nifique.
maid, s. (jeune) fille f.; bonne f.
mail, s. courrier m.
mail-boat, s. paquebot-poste m.
mail-van, s. wagon-poste m.
main, adj. principal.
mainland, s. terre f. fer-me.
mainly, adv. principale-ment.
mains, s. secteur (de cou-rant) m.
maintain, v.a. maintenir; soutenir.
maintenance, s. entretien m.
majesty, s. majesté f.
major, s. commandant m.; — adj. majeur.
majority, s. majorité f.; plupart f.
make, v.a. & n. faire; rendre; ~ away with détruire; ~ for se diriger vers; ~ off dé-camper; ~ out com-prendre; prouver; ~ over céder; ~ up (list) dresser; (invent) inventer; ~ up for com-penser; — s. forme f., fabrication f.
male, adj. mâle; masculin; — s. mâle m.
malice, s. méchanceté

f.

man, *s.* homme *m.*

manage, *v. a.* conduire, diriger, gérer, gouverner; *I shall* ~ *it* j'en viendrai à bout.

management, *s.* direction *f.;* gérance *f.*

manager, *s.* directeur *m.;* gérant *m.*

manicure, *s.* manicure *n. f.*

manifest, *adj.* manifeste; — *v.a.* manifester.

manipulate, *v.a.* manipuler.

manner, *s.* manière *f.;* air *m.;* ~*s* manières *f. pl.;* *(morals)* mœurs *f. pl.*

manœuvre, *s.* manœuvre *f.;* — *v.a.* faire manœuvrer.

manor, *s.* manoir *m.*

manual, *adj.* & *s.* manuel *(m.).*

manufacture, *s.* manufacture *f.;* — *v.a.* fabriquer.

manufacturer, *s.* manufacturier *m.;* fabricant *m.*

manure, *s.* fumier *m.*

manuscript, *s.* manuscrit *m.*

many, *adj.* beaucoup de.

map, *s.* carte *f.* géographique.

marble, *s.* marbre *m.*

march, *s.* marche *f.;* — *v.n.* marcher.

March, *s.* mars *m.*

mare, *s.* jument *f.*

margarine, *s.* margarine *f.*

marine, *s.* marine *f.;* — *adj.* marin; maritime.

mariner, *s.* marin *m.*

mark, *s.* marque *f.;* *(aim)* but *m.;* *(school)* point *m.;* *(coin)* marc *m.;* — *v.a.* marquer;

souligner.

market, *s.* marché *m.*

market-price, *s.* prix *m.* courant.

marmalade, *s.* marmelade *f.* (d'oranges).

marriage, *s.* mariage *m.*

married, *adj.* marié.

marry, *v. a.* épouser; *v. n.* *(get married)* se marier.

marsh, *s.* marais *m.*

marshal, *s.* maréchal *m.;* — *v.a.* ranger; conduire.

martial, *adj.* martial.

martyr, *s.* martyr *m.*

marvel, *s.* merveille *f.;* — *v.n.* s'étonner (de).

marvellous, *adj.* merveilleux.

masculine, *adj.* mâle; masculin.

mask, *s.* masque *m.*

mason, *s.* maçon *m.*

mass¹, *s.* masse *f.;* majorité *f.*

mass², *s.* *(eccles.)* messe *f.*

mast, *s.* mât *m.*

master, *s.* maître *m.;* — *v. a.* maîtriser

mat, *s.* *(door)* paillasson *m.;* *(table)* dessous de plat, *m.*

match¹, *s.* égal, -e *m. f.,* pareil, -le *m. f.,* mariage *m.;* *(pers.)* parti *m.;* *(sport)* match *m.;* — *v.a.* assortir; *v.n.* s'assortir.

match², *s.* allumette *f.*

mate, *s.* camarade *m.;* *(birds)* mâle *m.,* femelle *f.;* *(chess)* mat *m.;* *(ship)* second *m.;* — *v.a.* marier (à); *v.n.* s'accoupler.

material, *s.* matière *f.;* — *adj.* matériel.

maternal, *adj.* maternel.

mathematical, *adj.* mathématique.

mathematics, *s.* mathé-
matiques *f. pl.*

matinée, *s.* matinée *f.*

matron, *s.* mère de famille, *f.; (hospital)*
infirmière-en-chef *f.;*
surveillante *f.*

matter, *s.* matière *f.; affaire f.; sujet m.; chose
f.; as a ~ of fact* en
fait; *what is the ~?*
qu'est-ce qu'il y a?; —
v.n. importer; *it does
not ~* n'importe.

mattress, *s.* matelas *m.;
spring ~* sommier *m.,*
matelas *m.* à ressort.

mature, *adj.* mûr; — *v.a.*
& n. mûrir.

maturity, *s.* maturité *f.*

May, *s.* mai *m.*

may, *v. aux.* pouvoir; ~
I? vous permettez?

maybe, *adv.* peut-être.

mayor, *s.* maire *m.*

me, *pron. (acc.)* me;
(alone, with prep.) moi.

meadow, *s.* pré *m.*

meal, *s.* repas *m.*

mean¹, *s.* moyen terme,
m.; (math.) moyenne
f.; ~s moyens *m. pl.,
(way to do)* moyen *m.;
by ~s of* au moyen de:
by all ~s mais certainement; *by no ~s* en
aucune façon; — *adj.*
moyen.

mean², *v.a. (signify)*
vouloir dire, signifier:
(wish) vouloir (faire),
avoir l'intention (de);
destiner; *what does that
word ~?* que signifie
ce mot?; *what do you
~ by that?* qu'entendez-
vous par là?

mean³, *adj.* misérable,
pauvre; bas, vil; la-
dre.

meaning, *s.* intention *f.;*
sens *m.*

meantime, **-while,** *adv.
(in the ~)* dans l'in-
tervalle, pendant ce
temps-là.

measure, *s.* mesure *f.;* —
v.a. mesurer.

meat, *s.* viande *f.; (food)*
nourriture *f.*

mechanic, *s.* artisan *m.,*
mécanicien *m.*

mechanical, *adj.* mécanique.

mechanics, *s.* mécanique
f.

mechanism, *s.* mécanisme
m.

mechanize, *v.a.* mécaniser.

medal, *s.* médaille *f.*

medical, *adj.* médical;
~ student étudiant *m.*
en médicine.

medicine, *s.* médecine *f.*

meditate, *v.a. & n.* méditer.

medium, *s.* moyen terme
m.; milieu *m.;* — *adj.*
moyen.

meet, *v.a.* rencontrer
(qn.), se rencontrer
avec (qn.); *(face)* af-
fronter; *(expenses)*
faire face à; *~ sy at
the station* aller recevoir
qn. à la gare; — *v. n.*
se rencontrer; *~ with*
rencontrer; éprouver.

meeting, *s.* rencontre *f.;*
réunion *f.*

mellow, *adj.* mûr; moelleux.

melody, *s.* mélodie *f.*

melon, *s.* melon *m.*

melt, *v.a.* fondre.

member, *s.* membre *m.*

memorial, *s.* monument
m.; mémorial *m.*

memory, *s.* mémoire *f.;*
souvenir *m.*

mend, *v. a.* raccommoder;
réparer; corriger.

mental, *adj.* mental.

mention, *v. a.* mentionner; citer; *don't ~ it* il n'y a pas de quoi.

merchandise, *s.* marchandise *f.*

merchant, *s.* négociant *m.*; commerçant *m.*

merciful, *adj.* miséricordieux.

mercy, *s.* pitié *f.*; miséricorde *f.*

mere, *adj.* seul.

merely, *adv.* purement; simplement.

merit, mérite *m.*; — *v.a.* mériter.

merry, *adj.* gai.

mess, *s.* gâchis *m.*; *make a ~ of* gâcher.

message, *s.* message *m.*

messenger, *s.* messager *m.*

metal, *s.* métal *m.*

meteorology, *s.* météorologie *f.*

method, *s.* méthode *f.*

metre, *s.* mètre *m.*

microphone, *s.* microphone *m.*

microscope, *s.* microscope *m.*

middle, *s.* milieu *m.*; — *adj.* du milieu; moyen.

midnight, *s.* minuit *m.*

might, *s.* force *f.*; puissance *f.*

mighty, *adj.* fort; puissant

migrate, *v.n.* émigrer.

mild, *adj.* doux; bénin.

mile, *s.* mille *m.*

mileage, *s.* parcours *m.*; *(expense)* prix *m.* par mille.

military, *adj.* militaire.

milk, *s.* lait *m.*

milkman, *s.* laitier *m.*

mill, *s.* moulin *m.*; fabrique *f.*

miller, *s.* meunier *m.*

milliner, *s.* modiste *f.*

million, *s.* million *m.*

mince, *s.* hachis *m.*; *v.a.* hacher.

mind, *s.* esprit *m.*; *(remembrance)* souvenir *m.*; *(opinion)* pensée *f.*, avis *m.*; *change one's ~* changer d'avis; *make up one's ~ to* se décider à, se résigner à; — *v.a.* faire attention à, prendre garde à; écouter; *(look after)* garder; *(trouble about)* s'inquiéter de; *do you ~ my smoking?* est-ce que cela vous gêne que je fume?; *I don't ~* cela m'est égal; *never ~* ça ne fait rien.

mine¹, *s.* mine *f.*; — *v.a.* miner.

mine², *pron.* à moi; le mien.

miner, *s.* mineur *m.*

mineral, *adj. & s.* minéral *(m.)*.

minister, *s.* ministre *m.*

ministry, *s.* ministère *m.*

minor, *adj.* mineur.

minority, *s.* minorité.

mint, *s.* Hôtel *m.* de la Monnaie; *(plant)* menthe *f.*

minus, *adj.* en. moins; — *adv.* moins.

minute, *s.* minute *f.*; petit moment, *m.*; *~ hand* grande aiguille *f.*

miracle, *s.* miracle *m.*

mirror, *s.* miroir *m.*

miscarry, *v.n.* avorter.

miscellaneous, *adv.* divers.

mischief, *s.* mal *m.*; méchanceté *f.*

miser, *s.* avare *m.*

miserable, *adj.* misérable; malheureux.

misery, *s.* misère *f.*

misfortune, *s.* malheur *m.*

miss¹, *v.a.* manquer; ne pas entendre; ne pas voir; s'apercevoir

de l'absence (de); ~
out omettre; be ~ing
manquer.

miss², s. mademoiselle f.

missile, s. projectile m.

mission, s. mission f.

missionary, s. missionnaire m. f.

mist, s. brouillard m.,
brume f.

mistake, s. erreur f., mé-
prise f.; faute f.; —
v.a. se tromper de;
~ for prendre pour; be
~n se tromper.

mistress, s. maîtresse f.

(de maison).

mistrust, s. méfiance f.

misty, adj. brumeux.

misunderstand, v. a. comprendre mal.

mitten, s. mitaine f.

mix, v.a. mêler; mélanger; be ~ed up in être
mêlé à.

mixture, s. mélange m.;
mixture f.

moan, v.n. gémir; —
s. gémissement m.

mob, s. foule f., populace
f.

mobilization, s. mobilisation f.

mobilize, v.a. mobiliser.

mock, s. moquerie f.; —
adj. faux; — v.a.
railler.

mockery, s. moquerie f.

model, s. modèle m.

moderate, adj. modéré;
— v.a. modérer.

moderation, s. modération f.

modern, adj. moderne.

modest, adj. modeste.

modesty s. modestie f.

modify, v.a. modifier.

moist, adj. moite, humide.

moisten, v.a. humecter.

moisture, s. humidité f.

molecule, s. molécule f.

moment, s. moment m.

momentary, adj. mo-
mentané.

monarch, s. monarque m.

monarchy, s. monarchie f.

Monday, s. lundi m.

money, s. argent m.;
monnaie f.

money-order, s. mandat
m.

monk, s. moine m.

monkey, s. singe m.

monopolize, v.a. mono-
poliser.

monopoly, s. monopole m.

monotonous, adj. monotone.

monstrous, adj. mons-
trueux.

month, s. mois m.

monthly, adj. mensuel;
— adv. mensuellement.

monument, s. monument
m.

monumental, adj. mo-
numental.

mood, s. humeur f.; mode
m.

moon, s. lune f.

moonlight, s. clair m.
de lune

moor, s. bruyère f.

mop, balai m.; — v.a.
(also ~ up) éponger,
essuyer.

moral, s. morale f.; ~s
moeurs f. pl.; — adj.
moral; de morale.

more, adj. & pron. plus
de; davantage de;
~ than plus que; some
~ en ... davantage;
no ~ n'en ... pas
davantage, ne ...
plus; — adv. plus;
davantage; ~ and ~
de plus en plus.

moreover, adv. de plus.

morning, s. matin m.;
in the ~ le matin; —
adj. du matin.

mortal, *adj. & s.* mortel *(m., f.)*.

mortality, *s.* mortalité *f.*

mortgage, *s.* hypothèque *f.;* — *v. a.* hypothéquer.

mosquito, *s.* moustique *f.*

moss, *s.* mousse *f.*

most, *adj. & pron.* le plus (de), la plupart (de); *at the* ~ tout au plus; ~ *people* la plupart des gens; *make the* ~ *of* tirer le meilleur parti de; — *adv.* très, fort, bien.

mostly, *adv.* pour la plupart; principalement; la plupart du temps.

motel, *s.* motel *m.*

moth, *s.* mite *f.*

mother, *s.* mère *f.*

mother-in-law, *s.* belle-mère *f.*

mother-tongue, *s.* langue *f.* maternelle.

motion, *s.* mouvement *m.;* signe *m.;* *(proposal)* motion *f.*

motionless, *adj.* immobile.

motive, *s.* motif *m.*

motor, *s.* moteur *m.*

motor-bus, *s.* autobus *m.*

motor-car, *s.* auto(mobile) *f.*

motor-coach, *s.* autocar *m.*

motor-cycle, *s.* motocyclette *f.*

motor-scooter, *s.* scooter *m.*

motorway,, *s.* autoroute *f.*

mould, *s.* moule *m.;* — *v.a.* mouler.

mount, *s.* mont *m.;* — *v.a. & n.* monter.

mountain, *s.* montagne *f.*

mountaineering, *s.* alpinisme *m.*

mountainous, *adj.* montagneux.

mourn, *v. n. & a.* pleurer, (se) lamenter.

mouse, *s.* souris *f.*

moustache, *s.* moustache *f.*

mouth, *s.* bouche *f.;* *(beast)* gueule *f.*

move, *s.* mouvement *m.;* *(chess)* coup *m.;* — *v.a.* remuer; déplacer; *(goods)* transporter; *(affect)* émouvoir; *(motion)* proposer ~ *house (also:* ~*)* déménager; — *v.n.* se mouvoir, se déplacer; s'avancer; *(chess)* jouer; ~ *forward* s'avancer; ~ *in* emménager; ~ *out* déménager; ~ *on* avancer; *int.* circulez!

movement, *s.* mouvement *m.*

mow, *v.a.* faucher; tondre.

mower, *s.* faucheur *m.;* faucheuse (à moteur) *f.*

much, *adj. & pron.* beaucoup; — *adv.* beaucoup; très; *too* ~ trop.

mud, *s.* boue *f.*

muddle, *s.* fouillis *m.;* — *v.a.* embrouiller.

muddy, *adj.* boueux.

mug, *s.* timbale *f.*

mule, *s.* mulet *m.,* mule *f.*

multiple, *adj.* multiple.

multiplication, *s.* multiplication *f.*

multiply, *v.a.* multiplier.

multitude, *s.* multitude *f.*

municipal, *adj.* municipal.

murder, *s.* meurtre *m.*

murderer, *s.* meurtrier *m.*

murmur, *s.* murmure

m.

muscle, s. muscle m.

museum, s. musée m.

mushroom, s. champignon m.

music, s. musique f.

musical, adj. musical; ~ instrument instrument m. de musique.

music-hall, s. café m. concert.

musician, s. musicien, -enne m. f.

must, v. aux. il faut que; devoir.

mustard, s. moutarde f.

mute, adj. muet.

mutter, s. murmure m.; — v. n. murmurer.

mutton, s. mouton m.

mutual, adj. mutuel.

my, pron. mon, ma; mes (pl.).

myself, pron. moi-même; by ~ seul.

mysterious, adj. mystérieux.

mystery, s. mystère m.

mystic, adj. mystique.

myth, s. mythe m.

N

nail, s. (to hammer) clou m.; (on fingers) ongle m.; — v.a. clouer.

nail-brush, s. brosse f. à ongles.

naked, adj. nu; dénudé.

name, s. nom m.; — v.a. nommer; désigner.

namely, adv. savoir.

nap, s. somme m.

napkin, s. serviette f., (infant) couche f.

narrate, v. a. raconter.

narrow, adj. étroit.

nation, s. nation f.

national, adj. national.

nationality, s. nationalité

f.

nationalize, v.a. nationaliser.

native, adj. & s. natif, -ive (m. f.).

natural, adj. naturel.

naturalize, v.a. naturaliser.

nature, s. nature f.

naughty, adj. méchant.

nava l.adj. naval

navigate, v.n. naviguer.

navigator, s. navigateur m.

navy, s. marine f.

near, adv. près, proche; — prep. près de, auprès de; — adj. proche.

nearly, adv. (almost) presque.

neat, adj. propre; élégant.

necessary, adj. nécessaire.

necessity, s. néccesité f.

neck, s. cou m.

necklace, s. collier m.

necktie, s. cravate f.

need, s. besoin; — v.a. avoir besoin (de); demander.

needle, s. aiguille f.

needless, adj. inutile.

needy, adj. nécessiteux.

negative, adj. négatif; — s. négative f.; (photo) cliché m.; in the ~ négativement.

neglect, v. a. négliger (de).

negligence, s. négligence f.

negotiation, s. négociation f.

negro, -ess s. nègre m., négresse f.

neighbour, s. voisin, -e m. f.

neighbourhood, s. voisinage m.

neither, pron. & adj. ni l'un ni l'autre.

nephew, s. neveu m.

nerve, s. nerf m.

nervous, adj. nerveux.

nest, s. nid m.

net¹, s. filet m.
net², adj. net.
network, s. réseau m.
neutral, adj. neutre.
never, adj. (ne ...) jamais.
nevertheless, adv. néanmoins.
new, adj. neuf, neuve; nouveau,-el,-elle; *New Year* Nouvel An.
news, s. nouvelle f.
newspaper, s. journal m.
next, adj. le plus proche; prochain, suivant; ~ *door to* à côté de; adv. ensuite, après; — prep. ~ *to* à côté de.
nice, adj. agréable, bon; gentil.
niece, s. nièce f.
night, s. nuit f.; soir m.; *by* ~ de nuit; *good* ~! bonne nuit!
nightingale, s. rossignol m.
nine, adj. & s. neuf (m.).
nineteen, adj. & s. dix-neuf (m.).
ninety, adj. & s. quatre-vingt-dix (m.).
ninth, adj. neuvième; neuf.
nip, v.a. pincer.
nitrogen, s. azote m.
no, adj. ne ... pas (de), ne ... aucun.
noble, adj. noble.
nobleman, s. gentilhomme m.
nobody, no one, pron. personne ne (+ verb).
noise, s. bruit m.
noisy, adj. bruyant.
none, pron. ne ... aucun; personne ne (+ verb.)
nonsense, s. bêtise; m. no ~ pas de bêtises
non-smoker, s. compartiment m. pour non-fumeurs.

non-stop, adj. & adv. sans arrêt; sans escale.
noon, s. midi m.
nor, conj. ni; (and ... not) et ne ... pas, non plus.
normal, adj. normal.
north, s. nord m.; — adj. du nord.
north-east, adj. & s. nord-est m.
northern, adj. du nord.
north-west, adj. & s. nord-ouest m.
nose, s. nez m.
nostril, s. narine f.
not, adv. ne ... pas, ne ... point.
notable, adj. notable.
note, s. note f.; (letter and money) billet m.; (tone) ton m.; — v.a. noter; remarquer.
note-book, s. carnet m.
noted, adj. distingué.
nothing, pron. rien; ne ... rien.
notice, s. avis m.; attention f.; connaissance f.; *take* ~ *of* faire attention à.
notify, v.a. avertir, notifier.
notion, s. idée f.
noun, s. nom m.
nourish, v.a. nourrir.
novel, s. roman m.
novelist, s. romancier m.
novelty, s. nouveauté f.
November, s. novembre m.
now, adv. maintenant.
nowadays, adv. de nos jours.
nowhere, adv. ne ... nulle part.
nuclear, adj. nucléaire; ~ *energy* énergie f. nucléaire; ~ *physics* physique f. nucléaire; ~ *power station* centrale f. nucléaire.
nuisance, s. (pers.) peste

f.; (thing) ennui *m.*

number, *s.* nombre *m.,* numéro *m.*

number-plate, *s.* plaque *f.* matricule.

numerous, *adj.* nombreux.

nun, *s.* religieuse *f.*

nurse, *s.* nourrice *f.,* bonne (d'enfant) *f.; (hospital)* infirmier, -ère *m. f.; — v.a. (suckle)* allaiter; *(the sick)* soigner.

nursery, *s.* chambre *f.* des enfants.

nut, *s.* noix *f.,* noisette *f.*

nylon, *s.* nylon *m.; ~ stockings* (or *~s*) bas nylons *m. pl.*

O

oak, *s.* chêne *m.*

oar, *s.* rame *f.*

oat(s) *s. (pl).* avoine *f.*

oath, *s.* serment *m.*

obedience, *s.* obéissance *f.*

obedient, *adj.* obéissant.

obey, *v.a. & n.* obéir (à)·

object, *s.* objet *m.; but m.; (gramm.)* régime *m.; — v.a.* objecter; *v.n.* s'opposer (à).

objection, *s.* objection *f.*

objective, *adj. & s.* objectif *(m.).*

obligation, *s.* obligation *f.*

oblige, *v.a.* obliger.

obscure, *adj.* obscur.

observation, *s.* observation *f.*

observe, *v.a. & n.* observer.

obstacle, *s.* obstacle *m.*

obstinate, *adj.* obstiné.

obtain, *v.a.* obtenir.

obvious, *adj.* évident.

occasion, *s.* occasion *f.*

occasional *adj.* occasionnel.

occasionally, *adv.* de temps en temps.

occupation, *s.* occupation *f.*

occupy, *v.a.* occuper; *~ oneself with* s'occuper de.

occur, *v.n.* arriver; se trouver; *it ~red to me* il m'est venu à l'idée que.

occurrence, *s.* événement *m.*

ocean, *s.* océan *m.*

October, *s.* octobre *m.*

odd, *adj.* impair; dépareillé, déparié; *(strange)* non usuel, bizarre.

odds, *s. pl.* avantage *m.;* chances *f. pl.*

of, *prep.* de.

off, *adv.* à . . . de distance; *be ~* s'en aller; *be well ~* être à l'aise; *— prep.* de.

offence, *s* offense *f.*

offend, *v. a. & n.* offenser.

offensive, *s.* offensive *f.*

offer, *s.* offre *f.; — v.a.* offrir.

office, *s.* bureau *m.; (of pers.)* charge *f.;* fonction *f.*

officer, *s.* officer *m.; (police)* agent *m.*

official, *adj.* officiel; *— s.* fonctionnaire *m. f.*

often, *adv.* souvent.

oil, *s.* huile *f.;* pétrole *m.*

ointment, *s.* onguent *m.*

old, *adj.* vieux, -eil, -eille; âgé; ancien; *how ~ are you?* quel âge avez-vous?; *~ age* vieillesse *f.; grow ~* vieillir.

old-fashioned, *adj.* à l'ancienne mode.

omission, *s.* omission *f.*

omit, *v.a.* omettre (de).

on, *prep.* sur; *(prep. omitted with days etc.); ~ Monday* lundi; *~*

time à la minute.

once, *adv.* une fois; autre-fois; *at* ~ tout de suite.

one, *adj. & s.* un, une; — *pron.* (~, ~*s omitted if preceded by adj.*); (*peo-ple, they*) on; *this* ~ celui-ci; *that* ~ ce-lui-là; ~'*s* son, sa, ses; *which* ~? le-quel ...?

oneself, *pron,* soi-même; *by* ~ tout seul.

onion, *s.* oignon *m.*

onlooker, *s.* spectateur, -trice *m. f.*

open, *adj.* ouvert; dé-couvert; public; franc; — *v.a.* ouvrir; *v.n.* s'ouvrir.

opening, *s.* ouverture *f.*

opera, *s.* opéra *m.*

operate, *v.a. & n.* opérer; ~ *on* opérer (qn).

operating-theatre, *s.* salle *f.* d'opération.

operation, *s.* opération *f.*

operative, *adj.* actif.

opinion, *s.* opinion *f.;* *in my* ~ à mon avis.

opponent, *s.* adversaire *m.*

opportunity, *s.* occasion *f.*

oppose, *v.a.* s'opposer à; ~*d to* opposé à.

opposition, *s.* opposition *f.*

optional, *adj.* facultatif.

or, *conj.* ou; *whether* ... ~ ou ... ou.

oral, *adj.* oral.

orange, *s.* orange *f.*

orchard, *s.* verger *m.*

orchestra, *s.* orchestre *m.*

order, *s.* ordre *m.;* (*com-merce*) commande *f.;* (*ruling*) règlement *m.;* — *v.a.* ordonner; (*goods*) commander.

order-form, *s.* bon *m.* commande.

ordinary, *adj.* ordinaire *m.*

ore, *s.* minerai *m.*

organ, *s.* organe *m.;* (*music*) orgue *m.*

organic, *adj.* organique.

organization, *s.* organisa-tion. *f*

organize, *v.a.* organiser.

oriental, *adj.* oriental.

origin, *s.* origine *f.*

original, *adj.* original.

ornament, *s.* ornement *m.;* — *v.a.* orner.

ornamental, *adj.* orne-mental.

orphan, *adj. & s.* orphelin, -e *(m. f.).*

other, *adj. & pron.* autre.

otherwise, *adv.* autre-ment.

ought, *v. aux.* devoir.

ounce, *s.* once *f.*

our, *adj.* notre, *(pl.)* nos.

ours, *pron.* le, la nôtre; les nôtres.

ourself, *pron.* nous(-mê-mes); *ourselves* nous-(-mêmes); *by ourselves* seul, -s.

out, *adv.* dehors; — *prep.* ~ *of* hors de.

outdoors, *adv.* dehors, en plein air.

outfit, *s.* trousseau *m.*

outing, *s.* excursion *f.*

outline, *s.* contour *m.;* aperçu *m.;* — *v.a.* es-quisser.

outlive, *v.a.* survivre à.

outlook, *s.* perspective *f.*

output, *s.* production *f.*

outrageous, *adj.* outra-geant; atroce.

outset, *s.* début *m.; at the* ~ dès le commence-ment.

outside, *adv.* au dehors; — *prep.* en dehors de; — *adj.* du dehors; — *s.* extérieur.

outskirts, *s. pl.* banlieue

f.; lisière f.

outstanding, *adj.* non réglé, à payer; saillant; éminent.

outward, *adj.* extérieur.

outwards, *adv.* à l'extérieur, en dehors.

oven, *s.* four *m.*

over, *prep.* au-dessus de; *(motion)* par dessus; *(superior)* sur; *(more than)* plus de; *(across)* par; — *adv. (more)* davantage; *(finished)* fini, passé; *(too)* trop.

overcoat, *s.* pardessus *m.*

overcome, *v.a.* surmonter; vaincre.

overcrowded, *adj.* surpeuplé.

overdo, *v.a.* faire trop cuire; exagérer.

overexpose, *v.a.* surexposer.

overflow, *s.* débordement *m.;* — *v.a.* inonder; *v.n.* déborder.

overlook, *v.a. (look on to)* avoir vue sur; *(neglect)* négliger; *(superintend)* surveiller.

overpower, *v.a.* accabler; subjuguer.

oversea, *adj.* d'outre-mer; ~*s (adv.)* outre-mer.

oversight, *s.* inadvertence *f.*

overtake, *v.a.* rattraper; surprendre (par).

overthrow, *s.* renversement *m.;* — *v.a.* renverser.

overtime, *s.* heures *f. pl.* supplémentaires.

overwhelming, *adj.* accablant.

owe, *v.a.* devoir (à); être redevable (à).

owing, *adj.* ~ *to* à cause de.

owl, *s.* hibou *m.*

own, *adj.* propre; *of my*

~ à moi; — *v.a.* posséder.

owner, *s.* propriétaire *m. f.*

ox, *s.* bœuf *m.*

oxygen, *s.* oxygène *m.*

oyster, *s.* huitre *f.*

P

pace, *s.* pas *m.;* *v.a.* arpenter; *v.n.* aller au pas.

pack, *s.* paquet; *(cards)* jeu *m.; (wool)* balle; *(hounds)* meute *f.;* — *v.a.* emballer; faire: ~ *off* expédier.

package, *s.* colis *m.;* paquet *m.*

packet, *s.* paquet *m.*

pact, *s.* pacte *m.*

pad, *s.* bourrelet *m.;* tampon *m.;* bloc *m.;* *blotting* ~ buvard *m.*

paddle, *v.n.* pagayer.

page, *s.* page *f.*

pail, *s.* seau *m.*

pain, *s.* douleur *f.; take* ~*s* se donner de la peine.

painful, *adj.* douloureux.

paint, *s.* peinture *f.;* — *v. a.* peindre.

painter, *s.* peintre *m.*

painting, *s.* peinture *f.*

pair, *s.* paire *f.;* couple *m.*

palace, *s.* palais *m.*

palate, *s.* palais *m.*

pale, *adj.* pâle; *grow* ~ pâlir.

palm, *s.* palme *f.*

pan, *s.* poêle *f.*

pane, *s.* vitre *f.*

panel, *s.* panneau *m.*

panorama, *s.* panorama *m.*

pansy, *s.* pensée *f.*

pantry, *s.* office *f.*

pants, *s.pl.* caleçon *m.;* pantalon *m.*

paper, *s.* papier *m.;*

(newspaper) journal *m.; (essay)* étude *f.; (exam)* composition *f.*

parade, *s.* parade *f.;* — *v.n.* parader.

paraffin, *s.* pétrole *m.*

paragraph, *s.* paragraphe *m.*

parallel, *a.* *(line)* parallèle *f.; (comparison)* parallèle *m.;* — *adj.* parallèle.

paralysis, *s.* paralysie *f.*

parcel, *s.* paquet *m.*

pardon, *s.* pardon *m.; I beg your* ~ je vous demande pardon; *(I beg your)* ~? comment (dites-vous)?, pardon?; — *v.a.* pardonner.

parents, *s. pl.* père *m.* et mère *f.,* parents.

parish, *s.* paroisse *f.*
Parisian, *adj.* parisien; — *s.* Parisien, -enne *m.f.*

park, *s.* parc *m.; (car)* (parc de) stationnement *m.;* *v.a.* garer; stationner; *no* ~*ing* stationnement interdit.

parliament, *s.* parlement *m.*

parliamentary, *adj.* parlementaire.

parlour, *s.* petit salon *m.*

parrot, *s.* perroquet *m.*

part, *s.* part *f.;* partie *f.; (theatre)* rôle *m.; (region)* région *f.; on my* ~ de ma part; *take* ~ *in* prendre part à; — *v.a.* diviser; séparer; *v.n.* se diviser; *(pers.)* se séparer (de).

partial, *adj. (unfair)* partial; *(incomplete)* partiel.

participant, *s.* participant *m.*

participate, *v.n.* ~ *in* prendre part à.

participation, *s.* participation *f.*

participle, *s.* participe *m.*

particular, *adj.* particulier; — *s.* détail *m.*

partly, *adv.* en partie.

partner, *s.* associé, -e *m. f.;* partenaire *m. f.*

partridge, *s.* perdrix *f.*

party, *s.* parti *m.;* partie *f.;* groupe *m.;* réception *f.,* soirée *f.*

pass, *v.a.* passer; dépasser; surpasser; *(law)* voter; *(resolution)* prendre; *(exam)* être reçu (à); — *v. n.* passer; — *s.* défilé *m.;* laisser-passer *m.*

passage, *s.* passage *m.;* couloir *m.*

passenger, *s.* voyageur, -euse *m. f.;* passager, -ère *m. f.*

passer-by, *s.* passant *m.*

passion, *s.* passion *f.*

passionate, *adj.* passionné.

passive, *adj. & s.* passif *(m.).*

passport, *s.* passeport *m.*

past, *adj.* passé; dernier; — *s.* passé *m.*

paste, *s.* pâte *f.*

pastime, *s.* passe-temps *m*

pastry, *s.* pâtisserie *f.*

patch, *s.* pièce *f.*

patent, *s.* brevet *m.* d'invention.

path, -way, *s.* sentier *m.*

patience, *s.* patience *f.*

patient, *s.* malade *m. f.;* — *adj.* patient.

patriot, *s.* patriote *m. f.*

patrol, *s.* patrouille; — *v.n.* aller en patrouille.

patron, *s.* patron *m.;* client *m.*

pattern, *s.* modèle *m.*

pause, *s.* pause *f.;* — *v.n* faire une pause.

pave, *v.a.* paver.

pavement, *s.* trottoir *m.*

pavilion, *s.* pavillon *m.*
paw, *s.* patte *f.*
pay, *v.a.* payer; *(visit)*
faire; ~ off acquitter;
v.n. payer; — *s.*
paye *f.*, salaire *m.*
payable, *adj.* payable (à).
payment, *s.* payement *m.*
pea, *s.* pois *m.*
peace, *s.* paix *f.*
peaceful, *adj.* paisible.
peach, *s.* pêche *f.*
peacock, *s.* paon *m.*
peak, *s.* pic *m.*, cime *f.*
pear, *s.* poire *f.*
pearl, *s.* perle *f.*

peasant, *s.* paysan, -anne
m. f.
pebble, *s.* caillou *m.*
peck, *s.* coup *m.* de bec.
peculiar, *adj.* particulier.
pedestrian, *s.* piéton *m.*
peel, *s.* pelure *f.; — v.a.*
peler.
peer, *s.* pair *m.*
peg, *s.* pince *f.; piquet*
m.
pen, *s.* stylo *m.*
penalty, *s.* peine *f.*
pencil, *s.* crayon *m.*
penicillin, *s.* pénicilline *f.*
penknife, *s.* canif *m.*

penny, *s.* penny *m.*
pension, *s.* pension *f.*
people, *s.* peuple *m.;*
gens *m. pl.* [*f.* with *adj.*
before it]; famille *f.*
pepper, *s.* poivre *m.*
per, *prep.* par; ~ cent
pour cent.
perceive, *v.a.* percevoir.
perch, *s.* perchoir *m.; —*
v.n. se percher.
perfect, *adj.* parfait; —
v.a. rendre parfait;
achever.
perform, *v.a.* accomplir,
exécuter.
performance, *s.* représentation *f.*
perfume, *s.* parfum *m.*

perhaps, *adv.* peut-être.
peril, *s.* péril *m.*
period, *s.* période *f.*
periodical, *s.* périodique
m.
perish, *v.n.* périr.
perishable, *adj.* périssa-
ble.
permanent, *adj.* perma-
nent.
permission, *s.* permission
f.
permit, *s.* permis *m.; —*
v.a. permettre.
persecution, *s.* persécution *f.*
Persian, *adj.* persan.
persist, *v.n.* persister.
person, *s.* personne *f.*
personal, *adj.* personnel.
personality, *s.* personnalité *f.*
perspiration, *s.* transpiration *f.*
persuade, *v.a.* convaincre
(de), persuader.
pertain, *v.n.* appartenir
(à).
pet, *s.* enfant *m.f.* gâté, -e;
— *adj.* favori; ~
dog chien *m.* familier.
petrol, *s.* essence *f.*
petroleum, *s.* pétrole *m.*
petticoat, *s.* jupon *m.*
phase, *s.* phase *f.*
pheasant, *s.* faisan, -e
m. f.
phenomenon, *s.* phéno-
mène *m.*
philosopher, *s.* philosophe
m.
philosophy, *s.* philoso-
phie *f.*
phone, *s.* téléphone *m.;*
— *v.a. & n.* téléphoner.
photo(graph), *s.* photo-
graphie *f.* — *v.a.*
photographier.
phrase, *s.* phrase *f.*
physical, *adj.* physique.
physician, *s.* médecin *m.*
physicist, *s.* physicien *m.*

physics, s. physique f.
pianist, s. pianiste m. f
piano, s. piano m.
pick, v. a. cueillir; picoter; (teeth) curer; (bone) ronger; (choose) choisir; ~ out choisir; ~ up ramasser; prendre.
pickle, s. marinade f. ~s pickles m.
picnic, s. pique-nique m.
picture, s. tableau m.; portrait m.; film m.; ~s cinéma m.
pie, s. pâté m.
piece, s. morceau m.; partie f.; pièce f.; ~ of news nouvelle f.; ~ of work ouvrage m.
pier, s. jetée f.
pierce, v.a. percer.
pig, s. cochon m.
pigeon, s. pigeon m.
pile[1], s. tas m.; — v.a. (also ~ up) entasser, amasser.
pile[2], s. pieu m., pilot m.
pill, s. pillule f.
pillar, s. pilier m.
pillar-box, s. boîte f. aux lettres.
pillow, s. oreiller m.
pilot, s. pilote m.
pin, s. épingle f.
pinch, v.a. pincer.
pine, s. pin m.
pineapple, s. ananas m.
pink, adj. & s. rose (m.).
pint, s. pinte f.
pious, adj. pieux.
pipe, s. tuyau m.; (smoking) pipe f.
pistol, s. pistolet m.
pit, s. fosse f.; creux m.; (theatre) parterre m.
pitch, s. degré m.; ton m.; v.a. (tent) dresser; (camp) asseoir.
pity, s. pitié f.; dommage m.

place, s. lieu m., endroit m.; place f.; emploi m.; — v.a. mettre.
plain, adj. uni; simple; évident; ordinaire.
plait, s. tresse f.
plan, s. plan m.; projet m.; — v.a. faire le plan (de).
plane, s. plan m.; (tool) rabot m.; (aero-) avion m.; — v.a. raboter.
planet, s. planète f.
plank, s. planche f.
plant, s. plante f.; (works) usine f., fabrique f.; — v.a. planter.
plantation, s. plantation f.
plaster, s. (em)plâtre m.
plastic, adj. plastique; ~s plastiques m. pl.
plate, s. plaque f.; planche f.; (china) assiette f.; (silver) vaisselle f.
platform, s. quai m.
platinum, s. platine m.
platter, s. plat m.
play, s. jeu m.; pièce f. de théâtre; — v.a. & n. jouer.
player, s. joueur, -euse m. f.
playground, s. cour f. de récréation.
plea, s. excuse f.; défense f.
plead, v.a.&n. plaider
pleasant, adj. agréable.
please, v.a. & n. plaire (à); be ~ed with, to être content de; as you ~ comme vous voulez; if you ~ s'il vous plaît.
pleasure, s. plaisir m.
pledge, s. gage m.; — v.a. mettre en gage.
plenty, s. abondance f.; ~ of quantité de,

beaucoup de.

plot, s. *(land)* terrain m.; *(story)* intrigue f.; *(conspiracy)* complot m.; v. n. conspirer.

plough, s. charrue f.; — v.a.&n. labourer.

plug, s. tampon m.; prise f. de courant; — v.a. tamponner.

plum, s. prune f.

plume, s. plume f.; plumet m.

plunder, v.a. piller; — s. pillage m.

plunge, v.a. & n. plonger; — s. plongeon m.

plural, s. & adj. pluriel (m.).

plus, prep. plus.

ply, v.a. manier; s'appliquer (à); v.n. faire le service (entre).

pocket, s. poche f.

pocket-book, s. carnet m.; portefeuille m.

poem, s. poème m.

poet, s. poète m.

poetic(al), adj. poétique

poetry, s. poésie · f.

point, s. point m ; pointe f.; — v.a. & n. ~ out montrer du doigt; faire valoir (un fait); ~ to indiquer.

poison, s. poison m.; v.a. empoisonner.

poisonous, adj. vénéneux.

pole, s. pôle m.

Pole, s. Polonais, -e m. f.

police, s. police f.

policeman, -officer, s. agent (de police) m.

police-station, s. poste (de police) m.

policy, s. politique f.; *(insurance)* police f.

polish, s. poli m.; fig. politesse f.; — v. a. polir.

Polish, adj. polonais.

polite, adj. poli.

political, adj. politique.

politician, s. politique m.; politicien m.

politics, s. politique f.

poll, s. vote m.; liste f. (électorale); scrutin m.

pool[1], s. mare f.

pool[2], s. pool m.

poor, adj. pauvre; *(bad)* mauvais.

pope, s. pape m.

popular, adj. populaire.

popularity, s. popularité f.

population, s. population f.

pork, s. porc m.; ~ butcher charcutier m.

port, s. port m.; *(ship)* bâbord m.

portable, adj. portatif.

porter, s. portier m.; *(railw.)* porteur m.

portfolio, s. serviette f.

portion, s. portion f.; — v.a. partager.

portrait, s. portrait m.

Portuguese, adj. portugais; — s. Portugais, -e m. f.

position, s. position f.

positive, adj. & s. positif (m.).

possess, v.a. posséder.

possession, s. possession f.

possibility, s. possibilité f.

possible, adj. possible.

post[1], s. poteau m.; — v.a. afficher, placarder.

post[2], s. poste f.; courrier m. — v.a. mettre à la poste.

postage, s. port m., affranchissement; ~ paid port payé.

postal, adj. postal; ~ order mandat (de poste) m.

poster, s. affiche f.

post-free, *adj.* franco.
postman, *s.* facteur *m.*
post(-)office, *s.* bureau *m.* de poste
postpone, *v.a.* remettre.
postscript, *s.* post-scriptum *m.*
pot, *s.* pot *m.*
potato, *s.* pomme *f.* de terre.
pottery, *s.* poterie *f.*
pouch, *s.* blague *f.*
poultry, *s.* volaille *f.*
pound, *s.* livre *f.*
pour, *v.a.* verser.
pouring, *adj.* torrentiel.
poverty, *s.* pauvreté *f.*
powder, *s.* poudre *f.*
power, *s.* pouvoir *m.;* puissance *f.;* force *f.*
powerful, *adj.* puissant.
power-plant, -station, *s.* centrale *f.* électrique.
practical, *adv.* pratique.
practice, *s.* pratique *f.;* exercise *m.*
practise, *v.a.* pratiquer, exercer; étudier.
praise, *s.* louange *f.;* — *v.a.* louer.
pray, *v.a. & n.* prier.
prayer, *s.* prière *f.*
preach, *v.a. & n.* prêcher.
preacher, *s.* prédicateur *m.*
precede, *v.a.* précéder.
preceding, *adj.* précédent.
precious, *adj.* précieux.
precision, *s.* précision *f.*
predecessor, *s.* prédécesseur *m.*
predict, *v.a.* prédire.
prefabricated, *adj.* préfabriqué.
preface, *s.* préface *f.*
prefer, *v.a.* préférer *(to* à), aimer mieux.
preferable, *adj.* préférable (à).
preference, *s.* préférence *f.*
pregnant, *adj.* enceinte.
prejudice, *s.* préjugé *m.*
preliminary, *adj.* préliminaire.
premature, *adj.* prématuré.
premier, *s.* premier ministre *m., (in France)* président *m.* du conseil.
premises, *s. pl.* lieux *m. pl.;* local *m.,* immeuble *m.*
premium, *s.* prime *f.*
preparation, *s.* préparation *f.*
prepare, *v.a.* préparer, apprêter; — *v.n.* se préparer.
preposition, *s.* préposition *f.*
Presbyterian, *adj.* presbytérien.
prescribe, *v.a.* prescrire, ordonner; *v.n.* ~ *for* faire une ordonnance pour.
prescription, *s.* prescription *f.; (medical)* ordonnance *f.*
presence, *s.* présence *f.*
present[1], *adj.* présent; actuel; — *s.* présent *m.;* at ~ à présent.
present[2], *s. (gift)* cadeau *m.,* présent *m.;* — *v.a.* présenter; donner.
presently, *adv.* tout à l'heure.
preserve, *v.a.* préserver; *(fruits)* conserver; — *s.* confiture *f.;* conserve *f.*
president, *s.* président *m.*
press, *s.* presse *f.;* — *v.a.* presser; serrer.
pressure, *s.* pression *f.*
presume, *v.a.* présumer.
presumption, *s.* présomption *f.*
pretend, *v. a. & n.* feindre,

faire semblant; pré-
tendre (à).

pretention, *s.* prétension
f.

pretty, *adj.* joli.

prevail, *v.n.* prévaloir;
prédominer.

prevent, *v.a.* empêcher.

prevention, *s.* empêchement *m.*

previous, *adj.* antérieur
(à).

prey, *s.* proie *f.*

price, *s.* prix *m.; cours m.*

price-list, *s.* prix-courant
m., tarif *m.*

prick, *v.a.* piquer; —
s. piqûre *f.*

pride, *s.* orgueil *m.*

priest, *s.* prêtre *m.*

primary, *adj.* primaire.

prime, *adj.* ~ *minister*
see premier.

primitive, *adj.* primitif.

prince, *s.* prince *m.*

princess, *s.* princesse *f.*

principal, *adj.* principal;
— *s.* directeur *m.,*
patron, -ne *m.f.,* principal *m.*

principle, *s.* principe *m*

print, *s.* empreinte *f.;*
impression *f.; out of* ~
épuisé; — *v.a.* im-
primer; faire une em-
preinte (sur); *(photo)*
tirer; ~*ed matter* im-
primés *m. pl.*

printing-office, *s.* imprimerie *f.*

prison, *s.* prison *f.*

prisoner, *s.* prisonnier,
-ère *m. f.*

private, *adj.* particulier;
personel; privé.

privilege, *s.* privilège *m.*

prize, *s.* prix *m.*

probability, *s.* probabilité *f.*

probable, *adj.* probable.

probably, *adv.* probablement.

problem, *s.* problème *m.*

procedure, *s.* procédé *m.*

proceed, *v.n.* aller (à);
se mettre (à); avan-
cer; passer (à); pro-
céder; ~ *with* conti-
nuer.

process, *s.* développement *m.;* méthode *f.,*
procédé *m.;* — *v.n.*
aller en procession.

procession, *s.* cortège *m.;*
procession *f.*

proclaim, *v. a.* proclamer.

proclamation, *s.* proclamation *s.*

produce, *v.a.* produire.

producer, *s.* producteur,
-trice *m. f.*

product, *s.* produit *m.*

production, *s.* production
f.

profess, *v.a.* professer, déclarer.

profession, *s.* profession *f.*

professional, *adj.* professionnel; de profession.

professor, *s.* professeur *m.*

profit, *s.* profit *m.;* —
v.n. ~ *by* profiter de.

profitable, *adj.* profitable.

profound, *adj.* profond.

programme, *s.* programme *m.*

progress, *s.* progrès *m.;*
marche *f.;* — *v.n.*
s'avancer, faire des
progrès.

prohibit, *v.a.* défendre.

prohibition, *s.* prohibition *f.,* défense *f.*

project, *s.* projet *m.;*
— *v.a.* projeter; *v.n.*
saillir.

projector, *s.* projecteur
m.

prolong, *v.a.* prolonger.

prominent, *adj.* (pro)émi-
nent.

promise, *s.* promesse *f.;*
— *v.a.* promettre.

promote, *v.a.* donner de

l'avancement (à); encourager.

promotion, s. promotion f., avancement m.

prompt, adj. prompt; — v.a. (rheatre) souffler; inspirer.

pronoun, s. pronom m.

pronounce, v.a. prononcer.

pronunciation, s. prononciation f.

proof, s. preuve f.; épreuve f.

propeller, s. hélice f.

proper, adj. propre; convenable.

property, s. propriété f.

prophet, s. prophète m.

proportion, s. proportion f.

propose, v.a. proposer.

proposition, proposal, s. proposition f.

prose, s. prose f.

prospect, s. prospective f.

prospectus, s. prospectus m.

prosper, v.n. prospérer.

prosperity, s. prospérité f.

prosperous, adj. prospère.

protest, s. protestation f.; protêt m.; — v.a. protester.

Protestant, adj. & s. protestant, -e (m. f.).

proud, adj. fier, -ère.

prove, v.a. prouver; éprouver.

proverb, s. proverbe m.

provide, v.a. pourvoi de; fournir de; v.n. ~ for pourvoir à; ~d that pourvu que.

providence, s. prévoyance f.

province, s. province f.

provincial, adj. provincial.

provision, s. provision f.

provoke, v. a. provoquer (à).

prudent, adj. prudent.

psalm, s. psaume m.

psychological, adj. psychologique.

psychology, s. psychologie f.

public, adj. & s. public m.

publication, s. publication f.

publicity, s. publicité f.

publish, v.a. publier.

publisher, s. éditeur m.

pudding, s. pouding m.

pull, v.a. tirer; ~ down démolir; ~ out arracher; ~ up arrêter; v. n. tirer; ~ through s'en tirer; — s. traction f., tirage f.

pulpit, s. chaire f.

pulse, s. pouls m.

pump, s. pompe f.; — v. a. pomper.

punch¹, s. poinçon m.; — v.a. poinçonner, percer.

punch², s. punch m.

punctual, adj. ponctuel.

puncture, s. piqûre f.; (tyre) crevaison f.; — v.a.& n. crever.

punish, v.a. punir.

punishment,, s. punition f.

pupil¹, s. élève m. f.

pupil², s. (eye) pupille f.

puppy, s. petit chien m.

purchase, s. achat m.; — v.a. acheter.

pure, adj. pur.

purge, v.a. purger.

purify, v.a. purifier.

purity, s. pureté f.

purpose, s. but m.

purse, s. porte-monnaie m., bourse f.

pursue, v.a. (pour)sui-

vre.
pursuit, *s.* poursuite *f.*
push, *v.a.* & *n.* pousser;
~ *back* repousser; ~
on faire avancer; pous-
ser (jusqu'à); — *s.*
poussé *f.;* allant *m.*
puss, *s.* minet *m.*
put, *v.a.* mettre; *(express)* dire; ~ *back*
remettre; ~ *down* dé-
poser; attribuer; ins-
crire; ~ *off* remettre;
ôter; ~ *on* mettre; ~
out tendre; éteindre;
~ *up* ouvrir; loger;
~ *up with* s'accom-
moder.
puzzle, *v.a.* embarrasser.
pyjamas, *s. pl.* pyjama
m.
pyramid, *s.* pyramide *f.*

Q

quadrangle, *s.* quadrila-
tère *m.;* cour *f.*
quake, *v.n.* trembler.
qualification, *s.* qualification *f.;* compétence
f.
qualify, *v.a.* qualifier;
v.n. ~ *for* passer l'examen de.
quality, *s.* qualité *f.*
quantity, *s.* quantité *f.*
quarrel, *s.* querelle *f.;*
brouille *f.;* — *v.n.*
se brouiller; ~ *with*
se quereller avec.
quarter, *s.* quartier *m.;*
quart *m.;* ~s quar-
tiers *m.pl.*
quartet(te), *s.* quatuor *m.*
quay, *s.* quai *m.*
queen, *s.* reine *f.;* *(cards)*
dame *f.*
queer, *adj.* bizarre.
quench, *v.a.* éteindre.

question, *s.* question *f.;*
— *v.a.* interroger.
queue, *s.* queue *f.;* —
v.n. ~ *up* faire (la)
queue.
quick, *adj.* prompt, rapide; vif.
quick(ly), *adv.* vite.
quiet, *adj.* tranquille; calme; *be* ~ se taire.
quilt, *s.* courtepointe *f.*
quit, *v.a.* quitter.
quite, *adv.* tout à fait.
quiver, *v.n.* trembler.
quiz, *s.* mystification *f.;*
persifleur *m.;* *v.a.*
railler.
quotation, *s.* citation *f.*
quote, *v.a.* citer.

R

rabbi, *s.* rabbin *m.*
rabbit, *s.* lapin, -e *m. f.*
race[1], *s.* course *f.;* —
v.n. faire la course;
courir; lutter de vites-
se.
race[2], *s.* race *f.*
rack, *s.* râtelier *m.*
racket, *s.* raquette *f.*
radiate, *v.n.* rayonner,
irradier; *v.a.* dégager.
radiator, *s.* radiateur *m.*
radical, *adj.* radical.
radio, *s.* radio *f.*
radioactive, *adj.* radio-
actif.
radish, *s.* radis *m.*
rag, *s.* chiffon *m.*
rage, *s.* rage *f.*
raid, *s.* razzia *f.,* rafle
f.; raid *m.*
rail, *s.* barre *f.,* rampe *f.;*
rail *m.; by* ~ par che-
min de fer.
railway, *s.* chemin *m.*
de fer.
rain, *s.* pluie *f.;* — *v.n.*
pleuvoir.

rainy, *adj.* pluvieux.

raise, *v.a.* lever, élever; soulever; *(plants)* faire pousser, cultiver.

rake, *s.* râteau *m.*

rally, *v.n.* se rallier; — *s.* ralliement *m.*

ramify, *v.n.* ramifier.

random, *s. at ~* par hasard.

range, *s.* rangée *f.*; *(mountains)* chaîne *f.*; *(extent)* étendue *f.*; *(kitchen)* fourneau *m.*; — *v.a.* ranger.

rank, *s.* rang *m.*; grade *m.*

ransom, *s.* rançon *f.*; — *v.a.* payer rançon pour.

rap, *s.* tape *f.*; coup *m.*; — *v.a.* frapper.

rapid, *adj.* rapide.

rare, *adj.* rare.

rascal, *s.* coquin *m.*

rash, *adj.* téméraire; inconsidéré.

raspberry, *s.* framboise *f.*

rat, *s.* rat *m.*

rate, *s.* taux *m.*, cours *m.*, tarif *m.*; *(speed)* vitesse *f.*, allure *f.*; *(tax)* taxe *f.*; *at the ~ of* à la vitesse de; *at any ~* en tout cas, quoi qu'il en soit; — *v.a.* estimer; taxer.

rather, *adv.* plutôt; un peu.

ratify, *v.a.* ratifier.

ration, *s.* ration *f.*

rational, *adj.* raisonnable.

rattle, *s.* bruit *m.*; — *v.n.* faire du bruit.

raven, *s.* corbeau *m.*

raw, *adj.* cru; *~ material* matière *f.* première.

ray, *s.* rayon *m.*

razor, *s.* rasoir *m.*; *safety ~* rasoir de sûreté; *electric ~* rasoir électrique.

razor-blade, *s.* lame *f.* de rasoir.

reach, *v.a.* arriver (à); atteindre; *v. n.* atteindre; parvenir (à); — *s.* étendue *f.*; portée *f.*; *within ~* à portée.

react, *v.n.* réagir.

reaction, *s.* réaction *f.*

reactor, *s.* réacteur *m.*

read, *v.a.* lire; *(study)* étudier; *~ for (exam)* préparer.

reader, *s.* lecteur, -trice *m. f.*

reading, *s.* lecture *f.*

ready, *adj.* prêt (à); prompt (à); près (de); *get ~* (se) préparer.

real, *adj.* réel; véritable.

reality, *s.* réalité *f.*

realization, *s.* réalisation *f.*

realize, *v.a.* réaliser.

really, *adv.* vraiment.

realm, *s.* royaume *m.*; *fig.* domaine *m.*

reap, *v.a. & n.* moissonner.

reaper, *s.* moissonneur *m.*

rear, *adj.* de derrière; — *s.* arrière *m.*; queue *f.*; — *v.a.* élever; *v. n.* se cabrer.

reason, *s.* raison *f.*; — *v. a. & n.* raisonner.

reasonable, *adj.* raisonnable.

reasoning, *s.* raisonnement *m.*

rebellion, *s.* rébellion *f.*

rebuke, *s.* réprimande *f.*; — *v.a.* réprimander.

recall, *v.a.* rappeler; *(remember)* se rappeler.

receipt, *s.* reçu *m.*, quittance *f.*; recette *f.*

receive, *v.a.* recevoir.

receiver, s. destinataire m. f.; (phone, wireless) écouteur m., récepteur m., poste m.

recent, adj. récent.

recently, adv. récemment.

reception, s. réception f.

receptionist, s. portier m. d'auberge; employé à la réception.

recipe, s. recette f.

recital, s. récit m.; récital m.

recite, v.a. & n. réciter.

reckless, adj. insouciant.

reckon, v.a. compter.

recognize, v.a. reconnaître.

recollect, v. a. se rappeler.

recommend, v.a. recommander.

recommendation, s. recommandation f.

reconcile, v. a. réconcilier.

record, s. rapport m. officiel; souvenir m.; mention f.; archives f. pl.; (gramophone) disque m.; (sport) record m.; — v.a. enregistrer; rapporter.

recount, v.a. raconter.

recover, v.a. recouvrer: v.n. se remettre.

recreation, s. récréation f.

recruit, s. recrue f.; — v.a. recruter.

rectangle, s. rectangle m.

rector, s. recteur m.; curé m.

recur, v. n. revenir.

red, adj. rouge; roux.

redress, v.n. réparer; redresser.

reduce, v.a. réduire.

reduction, s. réduction f.

reed, s. roseau m.

reef, s. ris m.; récif m.

reel, s. dévidoir m.; bo-

bine f.; — v.n. tourner.

refer, v.a. référer; renvoyer; v.n. ~ to se rapporter à, s'en rapporter à, se référer à.

referee, s. arbitre m.; — v.a. arbitrer.

reference, s. renvoi m., référence f.; rapport m.; allusion f.; with ~ to à propos de; have ~ to se rapporter à.

refill, s. recharge f.

reflect, v.a. réfléchir; v.n. méditer (sur).

reflection, s. réflexion f.; image f.

reform, s. réforme f.; — v.a. réformer.

Reformation, s. Réforme f.

refrain, v.n. ~ from se retenir de.

refresh, v.a. rafraîchir.

refreshment, s. rafraîchissement m.; ~ room buffet m.

refrigerator, s. réfrigérateur m.

refuge, s. refuge m.; take ~ se réfugier.

refugee, s. réfugié, -e m. f.

refusal, refus m.

refuse, v.a. refuser.

refute, v.a. réfuter.

regain, v.a. reconquérir; regagner; reprendre.

regard, s. égard m.; with ~ to à l'égard de; kind(est) ~s meilleurs amitiés f. pl.; — v.a. regarder; tenir compte (de); considérer.

regent, s. régent m.

regime, s. régime m.

regiment, s. régiment m.

region, s. région f.

register, v. a. enregistrer.

regret, *v.a.* regretter;
— *s.* regret *m.*

regular, *adj.* régulier.

regulate, *v.a.* régler.

regulation, *s.* ordonnance
f.; réglementation *f.*

rehearsal, *s.* répétition *f.*

rehearse, *v.a.* répéter.

reign, *s.* règne *m.;* — *v. a.*
régner.

rein, *s.* rêne *f.*

reject, *v.a.* rejeter; refuser.

relate, *v.a.* raconter;
be ~ed to être appa-
renté à; *v.n.* ~ to
se rapporter à; *relat-
ing to* relatif à.

relation, *s.* relation *f.,*
rapport *m.* (à); *(rela-
tive)* parent, -e *m. f.*

relative, *s.* parent, -e
m. f.; — *adj.* relatif;
~ *to* au sujet de.

relax, *v.n.* se relâcher;
v. a. relâcher.

relay, *s.* relais *m.*

release, *s.* délivrance *f.;*
— *v.a.* libérer; dé-
charger (de).

reliable, *adj.* digne de
confiance.

relic, *s.* relique *f.*

relief[1], *s.* délivrance *f.;*
soulagement *m.;* se-
cours *m.*

relief[2], *s.* relief *m.*

relieve, *v.a.* soulager;
secourir; délivrer.

religion, *s.* religion *f.*

religious, *adj.* religieux.

rely, *v.n.* ~ *upon* compter sur.

remain, *v.n.* rester.

remark, *s.* remarque *f.;*
— *v.a.* remarquer;
v.n. faire une remar-
que.

remarkable, *adj.* remar-
quable.

remedy, *s.* remède *m.*

remember, *v.a.* se souvenir (de), se rappeler.

remembrance, *s.* souvenir
m.

remind, *v. a.* ~ *of* rappeler
(à), faire souvenir (de).

remit, *v.a.* remettre.

remittance, *s.* remise *f.*

remorse, *s.* remords *m.*

remote, *adj.* reculé.

removal, *s.* déménage-
ment *m.;* enlèvement;
(dismissal) renvoi *m.*

remove, *v.a.* déménager;
enlever; *(dismiss)* ren-
voyer, *(from school)*
retirer; *v.n.* démé-
nager; s'en aller.

Renaissance, *s.* Renais-
sance *f.*

render, *v.a.* rendre.

renew, *v.a.* renouveler.

renounce, *v.a.* renoncer
(à); dénoncer; répudier.

rent, *s.* *(house)* loyer
m.; — *v.a.* louer.

repair, *s.* réparation *f.;*
— *v.a.* réparer.

repay, *v.a.* rembourser.

repeat, *v.a.* répéter.

repentance, *s.* repentir *m.*

repetition, *s.* répétition *f.*

replace, *v.a.* replacer.

reply, *s.* réponse *f.;* —
v.a. & n. répondre.

report, *s.* rapport *m.,*
compte *m.* rendu; bruit
m.; bulletin *m.;* —
v.a. rapporter; rendre
compte (de).

reporter, *s.* reporter *m.*

represent, *v.a.* représenter.

representation, *s.* représentation *f.*

representative, *s.* re-
présentant *m.*

reproach, *s.* reproche *m.*

reproduce, *v.a.* repro-
duire.

reproduction, *s.* reproduction *f.*

reprove, *v.a.* réprimander.

republic, *s.* république *f.*

repulsion *s.* répulsion *f.*

repulsive, *adj.* repoussant.

reputation, repute, *s.* reputation *f.*

request, *s.* requête *f.;* — *v.a.* demander.

require, *v. a.* demander; exiger.

requirement, *s.* besoin *m.;* exigence *f.*

rescue, *s.* délivrance *f.;* secours *m.;* — *v.a.* délivrer; secourir.

research, *s.* recherche *f.*

resemble, *v.a.* ressembler (à).

resent, *v.a.* être froissé (de); ressentir.

reserve, *s.* réserve *f.;* — *v.a.* réserver.

reside, *v.n.* résider.

residence, *s.* résidence *f.*

resident, *s.* habitant *m.;* — *adj.* résidant.

resign, *v.a.* résigner, se démettre (de); *v.n.* donner sa démission.

resignation, *s.* résignation *f.;* démission *f.*

resist, *v. a.* résister (à).

resistance, *s.* résistance *f.*

resolution, *s.* résolution *f.*

resolve, *v.a.* résoudre; *v.n.* se résoudre (à), se décider (à faire).

resort, *s.* recours *m.;* ressource *f.;* — *v.n.* ~ *to* avoir recours à.

resource, *s.* ressource *f.*

respect, *s.* respect *m.;* rapport *m.; in this* ~ sous ce rapport; *with* ~ *to* concernant ...· — *v.a.* respecter.

respectful, *adj.* respectueux.

respective, *adj.* respectif.

respond, *v.n.* répondre.

response, *s.* réponse *f.*

responsibility, *s.* responsabilité *f.*

responsible, *adj.* responsable (de).

rest¹, *s.* reste *m.; the* ~ les autres.

rest², *s.* repos *m.;* pause *f.;* — *v.n.* se reposer.

restaurant, *s.* restaurant *m.*

restless, *adj.* sans repos; inquiet; agité.

restoration, *s.* restauration *f.*

restore, *v.a.* restaurer.

restrain, *v. a.* retenir; ~ *from* empêcher de.

restraint, *s.* contrainte *f.;* retenue *f.*

restrict, *v.a.* restreindre.

restriction, *s.* restriction *f.*

result, *s.* résultat *m.;* — *v.n.* ~ *from* résulter de; ~ *in* avoir pour résultat.

resume, *v. a.* reprendre.

retain, *v.a.* retenir.

retire, *v. n.* se retirer.

retreat, *s.* retraite *f.*

return, *v.n.* revenir, retourner; *v.a.* rendre; renvoyer; *(answer)* faire; — *s.* retour *m ;* renvoi *m.;* ~ *ticket* billet *m.* d'aller et retour.

reveal, *v.a.* révéler.

revenge, *s.* vengeance *f.;* — *v.a.* venger.

revenue, *s.* revenu *m.*

reverend, *adj.* révérend.

reverse, *adj.* inverse; — *s.* revers *m.*

review, *s.* revue *f.; (of book)* compte *m.* rendu, critique *f.;* — *v.a.* revoir; *(book)* faire la critique (d'un livre).

revision, *s.* révision *f.*

revolt, *s.* révolte *f.*

revolution, *s.* révolution

f.; (motor) tour *m.*

reward, *s.* récompense *f.; — v.a.* récompenser.

rheumatism, *s.* rhumatisme *m.*

rhyme, *s.* rime *f.*

rhythm, *s.* rythme *m.*

rib, *s.* côte *f.*

rice, *s.* riz *m.*

rich, *adj.* riche.

rid, *v.a.* get ∼ of ou débarrasser de.

riddle, *s.* énigme *f.*

ride, *v.n.* monter; aller à cheval *or* à bicyclette; *(bus)* voyager; aller (en autobus); *v. a.* monter; — *s.* promenade *f.*

ridge, *s.* crête *f.*

ridiculous, *adj.* ridicule.

rifle, *s.* fusil *m.*

right, *adj.* droit; correct, exact; juste, bon; bien; ∼ *side* endroit *m.; be* ∼ avoir raison; *that's* ∼ c'est ça; — *s.* droit *m.; (opposed to left)* droite *f.; — adv.* droit; bien; *(very)* très.

rim, *s.* bord *m.*

ring¹, *s.* anneau *m.;* cercle *m.; (sport)* ring *m.*

ring², *v.n. & a.* sonner; ∼ *up* appeler (au téléphone); — *s.* son *m.;* coup *m.* de sonnette; *there is a* ∼ *at the door* on sonne (à la porte).

rinse, *v.a.* rinser.

riot, *s.* émeute *f.*

rip, *v.a.* déchirer; ∼ *up* arracher; *v.n.* aller à toute vitesse.

ripe, *adj.* mûr.

rise, *v. n.* se lever; *(revolt)* se soulever; *(prices)* hausser; *(originate)* naître (de); — *s.* montée *f.; (salary)* augmentation *f.; give* ∼ *to*

donner lieu à.

risk, *s.* risque *m.; — v.a.* risquer.

rival, *adj. & s.* rival, -e *(m. f.); — v.a.* rivaliser (avec).

rivalry, *s.* rivalité *f.*

river, *s.* fleuve *m.,* rivière *f.*

road, *s.* route *f.,* chemin *m.*

road-map, *s.* carte *f.* routière. *f.*

roar, *s.* rugissement *m.; — v.n.* rugir; hurler.

roast, *v.a. & n.* rôtir; — *s.* rôti *m.*

rob, *v.a.* voler.

robber, *s.* voleur *m.*

robbery, *s.* vol *m.*

robe, *s.* robe *f.*

robin, *s.* rouge-gorge *m.*

rock, *s.* rocher *m.,* roc *m.*

rocket, *s.* fusée *f.*

rocky, *adj.* rocheux.

rod, *s.* baguette *f.*

rogue, *s.* coquin, -e *m. f.*

roll, *s.* rouleau *m.;* liste *f.; — v. a.* rouler.

roller-towel, *s.* essuie-mains *m.* à rouleau.

Roman, *adj.* romain; — *s.* Romain, -e *m. f.*

romantic, *adj.* romanesque; romantique.

roof, *s.* toit *m.*

room, *s.* chambre *f.;* salle *f.; (space)* place *f.*

root, *s.* racine *f.;* source *f.*

rope, *s.* corde *f.*

rose, *s.* rose *f.*

rotten, *adj.* pourri, carié.

rough, *adj.* rude; grossier; brut; *(sea)* gros.

roughly, *adv.* approximativement.

round, *adj.* rond; — *adv.* de tour, en rond, autour; *hand* ∼ faire circuler; *go* ∼ tourner;

turn ~ tourner, se retourner; — *prep.* autour de; — *s.* rond *m.*, cercle *m.*; tournée *f.;* tour *m.*

rouse, *v.a.* réveiller.

route, *s.* route *f.*

routine, *s.* routine *f.*

row[1], *s.* rang *m.*, rangée *f.;* ligne *f.*

row[2], *v.n.* ramer; *v.a.* faire aller (à la rame); — *s.* promenade *f.* en canot.

row[3], *s.* chahut *m.*, vacarme *m.*, querelle *f.;* réprimande *f.*

royal, *adj.* royal.

rub, *v.a.* frotter.

rubber, *s.* caoutchouc *m.*

rubbish, *s.* décombres *m. pl.*; ordure(s) *f.* *(pl)*, immondices *f. pl.*

ruby, *s.* rubis *m.*

rudder, *s.* gouvernail *m.*

rude, *adj.* rude.

ruffian, *s.* bandit *m.*

ruffle, *s.* ride *f.;* — *v.a.* rider; ébouriffer.

rug, *s.* couverture *f.;* tapis *m.*

ruin, *s.* ruine *f.;* — *v. a.* ruiner.

rule, *s.* autorité *f.;* règle *f.;* *(of the road)* code *m.;* *as a* ~ généralement; — *v.a.* gouverner; régler; guider; ~ *out* exclure.

ruler, *s.* gouverneur *m.*, souverain *m.;* *(for lines)* règle *f.*

rum, *s.* rhum *m.*

Rumanian, *adj.* roumain; — *s.* Roumain, -e *m. f.*

rumour, *s.* rumeur *f.*

run, *v.n.* courir; fuir, se sauver; *(flow)* couler; *(veh.)* marcher, faire le service; *(engine)* fonctionner; *(play in*

theatre) se jouer; *v.a.* faire fonctionner; mettre en service; faire marcher, faire aller; ~ *after* courir après; ~ *away* s'enfuir; ~ *down* descendre en courant; *(health)* s'affaiblir; ~ *in* *(motor)* roder; ~ *into* heurter, rencontrer; ~ *off* s'enfuir; s'écouler; ~ *out* se terminer; ~ *over* passer dessus; ~ *up* *(debts)* entasser; — *s.* course *f.;* voyage *m.*

runner, *s.* coureur, -euse *m. f.*

runway, *s.* piste (d envol) *f.*

rupture, *s.* rupture *f.*

rural, *adj.* rural.

rush, *v.n.* se précipiter, se jeter; *v.a.* entraîner à toute vitesse; — *s.* ruée *f.*, hâte *f.;* ~ *hours* heures *f.pl.* d'affluence, coup *m.* de feu.

Russian, *adj.* russe; — *s.* Russe *m. f.*

rust, *s.* rouille *f.*

rustic, *adj.* rustique.

rustle, *s.* bruissement *m.*

rye, *s.* seigle *m.*

S

sabre, *s.* sabre *m.*

sack, *s.* sac *m.*

sacrament, *s.* sacrement *m.*

sacrifice, *s.* sacrifice *m.*

sad, *adj.* triste.

saddle, *s.* selle *f.*

sadness, *s.* tristesse *f.*

safe, *adj.* sûr, en sûreté. sans danger; — *s.* coffre-fort *m.*

safely, *adv.* sain et sauf;

en sûreté.

safety, s. sûreté f.

sail, s. voile f.; — v.n. faire voile, naviguer.

sailor, s. marin m., matelot m.

saint, s. saint, -e m. f.

sake: for the ~ of pour l'amour de.

salad, s. salade f.

salary, s. traitement m., appointements m. pl.

sale, s. vente f.; (auction) vente f. aux enchères.

salesman, s. vendeur m.

saleswoman, s. vendeuse f.

salmon, s. saumon m.

saloon, s. salon m.; ~ bar bar m.

salt, s. sel m.

salt-cellar, s. salière f.

salvation, s. salut m.

same, adj. & pron. même.

sanatorium, s. sanatorium m.

sanction, s. sanction f.; — v.a. sanctionner.

sand, s. sable m.; the ~s la plage.

sandal, s. sandale f.

sandwich, s. sandwich m.

sanitary, adj. sanitaire.

sarcastic, adj. sarcastique.

sardine, s. sardine f.

Satan, s. Satan m.

satellite, s. satellite m.

satire, s. satire f.

satisfaction, s. satisfaction f.

satisfactory, adj. satisfaisant.

satisfy, v.a. satisfaire.

Saturday, s. samedi m.

sauce, s. sauce f.

sausage, s. saucisse f.

save, v. a. sauver; (spare) épargner, gagner; v.n. économiser.

savings-bank, s. caisse f. d'épargne.

Saviour, s. Sauveur m.

saw, s. scie f.; — v.a. & n. scier.

say, v. a. dire; that is to ~ c'est-à-dire.

scale¹, s. plateau (de balance) m.; (pair of) ~s balance f.; — v. a. peser.

scale², s. échelle f.; (music) gamme f.

scale³, s. (fish) écaille f.

scanty, adj. maigre.

scar, s. cicatrice f.

scarce, adj. rare.

scarcely, adv. à peine.

scare, s. panique f.; — v.a. effrayer.

scarf, s. écharpe f., foulard m.

scarlet, adj. écarlate.

scatter, v.a. disperser; éparpiller; dissiper.

scene, s. scène f.; behind the ~s dans les coulisses.

scenery, s. paysage m.; (theatre) décor m.

scent, s. odeur f.; parfum m.; (dog) flair m.

schedule, s. liste f.; cédule f.

scheme, s. plan m.; projet m.

scholar, s. (child) écolier, -ère m.f.; (learned) savant m.

scholarship, s. bourse f.

school, s. école f.; classe f.

schoolboy, -girl, s. écolier, -ère m. f.

schoolmaster, s. instituteur m., maître m. d'école.; (secondary) professeur m.

schoolmistress, s. maîtresse f. d'école; (secondary) professeur m.

schoolroom, s. (salle de) classe f.

science, s. science f.

scientific, *adj.* scientifique.

scientist, *s.* savant *m.*

scissors, *s. pl.* ciseaux *m. pl.*

scold, *v.a.* gronder.

scoop, *s.* écope *f.*

scooter, *s.* scooter *m.*

scope, *s.* portée *f.;* envergure *f.;* carrière *f.*

scorch, *v.a.* roussir, brûler.

score, *s.* entaille *f.; (sum)* compte *m.; (games)* points *m. pl.,* marque *f.,* score *m.; (twenty)* vingtaine *f.; (music)* partition *f.; — v.a.* marquer; ~ *out* rayer.

scorn, *s.* mépris *m.*

Scotch, Scottish, Scots, *adj.* écossais.

Scotsman, *s.* Écossais *m.*

scout, *s.* éclaireur *m.*

scrambled: ~ *eggs* œufs *m. pl.* brouillés.

scrap, *s.* morceau *m.;* bout *m.*

scrape, *v.a.* gratter; râcler; ~ *off* décrotter.

scratch, *v.a.* gratter; égratigner; *v. n.* griffer gratter; — *s.* égratignure *f.; m.* coup d'ongle.

scream, *v.n. & a.* crier; — *s.* cri *m.*

screen, *s.* écran *m.*

screw, *s.* vis *f.*

scrub, *v.a.* frotter; nettoyer à la brosse.

scrupulous, *adj.* scrupuleux.

sculptor, *s.* sculpteur *m.*

sculpture, *s.* sculpture *f.; — v.a.* sculpter.

scythe, *s.* faux *f.*

sea, *s.* mer *f.; by* ~ par (voie de) mer.

seal¹, *s. (animal)* phoque *m.*

seal², *s.* sceau *m.; — v.a.* sceller; cacheter.

seam, *s.* couture *f.*

seaport, *s.* port *m.* de mer.

search, *v.a.* chercher; — *s.* recherche *f.*

search-light, *s.* projecteur *m.*

seasickness, *s.* mal *m.* de mer.

seaside, *s.* bord *m.* de la mer.

season, *s.* saison *f.*

seat, *s.* siège *m.; — v.a.* asseoir; placer.

second, *adj.* second; deux; deuxième; — *s.* seconde *f.*

secondary, *adj.* secondaire; ~ *school* école *f.* secondaire.

second-hand, *adj.* de seconde main, d'occasion.

secret, *adj. & s.* secret *(m.).*

secretary, *s.* secrétaire *m. f.*

section, *s.* section *f.*

secular, *adj.* séculier.

secure, *adj.* en sûreté, sûr; — *v.a.* mettre en sûreté; obtenir; fixer.

security, *s.* sécurité *f.;* caution *f.;* sûreté *f.; securities* valeurs *f. pl.; social* ~ sécurité *f.* sociale.

sediment, *s.* sédiment *m.*

see, *v.a.* voir; *(understand)* comprendre; *(make sure)* s'assurer; *(accompany)* accompagner; ~ *about* s'occuper de; ~ *out* accompagner jusqu'à la porte; ~ *through* voir à travers, pénétrer; mener à bonne fin; ~ *to* veiller à, s'occuper de.

seed, s. semence f.; graine f.

seek, v.a. chercher.

seem, v.n. sembler, paraître.

seize, v.a. saisir; prendre.

seldom, adv. rarement.

select, v.a. choisir.

selection, s. choix m.

self, s. moi m.

self-conscious, adj. gêné.

self-control, s. maîtrise f. de soi-même.

selfish, adj. égoïste.

selfishness, s. égoïsme m.

self-respect, s. respect m. de soi.

self-service, adj. ~ restaurant restaurant à libre service.

sell, v.a. vendre; ~ out vendre tout son stock; v. n. se vendre.

seller, s. vendeur, -euse m. f.

semaphore, s. sémaphore m.

semicolon, s. point (et) virgule m.

senate, s. sénat m.

senator, s. sénateur m.

send, v.a. envoyer; (money) remettre; ~ back renvoyer; ~ for envoyer chercher: ~ forth exha er; ~ off expédier; ~ on faire suivre; ~ out lancer.

sender, s. expéditeur, -trice m. f.

sense, s. sens m.

senseless, adj. insensé; sans connaissance.

sensibility, s. sensibilité f.

sensible, adj. sensible; sensé, raisonnable.

sensitive, adj. sensible.

sensual, adj. sensuel.

sentence, s. jugement m.; sentence f.; phrase f.;

— v. a. condamner.

sentiment, s. sentiment m.

sentry, s. sentinelle f.

separate, adj, séparé; à part; — v.a. séparer; v.n. se séparer.

separation, s. séparation f.

September, s. septembre m.

serenade, s. sérénade f.

sergeant, s. sergent m.

series, a. séric f.

serious, adj. sérieux.

sermon, s. sermon m.

servant, s. serviteur, -vante m. f.; domestique m. f.

serve, v. a. & n. servir.

service, s. service m.; utilité f.

service-station, s. station-service f.

session, s. séance f., session f.

set, v.a. mettre, placer; (limb) remettre; (fashion) donner; (jewels) monter; (watch) régler; (problem) donner; (appoint) fixer; (trap) tendre; — v.n. (sun) se coucher; — ~ about se mettre à; ~ aside mettre de côté; ~ down déposer; noter; ~ forth exposer; ~ in commencer; ~ off, out partir; ~ on pousser (à); ~ up dresser; établir; ~ up for se donner pour. — s ensemble m., assortiment m., collection f.; (tea) service m.; (radio) poste m.; (ornaments) garniture f.; (tennis) set m.; (gang) bande f.; ~ of furniture ameublement m.; ~ of false teeth dentier m.

setting, s. mise f., pose f.; montage m.; installation f.; coucher m.

settle, *v. a.* fixer; arranger; régler, payer; décider, résoudre; *v.n.* s'établir; se poser (sur); se décider à; ~ *down* s'établir.

settlement, *s.* colonie *f.*

seven, *adj. & s.* sept.

seventeen, *adj.* dix-sept.

seventh, *adj.* septième.

seventy, *adj. & s.* soixante-dix.

several, *adj.* plusieurs; différent.

severe, *adj.* sévère.

sew, *v.a.* coudre.

sewing-machine, *s.* machine *f.* à coudre.

sex, *s.* sexe *m.*

sexual, *adj.* sexuel.

shabby, *adj.* usé, râpé.

shade, *s.* ombre *f.;* ombrage *m.;* — *v.a.* ombrager.

shadow, *s.* ombre *f.*

shady, *adj.* ombreux.

shaft, *s.* bois *m.;* trait *m.;* flèche *f.;* arbre *m.*

shake, *v.a.* secouer; ébranler; *(hands)* serrer; *v.n.* trembler; s'ébranler; — *s.* secousse *f.*

shaky, *adj.* tremblant, branlant; cassé; faible.

shall, *(future* see *Grammar);* *(command)* vouloir; *(duty)* devoir.

shallow, *adj.* peu profond.

shame, *s.* honte *f.*

shameless, *adj.* éhonté; honteux.

shampoo, *s.* shampooing *m.*

shank, *s.* jambe *f.*

shape, *s.* forme *f.;* — *v. a.* façonner; former; diriger; *v.n.* se développer; promettre.

shapeless, *adj.* sans forme.

share, *s.* part *f.;* action *f.;* have a ~ in contribuer (à); go ~s *(in)* partager; — *v. a. & n.* partager.

shareholder, *s.* actionnaire *m. f.*

sharp, *adj.* tranchant; aigu; aigre; piquant; perçant; — *s. (music)* dièse *m.;* — *adv.* net; 9.0 ~ 9 heures précises.

sharpen, *v.a.* aiguiser; tailler.

shatter, *v.a.* fracasser; déranger.

shave, *v.a.* raser; *v.n.* se raser.

shawl, *s.* châle *m.*

she, *pron.* elle.

shear, *v.a.* tondre; couper; — *s. (pair of)* ~s cisailles *f. pl.*

sheath, *s.* étui; fourreau *m.*

shed, *v.a.* verser; *(light)* répandre.

sheep, *s.* mouton *m.*

sheer, *adj.* pur; perpendiculaire.

sheet, *s.* drap *m.;* *(paper)* feuille *f.;* ~ *iron* tôle *f.*

shelf, *s.* rayon *m.*

shell, *s. (egg, nut)* coque *f.;* *(peas)* cosse *f.*

shelter, *s.* abri *m.;* *take* ~ s'abriter; — *v.a.* abriter (de); *v. n.* se mettre à l'abri (de).

shepherd, *s.* berger.

shield, *s.* bouclier *m.;* écu *m.*

shift, *s.* changement *m.;* *(work)* équipe *f.;* *make* ~ *to* s'arranger (de); — *v. n. & a.* changer de place.

shine, *v. n.* briller; rayonner (de); *the sun is shining* il fait du soleil.

ship, *s.* vaisseau *m.,* navire *m.;* — *v. a.* embarquer.

shipping, s. embarque-
ment m.; navires m. pl.;
~ company compagnie
f. de navigation.
shipping-agent, s. agent
maritime, m.; (goods)
expéditeur m.
shipwreck, s. naufrage
m.; — v.a. be ~ed
faire naufrage.
shipyard, s. chantier m. de
construction.
shirt, s. chemise f.
shiver, v.n. frissonner;
(cold) grelotter;
shock, s. choc m.; coup
m.; — v.a. choquer;
frapper d'horreur.
shocking, adj. affreux;
choquant.
shoe, s. soulier m.
shoeblack, s. décrotteur
m., cireur m.
shoe-lace, s. lacet m.
shoemaker, s. cordon-
nier m.
shoot, v.a. tirer, fusiller;
lancer; décharger;
(game) chasser; (plant)
pousser; (rays) darder;
(film) tourner; v.n.
tirer; se précipiter, se
lancer; (plant) pousser;
(pain) élancer.
shooting, s. tir m., fusillade f.; (game) chasse
f.; — adj. (pain) lan-
cinant.
shop, s. boutique f.,
magasin m.; — v.n. go
~ping faire des achats
or emplettes.
shop-assistant, s. commis
m.; demoiselle f., ven-
deur, -euse m. f.
shopkeeper, s. marchand,
-e m. f.; commerçant,
-e m. f.
shore, s. rivage m.; rive f.
short, adj. court; petit;
bref, brève; (lacking)
de manque; — adv.
be ~ of manquer de.
shorten, v. a. & n. raccourcir; abréger.
shorthand, s. sténogra-
phie f.
shortly, adv. sous peu;
bientôt; brièvement.
shot, s. coup m.; trait m.;
(bullet) balle f., (can-
non) boulet m.
shoulder, s. épaule f.
shout, s. cri m.; — v. a. &
n. crier.
shove, v.a. pousser.
shovel, s. pelle f.
show, v.a. montrer; in-
diquer; manifester; ex-
poser; expliquer; v.n.
se montrer; ~ in faire
entrer; ~ off étaler;
faire ressortir; se don-
ner des airs; ~ out
reconduire; ~ up res-
sortir; — s. blant m.;
spectacle m.; parade f.;
exposition f.
shower, s. averse f.; —
v.a. faire pleuvoir.
shower-bath, s. douche f.
shrill, adj. aigre; aigu, -ë.
shrine, s. châsse f.; lieu
saint m.
shrink, v. a. & n. rétrécir;
reculer.
shroud, s. linceul m.
shrub, s. arbrisseau m., ar-
buste m.
shrug, s. haussement
m. d'épaules; — v.a.
hausser.
shudder, s. frisson m.; —
v. n. frissonner (de).
shut, v.a. fermer; (also ~
in) enfermer; ~ off
couper; ~ up fermer;
se taire.
shutter, s. volet m.
shy, adj. timide.
sick, adj. malade; be ~
vomir; be ~ of être
dégoûté de; fall ~

tomber malade.

sickle, s. faucille f.

sickly, adj. maladif; malsain.

sickness, s. maladie f.

side, s. côte m.; bord m.; (team) équipe f.

siege, s. siège m.

sieve, s. crible m.

sift, v.a. cribler.

sigh, s. soupir m.; — v. n. soupirer.

sight, s. vue f.; spectacle m.; ~s curiosités f. pl.

sightseeing: go ~ visiter les curiosités.

sign, s. signe m.; enseigne f.; — v. a. & n. signer; ~ on engager.

signal, s signal m.; — v.a. signaler; v.n. faire des signaux.

signature, s. signature f.

significant, adj. significatif.

signify, v.a. signifier; v.n. importer.

signpost, s. poteau m. indicateur.

silence, s. silence m.

silent, adj. silencieux; muet.

silk, s. soie f.

silly, adj. sot.

silver, s. argent m.; — adj. d'argent; argenté.

similar, adj. semblable.

simple, adj. simple.

simultaneous, adj. simultané.

sin, s. péché m.; — v.n. pécher.

since, adv. & prep. depuis; — conj. depuis que; (because) puisque.

sincere, adj. sincère.

sinew, s. tendon m.

sinful, adj. pécheur.

sing, v. a. & n. chanter.

singer, s. chanteur, -euse m. f.; cantatrice f.

single, adj. simple; seul; célibataire; particulier; ~ ticket billet m. d'aller.

singular, s. singulier m.; — adj. remarquable; singulier.

sink, v. n. tomber au fond, sombrer; s'enfoncer; baisser; v. a. enfoncer; faire baisser; foncer; couler; — s. évier m.

sinner, s. pécheur, -eresse m. f.

sir, s. monsieur m.; Sir m.

sister, s. sœur f.; (nurse) infirmière f.

sister-in-law, s. belle-sœur f.

sit, v.n. s'asseoir; être assis; rester; ~ down s'asseoir; se mettre (à); ~ for (exam) se présenter à; ~ up se dresser; (at night) veiller.

site, s. emplacement m.; terrain m.; site m.

sitting-room, s. petit salon m.

situation, s. situation f.; (employment) position f.; emploi m.

six, adj. & s. six (m.).

sixteen, adj. & s. seize (m.).

sixth, adj. sixième; six.

sixty, adj. & s. soixante.

size, s. grandeur f., mesure f.; (shoes etc.) pointure f.; numéro m., taille f.; (pers.) taille f.

skate, v.n. patiner.

skating, s. patinage m.

sketch, s. croquis m.; esquisse f.; — v.a. esquisser.

ski, s. ski m.

skid, v.n. déraper.

skier, s. skieur m.

skiff, s. esquif m.

skilful, adj. adroit.

skill, s. adresse f.
skim, v.a. écrémer.
skin, s. peau f.; — v.a. écorcher; peler.
skip, v. a. & n. sauter.
skirt, s. jupe f.
skull, s. crâne m.
sky, s. ciel m. (pl. cieux).
slack, adj. lâche; négligent.
slacken, v.a. ralentir; relâcher; v.n. se relâcher; diminuer.
slacks, s. pl. pantalon m.
slander, s. calomnie f.; — v.a. calomnier.
slant, s. biais m.; — v. a. faire pencher; v. n. être en pente.
slap, s. claque f.; soufflet m.; — v. a. claquer; souffleter.
slate, s. ardoise f.
slaughter, s. massacre m.
slave, s. esclave m. f.
sledge, s. traîneau.
sleep, s. sommeil m.; go to ~ s'endormir; — v. a. & n. dormir.
sleeping-car, s. wagon-lit m.
sleepy, adj. somnolent; be ~ avoir sommeil.
sleeve, s. manche f.
slender, adj. mince, faible.
slice, s. tranche f.
slide, s. glissade f.; (photo) diapositive f.
slight, adj. mince; léger.
slim, adj. mince, svelte.
sling, s. fronde f.
slip, v.n. glisser; se glisser (dans); v.a. filer; pousser, glisser; ~ off ôter; ~ on mettre; ~ out s'esquiver; — s. glissade f.; (mistake) faux pas m.; (paper) fiche f.; (underwear) combinaison f.
slipper, s. pantoufle f.

slope, s. biais m.; pente f.; — v. n. incliner.
slot, s. fente f.
slow, adj. lent; (clock) en retard; (dull) peu intelligent; ~ to lent à; — v.n. & a. ~ down ralentir.
slumber, s. sommeil m.; — v.n. sommeiller.
slump, s. débâcle f.; (intrude) mévente f.; dépression f.
sly, adj. rusé.
small, adj. petit; faible; peu important; menu.
smart, adj. (clever) habile, débrouillard; (witty) spirituel; (dress, pers.) élégant, chic; pimpant; (society) élégant.
smash, v. a. briser; fig. écraser; — s. fracas m.; collision f.
smear, v.a. enduire; — s. tache f.
smell, s. odorat m.; odeur f.; — v. a. & n. sentir; ~ out flairer.
smile, s. sourire m.; — v.n. sourire (at à).
smoke, s. fumée f.; — v.a. & n. fumer.
smooth, adj. lisse; uni; doux, -ce; (sea) calme; — v.a. aplanir; lisser.
smuggle, v.a. ~ in faire passer en contrebande; v.n. faire la contrebande.
smuggler, s. contrebandier m.
snack, s. morceau (sur le pouce) m.; have a ~ casser la croûte.
snail, s. colimaçon m.
snake, s. serpent m.
snap, s. fermoir m.; coup m. de dents; claquement m.; (photo) instantané m.; — v. a. faire claquer; fermer;

~ *at* happer; ~ *off* casser.

snapshot, *s.* instantané *m.*

snatch, *s.* action de saisir, *f.;* accès *m.;* fragment *m.;* — *v. a.* saisir; ~ *at* saisir au vol.

sneeze, *v. n.* éternuer; — *s.* éternuement *m.*

sniff, *v.a.&n.* renifler.

snore, *v. n.* ronfler.

snow, *s.* neige *f.;* — *v.n.* neiger.

snug, *adj.* commode.

so, *adv.* ainsi; si; donc; ~ *that* de sorte que; afin que.

soak, *v.n.* tremper.

soap, *s.* savon *m.*

soar, *v.n.* prendre son essor; *fig.* s'élancer.

sob, *v.n.* sangloter; — *s.* sanglot.

sober, *adj.* sobre; sensé;

social, *adj.* social.

socialism, *s.* socialisme *m.*

society, *s.* société *f.*

sock, *s.* chaussette *f.*

socket, *s.* cavité *f.;* *(electric)* prise *f.* de contact.

soda-water, *s.* eau *f.* de Seltz.

sofa, *s.* canapé *m.*

soft, *adj.* mou, mol molle; doux, -ce.

soil, *s.* terroir; *(stain)* tache; — *v. a.* souiller.

soldier, *s.* soldat *m.*

sole¹, *s.* plante *f.;* semelle *f.;* *(fish)* sole *f.*

sole², *adj.* seul.

solicit, *v. a.* solliciter.

solicitor, *s.* avoué *m.* solicitor *m.*

solidarity, *s.* solidarité *f.*

solitude, *s.* solitude *f.*

solution, *s.* solution *f.*

solve, *v.a.* résoudre.

some, *adj.* quelque; de; — *pron.* quelques-uns; les uns; en *(+ verb)*

— *adv.* environ.

somebody, **-one**, *pron.* quelqu'un.

somehow, *adv.* d'une façon quelconque; ~ *or other* d'une façon ou d'une autre.

something, *s. & pron.* quelque chose *m.*

sometime, *adv.* quelque jour, autrefois.

sometimes, *adv.* quelquefois, parfois.

somewhere, *adv.* quelque part.

son, *s.* fils *m.*

song, *s.* chanson *f.*

son-in-law, *s.* gendre *m.*

soon, *adv.* bientôt.

sore, *adj.* douloureux; *have a* ~ ... avoir mal à ...; — *s.* plaie *f.*

sorrow, *s.* douleur *f.*

sorry, *adj. be* ~ *for* regretter; ~! pardon!

sort, *s.* sorte *f.;* genre *m.;* type *m.;* ~ *of* une espèce de.

soul, *s.* âme *f.*

sound¹, *s.* son *m.;* bruit *m.;* — *v. n.* sonner; — *v.a.* sonner; sonder; *(physician)* ausculter.

sound², *adj.* sain; solide; droit; profond; en bon état.

soup, *s.* potage *m.;(clear)* consommé *m.;* *(thick)* soupe *f.*

sour, *adj.* aigre; acide; *(milk)* tourné.

source, *s.* source *f.*

south, *s.* sud *m.*, midi *m.;* — *adj.* sud; du sud; — *adv.* vers le sud.

southeast, *adj. & s.* sud-est *(m.);* — *adv.* vers le sud-est.

southern, *adj.* du sud.

southwest, *adj. & s.* sud-ouest *(m.);* — *adv.* vers

le sud-ouest.

sovereign, *s.* souverain, -e *m. f.*

sow¹, *v. a.* & *n.* semer (de).

sow², *s.* truie *f.*

space, *s.* espace *m.*

space-craft, -ship, -ve-hicle, *s.* astronef *m.*

space-flight, *s.* navigation *f.* astronautique.

spaceman, *s.* cosmonaute *m.*, astronaute *m.*

spade, *s.* bêche *f.; (cards)* pique *m.*

span, *s.* empan *m.;* ouverture; — *v.a.* traverser; couvrir.

Spaniard, *s.* Espagnol, -e.

Spanish, *adj.* & *s.* espagnol *(m.).*

spanner, *s.* clef *f.*

spare, *adj.* maigre; disponible; de réserve; ~ *parts* pièces de rechange *f. pl.;* ~ *time* loisir *m.;* — *v.a.* épargner; économiser; *(evade)* éviter.

spark, *s.* étincelle *f.*

sparrow, *s.* moineau *m.*

speak, *v.n.* parler; *v.a.* dire; ~ *out* parler hardiment; ~ *up* parler plus haut; ... ~*ing* ici ...

spear, *s.* lance *f.*

special, *adj.* spécial.

specialist, *s.* spécialiste *m. f.*

specific, *adj.* spécifique.

specify, *v.a.* spécifier.

speck, *s.* grain *m.;* tache *f.*

spectacles, *s. pl.* lunettes *f.*

spectacular, *adj.* impressionnant.

spectator, *s.* spectateur, -trice *m. f.*

speech, *s.* parole *f.;* langage *m.; (address)* discours *m.*

speed, *s.* vitesse *f.*

speedy, *adj.* rapide;

prompt.

spell¹, *v.a.* & *n.* épeler; orthographier, écrire; *how is it spelt?* comment cela s'écrit-il?

spell², *s.* période *f.;* tour *m.*

spelling, *s.* ortographe *f.*

spend, *v.a.* dépenser; *(time)* passer; *v.n.* dépenser.

sphere, *s.* sphère *f.*

spice, *s.* épice *f.*

spider, *s.* araignée *f.*

spill, *v.a.* repandre; renverser.

spin, *v.a.* & *n.* filer; faire tourner.

spinach, *s.* épinards *m. pl.*

spine, *s.* épine (dorsale) *f.*

spinster, *s.* vieille fille *f.;* célibataire *f.*

spiral, *adj.* en spirale.

spire, *s.* flèche *f.*

spirit, *s.* esprit *m.;* âme *f.;* spectre *m.;* caractère *m.,* cœur *m.;* ~*s* spiritueux *m. pl.*

spiritual, *adj.* spirituel.

spit, *s.* crachat *m.;* — *v. a.* & *n.* cracher.

spite, *s.* dépit *m.; in* ~ *of* malgré.

splash, *s.* éclaboussement *m.;* — *v. a.* & *n.* éclabousser (de).

spleen, *s.* rate *f.*

splendid, *adj.* splendide.

splinter, *s.* éclat *m.; (bone)* esquille *f.*

split, *v. a.* fendre; (also ~ *up*) partager; *v.n.* se fendre; se diviser.

spoil, *v.a.* gâter; dépouiller (de); endommager; *v.n.* se gâter.

sponge, *s.* éponge *f.*

spontaneous, *adj.* spontané.

spoon, *s.* cuiller *f.*

spoonful, *s.* cuillerée *f.*

sport, *s.* sport *m.;* amuse-
ments *m. pl.*

sportsman, *s.* sportsman
m.

spot, *s.* tache *f.; (place)*
endroit *m.; — v.a.*
tacher; reconnaître.

spout, *s.* gouttière *f.;* bec
m.; — v.a. lancer.

sprain, *v.a.* donner une
entorse (à).

spray, *s.* embrun *m.,*
vaporisateur *m.;* ato-
miseur *m.; — v.a.* vapo-
riser, atomiser; arroser.

spread, *v.a.* étendre; répandre; *(cloth)* mettre;
(cover) couvrir; *(news)*
faire circuler; *v.n.*
s'étendre; — *s.* propa-
gation *f.;* étendue *f.*

spring¹, *s.* printemps *m.*

spring², *v.n.* sauter;
pousser; jaillir; prove-
nir (de), descendre (de),
naître (de); ~ up se
lever vite; jaillir; — *s.*
saut *m.; (watch etc.)*
ressort *m.*

sprinkle, *v.a.* répandre;
asperger (de), arroser.

sprout, *v. a. & n.* germer;
pousser; — *s.* pousse
f.; Brussels ~s choux
m. pl. de Bruxelles

spur, *s.* éperon *m.,* aiguillon *m.; — v. a.* éperon-
ner; ~ on pousser à.

spy, *s.* espion, -onne
m. f.; — v.n. espionner.

squander, *v. a.* gaspiller.

square, *s.* carré *m.; (town)*
place *f.; — adj.* carré;
honnête.

squeeze, *v.a.* serrer; presser.

squint, *v.n.* loucher; —
s. strabisme *m.*

squire, *s.* écuyer *m.;*
châtelain *m.*

squirrel, *s.* écureuil *m.*

stability, *s.* stabilité *f.*

stable, *s.* écurie *f.; — adj.*
stable.

stack, *s.* pile *f.;* meule *f.*

stadium, *s.* stade *m.*

staff, *s.* état-major *m.;*
bâton *m.;* hampe *f.;*
(institution) personnel
m.; ~ officer officier
d'état-major *m.*

stag, *s.* cerf *m.*

stage, *s.* scène *f.; (drama)* théâtre *m.; (pe-
riod)* période *f.; (platform)* estrade *f.; —
v.a.* mettre en scène.

stagger, *v.n.* chanceler;
v.a. bouleverser.

stain, *s.* tache *f.; — v.a.*
tacher; salir.

stair, *s.* marche; ~s
escalier *m.*

staircase, *s.* escalier *m.*

stake, *s.* pieu *m.; at ~*
en jeu; — *v.a.* garnir
de pieux; mettre au
jeu; jouer.

stale, *adj.* rassis.

stall, *s.* stalle *f.;* fauteuil
m.; (books) kiosque *m.*
à journaux.

stammer, *v. n.* bégayer.

stamp, *s.* timbre-poste *m.;*
estampe *f.;* contrôle
m.; empreinte *f.; —
v.a.* timbrer; estamper;
contrôler.

stand, *v.n.* être debout,
se tenir debout, se
soutenir; *(be situated)*
se trouver; *(remain)*
rester; ~ out ressortir;
~ up se lever; — *s.*
position *f.; (vehicles)*
station *f.; (stall)* étalage *m.;* stand *m.*

standard, *s.* étendard *m.;*
étalon *m.;* niveau *m.;*

— *adj.* régulateur; au
titre; *(authors)* clas-
sique.

star, *s.* étoile *f.*

stare, *v.n. (also ~ at)* regarder fixement.

start, *v.n.* partir; commencer; *v. a.* faire partir; faire lever; commencer; lancer; — *s.* commencement *m.*; départ *m.*

starve, *v.n.* mourir de faim; *v. a.* faire mourir de faim.

state, *s.* état *m.*; *v. a.* affirmer; porter; déclarer.

statement, *s.* déclaration *f.*

statesman, *s.* homme *m.* d'état.

station, *s.* poste *m.*; endroit *m.*; *(railway)* gare *f.*; *(police)* poste *m.* de police.

stationer, *s.* papetier *m.*; *~'s shop* papeterie *f.*

statistic(al), *adj.* statistique.

statistics, *s.* statistique *f.*

statue, *s.* statue *f.*

statute, *s.* statut *m.*; ordonnance *f.*

stay, *v.n.* rester; être installé; *~ away* rester absent; *~ up* veiller.

steady, *adj.* ferme; soutenu; *(pers.)* rangé; — *int.* attention!

steak, *s.* tranche *f.*; bifteck *m.*

steal, *v.a.* voler.

steam, *s.* vapeur *f.*

steamboat, *s.* bateau *m.* à vapeur

steam-engine, *s.* locomotive *f.*

steel, *s.* acier *m.*

steep, *adj.* raide, escarpé.

steeple, *s.* clocher *m.*

steer, *v.a.* gouverner; diriger.

steering-gear, *s.* appareil *m.* de direction.

steering-wheel, *s.* volant *m.*

stem, *s.* tige *f.*; queue *f.*

step, *s.* pas *m.*; *(stair)* marche *f.*; *(ladder)* échelon *m.; take ~s* faire des démarches; — *v.n.* faire un pas; marcher; aller, venir; *~ in* entrer.

stepmother, *s.* belle-mère *f.*

stereotype, *s.* cliché *m.*

sterile, *adj.* stérile.

stern, *s.* arrière *m.* — *adj.* sévère.

stew, *s.* ragoût *m.*; *(fruit)* compote *f.*; — *v.a. (meat)* faire un ragout de; *(fruit)* faire une compote de.

steward, *s.* régisseur *m.*; steward *m.*

stewardess, *s.* hôtesse *f.* de l'air.

stick, *s.* bâton *m.*, canne *f.*, petite branche *f.*; — *v.a.* coller; *v.n.* se coller; *~ on* attacher; *~ to* rester fidèle à.

sticky, *adj.* gluant.

stiff, *adj.* raide; dur.

still, *adj.* calme — *adv.* toujours; encore; cependant.

sting, *s.* aiguillon *m.*; — *v.a. & n.* piquer.

stink, *v.n.* puer; — *s.* puanteur *f.*

stipulate, *v.a.* stipuler.

stir, *v.a.* remuer; exciter; *v. n.* remuer; bouger; — *s.* remuement *m.*

stirrup, *s.* étrier *m.*

stitch, *s.* point *m.*; — *v.a. & n.* coudre.

stock, *s.* marchandises *f. pl.*; provision *f.*; *(tree)* tronc *m.*; *(cattle)* bestiaux *m. pl.; (finance)* valeurs *f. pl.; Stock Exchange* Bourse *f.*

stockholder, *s.* açtionnaire *m. f.*

stocking, *s.* bas *m.*

stomach, *s.* estomac *m.*

stone, *s.* pierre; *(fruit)* noyau *m.;* — *v.a.* lapider.

stony, *adj.* pierreux.

stool, *s.* tabouret *m.,* escabeau *m.*

stop, *v.a.* ¡arrêter; empêcher (de); *(teeth)* plomber; retenir suspendre, *v.n.* s'arrêter; cesser; — *s.* halte *f.;* arrêt *m.; (organ)* jeu *m.; (sign)* signe de ponctuation, *m.*

store, *s.* provision *f.;* ∼s grand magasin *m.;* — *v.a.* emmagasiner.

stork, *s.* cigogne *f.*

storm, *s.* orage *m.*

story[1]**,** *s.* histoire *f.*

story[2]**,** *s.* étage *m.*

stout, *adj.* fort; intrépide.

stove, *s.* poêle *m.;* fourneau *m.*

straight, *adj.* droit; honnête; d'aplomb; — *adv.* juste; droit.

straighten, *v.a.* (re)dresser; *v.n.* se redresser.

strain, *s.* effort *m.;* tension *f.;* — *v. a.* tendre; *(filter)* passer; *(muscle)* forcer.

strange, *adj.* étrange(r).

stranger, *s.* étranger -ère *m. f.*

strap, *s.* courroie *f.*

straw, *s.* paille *f.*

strawberry, *s.* fraise *f.*

stray, *adj.* égaré; — *v. n.* errer.

streak, *s.* raie *f.;* bande *f.*

stream, *s.* courant *m.;* — *v.n.* couler, ruisseler.

street, *s.* rue *f.*

strength, *s.* force *f.*

strengthen, *v.a.* fortifier.

stress, *s.* force *f.; (grammar)* accent *m.*

stretch, *s.* effort *m.;* étendue *f.;* — *v.a.* étendre; élargir.

stretcher, *s.* brancard *m.*

strew, *v.a.* semer.

strict, *adj.* strict.

stride, *s.* enjambée *f.;* grand pas *m.;* — *v. n.* enjamber.

strike, *v.a.* frapper; *(blow)* asséner; *(work)* cesser; *v.n.* frapper; *(clock)* sonner; *(workers)* se mettre en grève — *s.* grève *f.; be on* ∼ être en grève.

striking, *adj.* frappant.

string, *s.* ficelle *f.;* corde *f.*

strip, *s.* bande *f.;* bout *m.;* — *v. a.* déshabiller; *v.n.* se déshabiller.

stripe, *s.* bande *f.*

strip-lighting, *s.* éclairage *m.* par luminescent.

strive, *v. n.* s'efforcer (de).

stroke, *s.* coup *m.; (swimming)* brasse *f.; (pen)* trait *m.*

strong, *adj.* fort; vigoureux; puissant; solide.

structure, *s.* structure *f.*

struggle, *v.n.* lutter (avec); faire de grands efforts (pour); — *s.* lutte *f.;* mêlée *f.*

stub, *s.* souche *f.;* bout *m.*

stubborn, *adj.* obstiné.

stud, *s.* bouton *m.*

student, *s.* étudiant, -e *m. f.*

studio, *s.* atelier *m.*

study, *s.* étude *f.;* cabinet *m.* de travail —

v. a. & n. étudier.

stuff, *s.* étoffe *f.;* matériaux *m.pl.;* — *v.a.* remplir; fourrer.

stumble, *v.n.* trébucher; ~ *(up)on* tomber sur; — *s.* faux pas *m.*

stump, *s.* souche *f.;* — *v.a.* estomper.

stupid, *adj.* stupide.

style, *s.* style *m.*

subject, *s.* sujet, -te *m. f.;* — *adj.* ~ *to* sujet à; — *v.a.* assujettir (à).

submarine, *s.* sous-marin *m.*

submission, *s.* soumission *f.*

submit, *v.a.* soumettre.

subordinate, *adj. & s.* subordonné; — *v.a.* subordonner.

subscribe, *v.a. & n.* (~ *to)* souscrire (à); s'abonner (à).

subscriber, *s.* souscripteur *m.;* abonné; -e souscripteur *m.;* abonné, -e *m. f.*

subscription, *s.* souscription *f.;* abonnement *m.*

subsequent, *adj.* subséquent.

subsequently, *adv.* par la suite.

subsidy, *s.* subside *m.*

subsist, *v. n.* exister; subsister (de).

subsistence, *s.* subsistance *f.*

substance, *s.* substance *f.*

substantial, *adj.* substantiel.

substantive, *s.* substantif *m.*

substitute, *v.a.* substituer *(for* à).

substitution, *s.* substitution *f.*

subtle, *adj.* subtil.

subtract, *v.a.* soustraire.

subtraction, *s.* soustraction *f.*

suburb, *s.* faubourg *m.;* ~*s* banlieue *f.*

subway, *s.* souterrain *m.;* métro *m.*

succeed, *v.a.* succéder (à); *v.n. (be successful)* réussir (à); faire ses affaires; ~ *to* succéder à.

success, *s.* succès *m.*

successful, *adj.* heureux, *(exam)* reçu.

succession, *s.* succession *f.*

successive, *adj.* successif.

such, *adj.* tel, -le; ~ *and* ~ tel(le) ou tel(le); — *pron.* ~ *as* ceux, celles.

suck, *v.a. & n.* sucer; — *s.* give ~ *to* allaiter.

sudden, *adj.* soudain.

suddenly, *adv.* soudain.

suet, *s.* graisse *f.* de rognon.

suffer, *v. a. & n.* souffrir.

sufficient, *adj.* suffisant.

sufficiently, *adv.* suffisamment.

sugar, *s.* sucre *m.*

suggest, *v.a.* suggérer; proposer.

suggestion, *s.* suggestion *f.*

suicide, *s.* suicide *m.*

suit, *s. (clothes)* complet *m.; (cards)* couleur *f.; (law)* procès *m.; (request)* requête *f.;* — *v.a.* convenir (à); adapter (à); *v.n.* convenir (à); aller (avec).

suitable, *adj.* convenable; ~ *for* adapté à.

suitcase, *s.* mallette *f.,* valise *f.*

sum, *s.* somme *f.;* ~ *total* somme totale, *f.;*

— *v.a.* ~ *up* résumer

summary, *s.* résumé *m.*

summer, *s.* été *m.*

summon, *v.a.* convoquer; appeler.

sun, *s.* soleil *m.*

Sunday, *s.* dimanche *m.*

sunny, *adj.* ensoleillé; exposé au soleil.

sunrise, *s.* lever *m.* du soleil.

sunset, *s.* coucher *m.* du soleil.

sunshine, *s.* soleil *m.*

sunstroke, *s.* coup *m.* de soleil.

superannuate, *v. a.* mettre à la retraite.

superficial, *adj.* superficiel.

superfluous, *adj.* superflu.

superior, *s. & adj.* supérieur *(m.).*

supermarket, *s.* supermarché *m.*

supersonic, *adj.* supersonique.

superstition, *s.* superstition *f.*

superstitious, *adj.* superstitieux.

supervise, *v.a.* surveiller.

supervision, *s.* superveillance *f.*

supper, *s.* souper *m.*

supplement, *s.* supplément *m.;* — *v.a.* suppléer (à).

supplementary, *adj.* supplémentaire.

supply, *s.* provision *f.;* approvisionnement *m.;* ~ *and demand* l'offre et la demande; — *v.a.* fourner (de); suppléer.

support, *s.* appui *m.;* support *m.;* — *v.a.* supporter; soutenir; appuyer.

suppose, *v.a.* supposer.

supposition, *s.* supposition *f.*

suppress, *v.a.* supprimer.

suppression, *s.* suppression *f.;* répression *f.*

supreme, *adj.* suprême.

sure, *adj.* sûr; *be* ~ *to* ne pas manquer de; *make* ~ *that* s'assurer que.

surely, *adv.* sûrement.

surface, *s.* surface *f.*

surgeon, *s.* chirurgien *m.*

surgery, *s.* chirurgie *f.*

surname, *s.* nom *m.* de famille.

surpass, *v.a.* surpasser.

surprise, *s.* surprise *f.;* — *v.a.* surprendre.

surprising, *adj.* surprenant.

surrender, *s.* abandon *m.;* reddition *f.;* — *v.a.* rendre; renoncer; *v.n.* se rendre.

surround, *v.a.* entourer (de).

surroundings, *s. pl.* environs *m. pl.;* entourage *m.*

survey, *s.* vue *f.;* examen *m.;* — *v.a.* contempler, regarder; examiner; expertiser.

survive, *v. n. & a.* survivre (à).

suspect, *adj. & s.* suspect, -e *(m. f.);* — *v. a. & n.* soupçonner.

suspenders, *s. pl.* jarretelles *f. pl.*

suspicion, *s.* soupçon *m.*

suspicious, *adj.* soupçonneux; suspect.

swallow[1], *s.* hirondelle *f.*

swallow[2], *v. a.* avaler; gober.

swan, *s.* cygne *m.*

swarm, *s.* essaim *m.;* foule *f.;* — *v.n.* essaimer; s'assembler en foule.

swear, *v.a.* jurer; prêter; *v.n.* jurer.

sweat, *s.* sueur *f.;* — *v.a.* exploiter; *v.n.* suer.

Swede, *s.* Suédois, -e *m. f.*

Swedish, *adj.* & *s.* suédois *(m.).*

sweep, *v.a.* balayer; *(chimney)* ramoner; — *s.* coup *m.* de balai; courbe *f.;* grand geste *m.; (pers.)* ramoneur *m.*

sweet, *adj.* doux; *(pers.)* gentil; — *s.* bonbon *m.;* entremets *m.*

sweetheart, *s.* bien-aimé, -ée *m. f.;* ~! mon amour!, ma chérie!

swell, *v.n.* (s')enfler; se gonfler; grossir; *v.a.* gonfler; bouffir; — *s.* houle *f.;* élévation *f.*

swim, *v. n.* nager; aller à la nage; flotter; *v.a* nager; — *s. have a* ~ aller nager.

swimmer, *s.* nageur, -euse *m. f.*

swimming-pool, *s.* piscine *f.*

swine, *s.* cochon *m.*

swing, *s.* va-et-vient *m.;* rythme *m.; (for children)* escarpolette *f.* balançoire *f.;* — *v.a.* balancer; *v. n.* osciller; se balancer.

Swiss, *adj.* suisse; — *s.* Suisse *m. f.*

switch, *s.* badine *f.;* aiguille *f.;* interrupteur *m.,* commutateur *m.;* — *v.a.* cingler; aiguiller; couper; ~ *off* couper (le courant); ~ *on* donner (le courant), tourner (le bouton).

sword, *s.* épée *f.;* sa-

bre *m.*

syllable, *s.* syllabe *f.*

symbol, *s.* symbole *m.*

symmetrical, *adj.* symétrique.

symmetry, *s.* symétrie *f.*

sympathy, *s.* sympathie *f.*

symphony, *s.* symphonie *f.*

synagogue, *s.* synagogue *f.*

synthetic, *adj.* synthétique.

syringe, *s.* seringue *f.*

syrup, *s.* sirop *m.*

system, *s.* système *m.*

systematic(al), *adj.* systématique.

T

table, *s.* table *f.;* clear *the* ~ desservir; *lay the* ~ mettre le couvert.

table-cloth, *s.* nappe *f.*

table-spoon, *s.* cuiller *f.* à soupe.

tablet, *s.* tablette *f.*

tack, *s.* broquette *f.,* petit clou *m.*

tackle, *s.* attirail *m.;* apparaux *m. pl.;* — *v.a.* saisir à bras le corps; *(problem)* essayer de résoudre.

tact, *s.* tact *m.*

tag, *s.* ferret *m.;* étiquette (volante) *f.;* bout *m.*

tail, *s.* queue *f.*

tailor, *s.* tailleur *m.*

take, *v.a.* prendre; *(carry)* porter; *(walk)* faire; ~ *after* ressembler à; ~ *away* enlever; ~ *down* descendre, *(write)* prendre (par écrit); ~ *in (paper)* s'abonner à; ~ *off* ôter; *(v.n.)* prendre son élan; ~ *on* se charger

de; ~ *to* se mettre
à; ~ *up* ramasser,
relever.

tale, *s.* conte *m.*, histoire *f*

talent, *s.* talent *m.*

talk, *v.a. & n.* parler
(about, of de); ~*ing of*
à propos de; — *s.*
conversation *f.;* cau-
serie *f.*

tall, *adj.* grand; *how* ~ *is
he?* quelle est sa taille?

tame, *adj.* apprivoisé.

tan, *s.* tan *m.*

tank, *s.* réservoir *m.;* char
m. d'assaut.

t ankard, *s.* chope *f.*

tap, *s.* robinet *m.; (blow)*
tape *f.;* petit coup *m.;*
— *v.a.* mettre en
perce; *(strike)* frap-
per légèrement, taper.

tape, *s.* ruban *m.* (de coton).

tape-recorder, *s.* magnétophone *m.*

tapestry, *s.* tapisserie *f.*

target, *s.* cible *f.*

tariff, *s.* tarif *m.*

tart, *s.* tart *f.*

task, *s.* tâche *f.; (school)*
devoir *m.*

taste, *s.* goût *m.*

tasteless, *adj.* sans saveur.

tasty, *adj.* savoureux,
de bon goût.

tatter, *s.* lambeau *m.*

tavern, *s.* taverne *f.*

tax, *s.* impôt *m.;* ~ *free*
exempt d'impôts.

taxi, *s.* taxi *m.*

tea, *s.* thé *m.*

teach, *v.a.* enseigner,
instruire; *(how to)* ap-
prendre (à).

teacher, *s.* instituteur,
-trice *m. f.;* professeur
m. f.

teaching, *s.* enseignement
m.

team, *s.* équipe *f.*

tea-pot, *s.* théière *f.*

tear[1]**,** *s. (eye)* larme *f.*

tear[2]**,** *v.a.* déchirer; ~
away, down, out ar-
racher; ~ *up* déchirer;
— *s.* déchirure *f.*

tease, *v.a.* taquiner.

tea-spoon, *s.* cuiller *f.* à
thé.

technical, *adj.* technique.

technique, *s.* technique *f.*

technology, *s.* technologie *f.*

tedious, *adj.* ennuyeux.

teenager, *s.* adolescent,
-e *m. f.*

telecast, *v.a.* téléviser.

telegram, *s.* télégramme
m.

telegraph, *s.* télégraphe
m.

telephone, *s.* téléphone
m.; — *v.a. & n.* télé-
phoner *(to* à).

telescope, *s.* téléscope *m.;*
réfracteur *m.;* — *v.a.*
télescoper.

televise, *v.a.* téléviser.

television, *s.* télévision *f.*

television-set, *s.* appareil *m.* de TV, télé-
viseur *m.*

telex, *s.* télex *m.*

tell, *v.a.* dire; raconter; distinguer; ~ *s.o.*
to do sth. enjoindre,
dire à qn de faire qch.

temper, *s.* colère *f.;*
tempérament *m.*

temperature, *s.* température *f.*

temporary, *adj.* tempo-
raire.

tempt, *v.a.* tenter.

ten, *adj. & s.* dix *(m.).*

tenant, *s.* locataire *m. f.*

tend, *v.n.* tendre (à).

tendency, *s.* tendance *f.*

tender[1]**,** *v.a.* offrir; ~

for soumissionner; — s. soumission *f.*

tender², *adj.* tendre.

tennis, *s.* tennis *m.*

tension, *s.* tension *f.*

tent, *s.* tente *f.*

tenth, *adj.* dixième; dix.

term, *s.* terme *m.; (school)* trimestre *m.; be on good* ~s être bien (avec); — *v.a.* appeler.

terminate, *v.a.* terminer; *vn.* se terminer.

terminus, *s.* (gare *f.*) terminus *m.*

terrace, *s.* terrasse *f.*

terrible, *adj.* terrible.

territory, *s.* territoire *m.*

test, *s.* épreuve *f.;* examen *m.; (school)* composition *f., (oral)* épreuve *f.;* orale — *v.a.* mettre à l'épreuve.

testify, *v.a.* affirmer.

testimony, *s.* témoignage *m.*

text, *s.* texte *m.*

text-book, *s.* manuel *m.*

textile, *s.* textile *m.*

than, *conj.* que; *(with numbers)* de.

thank, *v.a.* remercier; ~ *you* merci; — *s.* ~s remerciements *m. pl.;* merci.

thankful, *adj.* reconnaissant.

that¹, *adj.* ce, cet, cette' ces; — *pron.* celui, celle, ceux; cela; ~'s *it* c'est cela.

that², *conj.* que.

the, *art.* le, la, les; ce, cet, cette; ces.

theatre, *s.* théâtre *m.*

their, *pron.* leur, leurs.

theirs, *pron.* le leur, la leur, les leurs; à eux, à elles.

them, *pron.* les; leur; eux, elles.

theme, *s.* thème *m.;* sujet *m.*

themselves, *pron.* se; eux-mêmes, elles-mêmes.

then, *adv.* alors; *(after that)* puis; *(consequently)* donc.

theology, *s.* théologie *f.*

theoretical, *adj.* théorique.

theory, *s.* théorie *f.*

there, *adv.* là; *(with verb)* y; ~ *is, are* il y a.

therefore *adv.* donc.

thermometer, *s.* thermomètre *m.*

thermos, *s.* thermos *f.*

they, *pron.* ils, elles; ~ *say* on dit

thick, *adj.* épais.

thief, *s.* voleur, -euse *m. f.*

thigh, *s.* cuisse *f.*

thimble, *s.* dé *m.*

thin, *adj.* mince; maigre; *fig.* pauvre.

thing, *s.* chose *f.;* ~s effets *m. pl.*

think, *v.a.* croire; concevoir; *v.n.* croire; penser *(about, of* à); ~ *out* élaborer; ~ *over* réfléchir à, penser.

third, *adj.* troisième; trois; — *s.* tiers *m.*

thirsty, *adj.* altéré; *be* ~ avoir soif.

thirteen, *adj.* & *s.* treize *(m.).*

thirty, *adj.* & *s.* trente *(m.).*

this, *pl.* these, *pron.* cela, — *adj.* ceci; ce, cet, cette; ces.

thorn, *s.* épine *f.*

thorough, *adj.* profond, complet; consommé.

thoroughfare, *s.* artère *f.* principal, grande rue *f.; no* ~ rue barrée, passage interdit.

thoroughly, *adv.* tout à fait, à fond.

though, *conj.* quoique, bien que; — *adv.* tout de même.

thought, *s.* pensée *f.*; idée *f.*; *(care)* souci *m.*

thoughtful, *adj.* pensif; attentif.

thoughtless, *adj.* étourdi; insouciant.

thousand, *s. & adj.* mille *(m.)*

thrash, *v.a.* battre.

thread, *s.* fil *m.*; — *v. a.* enfiler.

threat, *s.* menace *f.*

threaten, *v. a. & n.* menacer (de).

three, *adj. & s.* trois *(m.)*.

threshold, *s.* seuil *m.*

thrifty, *adj.* économe.

thrill, *s.* tressaillement *m.*; — *v. a.be ~ed with* frissonner de.

thrive, *v. n.* prospérer.

throat, *s.* gorge *f.*

throne, *s.* tône *m.*

through, *prep.* à travers; au travers de; par; par suite de; pendant; — *adv.* d'un bout à l'autre; *be ~ with* avoir fini qch.; — *adj.* direct.

throughout, *prep. & adv.* d'un bout à l'autre.

throw, *v.a.* jeter; *~ away* jeter, dissiper; *~ down* renverser; jeter à terre; *~ off* se débarrasser de; ôter; *~ out* rejecter; *~ over* abandonner; — *s.* jet *m.*

thrust, *v.a.* fourrer, pousser; enforcer; — *s.* poussée *f.*; botte *f.*

thumb, *s.* pouce *m.*

thunder, *s.* tonnerre *m.*; — *v.n.* tonner.

Thursday, *s.* jeudi *m.*

thus, *adv.* ainsi.

ticket, *s.* billet *m.*; étiquette *f.*

ticket-collector, *s.* contrôleur *m.*

tide, *s.* marée *f.*; courant *m.*

tidy, *adj.* propre; bien rangé; *(pers.)* ordonné; — *v.a.* *(also ~ up)* mettre en ordre.

tie, *v.a.* attacher; lier; nouer; *~ down* lier; *~ up* attacher; — *s.* lien *m.*; cravate *f.*; *(sport)* partie *f.* égale.

tiger, *s.* tigre, -esse *m. f.*

tight, *adj.* serré; tendu.

tighten, *v.a.* serrer.

tile, *s.* tuile *f.*

till, *prep.* jusqu'à; — *conj.* jusqu'à ce que.

tilt, *s.* inclinaison *f.*; — *v. n.* s'incliner, pencher; *v.a.* pencher.

time, *s.* temps *m.*; moment *m.*; *(clock)* heure *f.*; *(occasions)* fois; *at ~s* de temps en temps; *by the ~ that* avant que; *for the ~ being* actuellement; *what ~ is it?* quelle heure est-il?; *have a good ~* s'amuser bien; *keep good ~* marcher bien.

timely, *adj.* opportun.

timetable, *s.* horaire *m.*; indicateur *m.*; *(school)* emploi *m.* du temps.

tin, *s.* étain *m.*; *(conserve)* boîte *f.* (en fer blanc).

tinned, *adj.* en boîte; conservé.

tint, *s.* teinte *f.*

tinv. *adj.* tout petit.

tip[1], *s.* bout *m.*; — *v.a.*

renverser; *v.n.* (also ~ *over*) se renverser.

tip², s. *(money)* pourboire *m.;* — *v.a.* donner un pourboire (à).

tire¹, tyre, s. pneu(matique) *m.*

tire², *v.a.* fatiguer; *v.n.* se fatiguer.

tired, *adj. be* ~ *of* être las de.

tissue, s. tissu *m.*

tissue-paper, s. papier *m.* de soie.

title, s. titre *m.*

to, *prep.* à; vers; en,

toast, s. rôtie *f.; (bread, drink)* toast *m.;* — *v.a.* rôtir.

tobacco, s. tabac *m.*

tobacconist, s. marchand *m.* de tabac; ~'s débit *m.* de tabac.

today, *adv.* aujourd'hui.

toe, s. orteil *m.*, doigt *m.* du pied.

together, *adv.* ensemble; en même temps.

toil, s. travail *m.;* — *v.n.* travailler.

toilet, s. toilette *f.*

toilet-paper, s. papier *m.* hygiénique.

tomato, s. tomate *f.*

tomb, s. tombeau *m.*

tomorrow, *adv.* demain.

ton, s. tonne *f.*

tone, s. ton *m.*

tongs, s. *pl.* pincettes *f. pl.;* pince *f.*

tongue, s. langue *f.*

tonight, *adv.* cette nuit; ce soir.

tonsil, s. amygdale *f.*

too, *adv.* trop; *(also)* aussi.

tool, s. outil *m.;* instrument *m.*

tooth, s. dent *f.*

toothache, s. mal *m.* de dents.

toothbrush, s. brosse *f.* à dents.

toothpaste, s. pâte *f.* dentrifrice.

top, s. sommet *m.*, faîte *m.;* dessus *m.;* couvercle *m.;* tête *f.;* premier, -ère *m. f.;* — *v.a.* couronner; dépasser.

topic, s. sujet *m.;* ~s *of the day* actualités *f. pl.*

torch, s. torche *f.*

tortoise, s. tortue *f.*

toss, s. mouvement *m.;* — *v.a.* jeter; lancer en l'air; ballotter; ~ *up* lancer en l'air.

total, *adj.* & s. total *(m.).*

totter, *v.n.* chanceler.

touch, s. toucher *m.;* attouchement *m.;* touche *f.;* légère *f.* attaque,; — *v.a.* toucher.

tough, *adj.* dur; robuste; rude.

tour, s. voyage *m.;* tour *m.;* tournée *f.;* — *v.n.* voyager.

tourism, s. tourisme *m.*

tourist, s. touriste *m.*

tournament, s. tournoi *m.*

tow, s. étoupe *f.;* remorque *f.;* — *v.a.* remorquer.

toward(s), *prep.* vers; envers; pour.

towel, s. essuie-main(s) *m.*, serviette *f.*

tower, s. tour *f.*

town, s. ville *f.*

town-hall, s. hôtel *m.* de ville.

toy, s. jouet *m.;* — *v.n.* jouer (avec).

trace, s. trace *f.;* trait *m.;* — *v.a.* tracer; ~ *back* remonter à.

track, s. traces *f. pl.;* sentier *m.;* *(railw.)* voie *f.; (running)* piste

f.

tractor, *s.* tracteur *m.*

trade, *s.* commerce *m.;*
(occupation) métier *m.;*
v.n. commercer; ~ *in*
faire le commerce de.

trade-mark, *s.* marque
f. de fabrique.

tradesman, *s.* commer-
çant *m.*

trade(s)-union, *s.* syndicat *m.*

tradition, *s.* tradition *f.*

traditional, *adj.* traditionnel.

traffic, *s.* trafic *m.;* circulation *f.;* ~ *lights*
feux *m.pl.* de signa-
lisation.

tragedy, *s.* tragédie

tragic(al), *adj.* tragi-
que.

trail, *s.* trace *f.;* — *v.a.*
& *n.* traîner.

train, *s.* train *m.;* (series)
suite *f.;* — *v.a.* entraîner; ïormer.

trainer, *s.* entraîneur *m.*

traitor, *s.* traître *m.*

tram, *s.* tramway *m.*

tramp, *v.n.* aller à pied;
— *s.* bruit *m.* de pas;
(pers.) chemineau *m.*

transaction, *s.* transaction *f.*

transfer, *s.* transport *m.;*
— *v.a.* transférer.

transform, *v.a.* trans-
former (en).

transfusion, *s.* transfusion *f.*

transgress, *v.a.* trans-
gresser; *v.n.* pécher.

transistor, *s.* transistor
m.

transit, *s.* transit *m; in*
~ en cours de route.

translate, *v.a.* traduire.

translation, *s.* traduction
f.

translator, *s.* traducteur,

-trice *m. f.*

transmission, *s.* transmission *f.*

transmit, *v.a.* transmettre, émettre.

transmitter, *s.* (poste) é-
metteur *m.*

transparency, *s.* diapositive *f.*

transport, *s.* transport
m.; — *v.a.* transpor-
ter.

trap, *s.* piège *m.*

trash, *s.* rebut *m.;* ni-
aiseries *f. pl.*

travel, *v.n.* voyager; —
s. voyage *m.*

traveller, *s.* voyageur,
-euse *m. f.*

tray, *s.* plateau *m.*

treachery, *s.* trahison *f.*

tread, *s.* pas *m.;* — *v.n.*
& *a.* marcher (sur).

treasure, *s.* trésor *m.*

treasury, *s.* trésor *m.;*
trésorerie *f.*

treat, *v.a.* traiter.

treatment. *s.* traitement
m.

treaty, *s.* traité *m.*

tree, *s.* arbre *m.*

tremble, *v.n.* trembler.

tremendous, *adj.* terri-
ble; immense.

trench, *s.* tranchée *f.*

trend, *s.* tendance *f.*

trespass, *v.n.* envahir
sans autorisation; ~
against offenser; ~ *on*
abuser de; — *s.* offense *f.*

trial, *s.* essai *m.;* épreuve
f.; (law) procès *m.*

tribe, *s.* tribu *f.*

tribute, *s.* tribut *m.*

trick, *s.* ruse *f.;* tour *m.;*
truc *m.;* — *v.a.* du-
per.

trifle, *s.* bagatelle *f.;*
a ~ un peu; — *v.n.*
~ *with* traiter lé-
gèrement.

trim, s. état m.; tenue f.;
— adj. bien tenu; —
v.a. arranger; garnir,
orner; dresser.

trip, s. excursion f.;
voyage m.; — v.a. ~ up
faire trébucher.

triumph, s. triomphe m.;
— v.n. triompher.

triumphant, adj. triomphant.

trolley, s. fardier m.,
diable m.; trolley m.

trolley-bus, s. trolleybus
m.

troop, s. troupe f.

trophy, s. trophée m.

tropic(al), adj. tropique.

tropics, s. pl. tropiques
m. pl.

trot, s. trot m.; — v.n.
trotter.

trouble, s. affliction f.;
malheur m.; dérange-
ment m.; difficulté f.;
— v.a. inquiéter; dé-
ranger; affliger.

troublesome, adj. en-
nuyeux.

trousers, s. pl. pantalon m.

trout, s truite f.

truck, s. wagon m.

true, aaj. vrai; exact;
fidèle; come ~ se réali-
ser.

truly, adv. vraiment.

trumpet, s. trompette
f.; — v. a. proclamer.

trunk, s. melle f. (tree)
tronc m.

trunk-call, s. appel m. in-
terurbain.

trust, s. confiance f.;
espoir m.; dépôt m.;
trust m.; — v.a.
se confier (à); faire
crédit (à); v.n. espérer;
compter sur.

truth, s. vérité f.

try, v.a. essayer, éprouver; (law) mettre en
jugement; ~ on essa-
yer; — s. essai m.

tub, s. bac m.; (bath)
tub m.

tube, s. tube m.; tuyau
m.; métro m.

Tuesday, s. mardi m.

tug, s. effort m.; — v.a.
tirer; remorquer.

tug-boat, s. (bateau) remorqueur m.

tuition, s. enseignement
m.

tumble, v. n. tomber.

tumour, s. tumeur f.

tune, s. air m.; accord m.;
harmonie f.; in ~ d'ac-
cord; out of ~ faux; —
v.a.&n. accorder; ~
in to mettre sur; ~
up régler; s'accorder.

tunnel, s. tunnel m.

turbine, s. turbine f.

turbo-jet: ~ engine turboréacteur m.

turbo-prop, s. turbopropulseur m.

turkey, s. dindon, din-
de m. f.

Turkish, adj. turc, -que:
— s. Turc, -que m. f.;
(lang.) turc m.

turn, v.a. tourner, détourner; diriger; ".n.
tourner; se diriger; de-
venir; avoir recours (à);
~ about (se) tourner;
~ back retourner; ~
down plier, baisser;
repousser; ~ upside
down renverser; ~ in
se coucher; ~ off fer-
mer, serrer; éteindre;
~ on ouvrir; allumer;
~ over (se) renverser;
~ up arriver, appa-
raître — s. tour m.; dé-
tour m.; (mind, style)
tournure f.; (tide)
changement m.

turning, s. tournant m.
turnip, s. navet m.
turnover, s. chiffre m. d'affaires.
turret, s. tourelle f.
turtle, s. tortue f.
tutor, s. précepteur m.; — v.a. instruire.
twelfth, adj. douzième; douze.
twelve, adj. & s. douze (m.).
twentieth, adj. vingtième.
twenty, adj. & s. vingt (m.).
twice, adv. deux fois.
twig, s. brindille f.
twin, adj. & s. jumeau (m.), jumelle (f.).
twist, s. (road) coude f.; torsion f.; — v. a. tordre; dénaturer; v. n. s'entortiller.
twitter, v.n. gazouiller.
two, adj. & s. deux (m.).
type, s. type m.; caractère m.; — v.a. taper (à la machine).
type-script, s. manuscrit m. dactylographié.
typewriter, s. machine à écrire, f.
typical, adj. typique.
typist, s. dactilo(graphe) m. f.
tyre see tire.

U

udder, s. mamelle f.
ugly, adj. laid.
ulcer, s. ulcère m.
ultimate, adj. final, dernier.
umbrella, s. parapluie m.
umpire, s. arbitre m. f.
unable, adj. incapable; ~ to impuissant à faire qch.; dans l'impossibilité de.

unaccustomed, adj. inaccoutumé, peu habitué (à).
unaided, adj. sans aide.
unanimous, adj. unanime.
unassisted, adj. sans aide.
unaware: be ~ of ignorer.
unbearable, adj. insupportable.
uncertain, adj. incertain.
uncertainty, s. incertitude f.
unchangeable, adj. immuable.
uncle, s. oncle m.
uncomfortable, adj. peu confortable.
uncommon, adj. rare; extraordinaire.
unconditional, adj. sans conditions.
unconscious, adj. sans connaissance; ~ of sans conscience de.
uncover, v. a. découvrir.
undamaged, adj. non endommagé.
undefined, adj. non défini.
undeniable, adj. incontestable.
under, prep sous; au-dessous de; dans.
undercarriage, s. châssis m., train (d'atterrissage) m.
underclothes, s. pl. vêtements m. pl. de dessous.
underdeveloped, adj. sous-développe.
underdone, adj. pas assez cuit, saignant.
undergo, v.a. subir.
undergraduate, s. étudiant, -e (non diplomé) m. f.
underground, s. métro-(politain) m.
underline, v.a. souligner.

undermine, *v.a.* miner.

underneath, *prep. & adv.* au-dessous (de).

undersigned, *adj. & s.* soussigné, -e *(m. f.).*

understand, *v.a.&n.* comprendre; *it is understood that* il est convenu que.

understanding, *s.* entendement *m.;* intelligence *f.*

undertake, *v.a.* entreprendre; ~ *to* se charger de, s'engager à.

undertaking, *s.* entreprise *f.*

underwear, *s.* vêtements *m.pl.* de dessous.

undesirable, *adj.* peu désirable.

undo, *v.a.* défaire.

undress, *v. n.* se déshabiller.

undue, *adj.* indu.

uneasy, *adj.* inquiet; mal à l'aise; incommode.

uneducated, *adj.* sans instruction.

unemployed, *adj. & s.* sans travail; *the* ~ les chômeurs *m.*

unemployment, *s.* chômage *m.*

unequal, *adj.* inégal.

uneven, *adj.* inégal; impair.

unexpected, *adj.* inattendu; soudain.

unfair, *adj.* injuste; déloyal.

unfavorable, *adj.* défavorable.

unfortunate, *adj.* malheureux.

unfortunately, *adv.* malheureusement.

unhappy, *adj.* malheureux.

unhealthy, *adj.* maladif;

(place) insalubre.

uninhabited, *adj.* inhabité.

uninteresting, *adj.* peu intéressant,sans intérêt.

union, *s.* union *f.*

unique, *adj.* unique.

unit, *s.* unité *f.; (motor)* bloc *m.*

unite, *v.a.* unir; *v.n.* s'unir.

unity, *s.* unité *f.;* harmonie *f.*

universal, *adj.* universel.

university, *s.* université *f.*

unjust, *adj.* injuste.

unkind, *adj.* dur; peu aimable.

unknown, *adj.* inconnu.

unless, *conj.* à moins que... ne; à moins de.

unlike, *adj.* dissemblable.

unload, *v.a.* décharger.

unlock, *v.a.* ouvrir.

unmarried, *adj.* célibataire.

unnatural, *adj.* non naturel, dénaturé.

unnecessary, *adj.* inutile.

unnoticed, *adj.* inaperçu.

unoccupied, *adj.* inoccupé; libre; non occupé.

unpack, *v.a.* déballer.

unpaid, *adj.* impayé.

unparalleled, *adj.* incomparable.

unpleasant, *adj.* désagréable.

unprecedented, *adj.* sans exemple. *or.* précédent.

unprejudiced, *adj.* sans préjugés, impartial.

unprepared, *adj.* non préparé; *be* ~ *for* ne pas s'attendre à qch.

unprofitable, *adj.* peu profitable.

unpromising, *adj.* qui s'annonce mal; peu prometteur.

unqualified, *adj.* non qualifié; sans restriction.

unreal, *adj.* irréel.

unreasonable, *adj.* déraisonnable.

unsatisfactory, *adj.* peu satisfaisant.

unseen, *adj.* invisible; inaperçu.

unsettled, *adj.* non réglé; *(in mind)* indécis; incertain.

unskilled, *adj.* non spécialisé.

unsolved, *adj.* non résolu.

unspeakable, *adj.* inexprimable.

unsteady, *adj.* tremblant; peu fixe; chancelant; inconstant.

unsuccessful, *adj.* malheureux; infructueux.

unsuitable, *adj.* inconvenant; peu propre (à).

untidy, *adj.* sans ordre, malpropre; en désordre.

until, *prep.* jusqu'à; — *conj.* jusqu'à ce que; avant que.

unto, *prep.* jusqu'à.

unusual, *adj.* rare, peu commun.

unwell, *adj.* indisposé; souffrant.

unwilling, *adj.* peu disposé (à).

unworthy, *adj.* indigne.

unyielding, *adj.* inflexible.

up, *adv.* en montant, vers le haut; (en) haut; *go* ~ monter; *be* ~ *in* être fort en; *what's* ~? qu'est-ce qu'il y a?; — *prep.* vers le haut de; en haut; — *adj.* montant.

uphill, *adj.* montant; — *adv. go* ~ monter.

uphold, *v.a.* soutenir; appuyer.

upholsterer, *s.* tapissier *m.*

upon, *prep* sur.

upper, *adj.* supérieur; *(deck)* deuxième; *the* ~ *classes* les hautes classes.

upright, *adj.* droit; honnête.

upset, *v.a.* renverser; *fig.* troubler, bouleverser; — *adj.* renversé; *fig.* dérangé; *be* ~ être indisposé.

upside do ·n, *adv.* sens dessus dessous.

upstairs, *adv.* en haut; *go* ~ monter (l'escalier).

up-to-date, *adj* moderne, à la mode.

upwards, *adv.* en haut, vers le haut, en montant.

urge, *v.a.* prier instamment (de); recommander instamment; pousser en avant.

urgent, *adj.* urgent; pressant.

us, *pron.* nous.

usage, *s.* usage *m.*

use, *v.a.* se servir de; traiter; faire usage (de); consommer; ~ *up* user; consommer; ~*d to* habitué à; *get* ~*d to* s'habituer à; — *s.* usage *m.;* emploi *m.;* utilité *f.; be of* ~ être utile (à); *(of) no* ~ inutile; *out of* ~ hors d'usage *or* de service.

useful, *adj.* utile (à).

useless, *adj.* inutile.

usher, *s. (court)* (huissier) audiencier *m.*

usherette, *s. (theatre)* ouvreuse *f.*

usual, *adj.* usuel.

usually, *adv.* ordinairement.

utensil, s. ustensile m.

utility, s. utilité f.

utilize, v.a. utiliser.

utmost, adj. extrême; le plus grand; — s. le plus; tout son possible.

utter[1], adj. le plus grand; absolu.

utter[2], v.a. dire, prononcer; pousser.

utterance, s. prononciation. f.; expression f.; parole f.

V

vacancy, s. vacance f.

vacant, adj. vacant; vide; sans expression.

vacation, s. vacances f. pl.

vaccinate, v.a. vacciner.

vaccination, s. vaccination.

vacuum-cleaner, s. aspirateur m.

vague, adj. vague.

vain, adj. vain; vaniteux; in ~ en vain.

valid, adj. valide.

validity, s. validité f.

valley, s. vallée f.

valuable, adj. de valeur.

value, s. valeur f.; — v.a. évaluer; priser.

valve, s. soupape f.; lampe f., tube m.

van, s. fourgon m.; camion m. de livraison; wagon m.

vanish, v.n. disparaître; (also ~ away) s'évanouir.

vanity, s. vanité f.

variety, s. variété f.

various, adj. divers.

varnish, s. vernis m.

vary, v.a. & n. varier.

vase, s. vase m.

vast, adj. vaste.

vault, s. voûte f.; cave f., caveau m.

veal, s. veau m.

vegetable, s. légume m.

vehicle, s. véhicule m.

veil, s. voile m.

vein, s. veine f.

velvet, s. velours m.

venison, s. venaison f.

vent, s. ouverture f.; give ~ to donner libre cours à.

ventilation, s. ventilation f.

ventilator, s. ventilateur m.

venture, s. risque m.; hasard m.; — v.a. risquer; hasarder; v.n. ~ (up-) on se hasarder à, se risquer à.

verb, s. verbe m.

verdict, s. décision f., verdict m.

verge, s. bord m.

verify, v.a. vérifier.

verse, s. vers m.; strophe f.

version, s. version f.

vertical, adj. vertical.

very, adv. très; ~ good très bien; — adj. vrai; même.

vessel, s. vaisseau m.

vest, s. gilet m.; chemise f. américaine.

vestry, s. sacristie f.; assemblée f.

veterinary, adj. ~ surgeon vétérinaire m.

veto, s. véto m.; — v.a. mettre son véto (à).

vex, v.a. vexer.

vibrate, v.n. vibrer, osciller.

vibration, s. vibration f.

vicar, s. curé m.

vice-, prefix vice-.

vicinity, s. voisinage m.
victim, s. victime f.
victorious, adj. victorieux.
victory, s. victoire f.
victuals, s. pl. victuailles f. pl.
view, s. vue f.; avis m.; on ~ exposé; have in ~ se proposer (de); with a ~ to en vue de; point of ~ ~ point m. de vue; — v.a. voir; regarder; envisager.
viewer, s. spectateur, -trice m. f.
vigorous, adj. vigoureux.
vigour, s. vigueur f.
village, s. village m.
villain, s. scélérat m.
vine, s. vigne f.
vinegar, s. vinaigre m.
vineyard, s. vignoble m.
vintage, s. vendange f.
violate, v.a. violer.
violation, s. violation f.
violence, s. violence f.
violent, adj. violent.
violet, s. violette f.; (colour) violet m.; — adj. violet.
violin, s. violon m.
violinist, s. violoniste m. f.
violoncellist, s. violoncelliste m.
violoncello, s. violoncelle m.
virgin, s. vierge f.
virtue, s. vertu f.
visa, visé, s. visa m.
visibility, s. visibilité f.
visible, adj. visible.
vision, s. vision f., vue f.
visit, s. visite f.; séjour m.; be on a ~ to être en visite chez; — v.a. visiter.
visitor, s. visiteur, -euse m. f.
vital, adj. vital.
vitamin, s. vitamine f.
vocabulary, s. vocabu-

laire m.
vocation, s. vocation f.
voice, s. voix f.; — v.a. exprimer.
voltage, s. voltage m.
volume, s. volume m.
voluntary, adj. volontaire.
volunteer, s. volontaire m.; — v.n. s'engager (pour).
vomit, v.a. & n. vomir.
vote, s. voix; — v.a. & n. voter (sur).
voucher, s. pièce f. de dépense ; pièce f. de recette; bon m.
vow, s. vœu m.; — v. a. vouer; jurer; v. n. faire un vœu; jurer.
vowel, s. voyelle f.
voyage, s. voyage m.; — v. n. voyager (par mer).

vulgar, adj. vulgaire.

W

wade, v.a. passer à gué.
wafer, s. gaufrette f.; hostie f.
wag, v.a. hocher; (tail) agiter; v.n. s'agiter.
wage(s), s. (pl.) salaire m., gages m. pl.; — v.a. ~ war faire la guerre.
wag(g)on, s. wagon m.
waist, s. taille f.
waistcoat, s. gilet m.
wait, v. a. & n. attendre (for qn, qch).
waiter, s. garçon m. (de restaurant); head~ premier garçon m., maître m. d'hôtel.
waiting-room, s. salle f. d'attente.
wake, v.a. (also ~ up) réveiller; v.n. (also ~

up) s'éveiller.

waken, *v.a.* éveiller; *v.n.* s'éveiller .

walk, *s.* marche *f.;* promenade *f.; (path)* allée *f.; go for a ~* faire une promenade; — *v.n.* aller à pied; marcher; *(pleasure)* se promener; *~ off* s'en aller; *~ out* sortir.

wall, s. mur *m.*

wallet, *s.* portefeuille *m.*

walnut, *s.* noyer *m.; (fruit)* noix *f.*

waltz, *s.* valse *f.*

wander, *v.n.* errer; s'égarer (de); divaguer.

want, *s.* besoin *m.;* manque *m.; for ~ of* faute de; — *v.a.* avoir besoin (de); manquer (de); vouloir; demander; *v. n.* faire défaut; *be ~ing in* manquer de.

war, *s.* guerre *f.*

ward, *s.* pupille *m. f.; (hospital)* salle *f.*

warden, *s.* gouverneur *m.;* directeur *m.*

warder, *s.* gardien, -enne *m. f.*

wardrobe, *s.* armoire *f.*

ware, *s.* marchandise(s) *f. (pl.);* article *m.*

warehouse, *s.* magasin *m.;* dépôt *m.*

warm, *adj.* chaud; *be ~* avoir chaud; — *v.a.* chauffer; *~ up* réchauffer; *v.n.* se chauffer.

warmth, *s.* chaleur *f.*

warn, *v.a.* avertir; prévenir; mettre sur ses gardes (contre).

warning, *s.* avertissement *m.;* avis *m.*

warrant, *s.* autorisation *f.;* mandat *m.;*

— *v. a.* garantir; justifier.

wash, *v.a.* laver; *v.n.* se laver; *~ away* effacer; *~ up the dishes* faire la vaisselle; — *s.* lavage *m.;* lotion *f.;* toilette *f.;* lessive *f.*

wash-basin, *s.* cuvette *f.* (de lavabo).

washing-machine, *s.* machine *f.* à laver.

wasp, *s.* guêpe *f.*

waste, *s.* désert *m.,* *(money)* gaspillage *m.;* *(energy)* déperdition *f.;* *(loss)* perte *f.;* déchets *m. pl.; ~ of time* perte de temps *f.;* — *adj.* inculte; de rebut; *~ paper* papier *m.* de rebut; — *v.a.* gaspiller; perdre; ravager.

watch, *s.* garde *f.;* gardien *m.,* garde *m.;* *(to indicate time)* montre *f.;* — *v. a.* veiller, garder; observer; regarder; *v.n.* veiller; *~ out!* ouvrez l'œil!

watch-maker, *s.* horloger *m.*

water, *s.* eau *f.*

water-closet , *s.* cabinet *m.*

waterfall, *s.* chute *f.* d'eau

watering-place, *s.* station *f.* balnéaire; ville *f.* d'eaux.

waterproof, *adj.* imperméable; — *s.* caoutchouc *m.*

wave, *s.* vague *f.;* onde *f.;* — *v.a.* agiter; *(hair)* onduler; *v. n.* flotter; onduler.

wave-length, *s.* longueur *f.* d'onde.

waver, *v.n.* vaciller.

wax, *s.* cire *f.*

way, *s.* chemin *m.,* route

f.; distance *f.;* côte *m.; (means)* moyen *m.;* façon *f.,* manière *f.; which* ~*?* de quel côté?; *it's a long* ~ *to* il y a loin pour aller (à); *on the* ~ chemin faisant; ~ *in* entrée *f.;* ~ *out* sortie

f.; out of the ~ retiré; extraordinaire; *this* ~ de ce côté-ci, par ici; *by* ~ *of* par; *by the* ~ à propos; *in a* ~ à certains égards; *give* ~ *to* céder à.

we, *pron.* nous.

weak, *adj.* faible.

weakness, *s.* faiblesse *f.*

wealth, *s.* richesse *f.;* profusion *f.*

wealthy, *adj.* riche.

weapon, *s.* arme *f.*

wear, *v.a.* porter; ~ *away, down, out* (s')user; ~ *off* (s')effacer; — *s.* usage *m.;* usure *f.*

weary, *adj.* las, fatigué.

weather, *s.* temps *m.*

weather-forecast, *s.* prévisions *f. pl.* du temps; bulletin *m.* météorologique.

weave, *v. a.* tisser.

web, *s.* tissu *m.; (spider)* toile *f.*

wedding, *s.* mariage *m.*

wedding-ring, *s.* alliance *f.,* anneau *m.* de mariage.

wedge, *s.* coin *m.;* — *v.a.* coincer; caler.

Wednesday, *s.* mercredi *m.*

weed, *s.* mauvaise herbe *f.;* — *v.a.* sarcler.

week, *s.* semaine *f.*

week-day, *s.* jour *m.* de semaine; *on* ~*s* en semaine.

week-end, *s.* fin *f.* de semaine, week-end *m.*

weekly, *adj.* de la semaine; hebdomadaire; — *s.* (journal) hebdomadaire *m.*

weep, *v.n.* pleurer.

weigh, *v.a. & n.* peser; ~ *down* faire pencher, surcharger, accabler.

weight, *s.* poids *m.; put on* ~ prendre du corps.

welcome, *adj.* bienvenu; ~*!* soyez le bienvenu!; — *s.* accueil *m.:* — *v.a.* souhaiter la bienvenue (à); accueillir (avec plaisir).

well[1], *adv.* bien; ~, ~*!* allons, allons!; — *adj.* bien (portant).

well[2], *s.* puits *m.*

well-being, bien-être *m.*

well-informed, *adj.* bien informé, renseigné.

well-to-do, *adj.* aisé; *be* ~ être dans l'aisance

west, *s.* ouest *m.*

western, *adj.* de l'ouest.

westward, *adv.* vers l'ouest.

wet, *adj.* mouillé, humide; pluvieux; ~ *through* trempé jusqu'aux os; — *v.a.* mouiller; tremper.

whale, *s.* baleine *f.*

what, *rel. pron.* ce qui, ce que; — *interrog. pron.* qu'est-ce qui, que; — *int.* quoi!

wheat, *s.* blé *m.,* froment *m.*

wheel, *s.* roue *f.; (steering)* volant *m.*

when, *adv. & conj.* quand.

whenever, *adv.* toutes les fois que.

where, *adv.* où.

whereas, *conj.* tandis que;

vu que.

wherever, *adv.* partout où.

whether, *conj.* soit que; *(if)* si; ~ *or not* ... qu'-il en soit ainsi ou non...

which, *(interrogative) adj.* quel, quelle; *pron.* lequel; *(relative) adj.* lequel, laquelle; *pron.* qui, que, lequel.

while, *conj.* pendant que; *(whereas)* tandis que; *(as long as)* tant que; — *s.* temps *m.; be worth* ~ *to* cela vaut la peine de; — *v.a.* ~ *away* faire passer.

whip, *s.* fouet.

whisk, *v.a.* fouetter; — *s.* époussette *f.; (eggs)* fouet à œufs, *m.*

whisper, *s.* chuchotement *m.;* murmure *m.; v.a.* dire à l'oreille; *v.n.* chuchoter; murmurer.

whistle, *s.* sifflet *m.;* — *v.a. & n.* siffler.

white, *adj.* blanc, blanche; pâle.

Whit Sunday, dimanche *m.* de la Pentecôte.

who, *pron.* qui.

whole, *s.* tout *m.;* totalité *f.; on the* ~ à tout prendre; — *adj.* tout le, toute la; entier, -ère.

wholesale, *adj. & adv.* en gros.

wholesome, *adj.* sain.

wholly, *adv.* entièrement.

whom, *pron.* que; lequel; *interrog.* qui?, qui est-ce que?

whose, *pron.* dont; *interrog.* de qui?

why, *adv.* pourquoi.

wicked, *adj.* méchant.

wide, *adj.* large; étendue; *6 feet* ~ 6 pieds de largeur.

widow, *s.* veuve *f.*

widower, *s.* veuf *m.*

width, *s.* largeur *f.*

wife, *s.* femme *f.*

wild, *adj.* sauvage; déréglé; impétueux; frénétique.

wilful, *adj.* volontaire.

will, *s.* volonté *f.;* intention *f.;* testament *m.; at* ~ à volonté; *of one's own free* ~ de plein gré; — *v.n. & aux.* vouloir; *(future tense unexpressed,* see *grammar).*

willing *adj.* bien disposé; *be* ~ vouloir bien.

willingly, *adv.* volontiers.

win, *v. a. & n.* gagner.

winch, *s.* manivelle *f.*

wind[1], *s.* vent *m.;* souffle *m.*

wind[2], *v. a.* enrouler; dévider; ~ *up (clock)* remonter; *fig.* liquider; *v.n.* tourner, serpenter; s'enrouler.

window, *s.* fenêtre *f.; (car)* glace *f.*

windscreen, *s.* pare-brise *m.*

windy, *adj.* venteux.

wine, *s.* vin *m.*

wing, *s.* aile *f.;* vol *m.; take* ~ s'envoler.

wink, *s.* clin d'œil, *m.;* — *v.a.* clignoter.

winner, *s.* gagnant *m.*

winter, *s.* hiver *m.*

wipe, *v.a.* essuyer; ~ *out* effacer; — *s.* coup *m.* de torchon.

wire, *s.* fil *m.* (de fer); télégramme *m.; live* ~ fil *m.* en charge; — *v.a. & n.* télégraphier.

wireless, *s.* T.S.F.; télégraphie sans fil; ~ *set* poste *m.* (de T.S.F.).

wise, *adj.* sage; prudent.

wish, *s.* désir *m.*; ~es vœux *m. pl.*; — *v.a.* désirer (de); souhaiter; *(should like)* vouloir *(in conditional)*.

wit, *s.* esprit *m.*; *(pers.)* bel esprit *m.*

witch, *s.* sorcière *f.*

with, *prep.* avec; *(at)* chez.

withdraw, *v.n.* se retirer; *v.a.* retirer.

within, *adv.* dedans; — *prep. (time)* en; *(place)* dans; à.

without, *prep.* sans; *(place)* en dehors de.

witness, *s.* témoignage *m.*; *(pers.)* témoin *m.*; — *v.a.* être témoin de; *(attest)* témoigner; *(document)* signer (à).

witty, *adj.* spirituel.

wizard, *s.* sorcier *m.*

wolf, *s.* loup, louve *m. f.*

woman, *s.* femme *f.*

womb, *s.* matrice *f.*; *fig.* sein *m.*

wonder, *s.* étonnement *m.*; *(a thing)* merveille *f.*; — *v.n.* ~ at être étonné de; *(curious)* se demander; *I* ~ je me le demande.

wonderful, *adj.* étonnant.

wood, *s.* bois *m.*

wooden, *adj.* de bois.

woodman, *s.* bûcheron *m.*

wool, *s.* laine *f.*

woollen, *adj.* de laine.

word, *s.* mot *m.*; *(utterance)* parole *f.*; *(term)* terme *m.*; *(information* avis *m.*; *upon my* ~! ma parole!; *have a* ~ *with* avoir deux mots avec.

work, *s.* travail *m.*; *(achievement)* ouvrage *m.*; ~ *(of art)* œuvre *f.* d'art; ~s *(of s.o.)* œuvres *f.pl.*, *(factory)* usine *f.*; *set to* ~ se mettre à l'œuvre; — *v.a.* faire travailler; *(wood)* ouvrager; *v.n.* travailler; *(operate)* fonctionner, marcher.

worker, *s.* travailleur, -euse *m. f.*, ouvrier, -ère *m. f.*

workman, *s.* ouvrier *m.*

workshop, *s.* atelier *m.*

world, *s.* monde *m.*

world-war, *s.* guerre *f.* mondiale.

world-wide, *adj.* universel; mondial.

worm, *s.* ver *m.*

worry, *s.* ennui *m.*, tracas *m.*; — *v.a.* tracasser; importuner; *v. n.* se tracasser (de), se tourmenter; *don't* ~! soyez tranquille!

worse, *adj.* pire, plus mauvais; *grow* ~ empirer; — *adv.* pis.

worship, *s.* culte *m.*; — *v.a. & n.* adorer.

worst, *adj.* le, la pire; le, la plus malade; — *adv.* le plus mal; — *s.* pis *m.*

worth, *s.* valeur *f.*; — *adj. be* ~ valoir; *is it* ~ *while?* cela (en) vaut-il la peine?; *it is not* ~ *the trouble* cela ne vaut pas la peine.

worthless, *adj.* sans valeur, indigne.

worthy, *adj.* digne.

wound, *s.* blessure *f.*

wounded, *adj.* blessé; *the* ~ les blessés.

wrap, *s. (garment)* peignoir *m.*; *v.a.* ~ *up* envelopper; *fig.* être absorbé *(in* dans).

wrapper, *s.* toile d'emballage *f.; (book)* bande *f.*

wreck, *s.* naufrage *m.;* navire *m.* naufragé; *fig.* ruine *f.; v.a.* ruiner: *be ~ed* faire naufrage; être naufragé.

wrench, *s.* torsion *f.; (tool)* clef (à écrous) *f.; — v.a.* tordre; *(ankle)* fouler.

wrestle, *v.n.* lutter (avec).

wrestler, *s.* lutteur *m.*

wrestling, *s.* lutte *f.*

wring, *v.a.* tordre.

wrinkle, *s.* ride *f.; (crease)* faux pli *m.; — v.a.* rider.

wrist, *s.* poignet *m.*

writ, *s.* exploit *m.*

write, *v.a. & n.* écrire; *~ down* noter; *~ off* amortir; *~ out* transcrire.

writer, *s.* écrivain *m.*

writing, *s.* écriture *f.;* écrit *m.; in ~* par écrit.

writing-desk, *s.* bureau *m.*

wrong, *adj.* incorrect, faux; *be ~* avoir tort; se tromper (de); *take the ~ train* se tromper de train; *it is the ~ book* ce n'est pas le livre qu'il faut.

X

Xmas, *s.* Noël *m.*

x-ray, *adj. ~ treatment* radiothérapie *f.; ~photograph* radiograph e *f.*

Y

yacht, *s.* yacht *m.*

yard, *s.* yard *m.;* cour *f.*

yarn, *s.* fil *m*; histoire *f.*

yawn, *s.* baîllement *m.; — v.n.* bâiller.

year, *s.* an *m.;* année *f.*

yearly, *adv.* annuellement.

yearn, *v.n. ~ for* soupirer après.

yeast, *s.* levure *f.*

yell, *v. n.* hurler.

yellow, *adj.* jaune.

yes, *adv.* oui; *(after negation)* si.

yesterday, *adv.* hier.

yet, *adv.* encore; *not ~* pas encore; *as ~* jusqu'à présent; *— conj.* néanmoins.

yield, *v.a.* produire; accorder; rendre; *v.n.* céder (à); fléchir.

yoke, *s.* joug *m.*

yolk, *s.* jaune *m.*

you, *pron.* tu; vous.

young, *adj.* jeune; *(animal)* petit; *~er* plus jeune. cadet.

your, *adj.* votre, *(pl.)* vos.

yours, *pron.* à vous; le, la vôtre, les vôtres.

yourself, *pron.* vous-même, *-s.*

youth, *s.* jeunesse *f.; (pers.)* jeune homme *m.*

youth-hostel, *s.* auberge *f.* de la jeunesse.

Z

zeal, *s.* zèle *m.*

zealous, *adj.* zélé.

zero, *s.* zéro *m.*

zest, *s.* enthousiasme *m.;* goût *m.*

zigzag, *s.* zigzag *m.; — adv.* en zigzag.

zinc, *s*. zinc *m*.
zipper, *s*. fermeture éclair.
   f.

zone, *s*. zone *f*.
zoo, *s*. zoo *m*.
zoology, *s*. zoologie *f*.

FRENCH-ENGLISH

DICTIONARY

A

à, au, *prep.* to; at.

abaisser, *v. a.* lower, let down; s'~ stoop.

abandonner, *v. a.* forsake, abandon.

abat-jour, *s. m.* lampshade.

abbaye, *s. m.* abbey.

abbé, *s. m.* abbot.

abdication, *s. f.* abdication.

abdiquer, *v. n.* abdicate; *v. a.* renounce.

abeille, *s. f* bee.

abject, *adj.* abject, low.

abjurer, *v.a.* abjure; give up.

abolir, *v. a.* abolish.

abondance, *s. f.* plenty, abundance.

abondant, *adj.* abundant.

abonder, *v. n.* abound.

abonner: s'~ subscribe to, take in.

abord, *adv.* d'~ (at) first.

aboutir, *v. n.* end in, come to.

aboyer, *v. n.* bark.

abricot, *s. m.* apricot.

abrupt, *adj.* steep.

absence, *s. f.* absence; ~ d'esprit absence of mind.

absent, *adj.* absent.

absenter: s'~ leave, depart.

absolu, *adj.* absolute.

absorber, *v. a.* absorb;

absoudre*, *v. a.* absolve.

abstraction, *s. f.* abstraction.

abstrait, *adj.* abstract.

absurde, *adj.* absurd.

abus, *s. m.* abuse.

académie, *s. f.* academy.

accélérer, *v. a.* accelerate, hasten.

accent, *s.m.* accent, stress.

accentuer, *v.a.* accent.

accepter, *v. a.* accept; admit.

accès, *s. m.* access; fit.

accessible, *adj.* accessible.

accident, *s. m.* accident; par ~ accidentally.

accidentel, -elle, *adj.* accidental.

acclamer, *v.a.* acclaim.

acclimater, *v.a.* acclimatize; 's'~ become acclimatized.

accommoder, *v. a.* accommodate; fit up; s'~ put up with, come to terms.

accompagner, *v. a.* accompany.

accomplir, *v. a.* accomplish, carry out.

accord, *s. m.* agreement, accord, harmony.

accorder, *v.a.* grant, confer; agree.

accoutumer, *v. a.* accustom; s'~ get accustomed (to).

accréditer, *v. a.* accredit.

accrocher, *v. a.* hang up, hook; run against.

accroître, *v. a.* increase; s'~ increase.

accueil, *s. m.* reception.

accueillir, *v. a.* receive, welcome.

accumuler, *v. a.* accumulate, heap up.

accusation, *s. f.* accusation, charge.

accuser, *v.a.* accuse.

achat, *s. m.* purchase; faire des ~s go shopping.

acheter, *v.a.* purchase, buy.

achèvement, *s. m.* completion.

achever, *v.a.* complete finish; achieve.

acide, *adj.* acid, sour; — *s. m.* acid.

acier, *s. m.* steel.

acoustique, *s. f.* acoustics.

acquérir*, *v.a.* acquire, purchase; get.

âcre, *adj.* acrid, sour.

acte, *s. m.* action, deed, act; transaction, document, certificate; *(theatre)* act.

acteur, *s. m.* actor.

actif, -ive, *adj.* active; — *s.m.* assets *(pl.)*;

action, *s. f.* action; act, deed; effect; lawsuit; plot; story.

activité, *s. f.* activity.

actrice, *s. f.* actress.

actualité, *s. f.* topic of the hour; ~s current events; news-reel.

actuel, -elle, present, of present interest; actual.

adapter, *v.a.* adapt; s'~ adapt oneself.

addition, *s. f.* addition; bill.

additionner, *v. a.* add up.

adhérer, *v. a.* adhere, stick.

adieu, s. m. *(pl. -x)* goodbye; *faire ses* ~x take one's leave.

adjoint, *adj. & s. m.* assistant; deputy.

adjuger, *v. a.* adjuge.

administrateur, -trice,

s. m. f. manager, director.

administratif, -ive- *adj.* administrative.

administration, *s. f.* management, direction; administration.

administrer, *v.a.* administer; manage.

admirable, *adj.* admi-

rable.

admiration, *s. f.* admiration.

admirer, *v. a.* admire, wonder at.

admission, *s. f.* admission, admittance.

adolescent, *s. m.* adolescent, youth.

adopter, *v.a.* adopt, pass.

adoption, *s. f.* adoption.

adorer, *v.a.* adore.

adresse, *s. f.* address; skill, dexterity.

adresser, *v. a.* address, direct; s'~ apply (to).

adroit, *adj.* clever, skilful.

adulte, *adj. & s.* adult.

adversaire, *s. m.* adversary.

aérien, -enne, *adj.* aerial.

aérodrome, *s. m.* airport.

aéroport, *s. m.* airport.

affaiblir, *v. a.* weaken.

affaire, *s. f.* business, affair, matter; lawsuit.

affamé, *adj.* hungry.

affecter, *v. a.* affect, feign; move; assume.

affection, *s. f.* affection; disease.

affectueux, -euse, *adj.* affectionate.

affermir, *v. a.* strengthen; s'~ become stronger.

affiche, *s. f.* poster, bill.

afficher, *v. a.* post up, stick up, placard.

affiler, *v.a.* sharpen.

affirmatif, -ive, *adj.* affirmative.

affirmer, *v. a.* affirm.

affliger, *v. a.* afflict.

affluer, *v. n.* flow into.

affranchir, *v. a.* (set) free; stamp.

affreux, -euse, *adj.* dreadful, terrible.

affronter, *v.a.* face.

afin, *conj.* ~ *de* in order to; ~ *que* in order

that, so that.

africain (A.), *adj. & s. m.
f.* African.

âge, *s. m.* age; period;
quel ~ avez-vous? how
old are you?

agence, *s. f.* agency.

agent, *s. m.* agent; policeman.

aggraver, *v. a.* aggravate.

agile, *adj.* agile, active.

agilité, *s. f.* agility.

agir, *v. n.* act; take effect;
behave; s'~ be in
question.

agitation, *s. f.* agitation.

agiter, *v. a.* agitate.

agneau, *s. m.* lamb.

agonie, *s. f.* agony.

agréable, *adj.* agreeable.

agréer, *v. a.* accept, receive favourably.

agrément, *s. m.* consent,
approval; pleasure.

agressif, -ive, *adj.* aggres-
sive.

agression, *s. f.* aggression, attack.

agriculture, *s. f.* agriculture.

aide, *s. f.* help.

aider, *v. a.* help.

aïeux, *s. m. pl.* ancestors.

aigle, *s. m.* eagle.

aigre, *adj.* sour, acid.

aigrir: s'~ turn sour.

aigu, *adj.* pointed, sharp;
keen; *accent ~* acute
accent.

aiguille, *s. f.* needle; hand,
index; point, switch;
grande ~ minute hand.

aiguiser, *v. a.* sharpen.

ail, *s. m.* garlic.

aile, *s. f.* wing; flank;
aisle; mudguard.

ailleurs, *adv.* somewhere
else, elsewhere; *d'~*
in addition, besides.

aimable, *adj.* amiable,
pleasant, kindly.

aimer, *v. a. & n.* like, love,

be fond of, care to.

aîné, *adj. & s. m. f.* elder,
eldest; senior.

ainsi, *adv. & conj.* so,
thus; likewise; ~ *de
suite* and so on; ~ *que*
as well as.

air, *s. m.* air; look(s),
appearance, manner;
(music) air.

aisance, *s. f.* ease; comfort; facility; *être dans
l'~* be well off.

aise, *s. f.* ease, comfort.

aisé, *adj.* easy; well-off.

ajourner, *v.a.* adjourn.

alcool, *s. m.* alcohol.

alcoolique, *adj.* alcoholic.

algèbre, *s. f.* algebra.

aliment, *s. m.* aliment,
food.

alimentation, *s. f.* alimentation; feeding.

alimenter, *v. a.* feed.

aliter, *v. a. être alité* be
confined to bed, be laid
up.

allaiter, *v. a.* give suck
to; nurse.

allée, *s. f.* (garden) path,
lane, walk, alley.

alléger, *v.a.* lighten;
alleviate, soothe.

allégresse, *s. f.* gaiety,
delight.

allemand (A.), *adj. &
s. m. f.* German.

aller*, *v. n.* go, proceed;
get on; grow, get;
~ *à pied* walk; ~ *en
auto* drive; ~ *en avion*
fly; ~ *bien* be well;
comment allez-vous?
how are you?; *allons!*
come on!; *allez!* in-
deed; s'en ~ go away,
be off.

alliance, *s. f.* alliance,
union; wedding-ring.

allié, -e, *s. m. f.* ally; —
adj. allied.

allier, *v.a.* alloy; match;

unite; s'~ join with, unite.

allonger, *v. a.* lengthen, stretch out, prolong; ~ *le pas* step out; s'~ get longer.

allumer, *v. a.* light (up), set on fire; excite.

allumette, *s. f.* match.

allure, *s. f.* gait, pace; manner, behaviour; direction.

allusion, *s. f.* allusion, hint; reference.

alors, *adv.* then.

alpinisme, *s. m.* mountaineering.

altérer, *v. a.* alter, change; s'~ alter, degenerate.

alternance, *s. f.* alternation.

alternatif, -ive, *adj.* alternate, alternative.

alterner, *v. n. & a.* alternate.

altitude, *s. f.* altitude.

aluminium, *s. f.* aluminium.

amaigrir, *v.a.* make thin; s'~ grow thin.

amant, -e, *s. m. f.* lover.

amas, *s.m.* heap, mass, pile.

amateur, *s. m.* amateur, lover, fancier.

ambassade, *s. f.* embassy.

ambassadeur, *s. m.* ambassador.

ambassadrice, *s. f.* ambassadress.

ambitieux, -euse, *adj.* ambitious.

ambition, *s. f.* ambition.

ambulance, *s. f.* ambulance; ~ *(automobile)* ambulance(-car).

âme, *s. f.* soul; mind.

améliorer, *v. a.* ameliorate, improve; s'~ improve.

aménager, *v.a.* fit up, out.

amender, *v.a.* amend, improve.

amener, *v. a.* bring, draw; bring before, in, out; introduce; induce.

amer, -ère, *adj.* bitter.

américain, -e (A.), *adj. & s. m. f.* American.

ami, -e, *s. m. f.* friend; sweetheart; *bon* ~, *bonne* ~*e* sweetheart.

amical, *adj.* friendly, kind.

amiral, *s. m.* admiral.

amitié, *s. f.* friendship; affection; *meilleures* ~*s* kindest regards.

amortir, *v.a.* lessen, soften; pay (off), write off.

amortisseur, *s. m.* shockabsorber.

amour, *s. m.* love; *faire l'*~ court, make love to; *mon* ~ my darling.

amoureux, -euse, *adj.* in love *(de* with), enamoured *(de* of).

amplificateur, *s.m.* amplifier.

amplifier, *v. a.* amplify.

ampoule, *s. f.* blister; bulb.

amulette, *s. f.* amulet.

amusant, *adj.* amusing.

amusement, *s. m.* amusement, pastime, fun.

amuser, *v.a.* amuse, entertain; s'~ enjoy oneself.

an, *s. m.* year; *il y a un* ~ a year ago.

analogie, *s. f.* analogy.

analogue, *adj.* analogous.

analyse, *s. f.* analysis.

analyser, *v. a.* analyse.

ananas, *s. m.* pineapple.

anatomie, *s. f.* anatomy.

ancêtre, *s. m. f.* ancestor.

ancien, -enne, *adj.* ancient, old, antique.

ancre, *s. f.* anchor; *lever l'*~ weigh anchor.

âne, *s. m.* ass.

anéantir, *v. a.* annihilate.

anecdote, *s. f.* anecdote.

ange, s. m. angel.

anglais, -e (A.), adj. English; — s. m. f. Englishman, Englishwoman.

angle, s. m. angle, corner; bend.

angoisse, s.f. anguish.

animal, s.m. animal; beast.

anneau, s. m. circle, ring.

année, s. f. year; ~ scolaire school-year; bonne ~ a happy New Year!

annexer, v. a. annex.

anniversaire, s. m. anniversary, b rthday.

annonce, s. f. announcement, advertisement.

annoncer, v. a. announce, give notice of; advertise.

annuaire, s. m. year-book, annual, directory.

annuel, -elle, adj. annual.

annuler, v. a. annul.

anonyme, adj. anonymous; société ~ joint-stock company.

anormal, adj. abnormal.

anse, s. f. handle; creek.

antécédent, -e, adj. & s. m. antecedent.

antenne, s. f. aerial.

antérieur, adj. anterior, previous.

antibiotique, s. m. antibiotic.

antichambre, s. f. entrance hall.

anticiper, v. a. & n. anticipate; encroach.

antipathie, s.f. antipathy.

antiquaire, s. m. antiquarian.

antique, adj. antique, ancient.

antiquité, s. f. antiquity.

antiseptique, adj. & s. m. antiseptic.

anxiété, s. f. anxiety.

anxieux, -euse, adj. anxious.

août, s.m. August.

apaiser, v. a. appease, pacify, quiet.

apercevoir, v. a. perceive, catch sight of; remark, notice.

aplanir, v. a. smooth, level, even off; s'~ become level.

aplatir, v.a. fl atten.

apologie, s. m. apology, defence.

apoplexie, s. f. apoplexy.

apostolique, adj. apostolic(al).

apostrophe, s. f. apostrophe.

apôtre, s. m. apostle.

apparaître, v. n. appear.

appareil, s. m. apparatus, device, appliance, gear; camera; ~ de TV TV-set; ~ de direction steering-gear.

apparence, s. f. appearance, look(s); likelihood; en ~ apparenty.

apparent, adj. apparent.

apparition, s. f. appearance; apparition.

appartement, s.m. flat; apartment.

appartenir, v.n. belong, appertain (à to).

appel, s. m. call; appeal; faire l'~ call the roll.

appeler, v. a. call in, out, up, down; ring up; name, term; en ~ appeal; faire ~ send for; s'~ be called, call oneself.

appendice, s. m. appendix.

appendicite, s.f. appedicitis.

appesantir, v.a. make heavy, weigh down.

appétit, s. m. appetite.

applaudir, v. n. applaud, clap.

application, s. f. application; diligence.

appliquer, *v. a.* apply; lay on.

apporter, *v.a.* bring.

appréciation, *s.f.* appreciation; estimation.

apprécier, *v. a.* value.

appréhension, *s. f.* apprehension, fear.

apprendre, *v. a.* learn, acquire; hear of; teach.

apprentissage, *s. m.* apprenticeship.

apprêter, *v. a.* prepare; season; dress; s'~ prepare oneself, get ready.

approbation, *s.f.* approbation, approval.

approche, *s. f.* approach, advance.

approcher, *v.a.* bring toward, forward.

approprié, *adj.* appropriate.

approprier: s'~ appropriate, take; accommodate, adapt oneself.

approuver, *v. a.* sanction; approve.

approximatif, **-ive**, *adj.* approximate.

approximation, *s.f.* approximation.

appui, *s. m.* support.

appuyer, *v. a.* support; lean; *v. n.* ~ *sur* lay stress (up)on; s'~ lean, rest, rely (upon).

après, *adv.* after; behind; next (to); ~ *coup* too late; ~ *tout* after all; d'~ after, according to; by.

après-demain, *adv. & s. m.* (the) day after tomorrow.

après-midi, *s. m.* afternoon.

à-propos, *adv.* in good time; — *s. m.* timely word; fitness.

apte, *adj.* apt, suitable.

aptitude, *s. f.* aptitude, ability, talent.

aquarelle, *s.f.* water-color.

arabe (A.), *adj. & s. m. f.* Arab, Arabian; Arabic.

araignée, *s. f.* spider.

arbitre, *s. f.* arbiter, judge; umpire, referee.

arbre, *s. m.* tree; shaft; ~ *fruitier* fruit-tree; ~ *coudé* crank shaft.

arc, *s. m.* bow; arc(h).

arcade, *s. f.* arcade.

arche, *a. f.* arch, vault.

archet, *s.m.* bow.

archevêque, *s.m.* archbishop.

architecture, *s.f.* architecture.

archives *s. f. pl.* archives.

ardemment, *adv.* ardently.

ardent, *adj.* burning, fiery, ardent, eager.

ardeur, *s. f.* keenness; ardour, zeal.

arête, *s. f.* fish-bone; edge; ridge.

argent, *s. m.* silver; money; ~ *en caisse* cash in hand ~ *comptant* ready money; ~ *de la poche* pocket-money; *à-court* d'~ pressed for money.

argenterie, *s. f.* plate.

argentin[1], *adj.* silvery.

argentin[2], **-e (A.)**, *adj. & s. m. f.* Argentine.

argile, *s.f.* clay.

argot, *s. m.* slang.

argument, *s.m.* argument, proof, evidence.

aristocratie, *s.f.* aristocracy.

aristocratique, *adj.* aristocratic.

arme, *s.f.* arm, weapon; ~s *à feu* fire-arms; *faire des* ~s fence.

armée, *s. f.* army.

armer, *v.a.* arm; fortify; s'~ arm oneself.

armoire, *s. f.* cupboard;

wardrobe.

armure, s. f. armour; armature.

arracher, v.a. pull (out), tear up; extract, draw; remove from.

arrangement, s. m. arrangement; agreement, settlement; ~s terms.

arranger, v. a. arrange, settle, fix (up); s'~ come to an agreement, make arrangements (for); make shift (to).

arrestation, s. f. arrest.

arrêt, s. m. stop (of bus, tram etc.); pause; standstill; sentence; arrest; ~ facultatif request stop; sans ~ non-stop.

arrêter, v.a. check, stop; arrest; engage, book; decide, decree; settle; s'~ stop; draw up; leave off.

arrière. adv. behind, backward; en ~ back(ward); ~ s. m. back part, rear.

arriéré, adj. overdue; backward; under-developed; — s.m. arrears (pl.).

arrivée, s. f. arrival; à l'~ on arrival.

arriver, v. n. arrive, come; turn up; happen; occur; ~ à attain, arrive at, reach; le train arrive à the train is due at.

arrogance, s. f. arrogance.

arroser, v. a. water, sprinkle; baste.

art, s. m. art; les beaux ~s the fine arts.

artère, s.f. artery; thoroughfare.

article, s. m. article; ~s de grande consommation consumer(s') goods.

articulation, s. f. joint.

articuler, v.a. articulate.

artificiel, -elle, adj. artifi-cial.

artillerie, s. f. artillery.

artisan, s. m. craftsman.

artiste, s. m. & f. artist; player

ascenseur, s. m. lift.

asile, s. m. refuge, asylum.

aspect, s.m. aspect.

asperge, s. f. asparagus.

aspirateur, s.m. vacuum-cleaner.

aspiration, s. f. aspiration.

aspirer, v.a. inspire; v. n. aspire (à to).

assaillir*, v. a. assault.

assaisonner, v.a. season; dress.

assassin, s. m. assassin.

assassiner, v. a. assassi-nate, murder.

assaut, s.m. assault.

assemblage, s. m. assemblage, gathering, collection.

assemblée, s.f. assembly, meeting.

assembler, v. a. assemble; put together; gather; s'~ assemble.

asseoir*, v. a. seat; place; s'~ take a seat.

assez, adv. enough; pretty, fairly.

assiduité, s.f. assiduity.

assiéger, v.a. attack, besiege.

assiette, s. f. posture; seat; position; plate.

assimiler, v. a. assimilate (' to).

assistance, s.f. presence, attendance; audience; assistance, help.

assister, v. n. attend, be present (à at); v. a. assist, help.

association, s. f. association; partnership, company.

associer, v.a. associate, link up; share interests with; s'~ associate oneself *(avec* with).

assommant, *adj.* boring, dull.

assortir, *v.a.* match, assort; **s'~** be suitable, go well together.

assoupir, *v. a.* make drowsy, sleepy; **s'~** grow sleepy.

assujettir, *v.a.* subject, subjugate.

assumer, *v. a.* assume.

assurance, *s. f.* assurance; insurance; **~** *sur la vie* life-insurance.

assuré, *adj.* assured, confident, sure; insured.

assurer, *v. a.* assure, secure; insure; **s'~** make sure (of).

astre, *s. m.* star.

astronaute, *s. m.* astronaut, space man.

astronautique, *s. f.* astronautics, space travel.

astronef, *s. m.* spacecraft, space-ship.

atelier, *s.m.* workshop; studio.

athée, *s.m.f.* atheist.

athlète, *s.m.* athlete.

athlétique, *adj.* athletic.

atome, *s.m.* atom.

atomique, *adj.* atomic; *bombe* **~** atom(ic) bomb *énergie* **~** atomic energy.

attache, *s. f.* tie, fastener; bond, strap; *fig.* attachment.

attaché, *s. m.* attaché.

attacher, *v.a.* fasten, tie (up), attach; associate; engage; **s'~** attach (to), become attached (to).

attaque, *s. f.* attack.

attaquer, *v.a.* attack.

attarder, *v.a.* delay; *être attardé* be delayed.

atteindre*, *v. a.* attain, reach; hit, stirke.

atteinte, *s. f.* blow, stroke; fit; injury; *hors d'*~ out

of reach.

attendre, *v. a. & n.* await, wait for, expect; **s'~** hope for, expect.

attendrir, *v. a.* soften; *fig.* move, touch; **s'~** be moved.

attendrissement, *s.m.* compassino; tenderness.

attente, *s. f.* waiting; hope

attentif, **-ive,** *adj.* attentive, considerate.

attention, *s.f.* attention, notice, heed, care; *(pl.)* attentions; *faire* **~** be careful, mind, take notice of, take heed (to); **~***!* look out!

atténuer, *v. a.* extenuate, attenuate.

atterrir, *v. n.* land.

atterrissage, *s. m.* landing; *piste d'*~ landing-strip.

attester, *v.a.* attest.

attirail, *s. m.* implements *(pl.),* utensils *(pl.),* gear; tackle.

attirer, *v.a.* attract.

attitude, *s. f.* attitude.

attraction, *s. f.* attraction.

attrape, *s. f.* trap; catch.

attribuer, *v. a.* assign, allot; attribute, ascribe.

attribut, *s. m.* attribute.

au *(pl.* aux), to the, at the.

auberge, *s. f.* inn, tavern; **~** *de la jeunesse* youth hostel.

aucun, *adj. & pron.* no, none, no one, not any.

au-dessous, *adv.* below; **~** *de* under.

au-dessus, *adv. (***~** *de)* above, over.

audience, *s. f.* audience; public; sitting, session.

audiovisuel, **-elle,** *adj.* audio-visual.

auditeur, **-trice,** *s. m. f.* listener; auditor.

auditoire, *s. m.* audience;

congregation.

auge, *s.m.* trough; bucket.

augmentation, *s.f.* augmentation, increase; rise.

augmenter, *v. a.* augment, increase; s'~ increase.

aujourd'hui, *adv.* today.

auparavant, *adv.* previously, earlier; before.

auprès, *adv.* near, by, close by; ~ *de* near.

auquel, *rel.pron.* to whom, to which.

aurore, *s.f.* dawn.

aussi, *adv.* also, too; ~ ... *que* as ... as; — *conj.* and so, therefore; ~ *bien que* as well as; ~ *bien* in fact.

austère, *adj.* austere, severe.

autant, *adv. & conj.* as much, as many, as far; ~ *que* as far as, as much as.

autel, *s. m.* altar.

auteur, *s. m.* author.

authentique, *adj.* authentic, genuine.

auto, *s. f.* car.

autobus, *s.m.* (motor-)bus.

autocar, *s. m.* (motor-) coach.

automatique, *adj.* automatic; — *s.m.* dial-telephone.

automne, *s. m. f.* autumn.

automobile, *s. m. f.* motor-car.

autonomie, *s.f.* autonomy.

autorisation, *s. f.* authorization, permission; licence.

autoriser, *v.a.* authorize.

autorité, *s. f.* authority; rule.

autoroute, *s. f.* motorway.

auto-stop, *s. m.* hitch-hiking.

auto-stoppeur, -euse, *s. m. f.* hitch-hiker.

autour, *adv. & prep.* ~ *de* about, (a)round; *tout* ~ all round.

autre, *adj.* different, other, another, else; *un* ~ another; *d'* ~ *part* on the other hand; ~ *part* elsewhere; *de temps* ~ now and then, at times; *l'* ~ *jour* the other day; *l'un et l'* ~ both; *l'un l'* ~ each other.

autrefois, *adv.* formerly, long ago.

autrichien, -enne (A.), *adj. & s.m.f.* Austrian.

autrui, *pron.* others, other people.

avalanche, *s.f.* avalanche.

avaler, *v.a.* swallow; *fig.* endure, pocket.

avance, *s.f.* advance.

avancé, *adj.* advanced.

avancement, *s.m.* advance, progress; promotion.

avancer, *v.a.* advance, bring, put forward; pay in advance; — *v. n.* advance, proceed, move on; s'~ come, move ,go forward.

avant, *prep. & adv.* before, in front (of), in advance; ~ *tout* above all, before everything; *en* ~ forward, to the front; *mettre en* ~ bring forward; *en* ~ *de* in front of; — *s.m.* front (part); bow (of ship); forward.

avantage, *s. m.* advantage, benefit, profit; *(tennis)* vantage.

avantageux, -euse, *adj.* advantageous.

avant-hier, *adv.* day before yesterday.

avant-propos, *s. m.* foreword, preface.

avare, s. m. f. miser; — adj. avaricious, miserly.

avarice, s.f. avarice.

avec, prep. with.

avenir, s. m. future; à l'~ in the future.

aventure, s. f. adventure; chance, luck.

aventurer, v.a. risk; (s'~) venture.

aventurier, -ère, s. m. f. adventurer.

avenue, s. f. boulevard; avenue.

averse, s.f. shower (of rain).

aversion, v. f. aversion, dislike.

avertir, v.a. inform, let know; warn; faire ~ de give notice of.

avertissement, s. m. information, notification; advice; warning.

aveu, s. m. admission, confession; consent.

aveugle, adj. blind.

aveuglement, s. m. blindness.

avide, adj. greedy, eager.

avidité, s.f. avidity.

avilir, v.a. debase, disgrace, degrade.

avion, s.m. (aero)plane; ~ de ligne air-liner; ~ à réaction jet plane; par ~ by air-mail.

avis, s. m. opinion; advice; counsel; information, notice; hint; mind; changer d'~ change one's mind.

aviser, v.a. perceive; inform; let know; advise; s'~ de think, find.

avocat, s. m. barrister, advocate, counsel.

avoine, s.f. oat(s).

avoir*, v. a. have, possess; have on, wear;

feel; ~ raison be right; ~ faim be hungry; ~ de take after; ~ à have to; il y a there is, there are; ago.

avorter, v. n. miscarry, have a miscarriage.

avorton, s. m. abortion.

avoué, s. m. attorney, solicitor; lawyer.

avouer, v. a. & n. admit, confess; acknowledge; approve.

avril, s.m. April.

axe, s.m. axis; axle.

azote, s.m. nitrogen.

B

baccalauréat, s. m. baccalaureate, bachelor's degree.

bachelier, s. m. bachelor (of arts etc.).

bacille, s.m. bacillus.

bagage, s. m. luggage; plier ~ pack up one's kit.

bague, s.f. ring.

bai, adj. bay.

baie¹, s. f. bay.

baie², s. f. berry.

baigner: se ~ bathe.

baignoire, s.m. bath, bathtub; pit-box.

bâiller, v. n. yawn, gape.

bain, s. m. bath; salle de ~ bath-room.

baïonette, s.f. bayonet.

baiser, v.a. kiss.

baisse, s.f. fall; decline.

baisser, v.a. lower, let down; bring down; turn down; cast down; v.n. decline, fall; sink; se ~ stoop.

bal, s. m. ball; ~ costumé fancy-dress ball.

balai, s.m. broom, mop; (house-)brush; donner un coup de ~ sweep.

balance, *s. f.* balance, scales *(pl.)*.

balancer, *v.a.&n.* balance; weigh; swing, rock; give the sack; se ~ swing, wave; balance.

balayer, *v.a.* sweep (out), clear away.

balcon, *s. m.* balcony; dress-circle.

baleine, *s.f.* whale.

ballade, *s.f.* ballad.

balle, *s.f.* ball; bullet; bale.

ballon, *s.m.* balloon; (foot-)ball.

balnéaire, *adj.* pertaining to baths; *station* ~ watering place.

bambou, *s.m.* bamboo.

ban, *s. m.* ban; ~s *de mariage* banns.

banal *adj.* banal, common, ordinary.

banane, *s. f.* banana.

banc, *s. m.* bench, form; bank; pew; stand.

bande, *s.f.* band, strip; bandage; troop, gang, set; ~ *de papier* slip of paper; ~ *transporteuse* conveyer belt.

bander, *v. a.* bind up.

bandit, *s. m.* bandit.

banlieue, *s. f.* outskirts, suburbs *(pl.)*.

bannir, *v. a.* banish, exile.

banque, *s. f.* bank; *billet de* ~ banknote; *compte en* ~ bankaccount.

banquet, *s. m.* banquet, feast.

banquier, -ère, *s.m.f.* banker.

baptême, *s. m.* baptism.

baptiser, *v.a.* baptize.

barbare, *adj. & s.m.* barbarian.

barbarie, *s. f.* barbarousness, cruelty.

barbe, *s. f.* beard; *faire la* ~ *à* shave.

barbet, *s. m.* poodle.

barbier, *s. m.* barber.

baron, *s. m.* baron.

baronne, *s.f.* baroness.

barque, *s.f.* boat, barge.

barrage, *s.m.* barrier, barrage, dam.

barre, *s.f.* bar.

barreau, *s. m.* (small) bar; the Bar.

barrer, *v.a.* fasten, bar; cut off, shut out; steer.

barrière, *s.f.* barrier, town-gate, gate; bar; obstacle.

barrique, *s.f.* barrel, cask.

bas[1], *adj.* low; *à* ~ *prix* cheap; *terre* ~se lowland; *en* ~ (down) below, down(-wards), — *s. m.* bottom, lower part

bas[2], *s. m.* stocking; ~ *nylons* nylon stockings.

base, *s. f.* base; basis.

basique, *adj.* basic.

basse, *s.f.* bass; bass-viol.

bassesse, *s.f.* lowness, meanness.

basset, *s. m.* basset (dog).

bassin, *s. m.* basin, pool.

bataille, *s.f.* battle.

bataillon, *s. m.* battalion.

bateau, *s. m.* boat.

batelier, *s.m.* boatman.

bâtiment, *s. m.* building; building trade; ship.

bâtir, *v.a.* build, erect.

bâtisseur, -euse *s. m. f.* builder.

bâton, *s. m.* stick, staff.

batte, *s.f.* bat; beater.

battement, *s.m.* clap-(ping); flapping.

batterie, *s.f.* battery; fight, row; percussive instruments *(pl.)*; ~ *de cuisine* kitchen utensils *(pl.)*.

battre*, *v. a. & n.* beat, strike, thrash; se ~ fight.

battu, *adj.* beaten.

bavard, -e *s.m.f.* gossip.

bavarder, *v.n.* chat(ter), gossip.

bazar, *s.m.* bazaar.

beau, bel; belle; beaux, bolles, *adj.* beautiful, handsome, good-looking, fair; considerable; *il y a ~ temps que* it seems an age since; *un ~ jour* one fine day; — *s.m.* beauty.

beaucoup, *adv.* (~ *de*) a good deal, many, much; plenty (of); *à ~ près, de ~* by far.

beau-frère, *s. m.* brother-in-law.

beau-père, *s. m.* father-in-law.

beauté, *s. f.* beauty

beaux-arts, *s. m. pl.* (the) fine arts.

bébé, *s. m.* baby.

bec, *s. m.* beak, bill nib; mouth-piece; jet; ~ *de gaz* gas-burner, gas-jet.

bêche, *s. f.* spade.

bégayer, *v. n. &a.* stammer, stutter.

belge (B.), *adj. & s. m. f.* Belgian.

belle-fille, *s. f.* daughter-in-law; step-daughter.

belle-mère, *s. f.* mother-in-law; stepmother.

belle-sœur, *s. f.* sister-in-law.

bémol, *s. m. & adj.* flat *(music)*.

bénédiction, *s.f.* benediction, blessing.

bénéfice, *s. m.* benefit, advantage, profit.

bénir, *v. a.* bless; praise.

berceau, *s. m.* cradle; *fig.* origin.

bercer, *v. a.* rock, lull (to sleep); *fig.* lull (with promises).

béret, *s.m.* beret.

berger, *s. m.* shepherd.

bergère, *s. f.* shepherdess; deep easy chair.

bésicles, *s. f. pl.* spectacles; goggles.

besogne, *s. f.* (piece of) work, job, task.

besoin, *s. m.* need, want; requirement; *avoir ~ de* want, need; *être dans le ~* be poor.

bétail, *s. m.* cattle.

bête, *s. f.* beast; animal; — *adj.* foolish, silly, stupid, dull.

bêtise, *s. f.* foolishness, stupidity; nonsense; trifle.

beurre, *s. m.* butter.

biais, *s. m.* bias, slant, slope.

biaiser, *v. n.* slant, slope.

bibelot, *s. m.* trinket, gew-gaw.

biberon, *s. m.* feeding-bottle.

bible, *s. f.* Bible.

bibliothécaire, *s. m. f.* librarian.

bibliothèque, *s. f.* library; bookcase; bookstall.

bicyclette, *s. f.* bicycle, bike.

bicycliste, *s. m. f.* cyclist.

bien, *adv.* well, right, properly, fully; *assez ~* fairly; *faire du ~* benefit; *ou ~* or else; *très ~* very well, all right; ~ *avant* long before; very bad indeed; ~ *que* (al)though; — *s. m.* good, welfare, benefit; property, goods;

aller à ~ prosper, be successful.

bien-être, *s. m.* welfare, well-being.

bienfaisance, *s. f.* beneficence.

bienfaisant, *adj.* charitable, kind; humane.

bienfait, *s.m.* kindness; benefaction.

bientôt, *adv.* soon, shortly; *à* ~! so long!

bienveillance, *s.f.* benevolence, kindness.

bienveillant, *adj.* kind(ly), benevolent, charitable.

bienvenu, *adj.* welcome; *soyez le* ~ welcome!

bière, *s.f.* beer.

bifteck, *s. m.* beef-steak.

bijou, *s. m.* *(pl.* -x) jewel.

bijouterie, *s.f.* jewellery; jeweller's shop.

bijoutier, -ière *s. m. f.* jeweller.

bile, *s. f.* bile; *se faire de la* ~ worry, fret.

bille, *s. f.* billiard-ball.

billet, *s. m.* note; ticket; certificate; ~ *d'aller et retour* return ticket; ~ *d'entrée* admission ticket; ~ *de banque* banknote.

billot, *s. m.* block; yoke.

biographe, *s. m. f.* biographer.

biographie, *s. f.* biography.

biologie, *s. f.* biology.

biologiste, biologue, *s. m. f.* biologist.

bis, *int.* encore!

biscuit, *s. m.* biscuit.

bison, *s. m.* bison.

bistro, *s. m.* pub; wine-shop.

bizarre, *adj.* strange, odd.

blague, *s.f.* pouch.

blaireau, *s. m.* badger; shaving-brush.

blâme, *s. m.* blame, reprimand.

blâmer, *v. a.* blame; find fault with.

blanc, blanche, *adj.* white; hoary; blank.

blanchir, *v.a.* whiten, bleach; whitewash; *v.n.* turn white, whiten.

blasphème, *s. m.* blasphemy.

blasphémer, *v.a. & n.* blaspheme.

blé, *s. m.* wheat.

blême, *adj.* pale.

blesser, *v. a.* wound, injure, hurt; offend; se ~ wound oneself; be offended.

blessure, *s. f.* wound, injury; offence.

bleu, *adj. & s. m.* blue; ~ *marine* navy blue.

bloc, *s. m.* block; *en* ~ in the lump.

blond, *adj.* fair, blond.

bloquer, *v.a.* blockade; block (up); tighten.

blouse, *s.f.* blouse, smock.

bobine, *s. f.* bobbin, spool.

bœuf, *s. m.* ox, beef.

bohème, *adj.* bohemian.

boire*, *v. a. & n.* drink; swallow; ~ *à la santé de X* drink X's health; — *s. m.* drink(ing).

bois, *s. m.* wood; timber; *de, en* ~ wood(en).

boisson, *s. f.* drink, beverage.

boîte, *s. f.* box, case; can, tin; ~ *aux lettres* letter-box; ~ *de vitesse* gear-box; *en* ~ tinned.

boiteux, -euse *adj.* lame.

bombardement, *s. m.* bombardment.

bombarder, *v. a.* bombard, shell.

bombe, *s. f.* bomb, shell; ~ *H* H-bomb.

bon, bonne, *adj.* good; kind, nice; right; valid; *c'est ~!* (all) right!; *~ à rien* good for nothing; *~ne année!* happy new year!; *de ~ne heure* early; — *s. m.* good(ness); bond, order.

bonbon, *s. m.* bonbon, sweet.

bond, *o. m.* bound, leap.

bondé, *adj.* crowded.

bonder, *v. a.* load, cram.

bondir, *v. n.* bound, leap, spring.

bonheur, *s. m.* happiness; good fortune; success.

bonhomme, *s. m.* good-natured man; simple man; fellow.

bonjour, *s.m.* good morning; salutation.

bonne, *s. f.* maid-servant; *~ (d'enfants)* nursery-maid.

bonnet, *s. m.* cap, hood.

bonsoir, *s. m.* good evening.

bonté, *s. f.* goodness, kindness, benevolence.

bord, *s. m.* edge, border, brink, (b)rim, verge; side, board, bank; *à ~* on board; *monter à ~* go on board.

border, *v.a.* border, adjoin.

bordure, *s. f.* border, edging; verge; kerb.

borne, *s. f.* milestone; bound(ary), limit.

borner, *v. a.* bound, limit, restrict.

bosse, *s. f.* bump, protuberance; knob.

botanique, *adj.* botanical; — *s. f.* botany.

botte¹, *s.f.* (high) boot.

botte², *s.f.* bottle; truss.

bottine, *s.f.* boot.

bouche, *s. f.* mouth; orifice, muzzle.

boucher, *s. m.* butcher.

boucherie, *s. f.* butcher's (shop).

bouchon, *s. m.* plug, cork, stopper.

boue, *s. f.* mud, dirt.

bouger, *v. n.* stir, budge.

bougie, *s.f.* candle. (sparking-)plug.

bouillir*, *v. n. & a.* (also *faire ~*) boil.

bouillon, *s. m.* bubble; stock; *~ de bœuf* beef-tea.

bouillotte, *s. f.* kettle.

boulanger, -ère, *s. m. f.* baker; baker's wife.

boulangerie, *s. f.* bakery, baker's (shop).

boule, *s. f.* ball, bowl.

boulevard, *s. m.* boulevard.

bouleverser, *v. a.* overthrow, upset; turn upside down; distract.

boulon, *s. m.* bolt, pin.

bouquet, *s. m.* cluster, bunch; bouquet.

bourdonnement, *s.m.* buzz(ing), humming.

bourdonner, *v.n.* buzz, hum, drone.

bourg, *s. m.* (small) town; village.

bourgeois, e, *s. m. f.* citizen; townsman.

bourgeoisie, *s. f.* citizens *(pl.);* middle class.

bourse, *s. f.* purse; exchange; Stock Exchange; scholarship, bursary.

bousculade, *s. f.* hustling.

bousculer, *v. a.* upset, hustle, jostle; *se ~* hustle each other.

bout, *s. m.* end, extremity, tip, top, button; *un ~ de chemin* a short distance.

bouteille, *s. f.* bottle.

boutique, *s. f.* shop; booth, stall.

bouton, *s. m.* button; stud; bud; nipple; knob; ~*s de manchette* cuff-links.

boutonnière, *s. f.* button-hole.

boxer, *v. n.* box, fight.

boxeur, *s.m.* boxer.

bracelet, *s. m.* bracelet.

braconner, *v. n.* poach.

braconnier, *s. m.* poacher.

brancard, *s. m.* stretcher; shaft.

branche, *s.f.* branch.

branler, *v. a.* shake, totter, waver.

bras, *s. m.* arm; hand; branch.

braser, *v.a.* braze, solder

brasserie, *s. f.* brewery; beershop.

brave, *adj.* brave; honest. worthy, good.

braver, *v. a.* face, brave.

bravoure, *s. f.* bravery, courage.

brebis, *s. f.* ewe, sheep.

brèche, *s. f.* breach, gap.

bref, brève, *adj.* brief, short.

bretelles, *s. f. pl.* braces.

brevet, *s. m.* patent; certificate.

bride, *s. f.* bridle, reins.

brièveté, *s. f.* brevity.

brigade, *s. f.* brigade.

brigadier, *s. m.* corporal, overseer.

brigand, *s. m.* brigand, armed robber.

brillant, *adj.* brilliant, shiny, glittering.

briller, *v.n.* shine, glitter, sparkle.

brin, *s. m.* shoot, sprig, blade (of grass).

brioche, *s. f.* brioche.

brique, *s. f.* brick; bar (of soap).

briquet *s. m.* lighter.

briquette, *s. f.* briquette.

brise, *s. f.* breeze.

briser, *v. a.* break (to pieces), smash; *v. n.* break; se ~ break to pieces.

britannique, *adj.* British.

broche, *s. f.* brooch; knitting-needle; spindle spit.

brochure, *s. f.* pamphlet.

broder, *v. a.* embroider.

broderie, *s. f.* embroidery, braid.

bronchite, *s. f.* bronchitis.

bronze, *s. m.* bronze.

brosse, *s. f.* brush; ~ à barbe shaving-brush; ~ à dents tooth-brush; ~ à cheveux hairbrush; donner un coup de ~ a brush up.

brosser, *v.a.* brush; se ~ brush oneself.

brouillard, *s. m.* mist, fog.

brouille, *s.f.* quarrel.

brouiller, *v.a.* mingle, mix; confuse, embroil; shuffle (cards).

broyer, *v. a.* crush, pound.

bruire, *v.n.* rustle.

bruit, *s. m.* noise, din; fuss; rumour.

brûlant, *adj.* burning, hot, scorching; fiery.

brûler, *v. a. & n.* burn, schorch, roast; ~ de long for.

brume, *s. f.* mist, fog.

brumeux, -euse *adj.* foggy.

brun, *adj.* brown.

brusque, *adj.* sudden, curt, gruff.

brutal, *adj.* brutal, rude savage.

brute, *s. f.* brute.

bruyant, *adj.* noisy, loud.

budget, *s. m.* budget.

buffet, *s. m.* sideboard; buffet; refreshment room.

buisson, *s. m.* bush, shrub.

bulbe, *s. m.* bulb.
bulle, *s. f.* bubble; bull.
bulletin, *s.m.* bulletin.
bureau, *s. m.* (writing-) desk; bureau, office; department; board, committee; ~ *de location* box-office; ~ *de poste* post-office; ~ *de tabac* tobacconist's (shop); ~ *central* exchange.
burlesque, *adj.* burlesque, ridiculous; — *s.m.* burlesque.
but, *s. m.* butt, target; goal; aim, object, purpose; scope.
buter, *v.n.* stumble (*contre* against); se ~ grow obstinate.
butin, *s. m.* booty.

butte, *s. f.* hill, mound, knoll.

C

ça, *pron.* that; *comme* ~ in that way; — *adv.* here; — *int.* now then!
cabaret, *s. m.* tavern; wine-shop; night-club, music-hall.
cabine, *s. f.* cabin, berth; cage, car; ~ *téléphonique* call-box.
cabinet, *s. m.* small room; study; water-closet; office; business; cabinet (council); cabinet; ~ *de consultation* consulting room; surgery.
câble, *s. m.* rope, cable.
cabriolet, *s. m.* cabriolet,
cacao, *s. m.* cocoa.
cacher, *v.a.* hide, conceal; se ~ hide oneself.
cadeau, *s. m.* present, gift.
cadet, *adj. & s.m.* younger, junior; cadet.

café, *s. m.* coffee; café, coffee-house; ~ *au lait* white coffee; ~ *concert* music-hall.
cafetière, *s. f.* coffee-pot.
cage, *s.f.* cage; coop; case, crate.
cahier, *s. m.* exercise book.
caillou, *s.m.* pebble, stone.
caisse, *s.f.* box, case; cash(-box), till, cashier's office; drum; *en* ~ in hand.
caissier, -ère, *s.m.f.* cashier.
calcul, *s. m.* calculation, reckoning; arithmetic.
calculateur, *s. m.* calculator, computer.
calculer, *v.a. & n.* calculate, reckon, compute.
caleçon, *s. m.* pants (*pl.*); ~ *de bain* bathing-drawers (*pl.*).
calendrier, *s.m.* calendar.
calme, *adj.* quiet, calm; *fig.* cool; — *s. m.* calm.
calmer, *v. a.* quiet, calm.
calomnier, *v. a.* calumniate, slander.
calorie, *s. f.* calorie.
calorifère, *s. m.* heating apparatus.
calvaire, *s. m.* Calvary.
camarade, *s. m.* comrade, fellow; ~ *d'école* school-friend.
cambrioler, *v. a.* burgle, break into.
cambrioleur, *s.m.* burglar.
caméra, *s. f.* (cine-)camera.
camion, *s. m.* lorry.
camp, *s. m.* camp; side.
campagnard, *s. m.* countryman, peasant.
campagne, *s. f.* country-(side), fields (*pl.*); campaign, expedition.
camper, *v. n.* camp.

camping, *s. m.* camping; *(terrain de)* ~ camping site; *matériel de* ~ camping equipment; *faire du* ~ camp.

canal, *s. m.* canal; channel.

canapé, *s. m.* sofa, couch.

canard, *s. m.* duck, drake.

candidature, *s. f.* candidature, candidacy.

canif, *s. m.* penknife.

canne, *s. f.* stick, cane; ~ *à pêche* fishing-rod.

canon, *s. m.* gun, cannon

canot, *s. m.* boat.

cantine, *s. f.* canteen.

canton, *s.m.* canton, district.

cantonade, *s.f.* wings *(pl.); à la* ~ behind the scenes.

caoutchouc, *s.m.* rubber; waterproof, mackintosh.

capable, *adj.* capable, able; efficient; fit.

capacité, *s. f.* capacity, (cap)ability.

capitaine, *s. m.* captain, leader.

capital, *adj.* capital, chief; —*s.m.* main point; capital, fund.

capitale, *s.f.* capital; capital letter.

capitalisme, *s. m.* capitalism.

capituler, *v. n.* capitulate.

caprice, *s. m.* caprice.

capricieux, *adj.* capricious, fickle.

capsule, *s. f.* capsule.

captif, -ive, *adj. & s. m. f.* captive.

captiver, *v. a.* captivate.

capturer, *v. a.* capture.

car, *conj.* for, because.

caractère, *s. m.* character, temper; nature; type, print, letter.

caractériser, *v.a.* characterize, distinguish.

caractéristique, *adj. &. s.f.* characteristic.

cardinal, *s.m.* cardinal; — *adj.* chief, cardinal; *points card naux* cardinal points.

caresser, *v.a.* caress, fondle; foster.

caricature, *s. f.* caricature.

carnaval, *s. m.* carnival.

carnet, *s. m.* note-book, pocket-book; book of tickets; ~ *de chèques* cheque-book.

carotte, *s. f.* carrot.

carreau, *s. m.* square; (paving-)tile; tile flooring; pane; diamond.

carrière, *s.f.* career; race-course; race; quarry.

carrosserie, *s.f.* body.

carte, *s.f.* card; map; ticket; bill (of fare); *partie de* ~s game of cards; ~ *postale* postcard; ~ *routière* road-map; ~ *de visite* visiting-card; ~ *marine* chart; ~ *d'entrée* admission ticket; ~ *grise* driving licence; *à la* ~ à la carte.

carton, *s. m.* pasteboard, cardboard; (paper)box.

cas, *s.m.* case, event; instance, fact; *dans le* ~ *où, en* ~ *de* in case; *en tout* ~ in any case.

caserne, *s.f.* barracks *(pl.).*

casquette, *s. f.* cap.

casser, *v. a. & n.* break; crack, snap; annul; dismiss; *se* ~ break, get broken.

casserole, *s. v.* saucepan

casuel, -elle, *adj.* casual,

accidental.

catalogue, *s. m.* catalogue.

catastrophe, *s. f.* catastrophe, disaster.

catégorie, *s. f.* category,
class.

cathédrale, *s. f.* cathedral.

catholicisme, *s. m.* catholicism.

catholique, *adj.* catholic.

cause, *s. f.* cause, reason,
ground, case; *à ~ de*
on account of, owing to.

causer[1], *v. a.* cause.

causer[2], *v.n.* talk, converse, chat.

cavalerie, *s. f.* cavalry.

cavalier, *s. m.* horseman,
cavalier.

cave, *s. f.* cave; cellar.

caverne, *s. f.* cave(rn).

ce[1], c', *pron.* this, it.

ce[2], cet; cette; *dem. adj.*
(pl. ces) this *(pl.*
these); that *(pl.* those).

ceci, *pron.* this.

céder, *v. a.* give up, yield,
cede, make over; *v. n.*
yield, give in, up.

ceinture, *s. f.* belt, girdle.

cela, *pron.* that, it; *c'est*
~ that's right.

célébration, *s. f.* celebration.

célèbre, *adj.* celebrated.

célébrer, *v. a.* celebrate.

célibataire, *adj.* unmarried, single.

cellule, *s. f.* cell.

celtique, *adj.* Celtic.

celui, celle, *dem. pron.*
(pl. ceux, celles) he,
sie, they, those.

celui-ci, celui-là, celle-ci,
celle-là, *dem. pron.*

(pl. ceux-ci, -là, cel-
les-ci, -là) this one,
this person, the lat-
ter, these ones.

cément, *s. m* cement.

cendre, *s. f.* ash(es).

cendrier, *s. m.* ash-tray.

cent, *adj. & s. m.* hun-
dred; *pour ~* per cent.

centime, *s. m.* centime.

centimètre, *s. m.* cen-
timetre.

central, *adj.* central.

centrale, *s. f. ~ électri-*
que power-plant, -sta-
tion.

centre, *s. m.* centre.

cependant, *conj.* however,
yet, still, neverthe-
less; in the meantime;
~ que while.

céramique, *s. f.* ceramics;
— *adj.* ceramic.

cercle, *s. m.* circle, ring;
party, club.

cercueil, *s. m.* coffin.

cérémonie, *s. f.* cere-
mony.

cerf, *s. m.* stag, hart,

cerise, *s. f.* cherry.

certain, *adj.* certain, sure.

certainement, *adv.* cer-
tainly, surely.

certificat, *s. m.* certificate, testimonial.

certifier, *v. a.* certify.

certitude, *s. f.* certainty.

cerveau, *s. m.* brain(s).

ces *see* ce[2]

cesse, *s. f.* ceasing,
pause; *sans ~* unceas-
ingly.

cesser, *v. a. & n.* cease,
stop; give up; *faire ~*
put an end to.

c'est-à-dire, *conj.* that
is to say, viz., i.e.

cet *see* ce[2].

ceux *see* celui.

chacun, *pron.* each, each
one, every one; every-
body.

chagrin, *s. m.* grief, sorrow, vexation; — *adj.*
sad, sorrowful; sor-
ry; gloomy.

chaîne, *s. f.* chain; range
(of mountains); *~ de*

montage assembly line.

chair, *s. f.* flesh; pulp (of fruit).

chaire, *s. f.* chair; pulpit; seat, see.

chaise, *s. f.* chair.

châle, *s. m.* shawl.

chaleur, *s. f.* heat; fire.

chambre, *s.f.* room; bedroom; chamber; apartment; hall; ∼ à *coucher* bedroom; ∼ Haute Upper House; ∼ *de commerce* chamber of commerce.

chameau, *s.m.* camel.

champ, *s.m.* field, country; *fig.* space, opportunity, theme.

champagne, *s. m.* champagne.

champignon, *s. m.* mushroom.

champion, -onne, *s.m. f.* champion.

championnat, *s. m.* championship.

chance, *s. f.* chance, fortune, risk; luck.

chancelier, *s. m.* chancellor.

chancellerie, *s.f.* chancery.

chandail, *s. m.* sweater, pullover.

chandelle, *s. f.* candle.

change, *s. m.* change, changing; succession; (foreign) exchange, barter; *agent de* ∼ stockbroker; *bureau de* ∼ exchange office; *lettre de* ∼ bill of exchange.

changer, *v. a.* change, alter; exchange; *se* ∼ betransformed; change one's clothes.

chanson, *s. f.* song.

chant, *s. m.* singing; song, tune; chant(ing).

chanter, *v. a. & n.* warble; chant; praise.

chanteur, -euse, *s.m.f.* singer

chantier, *s.m.* yard, timber-yard, work-yard.

chapeau. *s.m.* hat; bonnet; cap.

chapelain, *s. m.* chaplain.

chapelle, *s. f.* chapel.

chapitre, *s.m.* chapter; subject, head.

chaque, *adj.* each, every.

charbon, *s. m.* coal; embers *(pl.)*; ∼ *de bois* charcoal.

charcuterie, *s. f.* pork-butchery.

charcutier, -ière, *s. m. f.* pork-butcher.

charge, *s. f.* load, burden; post, function, charge, office; attack; accusation.

charger, *v. a. & n.* load; burden; charge; entrust.

charité, *s. f.* charity.

charmant, *adj.* charming.

charme, *s. m.* charm.

charpente, *s.f.* timber-work.

charpentier, *s.m.* carpenter.

charrette, *s:f.* cart, wagon.

charrue, *s. f.* plough.

charte, *s. f.* charter.

chasse, *s. f.* chase, hunt(ing), shooting.

chasser, *v. a. & n.* chase, pursue, hunt, shoot, go shooting; drive out.

chasseur, *s.m.* hunter; page-boy.

chaste, *adj.* chaste, pure.

chat, *s. m.* (he-)cat.

châtaigne, *s. f.* chestnut.

château, *s.m.* castle; palace.

chatte, *s. f.* (she-)cat.

chaud, *adj. & adv.* hot, warm; ardent.

chauffage, *s. m.* heating,

warming; ~ *central* central heating.

chauffe-bain, *s. m.* geyser.

chauffer, *v. a. & n.* heat, warm; urge on; coach.

chauffeur, *s. m.* driver.

chausse, *s.f.* hose

chausser, *v. a. & n.* put on (shoes etc.), wear; se ~ put on one's stockings etc.

chaussette, *s. f.* sock.

chaussure, *s. f.* footwear, shoes *(pl.)*.

chauve, *adj.* bald.

chef, *s. f.* chief; ~ *de train* guard; ~ *d'orchestre* conductor.

chemin, *s. m.* road, way; lane; *se mettre en* ~ start; ~ *de fer* railway.

cheminée, *s. f.* chimney. fireplace, funnel.

chemise, *s. f.* shirt.

chêne, *s. m.* oak(-tree).

chèque, *s. m.* cheque; ~ *en blanc* blank cheque; ~ *de voyage* traveller's cheque.

cher, chère, *adj.* dear.

chercher, *v. a.* seek, look for, search for.

chéri, -e, *adj.* dear; — *s. m. f.* darling.

cheval, *s. m.* horse; *à* ~ on horseback; *monter à* ~ ride.

chevalerie, *s. f.* chivalry.

chevalier, *s. m.* knight.

chevelure, *s. f.* hair.

cheveu, *s. m.* hair; *en* ~ bareheaded.

cheville, *s.f.* wooden pin, peg; ankle.

chèvre, *s.f.* (she-)goat.

chevreau, *s.m.* kid- (leather).

chez, *prep.* at, in, at the house of; ~ X at X's.

chic, *adj.* smart, spruce, fashionable; — *s. m.* chic; trick; elegance.

chien, -enne, *s. m. f.* dog.

chiffon, *s. m.* rag, scrap; chiffon.

chiffre, *s. m.* figure, digit; number.

chignon, *s.m.* knot (of hair), bun.

chimie, *s.f.* chemistry.

chimique, *adj.* chemical.

chimiste, *s. m. f.* chemist.

chinois, -e (Ch.), *adj &* *s.m.f.* Chinese.

chirurgie, *s. f.* surgery.

chirurgien, -enne, *s.m.f.* surgeon.

choc, *s.m.* shock, clash, collision.

chocolat, *s. m.* chocolate.

chœur, *s. m.* chorus; choir.

choisir, *v.a.* choose, pick out, select.

choix, *s. m.* choice.

chômage, *s. m.* stoppage, cessation of work; unemployment.

choquer, *v. a.* run into, strike against, collide with; shock, offend; se ~ come into collision; be shocked.

chose, *s. f.* thing, object, matter; goods; event; *quelque* ~ something, anything.

chou, *s. m.* cabbage, cole.

chou-fleur, *s. m.* cauli- flower.

chrétien, -enne, *adj. & s.m. f.* Christian.

christianisme, *s.m.* Chris- tianity.

chronique, *adj.* chronic; — *s. f.* chronicle.

chuchoter, *v.n.&a.* whisper.

chute, *s. f.* fall, down- fall, descent; slope.

ci, *adv.* here.

ci-dessous, *adv.* below, underneath.

ci-dessus, *adv.* above; aforesaid.

cidre, s. m. cider.

ciel, s. m. (pl. **cieux**) heaven; sky; weather; climate.

cierge, s. m. wax candle.

cigare, s. m. cigar.

cigarette, s. f. cigarette.

cigogne, s. f. stork.

cil, s. m. eyelash.

cime, s. f. top, summit.

ciment, s. m. cement.

cimetière, s. m. cemetery; churchyard.

cinéma, s. m. cinema.

cinérama, s. m. cinerama.

cinq, adj. & s. m. five; fifth.

cinquante, adj. & s. m. fifty; fiftieth.

circonstance, s.f. circumstance; occurrence, occasion, event.

circuit, s. m. circuit.

circulation, s. f. circulation; currency; traffic.

circuler, v. n. circulate; circulez! move on!

cire, s. f. wax.

cirer, v. a. wax; polish.

ciseau, s.m. chisel.

ciseaux, s. m. pl. scissors.

citation, s.f. citation.

cité, s. f. city, town.

citer, v.a. cite; quote.

citoyen, -enne, s.m.f. citizen.

citron, s. m. lemon.

citronnade, s.f. lemon squash.

civil, adj. civil; — s. m. civilian.

civilisation, s. f. civilization, culture.

clair, adj. light, clear.

clapet, s. m. valve.

claquement, s. m. clap(ping); snap.

claquer, v. n. a. crack, clap; chatter; bang.

clarté, s. f. light, brightness; clearness.

classe, s. f. class; order, rank; form, class-room.

classer, v.a. class, rank.

classifier, v.a. classify.

classique, adj. classic(al).

clause, s. f. clause.

clé, clef, s. f. key; spanner, wrench; fig. clue; ~ de contact ignition key.

clerc, s. m. clerk; scholar.

clergé, s. m. clergy.

clérical, adj. clerical.

client, s. m. client, customer, patron.

clientèle, s. f. clients (pl.).

cligner, v. a. & n. wink.

clignotant, s. m. indicator.

clignoter, v.a.&n. blink, wink.

climat, s. m. climate.

clinique, adj. & s.f. clinic, clinical.

cloche, s. f. bell.

cloître, s. m. cloister.

clore*, v. a. shut, close.

clos, adj. closed.

clôture, s. f. enclosure, fence; close.

clou, s. m. nail, stud; boil, furuncle.

clouer, v. a. nail (down).

club, s. m. club.

cocher, s. m. coachman, driver.

cochon, s. m. pig, swine.

code, s. m. code; law, rule.

cœur, s. m. heart; fig. mind, soul, courage; par ~ by heart.

coffre, s. m. chest.

coffre-fort, s. m. safe.

cognac, s. m. cognac.

cogner, v. n. & a. beat, knock, strike; se ~ knock against.

coiffer, v. a. put on (hat); dress, do s.o.'s hair.

coiffeur, -euse, s.m.f. hairdresser.

coiffure, *s. f.* head-dress, cap; hair-do; *salon de* ~ hairdresser.

coin, *s. m.* corner; angle.

coïncider, *v.n.* coincide.

coke, *s.m.* coke.

col, *s.m.* collar; neck.

colère, *s.f.* anger.

colis, *s.m.* parcel; item (of luggage).

collaborateur, -trice, *s. m. f.* fellow worker; collaborator.

collaborer, *v.n.* work jointly, collaborate.

collectif, -ive, *adj.* collective.

collection, *s. f.* collection.

collège, *s.m.* college; grammar school.

collègue, *s.m.f.* colleague, fellow worker.

coller, *v.a.* stick, paste.

collet, *s.m.* collar; neck.

collier, *s.m.* necklace; collar.

colline, *s.f.* hill.

collision, *s.f.* collision; *entrer en* ~ collide.

colombe, *s. f.* dove.

colonel, *s.m.* colonel.

colonie, *s. f.* colony; dominion.

colonne, *s.f.* column.

coloré, *adj.* coloured; colourful.

colossal, *adj.* colossal.

combat, *s.m.* fight, combat.

combattre, *v.a.&n.* fight (against), combat (with).

combien, *adv.* (~ *de*) how much, how many, how far; ~ *de temps?* how long?

combinaison, *s.f.* combination.

combiner, *v.a.* combine, unite; contrive, devise.

comédie, *s.f.* comedy.

comédien, *s.m.* comedian, actor.

comestible, *adj.* edible.

comique, *adj.* comic; — *s. m.* comic actor.

comité, *s. m.* committee.

commandant, *s. m.* commander.

commande, *s.f.* order.

commandement, *s. m.* command, order; commandment.

commander, *v. a.* command, order; control.

comme, *adv. & conj.* as, like; as . . . as; while; ~ *il faut* decent, proper; *tout* ~ just like; ~ *si* as if, as though.

commémorer, *v.a.* commemorate.

commençant, -e, *s. m. f.* beginner; — *adj.* beginning.

commencement, *s.m.* beginning.

commencer, *v. a. & n.* begin, commence.

comment, *adv.* how, in what manner; why; ~ *allez-vous?* how are you?; ~ *(dites-vous)?* (I beg your) pardon?

commentaire, *s. m.* comment; commentary.

commenter, *v. a.* comment (on); criticize.

commerçant, -e, *s. m. f.* merchant, dealer.

commerce, *s. m.* commerce, trade; *voyageur de* ~ commercial traveller; ~ *de gros* wholesale trade; *faire le* ~ trade.

commercer, *v. n.* trade, deal with, in.

commercial, *adj.* commercial.

commettre, *v. a.* commit; *se* ~ commit oneself.

commis, *s.m.* clerk, employee.

commissaire, *s.m.* commisary; commissioner.

commissariat, *s.m.* police-station.

commission, *s. f.* commission; charge; committee; errand.

commode, *adj.* convenient, handy, comfortable; — *s. f.* chest of drawers.

commun, *adj.* common; joint; usual; vulgar; *peu* ~ unusual; — *s.m.* common people.

communauté, *s. f.* community.

commune, *s. f.* district.

communication, *s. f.* communication, message; call.

communier, *v. n.* communicate.

communion, *s.f.* communion.

communiqué, *s. m.* communiquè.

communiquer, *v. a. & n.* communicate.

compact, *adj.* compact.

compagnie, *s.f.* company.

compagnon, *s. m.* companion, fellow.

comparaison, *s. f.* comparison.

comparer, *v. a.* compare.

compartiment, *s. m.* compartment; ~ *de fumeurs* smoking compartment; ~ *pour non-fumeurs* non-smoker.

compas, *s.m.* compass(es).

compatriote, *s. m. f.* compartiot, (fellow) countryman.

compensation, *s. f.* compensation.

compenser, *v.a.&n.* com-

pensate.

compétent, *adj.* competent.

compétiteur, -trice, *s. m. f.* competitor.

compétition, *s. f.* competition.

compilation, *s. f.* compilation.

compiler, *v. a.* compile.

complainte, *s.f.* complaint.

complaisance, *s. f.* complaisance, kindness.

complaisant, *adj.* complaisant, obliging, kind.

complément, *s. m.* complement; object.

complémentaire, *adj.* complementary.

complet, -ète, *adj.* complete, full.

compléter, *v.a.* complete.

complexe, *adj.* complex, compound.

complication, *s. f.* complication.

compliment, *s. m.* compliment; congratulation.

compliquer, *v.a.* complicate.

comploter, *v.a.* plot.

composant, -e, *adj. & s. f.* component.

composer, *v. a.* compose, se ~ *de* be composed of, consist of.

compositeur, -trice ,*s. m. f.* composer.

composition, *s. f.* composition; paper.

comprendre, *v. a.* comprehend; unterstand.

comprimé, -e, *adj.* pressed; — *s. m.* tablet.

compromettre, *v. a.* compromise, commit; se ~ commit oneself.

compromis, *s. m.* compromise.

comptabilité, *s. f.* book-keeping, accounts *(pl.)*

compte, *s.m.* account; amount, sum; ~ *courant* current account; *faire le* ~ *de* count; *régler un* ~ settle an account; ~ *rendu* report, account, statement; review; *tenir* ~ *de* take into account.

compter, *v. a. & n.* count, reckon, calculate.

comptoir, *s. m.* counter.

computer, *v. a.* compute.

comte, *s. m.* count.

comtesse, *s. f.* countess.

concéder, *v. a.* grant.

concentration, *s. f.* concentration; reduction.

concentrer, *v. a.* condense, concentrate.

concept, -tion, *s. m. f.* concept(ion), idea.

concernant, *prep.* concerning.

concerner, *v. a.* concern, relate to.

concert, *s. m.* concert.

concevoir*, *v. a. & n.* conceive; think; imagine; apprehend.

concierge, *s. f. m.* porter.

concile, *s. m.* council.

concis, *adj.* concise.

conclure*, *v.a.&n.* conclude, end.

conclusion, *s.f.* conclusion, end.

concombre, *s. m.* cucumber.

concorder, *v.n.* agree.

concourir, *v. n.* contribute, concur; compte.

concours, *s. m.* concourse; help; assistance; competition.

concret, -ète, *adj.* concrete.

concurrence, *s. f.* competition; rivalry.

concurrent, *s. m.* competitor; rival.

condamnation, *s. f.* condemnation; sentence.

condamner, *v.a.* condemn, sentence.

condenser, *v. a.* condense.

condition, *s. f.* condition, state; service; stipulation, condition; *à* ~ *que* on condition that, provided that.

conditionnel, *adj.* conditional.

conditionnement, *s.m.* ~ *de l'air* air-conditioning.

conducteur, -trice, *s. m. f.* conductor; driver.

conduire*, *v. a. & n.* conduct, lead; drive; show (to), take (to); manage; *permis de* ~ driving licence.

conduit, *s. m.* pipe, tube.

conduite, *s. f.* conducting, leading; driving; behaviour, conduct.

cône, *s. m.* cone.

confection, *s. f.* readymade clothes *(pl.)*.

confédération, *s. f.* confederation, confederacy.

conférence, *s. f.* comparison; conference; lecture; *maître de* ~*s* lecturer; *faire une* ~ deliver a lecture.

conférencier, -ère, *s. m. f.* lecturer.

conférer, *v.a.* grant, confer, bestow; compare.

confesser, *v.a.* confess.

confession, *s. f.* confession.

confiance, *s. f.* confidence, trust, reliance; *avoir* ~ count on, trust.

confiant, *adj.* confident.

confidence, *s. f.* confidence.

confidentiel, -elle *adj.*

confidential.

confier, v.a. trust; entrust, give in charge.

confinement, s. m. imprisonment.

confiner, v. n. & a. confine.

confirmation, s.f. confirmation.

confirmer, v.a. confirm.

confiserie, s.f. confectionery, sweet-shop.

confiture, s.f. jam, preserve.

conflit, s. m. conflict.

confondre, v. a. confound.

conformer, v. a. conform, adapt; se ~ à conform oneself (to).

confort, s.m. comfort, ease.

confortable, adj. comfortable.

confrère, s.m. fellow-worker, colleague.

confronter, v. a. confront, compare.

confus, adj. confused.

confusion, s. f. confusion.

congé, s. m. leave, holiday; permission; discharge; warning, notice; donner ~ give notice (to); dismiss; prendre ~ de take leave of; être en ~ be on holiday.

congédier, v. a. dismiss.

congratulation, s. f. congratulation.

congrès, s.m. congress, assembly.

conjecture, s.f. conjecture.

conjecturer, v.a.&n. conjecture, guess.

conjonction, s.f. conjunction, union.

connaissance, s. f. knowledge; acquaintance; faire ~ avec get acquainted with.

connaître*, v.a. know, understand; be acquainted with.

connexion, s.f. connection.

conquérir*, v. a. & n. conquer; win (over).

conscience, s.f. consciousness; conscience; avoir la ~ de be conscious of, be aware of.

conscient, adj. conscious.

conscrit, s. m. conscript.

conseil, s. m. counsel, advice; adviser; council, board, staff.

conseiller¹, -ère, s. m. f. counsellor, councillor.

conseiller², v. a.&n. advise, counsel.

consentir, v. n. consent, agree (à to).

conséquence, s. f. consequence, result.

conséquent, adj. consistent; par ~ consequently.

conservatoire, s. m. conservatory.

conserver, v.a. keep, preserve; tin.

considérable, adj. considerable.

considération, s. f. consideration; esteem.

considérer, v. a. consider; esteem.

consigne, s. f. cloak-room, left-luggage office.

consigner, v.a. deposit.

consister, v.n. consist (of), be made (of).

consoler, v.a. console.

consommateur, -trice, s. m. f. consumer, customer.

consommer, v.a. consummate; consume.

consomption, s.f. consumption.

consonne, s. f. consonant.

conspiration, s.f. conspiracy.

conspirer, *v. a. & n.* conspire, plot.

constant, *adj.* constant, firm.

constipation, *s.f.* constipation.

constituer, *v. a.* constitute, compose.

constitution, *s. f.* constitution.

constitutionnel, -elle, *adj.* constitutional.

constructeur, *s. m.* builder.

construction, *s.f.* construction, building.

construire*, *v.a.* build, construct.

consul, *s. m.* consul.

consulat, *s. m.* consulate.

consulter, *v.a.* consult.

consumer, *v. a.* consume.

contact, *s.m.* contact, touch, switch.

contaminer, *v. a.* contaminate.

conte, *s.m.* story, tale.

contemplation, *s.f.* contemplation.

contempler, *v.a. & n.* contemplate.

contemporain, -e, *adj. &* *s. m. f.* contemporary.

contenance, *s. f.* capacity, contents *(pl.)*.

contenir, *v.a.* contain, hold; restrain; **se ~** restrain oneself.

content, *adj.* content.

contentement, *s. m.* content, satisfaction.

contenter, *v.a.* content, satisfy; **se ~** be contented, do with.

contenu, *s.m.* contents *(pl.)*.

conter, *v.a. & n.* tell, relate.

continent, *s. m.* continent.

continental, *adj.* continental:

continuation, *s.f.* con-

tinuation, continuance.

continuel, -elle, *adj.* continual.

continuer, *v.a. & n.* go on (with), keep on; **se ~** be continued.

contour, *s.m.* contour, outline.

contracter, *v. a.* contract, bargain for.

contradiction, *s. f.* contradiction.

contraindre*, *v. a.* compel, force; **se ~ ·** restrain oneself.

contrainte, *s.f.* constraint.

contraire, *adj. & s. m.* contrary; *au ~* on the contrary.

contrairement, *adv.* **~** *à* contrary to.

contraste, *s. m.* contrast.

contraster, *v. n.* contrast *(avec* with).

contrat, *s.m.* contract.

contre, *prep.* against.

contrée, *s.f.* country.

contrefaçon, *s. f.* counterfeit(ing); forgery.

contrefaire, *v. a.* counterfeit; pirate; forge.

contre-partie, *s. f.* counterpart.

contresigner, *v. a.* countersign.

contribuant, *s. m.* contributor.

contribuer, *v. n.* contribute *(à* to).

contribution, *s.f.* contribution, tax.

contrôle, *s.m.* control, check; hall-mark.

contrôler, *v.a.* control, check.

contrôleur, *s. m.* ticket-collector.

contusion, *s. f.* bruise.

convaincre, *v.a.* convince.

convenable, *adj.* suitable, appropriate.

convenance, *s.f.* suitability, convenience.

convenir, *v.n.* suit, be convenient (to), fit.

conventionnel, -elle, *adj.* conventional.

conversation, *s.f.* conversation, talk.

converser, *v. n.* converse.

convertir, *v.a.* convert.

conviction, *s. f.* conviction.

convier, *v.a.* invite.

convive, *s.m.* guest.

convoi, *s.m.* convoy; funeral procession.

convoquer *v.a.* convoke.

coopération, *s. f.* co-operation.

coopérer, *v. n.* co-operate.

copie, *s. f.* (fair) copy.

copier, *v.a.* copy.

coq, *s. m.* cock.

coquille, *s. f.* shell.

coquin, *s.m.* rogue.

corail, *s.m.* coral.

corbeau, *s. m.* raven.

corbeille, *s. f.* basket.

corde, *s.f.* cord, rope.

cordial, *adj.* cordial.

cordonnier, *s.m.* shoemaker.

corne, *s. f.* horn; hooter.

corneille, *s. f.* crow, rook.

cornet, *s. m.* horn; cornet.

cornichon, *s. m.* gherkin.

corporation, *s. f.* corporation.

corps, *s. m.* body, corpse; corporation, corps.

correct, *adj.* correct.

correction, *s. f.* correction.

correspondance, *s. f.* correspondence; relation; communication; connection.

correspondant, *adj.* corresponding.

correspondre, *v. n.* correspond; communicate.

corriger, *v.a.* correct.

corrompre, *v.a.* corrupt, spoil; se ~ become corrupted.

corruption, *s. f.* corruption.

corset, *s. m.* stays *(pl.)*.

cortège, *s. m.* escort.

cosmétique, *adj.* cosmetic; — *s. m.* ~s cosmetics.

cosmonaute, *s. m.* cosmonaut, spacemen.

costume, *s. m.* dress, costume; ~ *de bain (s)* bathing-costume.

côte, *s. f.* rib; slope; shore.

côté, *s. m.* side, part; *à* ~ by the side; *de* ~ on one side; *d'un* ~ on the one hand; *de l'autre* ~ on the other hand; *passer à* ~ pass by; *à* ~ *de* next (door) to; beside.

côtelette, *s. f.* chop.

coton, *s. m.* cotton.

cottage, *s. m.* cottage.

cou, *s. m.* neck.

couche, *s. f.* bed; napkin, diaper; coat; layer; *(pl.)* confinement.

coucher, *v. a.* put to bed; lay; *v.n.* lie down; sleep; *être couché* lie; se ~ go to bed, lie down; — *s. m.* bedtime; setting.

couchette, *s.f.* berth, bunk; napkin.

coude, *s. m.* elbow; angle, bend.

coudre*, *v. a. & n.* sew.

couler, *v.n.* flow, run, stream; leak; sink.

couleur, *s. f.* colour.

coulisse, *s. f.* groove; slip, wings *(pl.)*; *dans les* ~s behind the scenes.

couloir, *s.m.* passage; corridor; lobby.

coup, *s. m.* blow, stroke, knock; smack; pull;

kick; shot; draught; cast, move; *d'un seul* ~ at once; ~ *de feu* rush hours *(pl.)*; *de froid* chill; ~ *de main* sudden attack; ~ *d'œil* glance, look; ~ *de soleil* sunstroke.

coupe, *s.f.* wine-cup.

couper, *v.a.* cut; cut down, off, up; divide; cross; mix; se ~ cut oneself, cut one's (finger etc.).

couple, *s. f.* pair, brace; *m.* couple.

cour, *s. f.* (court)yard; court; courting, courtship; *faire la* ~ *à* court, make love to.

courage, *s. m.* courage.

courageux, -euse, *adj.* courageous, brave.

courant, *adj.* current; running; — *s.m.* current; stream; course run; ~ *d'air* draught.

courbe, *s. f.* curve, bend.

courbé, *adj.* curved; bent.

courber, *v. a. & n.* bend, bow; se ~ bend, be bent; bow.

courir*, *v. n.* run; hurry; flow; be curent.

couronne, *s.f.* crown.

couronner, *v.a.* crown.

courrier, *s. m.* messenger, courier, post, mail.

cours, *s. m.* course; current, flow; currency.

course, *s. f.* race, run; course; drive.

court, *adj.* short, brief; — *adv.* short; suddenly; — *s. m.* tennis-court.

courtiser, *v. a.* pay court to, court.

courtois, *adj.* courteous, polite.

courtoisie, *s. f.* courtesy.

cousin, -e *s. m. f.* cousin.

coussin, *s.m.* cushion.

coût, *s.m.* cost, price.

couteau, *s.m.* knife.

coûter, *v. n. & a.* cost.

coûteux, -euse, *adj.* costly, expensive, dear; *peu* ~ inexpensive.

coutume, *s.f.* custom, habit; *de* ~ customary.

couture, *s.f.* sewing, seam; needlework; scar.

couturière, *s.m.* dressmaker.

couvent, *s.m.* convent.

couver, *v.a.* brood (on), sit; hatch, breed.

couvercle, *s. m.* cover, lid, cap.

couvert, *adj.* covered; covert, sheltered; cloudy; secret; — *s.m.* set (of fork and spoon); cover; protection; *mettre le* ~ lay the table.

couverture, *s. f.* cover(ing); blanket; ~s bedclothes.

couvrir*, *v.a.* cover; load; protect; be sufficent for.

crabe, *s. m.* crab.

cracher, *v.n. & a.* spit.

craie, *s. f.* chalk.

craindre, *v.a.* fear, be afraid of.

crainte, *s. f.* fear; *de* ~ *de* for fear of; *de* ~ *que* lest.

crampe, *s.f.* cramp.

crampon, *s.m.* cramp.

crâne, *s. m.* skull; — *adj.* bold.

craquer, *v.n.* crack.

cravate, *s. f.* (neck)tie.

crayon, *s. m.* pencil; crayon.

créance, *s. f.* credence, belief, trust.

créancier, -ère, *s. m. f.* creditor.

création, *s. f.* creation.

créature, *s. f.* creature.

crèche, *s. f.* crèche.

crédit, *s. m.* credit; *à* ~ on credit.

créditer, *v.a.* credit.

crediteur, *s.m.* creditor.

créer, *v.a.* create, make.

crème, *s. f.* cream, custard; ~ *à raser* shaving cream.

crémerie, *s. f.* dairy.

crêpe, *s. m.* crape, crêpe.

creuser, *v. a.* dig; deepen.

creux, -euse, *adj.* hollow, empty; — *s. m.* hollow.

crevaison, *s. f.* puncture.

crever, *v. a. & n.* burst; puncture; die.

cri, *s. m.* cry, scream; call, shout.

crible, *s.m.* sieve, screen.

cric, *s. m.* jack.

crier, *v.a. & n.* cry (out).

crime, *s. m.* crime, guilt.

criminel, -elle, *adj. & s. m. f.* criminal.

crise, *s. f.* crisis.

crisper, *v.a.* contract, shrivel.

cristal, *s. m.* crystal.

critique, *adj.* critical; — *s.f.* criticism, critique; *s.m.f.* critic, reviewer.

crochet, *s. m.* hook; crochet(-work); hanger.

croire*, *v. a. & n.* believe, credit, trust; think.

croiser, *v.a.* cross; *v.n.* cruise.

croître*, *v.n.* grow, increase; grow up; *v.a.* increase.

croix, *s. f.* cross.

croquis, *s.m.* sketch.

crouler, *v. n.* fall (to pieces), fall in.

croûte, *s. f.* crust; *casser la* ~ have a snack.

croyance, *s.f.* belief, faith; creed.

croyant, -e, *s. m. f.* believer; — *adj.* faithful.

cru, *adj.* raw; crude.

cruauté, *s. f.* cruelty.

crue, *s. f.* rise, growth.

cruel, -elle, *adj.* cruel.

crypte, *s. f.* crypte.

cube, *s. m.* cube.

cueillir*, *v.a.* gather, pick, glean.

cuiller, -ère, *s. f.* spoon; ~ *à pot* ladle; ~ *à café* teaspoon.

cuir, *s. m.* skin; leather.

cuire*, *v. a. & n.* cook; boil; roast; burn; *faire trop* ~ overdo.

cuisine, *s. f.* kitchen; cooking, cookery; *batterie de* ~ kitchen utensils; *de* ~ culinary; *livre de* ~ cookery-book.

cuisinière, *s.f.* cook; kitchen range, cooker.

cuisse, *s. f.* thigh; leg.

cuit, *adj.* cooked, baked.

cuivre, *s. m.* copper.

cul, *s. m.* bottom.

culinaire, *adj.* culinary.

culotte, *s. f.* panties; breeches *(pl.)*.

culte, *s. m.* cult, worship.

cultivateur, -trice, *s. m. f.* farmer.

cultiver, *v.a.* cultivate, till; *fig.* improve.

culture, *s.f.* culture.

culturel, -elle, *adj.* cultural.

cure, *s. f.* care; cure.

curé, *s. m.* priest; vicar.

cure-dent, *s. m.* toothpick.

curieux, -euse, *adj.* curious, strange, inquisitive.

curiosité, *s. f.* curiosity; ~s sights.

cuve, *s. f.* tub, vat.

cuvette, *s. f.* ~ *(de lavabo)* wash-basin.

cycle, *s. m.* cycle.

cygne, *s. m.* swan.

cylindre, *s. m.* cylinder.

D

dactylo(graphe), *s. m. f.* typist.

dame, *s.f.* lady; queen.

danger, *s. m.* danger.

dangereux, -euse, *adj.* dangerous.

danois, -e (D.), *adj.* & *s. m. f.* Dane, Danish.

dans, *prep.* in, into; inside; during; ~ *le temps* formerly.

danse, *s. f.* dance.

danser, *v. n.* dance.

danseur, *s. m.* dancer.

danseuse: *s. f.* ballet-girl, dancer.

date, *s.f.* date; *prendre* ~ fix a day.

dater, *v. a.* & *n.* date.

datte, *s. f.* date.

davantage, *adv.* more, further; *bien* ~ much more; *pas* ~ no more; *en* ~ some more.

de, *prep.* of, from, out of, on account of.

dé, *s. m.* thimble.

déballer, *v. a.* unpack.

débarquer, *v. a.* & *n.* land, disembark, arrive.

débarrasser, *v. a.* clear (up), rid, free; *se* ~ get rid (of).

débat, *s. m.* debate.

débattre, *v. a.* & *n.* debate.

débit, *s. m.* sale; debit; output; utterance; ~ *de tabac* tobbaconist's shop.

déborder, *v. n.* & *a.* overflow, run over.

débouché, *s. m.* outlet, issue.

déboucher, *v. a.* uncork, open; *v. n.* run into.

débourser, *v. a.* disburse.

debout, *adv.* upright,

standing; *être* ~ stand.

début, *s.m.* start, outset; first appearance.

débuter, *v. n.* begin, start; make one's first appearance.

décadence, *s.f.* decadence.

décagramme, *s.m.* decagramme.

décéder, *v.n.* die, decease.

décembre, *s. m.* December.

déception, *s. f.* deception, deceit; disappointment.

décharge, *s. f.* discharge; outlet.

décharger, *v.a.* unload, unburden; release; discharge; *se* ~ unburden oneself.

déchausser, *v.a.* take off (shoes).

déchéance, *s.f.* decadence, decay; decline.

déchiffrer, *v.a.* decipher; make out.

déchirer, *v.a.* tear, rend.

dechoir*, *v.n.* fall off, decay.

décider, *v. a.* & *n.* decide, settle; *se* ~ make up one's mind; be settled.

décilitre, *s. m.* decilitre.

décimal, -e, *adj.* & *s. f.* decimal.

décimètre, *s.m.* decimetre.

décisif, -ive, *adj.* decisive, final.

décision, *s.f.* decision.

déclaration, *s.f.* declaration, statement.

déclarer, *v.a.* declare, state; *se* ~ declare itself.

décliner, *v.n.* decline.

décolletage, *s.m.* low neck.

décolleter, *v.a.* cut low

turn; *tour* *a* ~ turning lathe.

décomposer, *v. a.* decompose; spoil; se ~ decompose.

décomposition, *s. f.* decomposition.

décompte, *s. m.* discount; particulars *(pl.).*

décor, *s. m.* decoration; scene, environment; scenery.

décoratif, -ive, *adj.* decorative.

décorer, *v.a.* decorate; trim.

découper, *v.a.·* cut out, carve.

décourager, *v.a.* discourage

découverte, *s. f.* discovery.

découvrir*, *v. a.* discover, find out; uncover; se ~ uncover oneself, disclose oneself.

décret, *s. m.* decree, order.

décrier, *v.a.* cry down.

décrire, *v.a.* describe.

décrocher, *v.a.* unhook, take down.

décroissance, *s. m.* decrease.

décroître, *v. n.* decrease.

déçu, *adj.* disappointed.

dédain, *s.m.* disdain, scorn.

dedans, *adv.* within, inside; indoors, at home.

dédicace, *s. f.* dedication.

dédier, *v.a.* dedicate.

déduire*, *v.a.* deduct.

défaire, *v. a.* undo; break; unfasten; take off; defeat; se ~ come undone.

défaite, *s. f.* defeat

défaut, *s. m.* defect, deficiency, want; fault; flaw; *à* ~ *de* for want

of; *sans* ~ faultless.

défavorable, *adj.* unfavourable.

défendre, *v.a.* defend; forbid; se ~ defend oneself.

défense, *s.f.* defence, protection; prohibition; tusk; *se mettre en* ~ stand on one's guard.

défiance, *s.f.* distrust, mistrust.

défier, *v. a.* defy.

défigurer, *v. a.* disfigure, deface, spoil.

défiler, *v. n.* defile.

défini, *adj.* definite.

définir, *v. a.* define.

définitif, -ive, *adj.* definitive, final.

définition, *s. f.* definition.

défunt, -e, *adj. & s. m. f.* deceased, defunct.

dégager, *v. a.* redeem, release, disengage; emit.

dégorger, *v.a.* disgorge, discharge; *v.n.* discharge, overflow.

dégoût, *s. m.* disgust.

dégoûtant, *adj.* disgusting.

dégoûter, *v.a.* disgust; se ~ get tired of.

dégradation, *s. f.* degradation.

dégrader, *v.a.* degrade; damage.

degré, *s. m.* degree.

déguisement, *s.m.* disguise.

déguiser, *v.a.* disguise, hide.

dehors, *adv.* out, outside, out of doors; *au* ~ outside, abroad; *en* ~ *de* outside of, apart from.

déjà, *adv.* already; previously.

déjeuner, *s. m.* lunch(eon); *petit* ~ breakfast; — *v.n.* have breakfast; take lunch.

delà, *prep.* beyond; *au* ~
de beyond.

délai, *s. m.* delay; *à bref* ~
at short notice.

délégation, *s. f.* delegation.

déléguer, *v. a.* delegate.

délibération, *s. f.* delibera-
tion, resolution; *en* ~
under consideration.

délibérer, *v. n.* deliberate,
ponder; *v.a.* bring
under discussion.

délicat, *adj.* delicate;
feeble; fastidious, dain-
ty.

délicatesse, *s. f.* delicacy;
delicateness; dainti-
ness.

délice, *s. m.* delight.

délicieux, -euse, *adj.* delicious, delightful.

délier, *v. a.* untie; loosen.

délivrance, *s. f.* deliver-
ance.

délivrer, *v.a.* deliver,
(set) free.

déloyal, *adj.* disloyal, unfair.

demain, *adv.* tomorrow.

demande, *s.f.* request,
application, inquiry,
call, request, demand.

demander, *v.a.* ask, in-
quire (after); beg, de-
mand; request, require;
se ~ wonder.

démanger, *v.n.* itch.

démarche, *s. f.* walk, gait;
proceeding.

démasquer, *v. a.* unmask.

déménagement, *s. m.* re-
moval, moving.

déménager, *v.n.&a.*
move (house); remove.

démesuré, *adj.* immoder-
ate, excessive.

demeure, *s.f.* delay;
home, dwelling.

demeurer, *v.n.* live; stay.

demi, -e, *adj.* half; *à* ~ by
half; *une heure et* ~e

half past one; an hour
and a half; — *s. f.* half-
hour.

demi-cercle, *s. m.* semi-
circle.

demi-heure, *s. f.* half an
hour.

demi-jour, *s. m.* twilight.

démobiliser, *v.a.* demo-
bilize.

démocratie, *s. f.* democracy.

démocratique, *adj.* democratic.

démodé, *adj.* old-fash-
ioned.

demoiselle, *s.f.* young
lady, miss.

démolir, *v. a.* demolish,
pull down.

démon, *s. m.* demon.

démonstratif, -ive, *adj.*
demonstrative.

démonstration, *s.f.* de-
monstration.

démontrer, *v. a.* demon-
strate.

dénaturé, *adj.* unnatural.

dénombrer, *v. a.* number.

dénomination, *s. f.* denomination.

dénoncer, *v. a.* denounce.

dénoter, *v. a.* denote; indicate.

dense, *adj.* dense, com-
pact.

densité, *s. f.* density.

dent, *s. f.* tooth; *mal de* ~s
toothache.

dental, *adj.* dental.

dentelle, *s. f.* lace.

dentier, *s. m.* set of (false)
teeth, denture.

dentifrice, *s. m. pâte* ~
tooth-paste.

dentiste, *s. m. f.* dentist.

dénué, *adj.* destitute.

dénuement, *s. m.* destitu-
tion.

départ, *s. m.* departure.

département, *s. m.* department; territory.

départir, v. a. grant, allot; se ~ give up

dépasser, v. a. & n. pass, exceed, go beyond.

dépêche, s. f. despatch, wire, telegram.

dépêcher, v. a. dispatch; v. n. & se ~ hurry.

dépendance, s. f. dependance.

dépendant, -e, adj. dependent; — s. m. f. dependant.

dépendre, v. n. depend.

dépense, s. f. expense; larder.

dépenser, v. a. & n. spend; waste.

dépit, s. m. spite; en ~ de in spite of.

déplacement, s. m. displacement; shift.

déplacer, v.a. displace, move, shift; se ~ move.

déplaire, v.n. displease.

déplier, v.a. unfold, lay out.

déplorer, v. a. deplore.

déportation, s. f. transportation, deportation.

déposer, v. a. put down, set down; deposit; — se ~ settle.

dépôt, s.m. deposit; store-room, warehouse; lock-up.

dépourvu, adj. needy.

dépraver, v. a. deprave.

déprécier, v. a. depreciate.

dépression, s. f. depression.

déprimer, v. a. depress.

depuis, prep. since, from; ~ longtemps long since.

députation, s. f. deputation.

député, s.m. deputy; member of the French parliament.

dérangé, adj. deranged; upset.

déranger, v. a. upset, put out of order.

déraper, v. n. skid.

dérèglement, s. m. irregularity; disorder.

dérivation, s. f. derivation.

dériver, v.n. drift; be derived.

dernier, -ère, adj. & s. m. f. latter, last, latest; le ~ the latter.

dernièrement, adv. lately.

dérober, v. a. rob, steal. se ~ steal away.

déroger, v.n. derogate (from).

dérouler, v.a. unroll, unfold.

déroute, s.f. defeat.

derrière, adv. & prep. behind, back; — s. m. back (part); bottom.

dès, prep. from, as early as, since; ~ que as soon as.

désagréable, adj. disagreeable, unpleasant.

désarmer, v.a. disarm.

désastre, s.m. disaster.

désavantage, s. m. disadvantage.

descendance, s.f. descent.

descendant, adj. descending; en ~ downward, downhill.

descendre, v. n. descend, come down, go down; alight; ~ terre land; — v.a. take down.

descente, s.f. descent; landing.

description, s. f. description.

désert¹, s. m. desert.

désert², adj. deserted, desolate.

déserter, v. n. & a. leave, desert.

désespérer, v.n. despair,

give up.

désespoir, s. m. despair.

déshabiller, v. a. undress; take off clothes.

déshonneur, s.m. dishonour, disgrace.

déshonorer, v.a. dishonour, disgrace.

désigner, v. a. designate; denote; appoint.

desinfecter, v. a. disinfect.

désir, s. m. desire.

désirable: adj. desirable.

désirer, v. a. & n. desire, long for.

désireux, -euse, adj. desirous, anxious.

désobéir, v.n. disobey.

désobéissance, s.f. disobedience.

désobéissant, adj. disobedient.

désœuvré, adj. idle, unoccupied.

désolation, s. f. devastation; desolation.

désoler, v.a. desolate; afflict, distress; se ~ grieve, be sorry.

désordre, s.m. disorder.

dessert, s. m. dessert.

dessin, s.m. drawing, sketch; design; ~ animé cartoon.

dessiner, v.a. draw; sketch; design.

dessous, adv. & prep. under, underneath, below, beneath; — s. m. under-part; undies pl.

dessus, adv. & prep. on, upon, over, above, on top; — s. m. upper part, top.

destin, s. m. destiny, fate.

destinataire, s. m. f. receiver, addressee.

destination, s. f. destination.

destinée, s.f. destiny.

destiner, v.a. destine;

mean (for); se ~ be destined (á for).

détachement, s. m. disengagement; detachment.

détacher, v.a. loose(n), unfasten; detach; se ~ get loose, come undone.

détail, s.m. detail, particular; retail; en ~ in detail.

détention, s. f. detention.

détermination, s.f. determination.

déterminé, adj. definite, determinate; resolute; limited.

déterminer, v.a. determine, fix; limit; settle.

détestable, adj. hateful.

détester, v.a. detest.

détonation, s.f. detonation.

détour, s.m. turning, winding, turn; roundabout way; evasion.

détourner, v.a. turn aside; lead astray.

détroit, s. m. strait, pass.

détruire*, v.a. destroy, ruin; do away with.

dette, s. f. debt.

deuil, s.m. mourning.

deux, adj. & s. m. two; both.

deuxième, adj. second.

devancer, v. a. precede; anticipate.

devant, prep. adv. before; in front of; opposite to; ~ que before; au-~ de ~ in front of; — s. m. front; foreground.

dévaster, v. a. devastate, destroy.

développement, s. m. development, growth.

développer, v.a. (also se ~) develop.

devenir, v.n. become, get, turn, grow.

dévier, v. a. & n. deviate, turn away.

devise, *s. f.* device.

dévoiler, *v. a.* unveil, reveal.

devoir*, *v.a.* owe, be in debt for; have to, must, be bound to, ought to; — *s. m.* duty; task; work., prep.

dévorer, *v. a.* devour, eat up.

dévouement, *s. m.* devotion.

dévouer, *v. a.* devote, dedicate; se ~ devote oneself.

diable, *s. m.* devil; trolley, truck.

diacre, *s. m.* deacon.

diadème, *s. m.* diadem.

diagnostic, *s. m.* diagnosis.

dialecte, *s. m.* dialect.

dialogue, *s. m.* dialogue.

diamant, *s. m.* diamond.

diapositive, *s. f.* transparency, slide.

diarrhée, *s. f.* diarrhoea.

dictée, *s. f.* dictation.

dicter, *v. a.* dictate.

dictionnaire, *s. m.* dictionary.

diesel, *s. m.* diesel engine.

dieu, *s. m. (pl. -x)* God.

différence, *s. f.* difference.

différent, *adj.* different.

différer, *v.a.* defer, put off; *v.n.* differ, be different, vary.

difficile, *adj.* difficult, hard.

difficulté, *s. f.* difficulty, trouble.

diffusion, *s. f.* diffusion.

digne, *adj.* worthy; ~ *de* . . . worthy of . . .

dignité, *s.f.* dignity.

diligence, *s.f.* diligence.

diligent, *adj.* diligent.

dimanche, *s. m.* Sunday.

dimension, *s.f.* dimension.

diminuer, *v.a.* &. *n.* diminish, lessen, reduce.

dindon, *s.m.* turkey.

dîner, *s. m.* dinner; — *v. n.* dine.

diplomate, *s. m.* diplomat.

diplomatie, *s. f.* diplomacy.

diplomatique, *adj.* diplomatic.

diplôme, *s.m.* diploma.

dire*, *v.a.* say, tell; speak; ~ *à qn de faire qch.* tell s.o. to do sth.; *c'est à* ~ that is to say; *pour ainsi* ~ as it were; *vouloir* ~ mean; *dites donc!* look here!

direct, *adj.* direct.

directeur, *s.m.* director, manager; head master.

direction, *s.f.* direction; management; guidance; streering-gear.

directrice, *s. f.* directress; head mistress.

diriger, *v.a.* direct; lead, guide; manage; turn; steer.

disciple, *s.m.* disciple, follower.

discipline, *s. f.* discipline.

discorde, *s.f.* discord.

discours, *s.m.* discourse, speech.

discrédit, *s.m.* discredit.

discréditer, *v. a.* discredit.

discret, -ète *adj.* discreet; discrete.

discrètement, *adv.* discreetly.

discrétion, *s. f.* discretion.

discussion, *s. f.* discussion.

discuter, *v.a.* discuss, debate.

disparaître, *v.n.* disappear.

dispenser, *v. a.* dispense; se ~ *de* dispense with.

disposer, *v. a.* & *n.* dispose, lay out; se ~ prepare (to), be about (to); *bien disposé* willing.

disposition, *s. f.* disposition, arrangement; *la ~ de qn.* at s.o.'s disposal.

dispute, *s. f.* dispute.

disputer, *v. a. & n.* dispute, contest, argue; se ~ quarrel, dispute.

disqualifier, *v.a.* disqualify.

disque, *s. m.* disc, record; discus; ~ *microsillon* or *longue durée* long playing record.

dissimulation, *s. f.* dissimulation, dissembling.

dissimuler, *v.a. & n.* dissemble, conceal; se ~ conceal oneself.

dissolution, *s. f.* dissolution; undoing, breaking up.

dissoudre*, *v. a.* dissolve, disperse.

distance, *s. f.* distance; *à quelle ~ est-ce?* how far is it?

distant, *adj.* distant, far.

distiller, *v.a. & n.* distil.

distinct, *adj.* distinct, clear.

distinction, *s.f.* distinction.

distinguer, *v.a.* distinguish, discriminate; make out, tell.

distraction, *s. f.* abstraction; recreation; entertainment; distraction.

distraire, *v.a.* subtract; divert, distract; amuse, entertain.

distrait, *adj.* inattentive, absent-minded.

distribuer, *v. a.* distribute; deal out.

district, *s.m.* district.

divan, *s.m.* sofa, divan.

divergence, *s.f.* divergence; difference.

divers, *adj.* diverse, different, miscellaneous.

diversion, *s. f.* diversion.

divertir, *v. a.* divert, entertain; se ~ enjoy oneself.

divertissement, *s. m.* diversion; entertainment.

divin, *adj.* divine.

diviser, *v.a.* divide, separate.

division, *s.f.* division, department.

divorce, *s. m.* divorce.

divorcer, *v n. & n.* divorce, be divorced.

dix, *adj. s. m.* ten.

dix-huit, *adj. & s.m.* eighteen.

dixième, *adj. & s.f.* tenth.

dix-neuf, *adj. & s.m.* nineteen.

dix-sept, *adj. & s.m.* seventeen.

dizaine, *s. f.* ten.

docteur, *s. m.* doctor.

document, *s.m.* document.

documentaire, *s. m.* documentary (film).

dogme, *s. m.* dogma.

doigt, *s.m.* finger; toe.

dollar, *s.m.* dollar.

domaine, *s.m.* domain; landed property.

dôme, *s. m.* dome.

domestique, *adj. & s. m. f.* domestic, servant.

domicile, *s. m.* domicile, dwelling.

domination, *s. f.* domination, rule.

dominer, *v. a. & n.* dominate, rule.

dommage, *s. m.* damage; pity.

dompter, *v. a.* subdue, master, tame.

don, s. m. present, gift.
donateur, s.m. giver.
donc, conj. therefore, then, so; of course.
donne, s. f. deal.
donner, v. a. give, grant, present with, afford, hand over; ~ congé give notice to; se ~ pour claim to be.
dont, pron. whose, of whom; of which.
dormir*, v.n. sleep.

dortoir, s. m. dormitory.
dos, s. m. back.
dose, s. f. dose.
dossier, s. m. back-piece; record, file.
dot, s. f. dowry.
doter, v. a. endow.
douane, s.f. customs; custom-house; duty; déclaration de ~ customs declaration; droits de ~ customs duties; la visite de la ~ customs formalities.
douanier, s.m. custom-house officer.
double, s.m. double; en ~ duplicate; — adj. double, dual.
doubler, v. a. double (up); line; dub.
doublure, s.f. lining; understudy.
douce see doux.
douceur, s. f. sweetness; gentleness.
douche, s. f. shower-bath.
douer, v. a. endow, gift.
douleur, s. f. pain, ache.
douloureux, -euse, adj. painful.
doute, s. m. doubt; sans ~ no doubt, undoubtedly.
douter, v. n. doubt; se ~ suspect.
douteux, -euse, adj.

doubtful, dubious.
doux, douce, adj. sweet; mild, soft.
douzaine, s.f. dozen.
douze, adj. & s. m. twelve; twelfth.
douzième, adj. twelfth.
dramatique, adj. dramatic; l'art ~ drama.
drame, s.m. drama.
drap, s.m. cloth, sheet.
drapeau, s.m. flag.
dresser, v. a. set up, erect; prepare; se ~ stand up, get up.
drogue, s. f. drug.
droguerie, s.f. drugs pl.
droit, s. m. right; law; duty, due; avoir ~ à be entitled to; ~ de cité citizenship; ~ d'auteur, copyright; exempt de ~s duty-free; ~(s) de sortie, export duty; — adj. right, direct, straight.
droite, s. f. right hand.
drôle, adj. droll, funny, strange; — s. m. rogue.
du, art. of the, some, any.
dû, adj. & s. m. due.
duc, s. m. duke.
duchesse, s.f. duchess.
duel, s. m. duel.
duplicata, s. m. duplicate, copy.
dur, adj. hard, tough.
durable, adj. lasting.
durant, prep. during, for.
durcir, v. a. & n. harden.
durée, s.f. duration, term.
durer, v.n. & a. last, endure, hold out.
dureté, s. f. hardness.
dynastie, s.f. dynasty.

E

eau, s. f. (pl. -x) water;

~ *de mer* salt water;
~ *de Seltz* soda-water.

ébaucher, *v.a.* sketch; outline.

ébouriffer, *v.a.* ruffle.

ébullition, *s.f.* boiling.

écaille, *s.f.* scale.

écailler, *v.a.* scale.

écart, *s.m.* deviation; *à l'*~ aside, apart.

écarter, *v.a.* set aside; dispel, take away; s'~ turn aside.

ecclésiastique, *adj. & s. m.* ecclesiastic.

échafaud, *s. m.* scaffold-(ing).

échange, *s. m.* exchange.

échanger, *v. a.* exchange.

échapper, *v. n.* escape, get away.

échauder, *v.a.* scald.

échauffer, *v. a.* heat; s'~ get hot.

échéance, *s. f.* expiration.

échéant, *adj.* due.

échec, *s. m.* check.

échecs, *s. m. pl.* chess.

échelle, *s.f.* ladder; scale.

échine, *s.f.* backbone.

écho, *s.m.* echo.

échoir*, *v.n.* expire, fall due; happen.

éclabousser, *v. a.* splash, spatter with mud.

éclair, *s.m.* lightning; flash.

éclairage, *s. m.* lighting; ~ *au néon* strip-lighting.

éclaircir, *v. a.* make clear, clear up; clarify; throw light on; s'~ become clear, clear up.

éclairer, *v. a.* light, illuminate; enlighten.

éclaireur, *s. m.* boy scout.

éclat, *s.m.* splinter; burst; brightness.

éclatant, *adj.* bright.

éclater, *v. n.* split; burst; break out; flash.

éclipser, *v. a.* eclipse; s'~ be eclipsed; take French leave.

école, *s.f.* school; *maître d'*~ schoolmaster; ~ *normale* teachers' training college; ~ *secondaire* grammar-school.

écolier, *s. m.* schoolboy.

écolière, *s. f.* schoolgirl.

économe, *adj.* economical; — *s. m.* bursar.

économie, *s. f.* economy; thrift; ~ *politique* political economy; ~s savings; *faire des* ~s save up.

économique, *adj.* economic; economical.

économiser, *v. a. & n.* economize, save, spare.

écorce, *s. f.* bark; rind.

écossais, *adj.* Scottish, Scotch.

Écossais, *s. m.* Scotsman.

écouler, *v.a.* sell.

écouter, *v.a.* listen to; hear.

écouteur, *s.m.* headphone; receiver.

écran, *s.m.* screen; *le petit* ~ television.

écrier: s'~ cry out.

écrire*, *v. a.* write (down); *machine à* ~ typewriter.

écrit, *adj.* written; — *s. m.* writing; *par* ~ in writing.

écriture, *s.f.* writing, handwriting; style.

écrivain, *s.m.* writer, author.

écuelle, *s. f.* bowl, basin, dish.

écume, *s.f.* foam.

écureuil, *s.m.* squirrel.

écurie, *s.f.* stable.

édifice, *s.m.* building.

édifier, *v.a.* build, erect; edify.

édit, *s.m.* edict, decree.

éditer, *v. a.* publish; edit.

éditeur, *s. m.* publisher.

édition, *s. f.* publication; edition.

éducation, *s. f.* education; training.

effacer, *v. a.* efface, rub out; wipe out.

effectif, -ive *adj.* actual, real.

effectuer, *v.a.* effect, carry out.

effet, *s. m.* effect, result; impression; bill (of exchange); *(pl.)* clothes, belongings.

efficacité, *s. f.* efficacy.

effondrer: s'~ fall in, collapse.

effort, *s. m.* effort, exertion, endeavour.

effrayant, *adj.* frightful.

effrayé, *adj.* afraid.

effrayer, *v.a.* frighten; s'~ be frightened.

effroi, *s.m.* fright.

effroyable, *adj.* frightful.

effusion, *s.f.* effusion, gush.

égal, *adj.* equal, like, alike; (all the) same; even.

également, *adv.* equally.

égaler, *v.a.* equal.

égalité, *s.f.* equality.

égard, *s. m.* regard; à cet ~ on that account; à l'~ de with regard to; en ~ à considering.

égarer, *v. a.* mislead, misguide; s'~ lose one's way.

égayer, *v. a.* cheer (up); s'~ cheer up.

église (É), *s. f.* church.

égoïste, *adj.* egoistic, selfish.

égyptien, -enne (E.), *adj.* & *s.m.f.* Egyptian.

eh, *int.* ah!; ~ bien! well!

élaborer, *v. a.* work out, think out, elaborate.

élan, *s.m.* dash; run; élan, zest.

élancé, *adj.* slim.

élancer, *v. n.* shoot; s'~ bound, dash, rush; soar.

élargir, *v. a.* make wider, enlarge; set at liberty.

élastique, *adj.* & *s. m.* elastic.

électeur, -trice, *s. m. f.* voter.

élection, *s.f.* election.

électricien, -enne, *s. m. f.* electrician.

électricité, *s.f.* electricity; usine d'~ powerplant, -station.

électrique, *adj.* electric(al).

électron, *s.m.* electron.

électronique, *adj.* electronic.

élégance, *s.f.* elegance.

élégant, *adj.* elegant.

élément, *s. m.* element.

élémentaire, *adj.* elementary.

éléphant, *s. m.* elephant.

élévation, *s.f.* elevation.

élève, *s.m.f.* pupil.

élevé, *adj.* educated.

élever, *v. a.* raise, lift up; increase; bring up, educate; rear; s'~ rise; exalt oneself.

éliminer, *v. a.* eliminate

élire, *v. a.* choose; elect.

elle, *pron. (pl.* elles*)* she, it, her; they.

elle-même, *pron.* herself.

éloigné, *adj.* far, distant.

éloigner, *v.a.* remove; take away; set aside.

émail, *s. m.* enamel.

émaner, *v.n.* emanate.

emballer, *v.a.* pack up; pack off.

embarquement, *s. m.* embarking; shipment.

embarquer, *v.a.* ship, embark; *v.n.* go on board.

embarrasser, *v. a.* embarrass.

embellir, *v. a.* embellish.

embêter, *v.a.* bore; annoy.

emblème, *s. m.* emblem.

embouchure, *s. f.* mouthpiece; mouth (of river).

embranchement, *s.m.* branchline; junction.

embrasser, *v. a.* embrace; kiss; s'~ kiss.

embrayage, *s. m.* clutch, coupling.

embrouillement, *s.m.* tangle; muddle.

embrouiller, *v. a.* embroil, entangle; muddle; s'~ become confused.

émetteur, *s. m.* transmitter.

émettre *v. a.* emit; transmit, broadcast.

émigration, *s. f.* emigration.

émigré, -e, *s.m.f.* emigrant.

émigrer, *v.n.* emigrate.

éminent, *adj.* eminent.

emmener, *v.a.* take away.

émotion, *s.f.* emotion; feeling.

émouvoir, *v.a.* move, touch; s'~ be moved.

emparer: s'~ *de* get hold of, seize.

empêchement, *s. m.* hindrance.

empêcher, *v.a.* keep from; prevent; hinder.

empire, *s.m.* empire.

emplette, *s. f.* purchase.

emplir, *v.a.* fill (up).

emploi, *s.m.* employment, job; use.

employé, -e, *s.m.f.* employee; clerk; attendant.

employer, *v.a.* employ; use.

empoigner, *v.a.* grasp, grip; lay hands on.

empoisonner, *v. a.* poison.

emporter, *v.a.* carry, take away, carry off, remove; s'~ get angry, lose one's temper.

empreinte, *s. f.* stamp, print, impression.

empresser: s'~ hurry, hasten.

emprisonnement, *s.m.* imprisonment.

emprisonner, *v.a.* imprison.

emprunter, *v. a.* borrow.

en, *prep.* in; to; into; at; like, as; by, through; — *pron.* of him, of her, of it, of them, their; any, some.

encan, *s.m.* auction.

enceinte, *adj.* pregnant.

enchaîner, *v.a.* chain; link up; detain.

enchantement, *s. m.* spell; delight.

enchanter, *v.a.* charm, delight.

enclore, *v.a.* enclose.

enclose, *s. m.* enclosure; close.

enclume, *s.f.* anvil.

encombrement, *s. m.* stoppage; (traffic) jam.

encombrer, *v. a.* block up, jam.

encore, *adv.* yet, still; again; *pas* ~ not yet; ~ *une fois* once again; ~ *que* although; ~ *du* some more; ~ *quelque chose, Madame?* anything else, madam?

encouragement, *s. m.* encouragement.

encourager, *v. a.* encourage; cheer.

encre, *s.f.* ink.

encyclopédie, *s. f.* encyclopaedia.

endommager, *v.a.* damage; injure.

endormir, *v.a.* put to sleep; s'~ go to sleep, fall asleep.

endosser, *v.a.* endorse.

énergie, *s. f.* energy; ~ atomique atomic energy.

énergique, *adj.* energetic.

enfance, *s.f.* infancy, childhood.

enfant, *s. m. f.* infant, child; *chambre d'~s* nursery; *d'~s* juvenile.

enfermer, *v.a.* shut in, up, lock up.

enfin, *adv.* at last; finally; in short.

enflammer, *v. a.* set on fire; s'~ take fire.

enfler, *v. a.* swell (up); s'~ swell.

enflure, *s. f.* swelling.

engagement, *s. m.* obligation; commitment; engagement.

engager, *v. a. & n.* pledge; pawn; engage, sign on.

engloutir, *v. a.* swallow up, devour.

engraisser, *v.a.* fatten; *v.n.* grow fat.

enlèvement, *s.m.* removal.

enlever, *v.a.* remove, clear away, take away.

ennemi, *s.m.* enemy.

ennui, *s. m.* bore(dom); vexation; nuisance.

ennuyer, *v. a.* bore, weary; s'~ be bored.

ennuyeux, -euse, *adj.* boring, tedious.

énoncer, *v.a.* state.

énorme, *adj.* enormous.

enquérir: s'~ *de* inquire about.

enrager, *v. n.* be enraged.

enregistrer, *v. a.* register, enter, record.

enrhumer, *v.a. être enrhumé* have a cold; s'~ catch a cold.

enrôler, *v. a.* enrol, draft.

enroué, *adj.* hoarse.

enrouler, *v. a.* roll (up).

enseignement, *s. m.* instruction, tuition.

enseigner, *v.a. & n.* teach, instruct (in).

ensemble, *adv.* together; — *s. m.* whole, mass; unity; two-piece suit; set of furniture, suite.

ensuite, *adv.* then; next.

ensuivre: s'~ follow, ensue.

entasser, *v.a.* heap up.

entendement, *s. m.* understanding.

entendre, *v. a. & n.* hear; understand; ~ *parler de* hear of; *ne pas* ~ miss; *qu'entendez-vous par là?* what do you mean by that?; *bien entendu* of course; *c'est entendu!* that's settled!, agreed!

entente, *s.f.* meaning; understanding; agreement.

enterrement, *s. m.* burial.

enterrer, *v.a.* bury.

enthousiasme, *s. m.* enthusiasm.

enthousiaste, *adj.* enthusiastic; keen.

entier, -ère, *adj.* entire.

entièrement, *adv.* entirely, wholly.

entorse, *s.f.* sprain; *donner une* ~ *à* sprain one's (foot, ankle).

entourage, *s. m.* circle of friends; surroundings *(pl.)*; attendants *(pl.)*.

entourer, *v.a.* surround; encircle.

entracte, *s. m.* interval.

entrailles, *s. f. pl.* entrails.

entraîner, *v.a.* draw

along; carry away; involve, entail; coach.

entraîneur, s. m. trainer, coach.

entre, prep, between, among; into, in.

entrée, s. f. entry, entrance, beginning; free access; duty.

entremets, s. m. second course.

entreprendre, v.a. attempt, undertake, contract for; worry.

entrepreneur, s.m. contractor.

entreprise, s. f. undertaking, enterprise.

entrer, v. n. enter; come in, go in; get in; get into; faire ~ show in.

enveloppe, s. f. envelope; wrapper, cover.

envelopper, v. a. wrap up, do up; envelop.

envers, prep. towards, to.

enviable, adj. enviable.

envie, s. f. envy, desire.

envier, v. a. envy; desire.

environ, adv. & prep. about.

environner, v.a. surround.

environs, s. m. pl. surroundings.

envoi, s. m. sending; consignment, shipment.

envoler: s'~ fly away, take wing.

envoyer*, v.a. send, dispatch, forward.

envoyeur, s.m. sender.

épais, -aisse, adj. thick.

épaisseur, s. f. thickness.

épargne, s.f. savings (pl.).

épargner, v. a. save (up).

épaule, s.f. shoulder.

épée, s.f. sword.

éperon, s.m. spur.

épice, s. f. spice.

épicerie, s.f. grocery, grocer's (shop).

épicier, -ère, s. m. f. grocer.

épidémie, s. f. epidemic.

épinard, s.m. spinach.

épine, s. f. thorn; spine, backbone; obstacle.

épingle, s. f. pin; ~ de sûreté safety-pin.

épisode, s.m. episode.

éplucher, v. a. peel; pick; sift, preen, thin out.

éponge, s.f. sponge.

éponger, v. a. sponge; mop (up).

époque, s. f. period, age, epoch, time.

épouse, s.f. wife.

épouser, v.a. marry.

épouvante, s.f. fright.

époux, s. m. husband.

épreuve, s. f. test, trial; proof; print.

éprouver, v. a. test, prove; feel; experience.

épuisé, adj. exhausted; out of print.

épuiser, v. a. exhaust; use up; wear out.

équation, s.f. equation.

équilibre, s.m. balance, equilibrium.

équipage, s. m. suite, retinue; carriage; crew.

équipe, s. f. gang, shift; crew, team, side; train.

équipement, s. m. equipment.

équiper, v.a. equip.

équivalent, adj. equivalent.

ère, s.f. era.

errant, adj. wandering.

errer, v. n. stray; err.

erreur, s. f. error, mistake.

érudit, adj. learned.

érudition, s.f. learning.

escalateur, s. m. escalator.

escale, s.f. port; landing; sans ~ non-stop.

escalier, s. m. stairs (pl.), staircase; ~ de sauve-

tage fire-escape; ~ *de service* backstairs *(pl.)*; ~ *roulant* escalator.

escargot, *s.m.* snail.

escarpins, *s. m. pl.* pumps.

esclavage, *s.m.* slavery.

esclave, *s. m. f.* slave; — *adj.* slavish.

escrime, *s.f.* fencing; *faire de l'*~ fence.

escrimer, *v.n.* fence.

espace, *s. m.* space; room.

espagnol, -e (E.), *adj.* Spanish; — *s. m. f.* Spaniard; Spanish.

espèce, *s. f.* species, kind.

espérance, *s. f.* hope, expectation.

espérer, *v. a.* hope (for).

espion, -onne, *s.m.f.* spy.

espionnage, *s. m.* espionage, spying.

espoir, *s.m.* hope.

esprit, *s. m.* spirit; mind; character; wit; sense.

esquille, *s.f.* splinter.

esquiver, *v.a.* evade.

essai, *s.m.* trial, test; essay; attempt.

essayer, *v. a.* try, attempt; essay; assay.

essence, *s.f.* essence; petrol.

essentiel, -elle, *adj.* essential.

essieu, *s.m.* axle.

essor, *s.m.* flight.

essoreuse, *s. f.* spin-drier.

essuie-glace, *s. m.* windscreen wiper.

essuie-main(s), *s. m. (pl.)* towel; ~ *à rouleau* roller-towel.

essuyer, *v.a.* dust; wipe; dry; mop up.

est, *s.m.* cast.

esthétique, *adj.* aesthetic.

estime, *s.f.* esteem.

estimer, *v.a. & n.* estimate, value; esteem, regard; consider.

estomac, *s.m.* stomach.

estrade, *s.f.* platform.

estuaire, *s.m.* estuary.

et, *conj.* and; ~ ...~ both ... and.

étable, *s.f.* cow-shed; ~ *à porcs* pigsty.

établi, *s.m.* (joiner's) bench.

établir, *v.a.* establish, found, settle, set up; build; prove; s'~ settle (down).

établissement, *s. m.* establishment.

étage, *s. m.* floor, stor(e)y.

étagère, *s. f.* shelf.

étaler, *v.a.* display; spread (out); show off; s'~ stretch oneself out.

étang, *s.m.* pond.

étape, *s.f.* stage.

état, *s.m.* state; condition; profession, station office; statement; *homme d'*~ statesman; *coup d'*~ revolt.

été, *s.m.* summer.

éteindre*, *v. a.* put out, extinguish; turn off; s'~ be extinguished.

étendre, *v. a.* spread out; stretch out; extend; s'~ lie down; stretch one-self out.

étendu, *adj.* wide, vast, extensive.

étendue, *s.f.* expanse, reach, range; extent.

éternel, -elle, *adj.* eternal.

éternuement, *s. m.* sneeze.

éternuer, *v.n.* sneeze.

étincelle, *s.f.* spark.

étiquette, *s.f.* ticket, label; etiquette.

étoffe, *s.f.* cloth, material.

étoile, *s.f.* star.

étonnant, *adj.* astonishing, amazing.

étonnement, *s. m.* astonishment, wonder.

étonner, *v.a.* astonish,

amaze; s'~ be astonished.

étouffer, *v.a.* choke.

étrange, *adj.* strange.

étranger, -ère, *adj.* foreign, strange; — -*s.m.f.* foreigner; *u l'~* abroad.

être*, *v.n.* be, exist; *il est...* It is...; *~ bien* be good-looking; be well; *c'est que* the fact is; *~ à* belong to; — *s.m.* being.

étreindre*, *v.a.* clasp; press; embrace.

étreinte, *s.f.* embrace.

étrier, *s. m.* stirrup.

étroit, *adj.* narrow, strait; close.

étude, *s. f.* study; chambers *(pl.)*.

étudiant, -e, *s.m.f.* student, undergraduate.

étudier, *v. a.* study, read; practise.

étui, *s.m.* case, box.

étuver, *v.a.* stew, steam.

eucharistie, *s.f.* eucharist.

européen, -enne, *adj.* European.

eux, *pron. m.* they, them.

évader: s'~ escape; get away.

évaluer, *v. a.* value, estimate.

évangélique, *adj.* evangelical.

évangile, *s.m.* gospel.

évaporer, *v. a.* evaporate; s'~ evaporate.

éveil, *s. m. en ~* on the lookout.

éveiller, *v. a.* awaken; s'~ wake up.

événement, *s.m.* event.

éventail, *s.m.* fan.

éventuel, -elle, *adj.* eventual.

évêque, *s.m.* bishop.

évidemment, *adv.* evidently, obviously.

évidence, *s.f.* evidence.

évident, *adj.* evident, obvious.

éviter, *v. a.* avoid, evade.

évoluer, *v.n.* evolve.

évolution, *s. f.* evolution.

exact, *adj.* exact, accurate.

exactement, *adv.* exactly.

exactitude, *s.f.* exactitude, precision.

exagérer, *v. a.* exaggerate.

examen, *s. m.* exam(ination); test.

examiner, *v. a.* examine; investigate, look into.

excédent, *s.m.* surplus; ~s de bagages excess luggage.

excéder, *v. a.* exceed, surpass; tire out.

excellence, *s. f.* excellence; excellency.

excellent, *adj.* excellent.

excepté, *adj.* excepted; — *prep.* except(ing), but.

excepter, *v.a.* except.

exception, *s. f.* exception.

exceptionnel, -elle, *adj.* exceptional.

excès, *s. m.* excess.

excessif, -ive, *adj.* excessive.

excitation, *s.f.* excitement.

exciter, *v.a.* excite, stir up; urge on.

exclamation, *s.f.* exclamation.

exclure*, *v.a.* exclude.

exclusif, -ive, *adj.* exclusive.

excursion, *s. f.* excursion.

excursionniste, *s.m.f.* holiday-maker, tourist.

excuse, *s. f.* excuse; apology; *faire des ~s* apologize.

excuser, *v.a.* excuse; pardon; apologize for; s'~ apologize; ask to be

excused; *excusez-moi*
I beg your pardon;
excuse me.

exécuter, *v.a.* execute,
carry out, perform.

exécutif, -ive, *adj.* executive.

exécution, *s. f.* execution.

exemplaire, *s.m.* copy.

exemple, *s. m.* example;
par ~ for example;
sans ~ unprecedented.

exempt, *adj.* exempt, free
(de from).

exemption, *s.f.* exemp-
tion.

exercer, *v.a.* exercise;
practise; carry on; s'~
practise.

exercice, *s.m.* exercise.

exhibition, *s.f.* exhibition; display.

exigence, *s.f.* demand;
exigency.

exil, *s.m.* exile.

existence, *s. f.* existence.

exister, *v. n.* exist.

expansif, -ive, *adj.* expan-
sive.

expansion, *s. f.* expansion.

expédient, *s.m.* expedi-
ent, device.

expédier, *v.a.* forward,
send off.

expéditeur, -trice, *s. m. f.*
sender, shipping-agent.

expédition, *s. f.* consignment; expedition, for-
warding, dispatch.

expérience, *s. f.* experience; experiment; *faire
des* ~*s* to experiment.

expérimental, *adj.* experimental.

expert, *adj.* expert.

expirer, *v.n.* expire; die.

explication, *s. f.* explanation.

expliquer, *v.n.* explain,
account for, show.

exploration, *s. f.* exploration.

explorer, *v.a.* explore.

explosion, *s. f.* explosion.

exportateur, *s.m.* exporter.

exportation, *s. f.* export,
exportation.

exporter, *v. a.* export.

exposé, *s.m.* statement.

exposer, *v.a.* expose,
show; state; set forth.

exposition, *s. f.* exhibition, display; state-
ment, exposure; exposi-
tion.

exprès, *adv.* on purpose.

express, *adj.* express; —
s.m. express (train).

expression, *s. f.* expression

exprimer, *v.a.* express.

expulser, *v.a.* expel.

expulsion, *s.f.* expulsion.

extension, *s. f.* extension;
extent.

exténuer, *v.a.* tire out,
exhaust.

extérieur, *s. m.* exterior;
outside; à l'~ outwards
— *adj.* outward.

extinction, *s.f.* extinction; quenching.

extraire, *v. a.* extract;
draw, pull out.

extraordinaire, *adj.* extraordinary, unusual.

extravagant, *adj.* extravagant.

extrême, *adj.* extreme.

extrêmement, *adv.* ex-
tremely, very.

extrémité *s. f.* extremity;
last moment.

F

fabricant, *s.m.* manu-
facturer, maker.

fabrication, *s.f.* manu-
facture; fabrication.

fabrique, *s.f.* factory,
works.

fabriquer, *v.a.* manufacture, make.

façade, *s.f.* front.

face, *s.f.* face; look; *en ~ de* opposite, in front of.

facétieux, -euse, *adj.* facetious; humorous.

fâché, *adj.* offended.

fâcher, *v. a.* offend; make angry; se ~ get angry.

facile, *adj.* easy; fluent.

facilité, *s.f.* ease; facility; convenience.

faciliter, *v.a.* facilitate; make easy.

façon, *s. f.* making; fashion, shape; way, manner; *de ~ a* so as to; *de ~ que* so that; *en aucune ~* by no means; *d'une ~ quelconque* somehow.

facteur, *s.m.* factor; postman; porter, carrier; *fig.* circumstance.

faction, *s.f.* faction; sentry, watch.

facture, *s.f.* bill, invoice.

facultatif, -ive, *adj.* optional.

faculté, *s.f.* faculty.

fade, *adj.* flat, insipid.

faible, *adj.* weak; feeble.

faiblesse, *s. f.* weakness.

faiblir, *v. n.* become weak.

faillir, *v. n.* fail, fall short; err; ~ + *inf.* nearly; *j'ai failli manquer le train* I nearly missed the train.

faim, *s.f.* hunger; *avoir ~* be hungry.

faire*, *v.a.* make; do; build; cause; ~ *allusion* refer to; ~ *attention (a)* pay attention (to); ~ *une chambre* do a room; ~ *le commerce* trade; ~ *la cuisine* do the cooking; ~ *ses*

études study; be at school; ~ *la guerre* make war; ~ *un lit* make a bed; ~ *mal a* hurt; ~ *part a* let know; ~ *des progrès* make progress; ~ *une promenade* take a walk; ~ *queue* queue; ~ *savoir* let know, inform (of); ~ *usage (de)* make use (of); ~ *voir* show; *que ~?* what's to be done?; *qu'est-ce que cela fait?* what does it matter?; *n'avoir rien a ~* have nothing to do; *deux et deux font quatre* two and two make four; ~ *70 km. a l'heure* do 70 km. an hour; *il fait du vent* it is windy; *il fait chaud* it is warm; *il fait jour* it is daylight; — se ~ be made, be done; get used (to).

faisan, *s. m.* pheasant.

fait, *s. m.* fact; *en ~* in fact, after all, as a matter of fact.

falloir*, *v. impers.* be necessary, be required; must, have to, should, ought to; *comme il faut* proper, decent; *s'en ~* be wanting.

fameux, -euse, *adj.* famous.

familier, -ière, *adj.* familiar.

famille, *s. f.* family.

faner, *v.n.* fade.

fantaisie, *s.f.* fancy.

fantastique, *adj.* fantastic.

fardeau, *s.m.* burden.

farine, *s.f.* flour, meal.

fatal, *adj.* mortal, fatal.

fatigant, *adj.* fatiguing.

fatigue, *s.f.* fatigue.

fatigué, *adj.* tired, weary.

fatiguer, *v. a.* tire, weary,

fatigue.

faubourg, *s.m.* suburb.

faucher, *v.a.* mow, cut.

faucheuse, *s.f.* *(a moteur)* (lawn-)mower.

faucille, *s. f.* sickle.

faucon, *s.m.* falcon.

faute, *s. f.* mistake, error, fault; lapse; want; *faire* ~ fail.

fauteuil, *s. m.* arm-chair, easy chair; stall, dress-circle seat.

fauve, *s.m.* wild beast.

faux[1], fausse, *adj.* false.

faux[2], *s. f.* scythe.

faveur, *s. f.* favour; *en* ~ *de* in favour of, on behalf of.

favorable, *adj.* favourable.

favori, -ite, *adj.* favorite.

fécond, *adj.* fertile.

féconder, *v.a.* fertilize.

fédéral, *adj.* federal.

fédération, *s.f.* federation.

fédéré, -e, *adj. & s. m. f.* federate.

feindre*, *v. a. & n.* feign.

félicitation, *s.f.* congratulation.

félicité, *s.f.* happiness.

féliciter, *v.a.* congratulate.

féminin, *adj.* feminine.

femme, *s.f.* woman; wife.

fendre, *v. a.* split; rend.

fenêtre, *s. f.* window.

fente, *s. f.* crack, split.

fer, *s. m.* iron; ~ *à cheval* horseshoe.

férié, *adj. jour* ~ holiday.

ferme[1], *adj.* firm; — *adv.* fast; firmly.

ferme[2], *s. f.* farm.

fermé, *adj.* closed.

fermer, *v. a.* close, shut; *se* ~ close, be shut.

fermeté, *s. f.* firmness.

fermeture, *s. f.* shutting; shutter; ~ *éclair* zip fastener, zipper.

fermier, *s. m.* farmer.

féroce, *adj.* wild, cruel.

férocité, *s. f.* ferocity.

ferronnerie, *s.f.* iron-works.

fertile, *adj.* fertile.

fervent, *adj.* fervent.

ferveur, *s. f.* fervour.

fesse, *s.f.* buttock.

festin, *s.m.* feast.

fête, *s. f.* feast, holiday; birthday.

fêter, *v. a.* observe; celebrate.

fêteur, -euse, *s. m. f.* holiday-maker.

feu, *s. m.* fire, flame; light; *mettre le* ~ *à* set on fire; *prendre* ~ take fire; ~ *d'artifice* fireworks *(pl.);* ~*x de circulation* traffic lights; ~*x d'arrière* tail lights.

feuillage, *s.m.* foliage.

feuille, *s.f.* leaf; sheet.

février, *s.m.* February.

fiancé, -e, *s. m. f.* fiancè, -e.

fiancer, *v.a.* engage; *se* ~ be engaged.

fibre, *s. f.* fibre.

ficelle, *s. f.* string.

fiche, *s. f.* pin, peg; slip (of paper).

ficher, *v. a.* drive in, fix; do, work; deal (a blow).

fidèle, *adj.* faithful.

fidélité, *s. f.* fidelity.

fier: *se* ~ trust, count on.

fierté, *s. f.* pride.

fièvre, *s. f.* fever.

figue, *s. f.* fig.

figure, *s. f.* form, shape; face; figure.

figurer, *v.a.* figure, represent; *se* ~ imagine.

fil, *s.m.* thread, yarn; edge; clue; ~ *(de fer)* wire.

file, *s. f.* row, file, line.

filer, *v.a. & n.* spin.

filet, *s.m.* net; fillet; rack.

fille, *s. f.* daughter; girl; maid; *jeune* ~ young lady.

fillette, *s.f.* little girl.

filleul, -e, *s. m. f.* godson, god-daughter.

film, *s. m.* film; *le grand* ~ feature film; ~ *avec* film featuring ...; ~ *annonce* trailer.

fils, *s. m.* son.

fin[1], *s.f.* end; close; *à la* ~ in the end, finally; *mettre* ~ *à* put an end to; *tirer à sa* ~ come to an end; ~ *de semaine* week-end.

fin[2], *adj.* fine; nice.

final, *adj.* final.

finance, *s. f.* finance.

financier, *adj.* financial.

fini, *adj.* finished; ended; over.

finir, *v. a. & n.* end, finish, put an end to; eat up.

finlandais, -e (F.), *adj.* Finnish; — *s. m. f.* Finn; Finnish.

fixe, *adj.* fixed, firm.

fixer, *v.a.* fix, fasten; stare at; settle.

flacon, *s. m.* flagon, bottle.

flagrant, *adj.* flagrant.

flairer, *v. a.* smell, scent.

flambeau, *s. m.* torch.

flamboyer, *v.n.* flame, flare.

flamme, *s.f.* flame.

flanelle, *s. f* flannel.

flanquer, *v.a.* fling.

flatter, *v. a.* caress; flatter.

flatterie, *s.f.* flattery.

flèche. *s. f.* arrow.

fléchir, *v. a.* bend, bow; *fig.* move.

fleur, *s. f.* flower, blossom.

fleurir, *v.n.* flower, blossom.

fleuve, *s. m.* river.

flirter, *v. n.* flirt.

flocon, *s. m.* flake *(snow etc.).*

flot, *s. m.* wave; flood; *être à* ~ be floating.

flottant, *adj.* floating.

flotte, *s.f.* fleet; navy.

flotter, *v.n. & a.* float.

fluide, *s. m. & adj.* fluid.

flute, *s. f.* flute.

foi, *s.f.* faith, belief; credit.

foie, *s. m.* liver.

foin, *s.m.* hay; grass.

foire, *s.f.* fair, market.

fois, *s.f.* time; *une* ~ once; *encore une* ~ again; *deux* ~ twice; *à la* ~ at same time; *chaque* ~ every time.

folie, *s. f.* folly, madness.

folle *see* **fou.**

foncer, *v. a.* sink; darken, deepen.

fonction, *s.f.* function, duty.

fonctionnaire, *s.m.f.* functionary, official.

fonctionner, *v.n.* function, operate, work.

fond, *s. m.* bottom, ground, foundation; *à* ~ thoroughly.

fondamental, *adj.* fundamental, basic.

forcer, *v. a.* force; break open; compel, impel.

forêt, *s. f.* forest.

forger, *v. a.* forge.

formalité, *s. f.* formality.

forme, *s. f.* form, shape.

formel, -elle, *adj.* formal, express; flat.

former, *v. a.* form, shape.

formidable, *adj.* formidable, terrible.

formule, *s.f.* formula.

formuler, *v. a.* formulate, draw up.

fort, *adj.* strong, robust; fat; stout, stiff; skilful; heavy; *être ~ en* be well up in; — *adv.* very (much), highly, hard; *~ bien* very well; — *s. m.* strong man; stronghold.

forteresse, *s.f.* fortress.

fortification, *s. f.* fortification.

fortifier, *v. a.* strengthen, fortify.

fortune, *s.f.* fortune; chance; luck; wealth, property.

fou, fol, folle, *adj.* mad, foolish; crazy.

foudre, *s.f.* lightning, thunderbolt.

fouille, *s. f.* excavation.

fouiller, *v. a. & n.* dig, excavate.

fouillis, *s.m.* muddle, mess.

foule, *s. f.* crowd, mass.

four, *s. m.* oven, furnace.

fourchette, *s.f.* fork *(table)*.

fourgon, *s. m.* (delivery) van; wagon; *~ (aux bagages)* luggage-van.

fourmi, *s.f.* ant.

fourneau, *s.m.* stove, range; *~ à gaz* gas-ring, -stove; *~ électrique* electric cooker.

fourniment, *s.m.* outfit, kit.

fournir, *v.a.* furnish (with), supply; provide (with).

fourreau, *s.m.* sheath, case, scabbard.

fourreur, *s.m.* furrier.

fourrure, *s.f.* fur.

foyer, *s.m.* fireside, home; foyer, lounge.

fracas, *s.m.* crash; uproar; fuss; noise.

fracasser, *v.a.* shatter, smash.

fraction, *s.f.* fraction; portion; instalment.

fracture, *s.f.* fracture.

fragile, *adj.* fragile.

frais[1], fraîche, *adj.* fresh, cool; chilly.

frais[2], *s. m. pl.* expenses, charges, fees.

fraise, *s.f.* strawberry.

framboise, *s. f.* raspberry.

franc, franche, *adj.* frank, free, open.

français (F.), *adj.* French; — *s. m.* Frenchman; French (language).

Française, *s.f.* Frenchwoman.

franchir, *v.a.* clear, jump over, cross.

franchise, *s. f.* exemption; frankness.

frapper, *v.a.* strike, hit, knock; impress; surprise.

frein, *s. m.* bit (of bridle); brake; *fig.* check.

frêle, *adj.* weak, frail.

fréquent, *adj.* frequent.

frère, *s.m.* brother.

fricassée, *s.f.* fricassee.

friction, *s.f.* friction.

frigidaire, *s.m.* refrigerator.

frigo, *s.m.* fridge.

frileux, -euse, *adj.* chilly.

frire*, *v.n. & a.* fry.

friser, *v.a. & n.* curl.

frissonner, *v. n.* shiver, tremble.

frivole, *adj.* frivolous, flimsy.

froid, *s. m.* cold; *avoir ~* feel cold; — *adj.* cold, cool; *il fait froid* it is cold.

froisser, *v.a.* rumple, crumple; bruise; *fig.* offend, hurt; *se ~* take offence.

frôler, *v.a.* graze.

fromage, *s.m.* cheese.

front, *s.m.* forehead; face; front (part).

frontière, *s.f.* frontier, border.

frotter, *v. a.* rub.

fruit, *s.m.* fruit; produce.

fruitier, *s.m.* fruiterer, greengrocer.

fuir*, *v. n. & a.* run away, flee.

fuite, *s. f.* flight; leakage, leak.

fumée, *s.f.* smoke.

fumer, *v. a. & n.* smoke.

fumeur, **-euse** *s.m.f.* smoker.

fumier, *s.m.* dung.

funèbre, *adj.* funereal.

funérailles, *s.f.pl.* funeral.

funiculaire, *s.m.* rope railway.

fureur, *s.f.* fury, rage.

furie, *s. f.* fury.

furieux, **-euse,** *adj.* furious.

furoncle, *s.m.* boil, furuncle.

fusée, *s.f.* fuse; rocket.

fusil, *s.m.* gun.

fusillade, *s.f.* firing, shooting.

futur, *adj. & s. m.* future.

fuyant, *adj.* flying, fleeing; passing.

G

gâchis, *s.m.* mortar; mire; *fig.* muddle, mess.

gaffe, *s. f.* blunder.

gage, *s. m.* pledge; security; **~s** wages.

gagner, *v. a.* gain; win.

gai, *adj.* gay, cheerful.

gaieté, *s.f.* gaiety.

gain, *s.m.* gain, profit.

galant, *adj.* courteous.

galerie, *s. f.* gallery.

galop, *s. m.* gallop.

gamin, *s.m.* urchin.

gamme, *s. f.* scale; range.

gant, *s. m.* glove.

garage, *s.m.* garage; siding.

garantie, *s. f.* guarantee.

garantir, *v. a.* guarantee.

garçon, *s. m.* boy; young man; fellow; bachelor; waiter.

garde[1], *s. f.* guard; watch; police; nurse.

garde[2], *s.m.* warden, guardian; watch.

garde-bébé, *s. m.* baby-sitter, sitter-in.

garde-boue, *s.f.* mudguard.

garde-chasse, *s. m.* gamekeeper.

garder, *v.a.* keep, take care of; attend (to).

garde-robe, *s.f.* wardrobe.

gardien, **-enne,** *s.m.f.* guardian, keeper; warden; watch(man); **~** *de la paix* constable; **~** *(de but)* goalkeeper.

gare, *s. f.* station; depot; **~** *des marchandises* goods station; *aller recevoir qn à la* **~** meet sy at the station.

garni, *s.m.* furnished lodgings *(pl.)*, digs.

garnir, *v. a.* furnish; fit up, trim.

garnison, *s. f.* garrison.

garniture, *s.f.* fittings *(pl.)*; set; garnishing.

gâteau, *s. m.* cake.

gâter, *v. a.* waste, impair; spoil.

gauche, *adj.* left.

gaz, *s. m.* gas; *usine à* **~** gas-works.

gazon, *s. m.* grass; lawn.

géant, *s. m.* giant.

gelée, *s. f.* jelly.

gémir, *v. n.* groan.

gênant, *adj.* inconvenient, annoying.

gendre, *s. m.* son-in-law.

gêne, *s. f.* inconvenience;

trouble; *être dans la* ~ be hard-up.

gêné, *adj.* uneasy; stiff; embarrassed.

gêner, *v.n.* inconvenience; be in the way of; interfere with.

général, *adj. & s. m.* general; *en* ~ in general, generally.

généraliser, *v.a. & n.* generalize.

générateur, *s.m.* generator.

génération, *s.f.* generation.

généreux, -euse, *adj.* generous.

générosité, *s.f.* generosity.

génie, *s. m.* genius; corps of engineers.

genou, *s.m.* *(pl. -x)* knee; *(pl.)* lap; *se mettre à* ~*s* kneel down.

genre, *s. m.* genus, kind.

gens, *s.m. f.* people; attendants.

gentil, -ille, *adj.* gentle.

géographie, *s.f.* geography.

géographique, *adj.* geographic(al).

géologie, *s. f.* geology.

géométrie, *s. f.* geometry.

géométrique, *adj.* geometric(al).

gérant, -e, *s. m. f.* manager; manageress.

gérer, *v. a.* manage.

germanique, *adj.* Germanic.

germe, *s.m.* germ.

gésir*, *v.n.* lie.

geste, *s.m.* gesture.

gesticuler, *v. n.* gesticulate.

gibier, *s. m.* game.

gifle, *s. f.* slap, box on the ear.

gifler, *v. a.* give s.o. a slap (in the face).

gilet, *s.m.* waistcoat, vest.

girafe, *s. f.* giraffe.

glace, *s. f.* ice; ice-cream; mirror; *mer de* ~ glacier.

glacer, *v. a.* freeze, chill.

glacial, *adj.* icy, glacial.

glacier, *s. m.* glacier.

glissade, *s. f.* slide; slip.

glissant, *adj.* slippery.

glisser, *v.n.* slide; slip; glide over; se ~ slip, creep (into).

globe, *s. m.* globe; earth.

gloire, *s. f.* glory, fame.

glorieux, -euse, *adj.* glorious; proud.

gober, *v.a.* swallow.

golfe, *s. m.* gulf.

gomme, *s. f.* gum; india-rubber.

gommer, *v. a.* gum.

gonfler, *v.a.* inflate.

gorge, *s.f.* throat, gullet.

gorgée, *s. f.* gulp.

gosse, *s.m.* kid, brat.

gothique, *adj.* Gothic.

goudron, *s. m.* tar.

gourmand, *adj.* greedy.

goût, *s. m.* taste; savour.

goûter, *v. a.* taste; relish, enjoy; — *s.m.* tea *(meal)*.

goutte, *s. f.* drop.

gouvernail, *s. m.* rudder, helm.

gouvernante *s. f.* governess.

gouvernement, *s.m.* government.

gouverner, *v. a.* govern, control, rule; manage; steer.

gouverneur, *s. m.* governor; tutor, preceptor.

grâce, *s. f.* grace; pardon; thanks *(pl.)*; favour.

gracieux, -euse, *adj.* graceful; gracious.

grade, *s. m.* rank, grade.

grain, *s. m.* grain, berry, corn; a touch (of).

graine, *s. f.* seed, berry.

graissage, *s. m.* lubrication.

graisse, *s. f.* fat, grease, lard.

graisser, *v.a.* grease, lubricate.

grammaire, *s. f.* grammar.

grammatical, *adj.* grammatical.

gramme, *s. m.* gramme.

gramophone, *s. m.* gramophone.

grand, *adj.* great; large; big; tall; grand.

grandeur, *s.f.* size; length; breadth; greatness.

grandir, *v.n.* grow (up); grow big, tall.

grand'mère, *s. f.* grandmother.

grand-père, *s. m.* grandfather.

granit, *s. m.* granite.

grappe, *s. f.* bunch; ~ *de raisin* bunch of grapes.

gras, grasse, *adj.* fat; thick.

gratitude, *s.f.* gratitude.

gratter, *v. a. & n.* scratch, overtake; brush.

gratuit, *adj.* free (of charge).

grave, *adj.* grave; heavy.

graver, *v.a.* engrave.

gravure, *s.f.* engraving.

grec, grecque (G.), *adj. & s. m. f.* Greek.

grêle, *adj.* slender, delicate, slim.

grelotter, *v.n.* shiver.

grenier, *s. m.* loft; granary.

grenouille, *s. f.* frog.

grève, *s. f.* strike; beach.

grief, *s. m.* grievance.

griffe, *s. f.* claw; clutch.

grill, *s. m.* grill, gridiron.

grille, *s. f.* iron railing, grating.

griller, *v.a.* grill, toast.

grimace, *s.f.* grimace.

grimacer, *v.n.* grimace.

grimper, *v. n. & n.* climb.

grincer, *v. n. & a.* grind, grate; creak.

grippe, *s.f.* influenza.

gris, *adj.* gray.

grogner, *v.n.* groan; grunt, grumble.

gronder, *v. n.* roar; rumble; *v.a.* scold.

gros, grosse, *adj.* large, big; stout; great; thick; — *s. m.* bulk; wholesale; *en* ~ roughly; wholesale.

grossier, *adj.* coarse, gross.

grossir, *v. a.* make bigger; increase; *v. n.* grow bigger.

grotesque, *adj.* grotesque.

groupe, *s.m.* group.

grouper, *v.a.* group.

grue, *s.f.* crane.

gué, *s. m.* ford (*across river*).

guêpe, *s. f.* wasp.

guérir, *v.a.* cure, heal; *v. n. & se* ~ be cured, get well again.

guerre, *s. f.* war.

gueule, *s. f.* mouth, jaws (*pl.*); opening.

guichet, *s.m.* ticket window; counter; booking-office.

guide, *s. m.* guide; conductor; guide-book.

guider, *v. a.* guide, lead.

guillemets, *s. m. pl.* inverted commas.

guise, *s. f.* way, manner; *à votre* ~ as you like.

guitare, *s. f.* guitar.

gymnastique, *s. f.* gymnastics.

H

habile, *adj.* able, clever.

habileté, *s. f.* skill, cleverness; ability.

habiller, *v. a.* clothe; dress (up); s'~ dress, put on one's clothes.

habit, *s. m.* (dress-)suit; coat; ~s clothes.

habitant, -e, *s.m.f.* inhabitant.

habitation, *s. f.* habitation, dwelling.

habiter, *v. a. & n.* inhabit, live in, dwell in.

habitude, *s. f.* habit, use.

habituel, -elle, *adj.* habitual, usual.

habituer, *v. a.* accustom; s'~ *a* get accustomed to, get used to.

hache, *s. f.* axe.

hacher, *v.a.* chop, cut up, hack, mince.

hachis, *s. m.* hash.

haine, *s. f.* hate, hatred.

haïr*, *v.a.* hate.

haleine, *s. f.* breath.

hall, *s. m.* lounge; ~ *de montage* erecting shop.

halle, *s.f.* market-hall.

hanche, *s.f.* haunch, hip.

hangar, *s. m.* shed, hangar.

happer, *v.a.* snap up.

harasser, *v.a.* harass.

hardi, *adj.* bold, daring.

hareng, *s.m.* herring.

haricot, *s.m.* bean; ~s *verts* French-beans.

harmonie, *s. f.* harmony.

harmonieux, -euse, *adj.* harmonious.

harnais, *s.m.* harness.

harpe, *s.f.* harp.

hasard, *s. m.* hazard, risk; *par* ~ by chance.

hasarder, *v.a.* hazard, risk, stake.

hasardeux, -euse, *adj.* risky; unsafe.

hâte, *s. f.* haste, hurry, rush; *a la* ~ in a hurry.

hâter, *v. a.* hasten, urge on; se ~ hurry (up).

hausse, *s. f.* rise.

hausser, *v. a. & n.* raise, lift; se ~ rise.

haut, *adj.* high; elevated; upright; loud; upper; *terre* ~e highland; *à voix* ~e aloud: — *adv.* high, highly, up; aloud; *en* ~ at the top; upstairs; — *s. m.* top, height, summit.

hauteur, *s.f.* height, altitude.

haut-parleur, *s. m.* loudspeaker.

havresac, *s.m.* haversack, knapsack.

hebdomadaire, *adj. & s. m.* weekly.

hébreu (H.), *adj. & s. m.* Hebrew.

hectare, *s.m.* hectare.

hélice, *s.f.* air-screw, propeller.

hélicoptère, *s.m.* helicopter.

herbe, *s.f.* herb, grass; pot-herb.

herbeux, -euse, *adj.* grassy.

hérédité, *s.f.* heredity.

hérisser, *v.a.* bristle; ruffle; se ~ bristle up, stand on end.

hérisson, *s. m.* hedgehog.

héritage, *s. m.* inheritance, heritage.

hériter, *v.a. & n.* inherit.

héritier, *s.m.* heir.

héritière, *s.f.* heiress.

héroïne, *s.f.* heroine.

héros, *s. m.* hero.

hésitation, *s.f.* hesitation.

hésiter, *v.n.* hesitate.

heure, *s. f.* hour, time; *quelle ~ est-il?* what time is it?; *il est dix ~s moins le quart* it's a quarter to ten; *dix ~s* ten o'clock; *dix ~s et quart* a quarter past ten; *dix ~s et demie* half past ten; *de bonne ~* early; *~s de pointe* rush hours; *~s d'ouverture* business hours; *~s supplémentaires* overtime.

heureux, -euse, *adj.* happy, fortunate, successful.

heurter, *v. a. & n.* knock against, hit, run into, against; **se ~** run, hit, dash against, collide.

hibou, *s. m. (pl. -x)* owl.

hideux, -euse, *adj.* hideous, terrible.

hier, *adv.* yesterday; *~ soir* last night.

hirondelle, *s. f.* swallow.

histoire, *s. f.* (hi)story,

historique, *adj.* historic.

hiver, *s.m.* winter.

hollandais, -e (H.), *adj. & s. m. f.* Dutch(man), Dutch-woman.

homard, *s.m.* lobster.

homme, *s.m.* man; *~ d'affaires* business man; *~ d'état* statesman.

hongrois, -e, (H.), *adj. & s.m.f.* Hungarian.

honnête, *adj.* honest.

honnêteté, *s. f.* honesty.

honneur, *s.m.* honour; credit.

honorable, *adj.* honourable.

honoraires, *s. m. pl.* fee(s).

honorer, *v.a.* honour.

honte, *s.f.* shame; *avoir ~ de* be ashamed of.

honteux, -euse, *adj.* shameful, disgraceful.

hôpital, *s. m. (pl. -aux)* hospital.

hoquet, *s.m.* hiccup.

horaire, *s.m.* time-table.

horizon, *s.m.* horizon.

horizontal, *adj.* horizontal.

horloge, *s.f.* clock.

horloger, *s.m.* watch-maker.

horreur, *s.f.* horror.

horrible, *adj.* horrible.

hors, *adv.* out, outside; *— prep.* out of, outside.

hospitalité, *s. f.* hospitality.

hostie, *s. f.* wafer (Church).

hostile, *adj.* hostile.

hostilité, *s.f.* hostility.

hôte, *s.m.* host; guest.

hôtel, *s.m.* hotel; large house; *~ de ville* town-hall.

hôtesse, *s. f.* hostess; *~ de l'air* air-hostess.

houe, *s. f.* hoe.

houillère, *s.f.* colliery.

hublot, *s.m.* window.

huile, *s. f.* oil.

huissier, *s. m.* usher.

huit, *adj. & s. m.* eight.

huitième, *adj.* eighth.

huître, *s. f.* oyster.

humain, *adj.* human.

humanité, *s. f.* humanity.

humble, *adj.* humble.

humecter, *v.a.* wet.

humer, *v. a.* inhale, suck in.

humide, *adj.* humid, wet.

humidité, *s. f.* humidity.

humiliation, *s. f.* humiliation.

humilier, *v. a.* humiliate.

humilité, *s. f.* humility.

humoristique, *adj.* humorous.

humour, *s. m.* humour.

hurlement, *s. m.* howl(ing), roar(ing).

hurler, *v.n.* howl, roar.

hutte, *s.f.* hut, cabin.

hydrogène, *s. m.* hydrogen.

hygiène, s. f. hygiene.
hymne, s. m. hymn.
hypocrite, s. m. f. hypo-
crite; — adj. hypocriti-
cal.
hypothèse, s. f. supposi-
tion; hypothesis.
hystérique, adj. hysterical.

I

ici, adv. here; d'~ from
here; par ~ this way.
idéal, -e, adj. ideal.
idéalisme, s. m. idealism.
idéaliste, s. m. f. idealist.
idée, s. f. idea, notion;
il m'est venu à l'~
it occurred to me.
identique, adj. identical.
identité, s.f. identity.
idiome, s. m. language,
dialect.
idiot, adj. idiotic; — s. m.
idiot.
idiotisme, s. m. idiom.
ignition, s. f. ignition.
ignorance, s. f. ignorance.
ignorant, adj. ignorant.
ignorer, v.a. not know,
be ignorant of, be
unaware of.
il, elle, pron. (pl. ils,
elles) he, she, it; they;
there.
île, s. f. island.
illégal, adj. illegal.
illicite, adj. illicit, un-
lawful.
illumination, s. f. illumination; ~ par projec-
teurs flood-lighting.
illuminer, v. a. illuminate,
light up; ~ par projec-
teurs flood-light.
illusion, s.f. illusion,
delusion.
illustration, s. f. illustration.
illustrer, v.a. illustrate,
explain.

image, s. f. image, pic-
ture, likeness.
imagé, adj. vivid.
imaginaire, adj. imagi-
nary, fantastic.
imaginatif, -ive, adj.
imaginative.
imagination, s. f. imagination, fancy.
imaginer, v.a. s'~ im-
agine.
imbécile, s.m. f. fool,
idiot; — adj. foolish.
imitation, s.f. imita-
tion, copy.
imiter, v. a. imitate, copy.
immédiat, adj. immediate.
immense, adj. immense.
immeuble, s. m. real
estate, landed property.
immigrant, -e, adj. &
s. m. f. immigrant.
immigration, s.f. im-
migration.
immigrer, v. a. immigrate.
immobile, adj. immobile.
immoral, adj. immoral.
immortel, -elle, adj. im-
mortal.
imparfait, adj. & s. m.
imperfect.
impartial, adj. impartial.
impatience, s. f. impa-
tience.
impatient, adj. impatient.
impayé, adj. unpaid.
impératif, -ive, adj. &
s. m. imperative.
impératrice, s. f. empress.
imperfection, s.f. im-
perfection.
impérial, adj. imperial.
impérialisme, s.m. im-
perialism.
imperméable, adj. im-
permeable; waterproof.
impertinent, adj. im-
pertinent.
impétueux, -euse, adj.
impetuous, headlong.
impliquer, v. a. implicate,

involve, imply.

implorer, *v.a.* implore, beg.

impoli, *adj.* impolite.

impopulaire, *adj.* unpopular.

importance, *s.f.* importance.

important, *adj.* important.

importateur, -trice, *s.m.f.* importer.

importation, *s.f.* importation; ~s imports.

importer, *v.n.* matter, be of moment; *n'importe* it does not matter.

importun, *adj.* troublesome, importunate.

importuner, *v.a.* annoy, molest, worry.

imposer, *v.a.* impose, inflict, lay (on); levy.

impossible, *adj.* impossible.

impôt, *s. m.* tax, duty.

impression, *s. f.* impression; print, edition; *faute d'*~ misprint.

impressionner, *v. a.* impress, affect.

imprimé, *s.m.* printed matter.

imprimer, *v. a.* (im)print, impress; publish.

imprimerie, *s. f.* printing; printing office.

impropre, *adj.* unfit, improper.

imprudent, *adj.* imprudent.

impuissant, *adj.* powerless, ineffectual, helpless.

impulsion, *s. f.* spur, impulse.

inaccoutumé, *adj.* unaccustomed.

inachevé, *adj.* unfinished.

inanimé, *adj.* inanimate.

inapplicable, *adj.* inapplicable, irrelevant.

inattendu, *adj.* unexpected.

inattentif, -ive, *adj.* inattentive, heedless.

incapable, *adj.* incapable, unable, inefficient.

incendie, *s. m.* fire.

incendier, *v. a.* set fire to.

incertain, *adj.* uncertain.

incessant, *adj.* incessant.

incident, *s. m.* incident; — *adj.* incidental.

inciter, *v.a.* incite, urge.

inclinaison, *s. f.* inclination, gradient.

inclination, *s. f.* inclination; bent; love.

incliner, *v. a. & n.* incline, bend; slope; slant; s'~ bow down, bend.

inclusif, -ive *adj.* inclusive.

incommode, *adj.* inconvenient, uncomfortable.

incommoder, *v.a.* inconvenience, annoy.

incomparable, *adj.* incomparable.

incompatible, *adj.* incompatible.

incompétent, *adj.* incompetent.

incomplet, *adj.* incomplete, imperfect.

inconscient, *adj.* unconscious.

inconséquent, *adj.* inconsistent.

inconvenant, *adj.* improper, unsuitable.

inconvénient, *s.m.* inconvenience.

incorrect, *adj.* incorrect.

incroyable, *adj.* incredible.

incurable, *adj.* incurable.

indécis, *adj.* uncertain.

indécision, *s. f.* indecision.

indéfini, *adj.* indefinite,

underïned.

indépendance, *s.f.* independence.

index, *s.m.* forefinger, index.

indicateur, *s. m.* indicator, gauge; time-table.

indication, *s. f.* indication; direction; sign.

indice, *s. m.* sign, token, mark; index.

indien, -enne (I.), *adj.* & *s.m.f.* Indian.

indifférent, *adj.* indifferent.

indigestion, *s. f.* indigestion.

indignation, *s. f.* indignation.

indiquer, *v.a.* indicate, point out, show.

indirect, *adj.* indirect.

indiscret, -ète, *adj.* indiscreet.

indiscrétion, *s. f.* indiscretion.

indispensable, *adj.* indispensable, essential.

indisposé, *adj.* unwell; upset.

individu, *s. m.* individual, person.

individuel, -elle, *adj.* individual.

indulgence, *s. f.* indulgence.

indulgent, *adj.* indulgent.

industrie, *s. f.* industry.

industriel, -elle, *adj.* industrial; — *s. m.* manufacturer.

inefficace, *adj.* inefficient.

inégal, *adj.* unequal.

inégalité, *s. f.* inequality.

inerte, *adj.* inert; dull.

inévitable, *adj.* inevitable.

inexpérimenté, *adj.* inexperienced.

inexplicable, *adj.* inexplicable.

infâme, *adj.* infamous.

infanterie, *s. f.* infantry.

infection, *s. f.* infection.

inférieur, *adj.* inferior.

infinitif, *s. m.* infinitive.

infirmerie, *s. f.* infirmary.

infirmier, -ère, *s. m. f.* nurse.

influence, *s. f.* influence.

influencer, *v. a.* influence.

information, *s. f.* information.

informer, *v. a.* inform, let know; s'~ *de* inquire about.

infructueux, -euse, *adj.* unsuccessful.

ingénieur, *s. m.* engineer.

ingénieux, -euse, *adj.* ingenious.

ingéniosité, *s. f.* ingenuity.

ingrat, *adj.* ungrateful.

ingrédient , *s. m.* ingredient.

inhabité, *adj.* uninhabited.

inintéressant, *adj.* uninteresting.

initial, -e, *adj.* & *s. f.* initial.

initiative, *s. f.* initiative; *syndicat d'~* tourist office.

injection, *s. f.* injection.

injure, *s.f.* injury.

injurier, *v.a.* insult.

injurieux, -euse, *adj.* injurious.

injuste, *adj.* unjust.

injustice, *s. f.* injustice.

innocence, *s. f.* innocence.

innocent, *adj.* innocent.

innombrable, *adj.* innumerable, countless.

inoccupé, *adj.* unoccupied.

inoculer, *v.a.* inoculate.

inondation, *s. f.* flood.

inonder, *v. a.* flood.

inquiet, -ète, *adj.* anxious, restless, uneasy.

inquiéter, *v.a.* worry.

insecte, *s.m.* insect.

insensé, *adj.* insane, mad.

insensible, *adj.* insensible.
inséparable, *ad.j* inseparable.
insigne, *s. m.* badge.
insignifiant, *adj.* insignificant.
insipide, *adj.* dull, flat.
insister, *v. a.* insist, lay stress on.
insolence, *s. f.* insolence.
insolent, *adj.* insolent.
insouciant, *adj.* careless.
inspecter, *v.a.* inspect, survey.
inspiration, *s. f.* inspiration.
inspirer, *v.a.* inspire, suggest; inhale.
installation, *s. f.* installation; fitting up.
installer, *v.a.* install; fit up; *v.n.* **s'~** to settle down.
instant, *adj.* instant, pressing; — *s.m.* instant, moment; *a l'~* instantly, at once.
instantané, *s.m.* snap(shot).
instinct, *s. m.* instinct.
instituer, *v.a.* institute.
institut, *s.m.* institute.
institution, *s. f.* institution; boarding-school.
instruction, *s. f.* instruction, tuition; knowledge, learning; direction; inquiry.
instruire*, *v.a.* instruct, teach.
instrument, *s. m.* instrument, implement, tool.
instrumental, *adj.* instrumental.
insuffisance, *s. f.* insufficiency.
insuffisant, *adj.* insufficient, deficient.
insulte, *s. f.* insult.
insulter, *v. a. & n.* insult.
insupportable, *adj.* intolerable, unbearable.

intact, *adj.* intact, entire.
intégral, *adj.* integral.
intégrité, *s.f.* integrity.
intellectuel, -elle, *adj. & s.m.* intellectual.
intelligence, *s. f.* intelligence, understanding.
intelligent, *adj.* intelligent, clever.
intendant, *s. m.* manager.
intense, *adj.* intense.
intensité, *s. f.* intensity.
intention, *s. f.* intention, purpose; *avoir l'~* intend, mean.
interdire, *v. a.* forbid.
intéressant, *adj.* interesting; *peu ~* uninteresting.
intéressé, *adj.* interested, concerned.
intéresser, *v. a. & n.* interest; concern; **s'~** take an interest (*à* in); be concerned.
intérêt, *s.m.* interest; concern; share; *avoir ~ à* have an interest in.
intérieur, *s.m.* inside, interior; *à l'~* inside, indoors; *Ministre de l'Intérieur* Home Secretary.
intermédiaire, *adj.* intermediate; — *s. m. f.* intermediary.
international, *adj.* international.
interne, *adj.* internal, inward.
interpellation, *s. f.* interpellation.
interpeller, *v. a.* interpellate, question.
interposer, *v. a.* interpose.
interprétation, *s. f.* interpretation.
interprète, *s. m. f.* interpreter.
interpréter. *v.a.* inter

pret; render.

interrogation, s. f. interrogation; inquiry.

interrogatoire, s.m. (cross-)examination.

interroger, v.a. interrogate, cross-examine, question.

interrompre, v.a. interrupt.

interrupteur, s. m. interrupter; switch.

interruption, s. f. interruption.

intervalle, s.m. interval; dans l'~ in the meantime.

intervenir, v.n. intervene, interfere, go between.

intervention, s. f. intervention.

interview, s. f. m. interview.

intime, adj. intimate.

intimité, s.f. intimacy.

intolérable, adj. intolerable.

intrigue, s.f. intrigue.

intriguer, v.n. & n. intrigue.

introduction, s. f. introduction.

introduire, v.a. introduce; show in.

inutile, adj. useless.

invalide, adj. invalid, disabled.

invasion, s. f. invasion.

inventer, v.a. make up.

inventeur, s. m. inventor.

invention, s. f. invention.

investigation, s. f. investigation, inquiry.

invisible, adj. invisible.

invitation, s.f. invitation.

invité, -e, s. m. f. guest.

inviter, v. a. invite.

iris, s. m. iris.

irlandais (I.), adj. Irish; — s. m. Irishman.

ironie, s. f. irony.

ironique, adj. ironical.

irradier, v. a. (ir)radiate.

irréel, adj. unreal.

irrésistible, adj. irresistible.

irritation, s. f. irritation.

irriter, v.a. irritate.

isolement, s. m. isolation.

isoler, v.a. isolate.

isotope, s.m. isotope.

issue, s. f. issue, outlet, way out.

italien, -enne (I.), adj. & s. m. f. Italian.

itinéraire, adj. itinerary; — s.m. guide-book.

ivre, adj. drunk.

J

j' see je.

jadis, adv. once, long ago, formerly.

jalousie, s.f. jealousy; blind.

jaloux, -se, adj. jealous.

jamais, adv. never, ever.

jambe, s. f. leg, shank.

jambon, s. m. ham.

janvier, s. m. January.

japonais, -e (J.), adj. & s. m. f. Japanese.

jardin, s. m. garden.

jardinier, -ère, s. m. f. gardener.

jarre, s. f. jar.

jarretière, s. f. garter.

jauge, s. f. gauge.

jauger, v. a. gauge.

jaune, adj. yellow; — s. m. yolk.

je, j', pron. I.

jersey, s. m. jersey.

jet, s.m. throw(ing).

jeter, v.a. throw, throw away, down; cast,

fling; shoot; discharge;
se ~ rush.

jeton, s. m. counter.

jeu, s.m. game, play, set.

jeudi, s. m. Thursday.

jeune, adj. young.

jeûne, s.m. fast(ing).

jeûner, v.n. fast.

jeunesse, s. f. youth.

joie, s. f. joy, delight

joindre*, v. a. & n. join,
unite; se ~ join.

joint, s. m. joint, arti-
culation.

jointure, s. f. joint.

joli, adj. pretty, nice.

jonction, s. f. junction.

jongleur, s. m. juggler.

joue, s. f. cheek (face).

jouer, v. a. & n. play;
gambol; gamble.

jouet, s. m. toy.

joueur, -euse, s. m. f.
player; gambler.

joug, s. m. yoke.

jouir, v.n. (~ de) en-
joy.

jouissance, s.f. enjoy-
ment, pleasure, joy.

jour, s. m. day; daylight,
light; life; ~ de fête
holiday; ~ de semaine
week-day; un ~ some
day; tous les ~s every
day; à ~ up to date.

journal, s. m. (news)pa-
per; journal; diary.

journalier, -ère, adj. daily;
— s.m. day-labour-
er.

journaliste, s. m. f. journalist.

journée, s. f. day; day's
wages (pl.); day's
work.

joyau, s. m. jewel.

joyeux, -euse, adj. joy-
ful, merry.

judiciaire, adj. judicial,
legal.

judicieux, -euse, adj. ju-

dicious, sensible, rea-
sonable.

juge, s. m. judge.

jugement, s. m. judg(e)-
ment; sentence.

juger, v. a. & n. judge.

juif, -ive (J.), adj. Jew-
ish; — s. m. f. Jew.

juillet, s. m. July.

juin, s. m. June.

jumeau, -elle adj. s. m. f.
twin; f. pl. binoculars.

jungle, s. f. jungle.

jupe, s. f. skirt.

juré, s. m. juryman.

jurer, v. a. & n. swear.

jurisprudence, s..f ju-
risprudence.

juron, s. m. oath.

jury, s. m. jury.

jus, s.m. juice.

jusque, jusqu'à, prep.
till; as far as.

juste, adj. just, right;
fair.

justice, s.f. justice.

justification, s.f. justification.

justifier, v.a. justify.

juvénile, adj. juvenile.

K

kangourou, s. m. kanga-
roo.

kayak, s. m. kayak.

képi, s. m. cap.

kilogramme, s.m. kil-
ogram(me).

kilomètre, s.m. kilo-
metre.

kiosque, s. n. kiosk.

L

l' = le or la.

la, *art.* the; —*pron.* her, it.

là, *adv.* there; here.

labeur, *s.m.* labour, work.

laboratoire, *s.m.* laboratory.

laborieux, -euse, *adj.* laborious, hard-working.

labourer, *v.a.* plough.

lac, *s. m.* lake.

lacer, *v. a.* lace.

lacet, *s. m.* lace; braid; bowstring; shoe-lace.

lâche, *adj.* loose; cowardly; — *s. m.* coward.

lâcher, *v.a.* loosen, slacken; let go.

lactation, *s. f.* lactation.

laid, *adj.* ugly; plain.

laideur, *s. f.* ugliness.

lainage, *s.m.* woollen goods *(pl.);* wool.

laine, *s. f.* wool; *pure* ~ all wool.

laïque, *adj.* lay.

laisser, *v.a.* leave, quit; give up; let alone; leave behind, off; ~ *aller* let go, neglect.

lait, *s. m.* milk.

laiterie, *s. f.* dairy.

laitier, *s. m.* milkman, dairyman.

laitière, *s. f.* dairymaid.

laitue, *s. f.* lettuce.

lambeau, *s. m.* rag, strip.

lame, *s. f.* blade; plate, sheet; ~ *de rasoir* razor-blade.

lamentation, *s. f.* lamentation.

lampe, *s. f.* lamp.

lancement, *s.m.* throwing; launching.

lancer, *v. a.* throw, fling; se ~ dart, rush.

langage, *s. m.* language, tongue; speech, way of speaking.

lange *s. m.* baby's nappy.

langue, *s. f.* tongue; language; ~ *maternelle* mother-tongue.

laper, *v. a.* lap (up).

lapin, *s. m.* rabbit.

laps, *s. m.* lapse, space (of time).

lapsus, *s. m.* lapse, slip.

laque, *s. f.* lacquer.

lard, *s. m.* bacon.

large, *adj.* broad, wise; generous; liberal; — *s.m.* room, breadth.

largeur, *s. f.* width.

larme, *s. f.* tear.

las, lasse, *adj.* weary.

lasser, *v.a.* tire, wear out; se ~ *de* get tired of.

latéral, *adj.* lateral, side.

latin, -e, *adj. & s. m. f.* Latin.

latitude, *s.f.* latitude; scope, freedom.

lavable, *adj.* washable.

lavabo, *s. m.* wash-basin; lavatory.

lavage, *s.m.* washing; ~ *de vaisselle* washing-up.

lavande, *s. f.* lavender.

laver, *v. a.* wash; se ~ wash (oneself); *machine à* ~ washing-machine.

layette, *s. f.* baby-linen.

le, la, l', *art.* the; —*pron.* (*pl.* les) him, her, it; them.

lécher, *v. a.* lick, lap.

leçon, *s. f.* lesson; lecture.

lecteur, -trice, *s. m. f.* reader; lector.

lecture, *s. f.* reading.

légal, *adj.* legal, lawful.

légende, *s. f.* legend.

léger, -ère, *adj.* light, slight; loose.

légèreté, *s. f.* lightness; ease.

légion, *s. f.* legion.

législation, *s.f.* legislation.

législature, *s. f.* legislature.

légitime, *adj.* legitimate, lawful.

légume, *s.m.* vegetable.

lendemain, *s.m.* next day, day after.

lent, *adj.* slow; tardy.

lenteur, *s.f.* slowness.

lentille, *s.f.* lentil; lens.

léopard, *s.m.* leopard.

lequel, laquelle, *rel. pron.* *(pl.* **lesquels, lesquelles)** who, whom; which, that.

lettre, *s.f.* letter; type character; ~s literature; arts; *à la* ~ literally, word for word; ~ *de change* bill of exchange; ~ *de crédit* letter of credit; ~ *recommandée* registered letter; *boîte aux* ~s letter-box.

lettré, *adj.* learned; literary.

leur, *poss. adj.* *(pl.* **-s)** their; — *pron.* to them, them; *le or la* ~, *les* ~s theirs, their own.

levée, *s. f.* raising; removal; levy.

lever, *v. a.* lift (up), raise; hoist; *v. n.* rise; *se* ~ rise get up.

levier, *s. m.* lever; ~ *des vitesses* gear-lever.

lèvre, *s. f.* lip.

lexique, *s.m.* lexicon.

liaison, *s.f.* joining, junction; union; connection; tie; liaison.

libéral, *adj.* liberal.

libérer, *v.a.* liberate.

liberté, *s.f.* liberty.

libraire, *s.m. f.* bookseller.

librairie, *s. f.* bookshop.

libre, *adj.* free; unoccupied.

licence, *s.f.* licence, degree.

licencié, -e, *s. m. f.* licenciate; licensee.

licencieux, -euse, *adj.* licentious.

lie, *s. f.* dregs, grounds *(pl.).*

liège, *s.m.* cork.

lien, *s.m.* tie, bond; band, strap, cord; link.

lier, *v. a.* bind, tie (up); fasten; link up.

lieu, *s. m.* place; *au* ~ *de* instead of; *avoir* ~ take place.

lieutenant, *s. m.* lieutenant.

lièvre, *s. m.* hare.

ligne, *s. f.* line; ~ *aérienne* air-line.

lilas, *s. m.* lilac.

limace, *s. f.* slug.

limaçon, *s. m.* snail.

lime, *s. f.* file.

limer, *v. a.* file.

limite, *s.f.* bound(s), border, limit.

limiter, *v.a.* limit, restrict.

limon, *s.m.* mud, silt.

limonade, *s. f.* lemonade.

lin, *s. m.* flax.

linge, *s. m.* linen.

linger, -ère, *s.m.f.* linendraper.

lingerie, *s. f.* ladies' underclothing, lingerie.

lion, *s. m.* lion.

liqueur, *s. f.* liqueur.

liquide, *adj.* liquid.

liquider, *v.a.* liquidate.

lire*, *v.a.* read.

liste, *s. f.* list, roll; panel.

lit, *s. m.* bed.

litre, *s. m.* litre.

littéraire, *adj.* literary.

littérature, *s.f.* literature.

livraison, *s.f.* delivery; part (of book).

livre[1], *s. m.* book; work; *teneur de ~s* book-keeper.

livre[2], *s. f.* pound.

livrer, *v.a.* deliver; give up.

local, *s.m.* spot, premises; — *adj.* local.

localité, *s. f.* place, spot.

locataire, *s. m. f.* tenant, lodger.

location, *s. f.* letting out; hiring, renting; *prendre en ~* hire; *bureau de ~* box-office; *~ des places* seat reservation.

locomotive, *s.f.* (railway) engine.

loge, *s.f.* hut. cabin; box.

logement, *s. m.* lodging.

loger, *v.a.* accommodate, lodge; house; *v. n.* reside, live (in).

logeur, *s. m.* landlord.

logeuse, *s. f.* landlady.

logique, *s. f.* logic; — *adj.* logical.

loi, *s.f.* law, statute; *projet de ~* bill, draft.

loin, *adv.* far, far off, away; *au ~* far off.

lointain, *adj.* far, remote.

loisif, *s. m.* spare time, leisure.

long, longue, *adj. & s. m. f.* long; *être ~ à* be long in.

longitude, *s. f.* longitude.

longtemps, *adv.* long, a long time; *depuis ~* for a long time, long since.

longueur, *s. f.* length.

loquet, *s. m.* latch.

lors, *adv.* then; *dès ~* from that time.

lorsque, *conj.* when.

lot, *s. m.* lot, fate; prize.

loterie, *s. f.* lottery.

lotion, *s. f.* lotion.

louage, *s.m.* hiring; hire.

louche, *s.f.* ladle.

louer[1], *v.a.* hire (out); let; *à ~* for hire; to let.

louer[2], *v. a.* praise.

loup, *s. m.* wolf.

lourd, *adj.* heavy; clumsy.

louve, *s. f.* she-wolf.

loyal, *adj.* loyal, true.

loyauté, *s.f.* honesty.

loyer, *s. m.* rent; hire.

lubrifier, *v.a.* lubricate.

lucratif, -ive, *adj.* lucrative.

luge, *s. f.* sledge.

lugubre, *adj.* dismal.

lui, *pron.* (to) him, (to) her, (to) it.

lui-même, *pron.* himself.

luire*, *v. n.* shine, gleam.

lumière, *s. f.* light, daylight.

lumineux, -euse, *adj.* luminous, bright.

lundi, *s. m.* Monday.

lune, *s.f.* moon; *~ de miel* honeymoon.

lunette, *s. f.* telescope; *(pl.)* spectacles, specs; *~s de soleil* sun-glasses.

luthérien, -enne, *adj. & s. m. f.* Lutheran.

lutte, *s. f.* wrestling; fight, struggle.

lutter, *v.n.* wrestle, fight.

lutteur, *s. m.* wrestler.

luxe, *s. m.* luxury.

luxeux, -euse, *adj.* luxurious.

lycée, *s.m.* secondary

school, grammar-school.

M

m' *see* me.

ma *see* mon.

mâcher, *v. a.* chew.

machine, *s. f.* machine, engine, apparatus; ~ à coudre, sewing-machine.

mâchoire, *s. f.* jaw.

maçon, *s m.* mason.

madame, *s. f. (pl.* mesdames) madam.

mademoiselle, *s. f. (pl.* mesdemoiselles) miss.

magasin, *s.m.* shop; store; warehouse; *grand* ~ department store.

magique, *adj.* magic.

magnétique, *adj.* magnetic.

magnétophone, *s.m.* tape-recorder.

magnifique, *adj.* magnificent.

mai, *s. m.* May.

maigre, *adj.* lean, thin.

maigrir, *v.n.* grow lean, get thin.

maille, *s. f.* stitch; knot.

maillot, *s.m.* tights *(pl.);* ~ *(de bain)* bathing-costume.

main, *s. f.* hand; lead; *en* ~ in hand; *se donner la* ~ shake hands; *tenir la* ~ à see to, see that; *de seconde* ~ second-hand.

maintenant, *adv.* now, at present

maintenir, *v. a.* (up)hold, support, keep (up), maintain.

maintien, *s. m.* maintenance.

maire, *s. m.* mayor.

mais, *conj.* but.

maïs, *s. m.* maize.

maison, *s. f.* house, residence; home; firm; *à la* ~ at home, indoors; *tenir* ~ keep house.

maître, *s.m.* master; proprietor; teacher; ~ d'école schoolmaster; ~ de maison host.

maîtresse, *s. f.* mistress; (land)lady; sweetheart; ~ d'école schoolmistress.

maîtrise, *s.f.* mastery, control.

maîtriser, *v.a.* master.

majesté, *s. f.* majesty.

majeur, *adj.* major; main; chief; — *s. m.* major.

majorité, *s. f.* majority.

majuscule, *s. f.* capital letter.

mal, *s. m.* ill, evil, wrong; pain, harm; trouble, hardship; *avoir* ~ à have a pain in; — *adv.* wrong, badly, ill.

malade, *adj.* sick, ill; *tomber* ~ fall ill, be taken ill; — *s. m. f.* invalid, patient.

maladie, *s.f.* illness; sickness; disease.

maladroit, *adj.* awkward, clumsy.

malaise, *s. m.* uneasiness.

malchance, *s.f.* bad luck.

mâle, *s. m.* male.

malentendu, *s. m.* misunderstandig.

malgré, *prep.* in spite of; ~ *tout* for all that.

malheur, *s.m.* misfortune, ill luck; mischance; accident.

malheureux, -euse, *adj.* unfortunate, unlucky.

malice, *s. f.* malice.

malin, maligne, *adj.* malicious, malignant; evil.

malle, *s. f.* trunk; mail;

faire la ~ pack.

mallette, *s.f.* suit-case.

malpropre, *adj.* dirty, filthy; untidy.

malsain, *adj.* unhealthy.

malveillant, *adj.* male-volent, evil-minded.

maman, *s.f.* mamma.

manche¹, *s.m,* handle. holder.

manche², *s. f.* sleeve.

Manche, *s.f.* English Channel.

manchette, *s. f.* cuff.

mandat, *s. m.* mandate; money-order.

manger, *v.a.* eat; *donner à* ~ feed; *salle à* ~ dining-room; — *s. m.* eating; food.

manicure, *s. m. f.* manicure.

manier, *v.a.* handle.

manière, *s. f.* manner, way, fashion; *(pl.)* manners.

manifestation, *s. f.* manifestation.

manifester, *v.a.* manifest, show; **se** ~ manfest oneself.

manipuler, *v. a.* manipulate, operate.

manœuvre, *s.f.* action; proceeding; manœuvre; *s. m.* labourer.

manœuvrer, *v. a. & n.* handle, manœuvre, work.

manoir, *s. m.* manor.

manque, *s.m.* want; deficiency.

manquer, *v. a.* miss; *v. n.* fail; be missing, be wanting.

mansarde, *s.f.* garret.

manteau, *s. m.* coat.

manuel, -elle, *adj.* manual; — *s. m.* manual, handbook.

manufacture, *s. f.* manufacture; factory.

manufacturer, *v. a.* manufacture.

manuscrit, *s. m.* manuscript.

maquillage, *s.m.* make-up.

marbre, *s. m.* marble.

marchand, -e, *s. m. f.* merchant, tradesman; shopkeeper.

marchandise, *s. f.* merchandise, goods *(pl.)*.

marche, *s. f.* walk; march; progress; move.

marché, *s. m.* market; bargain; agreement: *bon* ~ cheap.

marcher, *v.n.* walk; travel; march; work; run; proceed.

mardi, *s. m.* Tuesday; ~ *gras* Shrove Tuesday.

mare, *s.f.* pool, pond.

maréchal, *s. m.* marshal.

marée, *s.f.* tide, flood.

margarine, *s. f.* margarine.

marge, *s. f.* margin.

mari, *s.m.* husband.

mariage, *s. m.* marriage.

marié, -e, *adj.* married; — *s. m. f.* bridegroom, married man; bride, married woman.

marier, *v. a.* marry; match; — **se** ~ marry, get married.

marin, *adj.* marine; — *s.m.* seaman, sailor, mariner.

marmelade, *s. f.* marmalade.

marque, *s. f.* mark, imprint; trade-mark.

marquer, *v.a.* mark; stamp; brand.

marron, *s. m.* chestnut.

mars, *s. m.* March.

marteau, *s. m.* hammer.

martyr, -e, *s.m.f.* martyr.

masque, s. m. mask.

masquer, v.a. mask.

massacre, s. m. massacre.

massage, s. m. massage.

masse, s. f. mass; heap.

massif, -ive, adj. massive, bulky, clumsy.

mât, s. m. mast.

match, s. m. match.

matelas, s. m. mattress.

matelot, a.m. sailor, seaman.

matérialisme, s. m. materialism.

matériaux, s.m.pl. material(s).

matériel, -elle, adj. material; — s. m. matter; material; implements (pl.).

maternel, -elle, adj. maternal; motherly; école ~le infant-school.

mathématicien, -enne, s. m. f. mathematician.

mathématique, adj. mathematical; — s. f. mathematics.

matière, s.f. matter; material; substance; ~ première raw material.

matin, s.m. morning; le ~ in the morning; du ~ a.m.

matinal, adj. morning.

matinée, s.f. morning; matinée.

matrice, s. f. womb.

maturité, s. f. maturity.

maudire*, v.a. curse.

mauvais, adj. bad, ill, evil; — s. m. bad.

me, m' pron. (to) me; (to) myself.

mécanicien, s. m. mechanic; engine-driver.

mécanique, adj. mechanic(al); — s.m. mechanics; machine; mechanism.

mécaniser, v. a. mechanize.

mécanisme, s. m. mechanism; machinery.

méchant, adj. evil, bad.

mécontent, adj. displeased, dissatisfied, unhappy.

mécontenter, v. a. dissatisfy.

médaille, s. f. medal.

médecin, s.m. doctor, physician.

médecine, s. f. medicine.

médical, adj. medical.

médicament, s. m. medicament; medicine.

médiéval, adj. medieval.

méditation, s. m. meditation.

méditer, v. a. & n. meditate.

méfiance, s. f. mistrust.

méfier: se ~ be suspicious (de of); mistrust.

meilleur, -e, adj. better; — s. m. f. the best.

mélancolie, s. f. melancholy, gloom.

mélancolique, adj. melancholy, sad.

mélange, s.m. mixture, blend.

mélanger, v.a. mix, blend.

mêler, v.a. mix (up), mingle; se ~ mingle, be mixed; interfere with.

mélodie, s. f. melody.

melon, s.m. melon.

membre, s.m. member, limb.

même, adj. same; self; — adv. even, also, likewise; de ~ in the same way; de ~ que as well as; quand ~ even if.

mémoire, s.f. memory; s.m. memorandum; bill; (pl.) memoirs.

menace, *s.f.* menace.

menacer, *v.a.* threaten.

ménage, *s. m.* housekeeping; household.

ménager, *v. a.* be sparing of; take care of; manage.

ménagère, *s.f.* housewife, housekeeper.

mendiant, -e, *s.m.f.* beggar.

mendier, *v. a. & n.* beg.

mener, *v.a.* guide, conduct, lead.

mensonge, *s.m.* lie.

mensuel, *adj.* monthly.

mental, *adj.* mental.

mention, *s.f.* mention.

mentionner, *v. a.* mention.

mentir*, *v.n.* lie, tell a lie.

menton, *s.m.* chin.

menu, *adj.* slim; small; minute; — *s. m.* bill of fare, menu.

menuisier, *s. m.* joiner, carpenter.

méprendre: se ~ make a mistake, be mistaken.

mépris, *s.m.* contempt.

mer, *s.f.* sea; *par* ~ by sea; *bord de la* ~ seaside.

mercerie, *s. f.* haberdashery.

merci, *s. f.* mercy; — *int.* thanks!, (no) thank you!

mercredi, *s. m.* Wednesday.

mercure, *s.m.* mercury.

mère, *s.f.* mother.

mérite, *s. m.* merit, worth.

mériter, *v.a.* merit, deserve.

merveille, *s.f.* wonder.

merveilleux, -euse, *adj.* wonderful.

message, *s.m.* message.

messe, *s.f.* mass.

mesure, *s.f.* measure,

gauge, measurement; size; metre.

mesurer, *v.a.* measure.

métal, *s.m.* metal.

métallique, *adj.* metallic.

météorologie *s. f.* meteorology.

méthode, *s.f.* method.

méthodique, *adj.* methodical, systematic.

métier, *s. m.* trade; business; employment, occupation.

mètre, *s. m.* metre.

métro, *s. m.* tube, underground.

métropolitain, *adj.* metropolitan; underground.

mets, *s.m.* dish, food.

mettre*, *v.a.* put, set, place; put in, on; bring; ~ *de c té* set aside, save; ~ *en ordre* set in order, tidy up; se ~ sit down; *se ~ à* set about, take to.

meuble, *s. m.* (piece of) furniture; — *adj.* movable; *biens* ~s personal property.

meubler, *v.a.* furnish, fit up.

meunier, *s.m.* miller.

meurtre, *s.m.* murder.

meurtrier, *s. m.* murderer.

meurtrir, *v.a.* bruise, injure.

mi-, half, mid.

microbe, *s. m.* microbe.

microphone, *s. m.* microphone.

microscope, *s. m.* microscope.

midi, *s. m.* noon, midday; south.

miel, *s. m.* honey.

mien, *pron.* mine, my own.

miette, *s. f.* crumb.

mieux, *adv.* better.

mignon, -onne, *adj.* tiny; — *s.m.f.* darling.

migraine, *s. f.* headache.

milieu, *s.m.* middle, centre; environment.

militaire, *adj.* military; — *s. m.* soldier.

mille[1], *adj. & s.m.* thousand.

mille[2], *s. m.* mile (= 1609 metres).

millier, *s.m.* thousand.

million, *s.m.* million.

millionaire, *s. m. f.* millionaire.

mince, *adj.* thin, slim.

mine[1], *s.f.* mine.

mine[2], *s.f.* look(s); *bonne ~* good-looki ...

miner, *v. a.* (under)mine.

minerai, *s.m.* ore.

minéral, *adj.* mineral.

mineur[1], *s.m.* miner.

mineur[2], -e, *adj. & s. m. f.* minor.

ministère, *s. m.* ministry.

ministre, *s. m.* minister; *premier ~* prime minister, premier.

minorité, *s. f.* minority.

minuit, *s.m.* midnight.

minuscule, *s.f.* small letter.

minute, *s.f.* minute; instant.

miracle, *s.m.* miracle.

miraculeux, -euse, *adj.* miraculous, wonderful.

miroir, *s.m.* mirror.

misérable, *adj.* miserable.

misère, *s. f.* misery.

miséricorde, *s. f.* mercy.

mission, *s.f.* mission.

missionnaire, *adj. & s. m. f.* missionary.

mite, *s. f.* moth.

mobile, *adj.* movable, mobile.

mobilier, *s. m.* furniture, suite.

mobilisation, *s. f.* mobilization.

mobiliser, *v.a.&n.* mobilize.

mode[1], *s.f.* fashion, vogue; *à la ~* in vogue, in fashion.

mode[2], *s. m.* mode, way; mood.

modèle, *s.m.* model.

modération, *s. f.* moderation.

modérer, *v.a.* moderate.

moderne, *adj* modern.

modeste, *adj.* modest.

modestie, *s.f.* modesty.

modification, *s. f.* modification, change.

modifier, *v.a.* modify.

modiste, *s.f.* milliner.

moelleux, -euse, *adj.* soft, mellow.

mœurs, *s. f. pl.* manners, customs, ways.

moi, *pron.* me, to me.

moi-même, *pron.* myself.

moindre, *adj.* less, lesser, smaller; *le ~* the least.

moineau, *s. m.* sparrow.

moins, *adv. & s. m.* less (*que, de* than); fewer (*de* than); minus; *le ~* the least; *à ~ que* unless; *au ~* at least.

mois, *s. m.* month; *par ~* monthly; a month.

moisson, *s.f.* harvest, crop.

moissonner, *v. a.* harvest, reap.

moitié, *s.f.* half.

molécule, *s. f.* molecule.

mollet, *s. m.* calf (*of leg*).

moment, *s. m.* moment, instant.

mon, ma, *pron. (pl. mes)* my.

monarchie, *s. f.* monarchy

monastère, *s. m.* monastery, convent.

mondain, *ad²* worldly.

monde, *s.m.* ...rld; people, company; *mettre au ~* give birth to; *tout le ~* everybody.

monnaie, *s.f.* money, coin, change; currency; ~ *légale* legal tender; ~ *étrangère* foreign currency.

monopole, *s.m.* monopoly.

monotone, *adj.* monotonous.

monseigneur, *s.m.* my lord, your lordship.

monsieur, *s. m.* gentleman; M. Mr.

monstrueux, -euse, *adj.* monstrous.

mont, *s. m.* mountain.

montage, *s. m.* carrying up; mounting, setting; wiring.

montagne, *s. f.* mountain.

montagneux, -euse, *adj.* mountainous.

montant, *adj.* ascending, uphill; *en* ~ upwards.

monte-charge, *s. m.* goods lift.

montée, *s. f.* rise, slope.

monter, *v.n.* go up, come up, ascend, climb; mount; ride; amount *(à* to); equip, fit up; ~ *à cheval* ride; *faire* ~ *qn. (dans sa voiture)* give s.o. a lift.

montre¹, *s.f.* watch.

montre², *s.f.* display, show; show-window.

montrer, *v.a.* show, display, point out; se ~ show oneself.

montueux, -euse, *adj.* hilly, steep.

monument, *s. m.* monument.

monumental, *adj.* monumental.

moquerie, *s. f.* mockery.

moral, _ *adj.* moral.

morale, *s. f.* ethics; morality.

moralité, *s. f.* morality, morals *(pl.).*

morceau, *s. m.* piece,

morsel, bit; snack.

mordre, *v. a.* bite; gnaw.

mors, *s. m.* bit; *fig.* check.

mort, *s. f.* death; — *adj.* dead, lifeless.

mortel, -elle, *adi.* mortal; boring, tedious.

mot, *s. m.* word; short note; ~s *croisés* crossword (puzzle).

motel, *s. m.* motel.

moteur, *s. m.* motor, engine.

motif, *s. m.* motive; cause.

motion, *s.f.* motion, movement.

motocyclette, *s. f.* motor-(bi)cycle, motor-bike.

mou, mol, molle, *adj.* soft; loose.

mouche, *s. f.* fly.

moucher: se ~ blow one's nose.

mouchoir, *s. m.* handkerchief.

moudre*, *v.a.* grind.

mouette, *s.f.* gull.

mouiller, *v.a.* & *n.* soak, wet.

moule, *s. m.* mould, cast.

moulin, *s. m.* mill; ~ *à vent* windmill; ~ *à café* coffee-mill.

mourant, *adj.* dying, expiring.

mourir*, *v. n.* die, expire.

mousse, *s. f.* foam, froth, lather; moss.

moustache, *s. f.* moustache.

moustique, *s.m.* mosquito.

moutarde, *sf.* mustard.

mouton, *s.m.* sheep; mutton.

mouvement, *s. m.* movement, motion, move.

mouvoir*, *v.a.* move; start; se ~ move, stir.

moyen, -enne, *adj.* mean, middle, average; *le* ~ *âge* the Middle Ages; — *s. m.* means, way, manner; *au* ~ *de* by means of; *avoir les* ~*s de* can afford.

moyenne, *s. f.* average, mean; *en* ~ on the average.

muet, -ette, *adj.* dumb, mute; speechless.

multiplication, *s. f.* multiplication.

multiplier, *v.a.&n.* multiply.

multitude, *s. f.* multitude, crowd.

municipal, *adj.* municipal, city.

munir, *v.a.* provide *(de* with).

munition, *s. f.* (am)munition.

mur, *s. m.* wall.

mûr, *adj.* ripe; mature.

mûrir, *v. a. & n.* ripen.

murmure, *s.m.* murmur.

murmurer, *v.n.* murmur.

muscle, *s.m.* muscle.

muse, *s. f.* muse.

museau, *s. m.* muzzle. musician; — *adj.* musical.

musical, *adj.* musical.

musicien, -enne, *s. m. f.*

musique, *s.f.* music; *instrument de* ~ musical instrument.

mutuel, -elle, *adj.* mutual.

myope, *adj.* short-sighted.

mystère, *s.m.* mystery.

mystérieux, -euse, *adj.* mysterious.

mystification, *s. f.* mystification.

mystique, *adj.* mystic.

N

nacre, *s.f.* mother-of-pearl.

nage, *s.f.* swimming; rowing, paddling.

nager, *v.n.* swim; float; row.

nageur, -euse, *s. m. f.* swimmer.

naïf, -ïve, *adj.* naïve.

nain, -e, *s. m. f.* dwarf.

naissance, *s. f.* birth; *lieu de* ~ birth-place.

naître*, *v. n.* be born; arise (from).

nappe, *s.f.* table-cloth.

narine, *s.f.* nostril.

nasal, *adj.* nasal.

natal, *adj.* natal, native, birth.

natif, -ive, *adj. & s. m. f.* native.

nation, *s.f.* nation.

national, *adj.* national.

nationalité, *s.f.* nationality.

naturaliser, *v.a.* naturalize.

nature, *s.f.* nature.

naturel, -elle, *adj.* natural, native.

naturellement, *adv.* naturally, of course.

naufrage, *s. m.* shipwreck; *faire* ~ be shipwrecked.

nausée, *s.f.* nausea.

nautique, *adj.* nautical.

naval, *adj.* naval.

navigateur, *s.m.* navigator.

navigation, *s.f.* navigation; sailing; *compagnie de* ~ shipping company; ~ *spatiale* space-flight.

naviguer, *v. a. & n.* navigate.

navire, *s.m.* ship; ~*s*

shipping.

ne, n', *adv.* not; ~... *pas* not; ~ ... *que* only.

né, -e, *adj.* born; née.

nécessaire, *adj.* necessary.

nécessité, *s. f.* necessity.

nécessiter, *v.a.* necessitate, make necessary.

nef, *s. f.* ship, vessel; nave; ~ *latérale* aisle.

négatif, -ive, *adj. & s. m.* negative.

négative, *s. f.* negative.

négligence, *s. f.* neglect, negligence.

négligent, *adj.* negligent.

négliger, *v.a.* neglect.

négociant, -e, *s. m. f.* merchant, trader.

négociation, *s. f.* negotiation, transaction.

nègre, *s.m.* negro.

neige, *s.f.* snow.

neiger, *v.n.* snow.

neigeux, -euse, *adj.* snowy

néon, *s. m.* neon.

nerf, *s. m.* nerve; sinew.

nerveux, -euse, *adj.* nervous.

net, nette, *adj.* clean, neat, clear, tidy; net; — *adv.* flatly, point-blank.

nettoyage, *s. m.* cleaning, cleansing.

nettoyer, *v.a.* clean, cleanse, clear.

neuf[1], *adj. & s. m.* nine.

neuf[2], neuve, *adj.* new.

neutre, *adj.* neutral.

neuvième, *adj.* ninth.

neveu, *s.m.* nephew.

nez, *s.m.* nose.

ni, *conj.* ~... ~ (n)either ... (n)or; ~ *l'un* ~ *l'autre* neither (one).

nid, *s.m.* nest; berth.

nièce, *s.f.* niece.

nier, *v.a.* deny.

niveau, *s. m.* level.

noble, *adj.* noble.

noblesse, *s.f.* nobility.

noce, *s. f. (often pl.)* wedding; *(sing.)* revelry.

Noël, *s. m.* Christmas; *veillée de* ~ Christmas eve.

nœud, *s. m.* knot, bow, tie.

noir, *adj.* black.

noix, *s. f.* (wal)nut; ~ *de coco* coconut.

nom, *s. m.* name, surname; fame; noun; ~ *de famille* surname.

nombre, *s.m.* number.

nombreux, -euse, *adj.* numerous.

nomination, *s. f.* nomination, appointment.

nommer, *v. a.* name, give name to; appoint, nominate.

non, *adv.* no, not.

nonne, *s. f.* nun.

nord, *s. m.* north; *du* ~, *au* ~ northern.

nord-est, *s. m.* northeast.

nord-ouest, *s. m.* northwest.

normal, *adj.* normal.

norvégien, -enne (N.), *adj. & s. m. f.* Norwegian.

nos, *poss. adj.* our.

notable, *adj.* notable, remarkable.

notaire, *s. m.* notary (-public).

note, *s. f.* note, mark; bill, account; note *(music)*; ~ *(au bas de la page)* foot-note.

noter, *v.a.* note, jot down; notice.

notice, *s. f.* notice.

notion, *s. f.* notion, idea.

notre, *poss. adj.* our.

nôtre, *pron. poss.* ours, our own.

nourrir, *v.a.* nourish, feed.

nourriture, *s. f.* nourishment food.

nous, *pron.* we; us.

nous-mêmes, *pron.* ourselves.

nouveau, -el, -elle, *adj.* new; further; *de ~* again.

nouvelle, *s.f.* news; short story.

novembre, *s. m.* November.

noyau *s.m.* stone, kernel; nucleus, core.

noyer[1], *v. a.* drown; *se ~* be drowning; drown oneself.

noyer[2], *s. m.* walnut-tree.

nu, *adj.* naked, bare.

nuage, *s. m.* cloud.

nuageux, -euse, *adj.* cloudy, clouded.

nuance, *s. f.* shade, tint, nuance.

nucléaire, *adj.* nuclear.

nuire*, *v. n.* hurt, harm, be harmful.

nuit, *s. f.* night; *il (se) fait ~* it is night, it is getting dark; *de ~* by night; *la ~* at night, *bonne ~!* good night!

nul, nulle, *adj.* not one, not any; null, nil; — *pron.* no one, nobody.

numéro, *s. m.* number, size; ticket; copy, issue.

nu-pied, *adv.* barefoot.

nylon, *s. m.* nylon.

O

obéir, *v.n.* obey.

obéissance, *s. f.* obedience.

objectif, -ive, *adj.* objective; — *s. m.* object, purpose; lens.

objection, *s. f.* objection.

objet, *s. m.* object, thing, article; purpose; *~*

d'art work of art.

obligation, *s. f.* obligation.

obligatoire, *adj.* compulsory, obligatory.

obliger, *v.a.* oblige, compel.

obscur, *adj.* dark, dim.

obscurité, *s. f.* darkness, dimness; *dans l'~* in the dark.

observation, *s. f.* observation; remark.

observer, *v. a. & n.* observe, watch; keep.

obstacle, *s. m.* obstacle; hindrance; bar.

obstine, *adj.* obstinate.

obtenir, *v. a.* obtain, get.

occasion, *s. f.* occasion, chance, event; *a l'~* if need be, eventually; *d'~* second-hand.

occidental, *adj.* western, occidental.

occupant, -e, *s. m. f.* occupier, occupant.

occupation, *s. f.* occupation; pursuit.

occupé, *adj.* occupied, busy, engaged; *non ~* unoccupied.

occuper, *v.a.* occupy, employ; *s'~* occupy oneself *(de* with), be engaged; think *(de* of).

occurrence, *s.f.* occurrence; *en l'~* in this case.

océan, *s.m.* ocean.

octobre, *s.m.* October.

odieux, -euse, *adj.* odious.

œil, *s. m. (pl.* **yeux)** eye, sight; *coup d'~* glance; *au premier coup d'~* at first sight, at a glance; *ouvrez l'~!* look out!

œillet, *s.m.* carnation; eyelet.

œuf, *s.m.* egg; *~ à la coque* boiled egg; *~s*

brouillés scrambled eggs; ~s *durs* hard-boiled eggs; *blanc d'*~ white of egg; *jaune d'*~ egg-yolk.

œuvre, *s. f.* work; composition; ~ *d'art* work of art.

offense, *s. f.* offence, insult; trespass.

offenser, *v.a.* offend, shock, injure; s'~ take offence, be offended *(de* with), be angry.

office, *s.m.* office; service; post; agency; *exercer un* ~ hold an office.

officiel, -elle, *adj.* official.

officier, *s.m.* officer.

offre, *s. f.* offer, tender.

offrir*, *v. a.* offer, present, hold out; s'~ offer, propose oneself.

oh!, *int.* oh!, O!, indeed!

oie, *s.f.* goose.

oignon, *s. m.* onion; bulb.

oiseau, *s. m.* bird.

olympique, *adj.* Olympic; *les jeux* ~ the Olympic games.

ombre, *s.m.* shade; ghost; obscurity, darkness.

ombreux, -euse, *adj.* shady, shaded.

omelette, *s.f.* omelet.

omettre, *v. a.* omit.

omission, *s. f.* omission, oversight.

omnibus, *s. m.* bus; — *adj.* slow; *train* ~ slow train.

on, *pron.* one, we, people *(pl.);* you; they; somebody; some one; ~ *dit* they say, it is said, people say; *ferme!* closing time!

oncle, *s.m.* uncle.

onde, *s. f.* wave; undulation;

ondulation, *s. f.* undulation; waving.

onduler, *v. a. & n.* undulate, wave; ripple.

ongle, *s. m.* nail *(finger).*

onze, *adj. & s. m.* eleven; eleventh.

opéra, *s. m.* opera; opera-house; ~ *comique* comic opera.

opérateur, *s. m.* operator; cameraman.

opération, *s. f.* operation; *salle d'*~ operating-theatre.

opérer, *v. a. & n.* operate (on); *se faire* ~ undergo an operation.

opérette, *s.f.* operetta.

opinion, *s.f.* opinion.

opportun, *adj.* opportune, timely.

opposer, *v.a.* oppose.

opposition, *s. f.* opposition.

oppression, *s. f.* oppression.

opprimer, *v. a.* oppress.

optimiste, *adj.* optimistic; — *s. m. f.* optimist.

optique, *adj.* optic(al); — *s. f.* optics.

or, *s. m.* gold: *d'*~, *en* ~ golden.

orage, *s.m.* storm.

orange, *s.f.* orange.

orateur, *s.m.* speaker.

orbite, *s. f.* orbit.

orchestre, *s. m.* orchestra.

ordinaire, *adj.* ordinary, usual, common.

ordinairement, *adv.* usually, generally.

ordonnance, *s. f.* order; statute; prescription.

ordonner, *v.a.* order, command.

ordre, *s. m.* order, command; *mettre en* ~ arrange, clear up.

ordure, *s. f.* refuse, rubbish.

oreille, *s. f.* ear; hearing; *prêter l'~ a* listen to, lend an ear to.

oreiller, *s.m.* pillow.

organe, *s.m.* organ.

organique, *adj.* organic.

organisation, *s. f.* organization, arrangement.

organiser, *v. a.* organize.

organisme, *s. m.* organism, system.

orgue, *s.m.* organ.

orgueil, *s.m.* pride.

orient, *s. m.* the East; *de l'~* eastern.

oriental, *adj.* oriental, eastern.

original, *adj.* original.

origine, *s. f.* origin, source; *avoir ~* come from.

ornement, *s. m.* ornament, adornment.

orner, *v. a.* adorn, ornament, trim, decorate.

orphelin, -e, *s. m. f.* orphan.

orthographie, *s. f.* spelling.

os, *s. m.* bone.

osciller, *v.n.* oscillate.

oser, *v. a. & n.* dare, venture.

ôter, *v.a.* take away, take off, remove, pull off; *s'~* remove oneself.

ou, *conj.* or, either, else.

où, *adv.* where; whence; at which, in which; *n'importe ~* anywhere.

ouate, *s.f.* cotton-vool

oublier, *v. a. & n.* forget; overlook.

ouest, *s. m.* west; *à l'~* to, in the west, westward; *de l'~* western.

oui, *adv.* yes.

ouragan, *s. m.* hurricane.

ours, *s.m.* bear.

ourse, *s.f.* she-bear.

outil, *s.m.* tool.

outré, *adj.* exaggerated.

ouvert, *adj.* open; free; open-hearted; *à bras ~s* with open arms.

ouverture, *s. f.* opening; overtures *(pl.)*, proposal; overture.

ouvrage, *s. m.* (piece of) work.

ouvre-boîte, *s. m.* tin-opener.

ouvreuse, *s.f.* box-opener, attendant.

ouvrier, -ère, *s. m. f.* workman, worker; workwoman; hand; *premier ~* foreman.

ouvrir*, *v. a. & n.* open (up); break open; *s'~* be opened, open.

oxygène, *s. m.* oxygen.

P

pacifique, *adj.* pacific, peaceful; *l'Océan ~* the Pacific Ocean.

pacte, *s. m.* pact.

page[1], *s. f.* page; *être à la ~* be up to date.

page[2], *s. m.* page *(boy)*.

paiement *see* payement.

paille, *s. f.* straw, chaff.

pain, *s.m.* bread, loaf; cake, tablet.

pair[1], *adj.* equal, even; *au ~* at par; "au pair".

pair[2], *s. m.* peer.

paire, *s. f.* pair; couple.

paisible, *adj.* peaceful.

paître*, *v. a. & n.* graze, feed.

paix, *s. f.* peace; calm.

palais[1], *s. m.* palace.

palais[2], *s. m.* palate.

pâle, *adj.* pale.

paletot, *s. m.* overcoat.

pâleur, s. f. pallor.

pâlir, v. n. & a. (grow) pale.

palmier, s.m. palm-tree.

palpiter, v.n. palpitate.

pamphlet, s.m. pamphlet.

pamplemousse, s. m. grapefruit.

pan, s. m. flap; coat-tail.

panache, s.m. plume.

panier, s. m. basket.

panique, s. f. panic.

panne, s. f. break-down; power-cut.

panneau, s. m. panel.

panorama, s. m. panorama.

pansement, s. m. dressing, bandage.

pantalon, s. m. trousers (pl.).

pantoufle(s), s. f. (pl.) slipper(s).

papa, s. m. dad, daddy.

papauté, s. f. papacy.

pape, s. m. pope.

papeterie, s. f. paper-mill; stationery.

papetier, s. m. stationer.

papier, s.m. paper; ~ hygiénique toilet-paper; ~ peint wallpaper.

papillon, s. m. butterfly.

pâques, s. m. pl. Easter.

paquet, s.m. packet, parcel.

par, prep. by, by way of, by means of; across; through; per; for.

parade, s. f. parade, show.

paragraphe, s. m. paragraph.

paraître*, v.n. appear, come in sight; come out; faire ~ publish.

parallèle, adj. & s. f. parallel.

paralysie, s. f. paralysis.

paralytique, s. m. f. paralytic.

parapluie, s. m. unbrella.

paratonnerre, s. m. lightning-conductor.

parbleu, int. indeed!

parc, s. m. park; fold.

parce que, conj. because, on account of.

parcourir, v.n. travel through, go over; cover; run over, look over.

parcours, s.m. course, run; distance; mileage.

pardessus, s. m. overcoat.

par-dessus, prep. above.

pardon, s. m. pardon; je vous demande ~! I beg your pardon!; pardon me!; excuse me!; ~? (I beg your) pardon?

pardonner, v.a. pardon.

pare-boue, . s.m. mud-guard.

pare-brise, s.m. wind-screen.

pare-choc, s. m. bumper.

pareil, -eille, adj. like, similar; such; same.

parent, s. m. f. relative, relation; ~s parents; relatives.

parer, v. a. adorn, trim; parry, ward off.

paresseux, -euse, adj. lazy, idle.

parfait, adj. & s. m. perfect.

parfaitement, adv. perfectly; ~! quite so!

parfois, adv. sometimes.

parfum, s. m. perfume.

parfumer, v. a. perfume.

parfumerie, s. f. perfumery.

parier, v. a. bet, stake.

parisien, -enne, adj. & s. m. f. Parisian.

parlement, s. m. parliament.

parlementaire, adj. parliamentary.

parler, v. n. & a. speak, talk; — s. m. speech, utterance; parlance.

parmi, *prep.* among.

paroi, *s. f.* wall, partition.

paroisse, *s. f.* parish.

parole, *s. f.* speech, utterance; language; word.

parquet, *s. m.* parquet.

part, *s. f.* part, share; side; *prendre ~ à* take part in, participate; *faire ~ à* inform (of), let know; *à ~* apart; *d'une ~ ... d'autre ~* on the one hand ... on the other (hand).

partager, *v.a.* divide, share out; share.

partenaire, *s. m. f.* partner.

parterre, *s. m.* flower-bed; pit.

parti, *s. m.* party; side.

participant, -e, *s. m. f.* & *adj.* participant.

participation, *s. f.* participation, share.

participe, *s. m.* participle; *~ passé* past participle.

participer, *v.n.* participate, take part (*à* in).

particulier, -ère, *adj.* particular, special, specific; peculiar; private;

— *s. m. f.* private person; *en ~* in particular.

partie, *s. f.* part; match, game; party; *en ~* partly, in part.

partir*, *v. n.* start, leave, go (away), set out.

partisan, *s. m.* partisan, follower.

partition, *s. f.* score.

partout, *adv.* everywhere.

parure, *s. f.* ornament; set.

parvenir, *v. n.* attain (*à* to), reach.

pas[1], *s. m.* step, pace.

pas[2], *adv.* no, not, not any; *~ du tout* not at all; *~ nécessaire* unnecessary.

passage, *s. m.* passing; passage; corridor; crossing; thoroughfare; *~ clouté* pedestrian crossing; *~ à niveau* level-crossing; *~ interdit* no thoroughfare.

passager, -ère, *adj.* passing, transient, fugitive; — *s. m. f.* passenger.

passant, -e, *adj. en ~* by the way, cursorily; — *s. m. f.* passer-by.

passe, *s. f.* pass, passage; channel; permit.

passé, *adj.* past; — *prep.* after, beyond.

passeport, *s. m.* passport.

passer, *v. n.* & *a.* pass; pass along, by; cross; go on, pass on; hand; pass away; omit; forgive; strain; *en par là* submit to it; *~ un examen* take an examination; *~ la nuit* spend the night; *se ~* happen; disappear; do without.

passif, -ive, *adj.* passive — *s. m.* liabilities *(pl.).*

passion, *s. f.* passion.

passionné *adj.* passionate.

pastel, *s. m.* pastel.

pastille, *s.f.* pastille.

pâte, *s. f.* paste; dough.

pâté, *s. m.* pie, pasty; block (of buildings); blot.

patente, *s.f.* patent, licence.

patience, *s. f.* patience.

patient, -e, *adj.* & *s. m. f.* patient.

patin, *s. m.* skate.

patinage, *s. m.* skating.

patiner, *v.n.* skate.

patinoire, *s.f.* skating-rink.

pâtisserie, *s.f.* pastry; pastry-shop, cake-shop.

pâtissier, -ère, s. m. f. pastry-cook.

pâtre, s. m. shepherd.

patrie, s. f. country.

patriote, adj. patriotic; — s. m. f. patriot.

patron[1], -onne, s. m. f. patron; employer, boss.

patron[2], s. m. model, pattern.

patronage, s. m. patronage, support.

patronner, v. a. patronize, protect.

patrouille, s. f. patrol.

patte, s. f. paw, foot.

pâture, s. f. fodder, pasture.

paume, s. f. palm.

paupière, s. f. eyelid.

pause, s. f. pause, stop, break; rest.

pauvre, adj. poor.

pauvreté, s. f. poverty.

pavé, s. m. paving-stone; pavement; street.

paver, v. a. pave.

pavillon, s. m. pavilion, summer-house; flag.

payable, adj. payable, due.

paye, s.f. pay, wages pl.

payement, paiement, s. m. payment.

payer, v.a. pay; pay down, for, off; repay.

pays, s. m. country, land; home; nation; district, region.

paysage, s. m. landscape; scenery.

paysan, -anne, s. m. f. peasant, countryman; countrywoman.

peau, s. f. skin; hide; leather.

pêche[1], s. f. peach.

pêche[2], s. f. fishing; angling; ~ à la ligne angling.

péché, s. m. sin, trespass.

pécher, v. n. sin, trespass.

pêcher, v. a. & n. fish, angle.

pécheur, -eresse, s. m. f. sinner.

pêcheur, s.m. angler, fisher.

pécuniaire, adj. pecuniary.

pédagogie, s. f. pedagogy.

pédale, s. f. pedal.

pédant, adj. pedant.

pédicure, s. m. pedicure.

peigne, s. m. comb.

peigner, v. a. comb.

peignoir, s.m. wrapper, dressing-gown.

peindre*, v.a. paint.

peine, s. f. punishment; pain, grief; trouble.

peintre, s. m. painter.

peinture, s. f. painting.

pêle-mêle, adv. pell-mell, in a muddle.

pelle, s. f. shovel, spade.

pellicule, s. f. film.

pelote, s. f. ball.

pelouse, s. f. lawn.

pelure, s. f. rind, peel.

pénalité, s. f. penalty.

penchant, s. m. slope, slant; bent, liking.

pencher, v. a. & n. incline, bend; stoop; lean (towards).

pendant[1], adj. hanging, pendent; — s. m. pendant; match.

pendant[2], prep. during; ~ que while.

pendre, v. a. & n. hang (up), suspend; hang down; be hanging.

pendule, s. f. clock.

pénétrer, v. a. & n. penetrate, go through; search; see through.

pénitence, s. f. penitence.

pensée, s.f. thought, thinking; mind; pansy.

penser, v. n. & a. think.

pension, s.f. pension; board (and lodging);

boarding-house; boarding-school; life annuity; ~ *et chambre(s)* board and lodging; ~ *pour étudiants* hostel.

pensionnaire, *s.m.f.* boarder; paying guest.

pensionnat, *s. m.* boarding-school.

pente, *s. f.* slope, descent; *en* ~ downhill.

Pentecôte, *s.f.* Whitsuntide; *dimanche de la* ~ Whit Sunday.

pépier, *v.n.* chirp.

pépin, *s. m.* pip, stone.

perçant, *adj.* piercing.

perception, *s.f.* perception.

percer, *v. a. & n.* pierce, bore; punch; tap.

percevoir, *v. a.* perceive, understand.

perdre, *v. a. & n.* lose; waste; be the ruin of; se ~ get lost, disappear; be ruined.

perdrix, *s. f.* partridge.

père, *s. m.* father.

perfection, *s.f.* perfection.

perforation, *s. f.* perforation.

perforer, *v.a.* perforate.

peril, *s.m.* peril, danger.

période, *s. f.* period, term.

périodique, *adj.* periodic, periodical.

périr, *v. n.* perish.

perle, *s. f.* pearl, bead.

permanent, *adj.* permanent.

permanente, *s. f.* perm.

permettre, *v.a.* allow, permit, let; *permettez-moi de* allow me to; *vous permettez?* may I?

permis, *s.m.* permit, licence.

permission *s. f.* permission, leave (of absence).

perron, *s. m.* stair, steps *(pl.)*.

perroquet, *s. m.* parrot.

persan, -e (P.), *adj. & s. m. f.* Persian.

persécuter, *v. a.* persecute.

persécution, *s. f.* persecution.

persil, *s. m.* parsley.

persister, *v.n.* persist.

personnage, *s. m.* personage, person.

personnalité, *s. f.* personality.

personne, *s.f.* person; *grande* ~ grown-up; — *pron.* any one; anybody; no one.

personnel, -elle, *adj.* personal; — *s. m.* personnel, staff.

perspective, *s. f.* perspective, prospect, outlook.

persuader, *v. a.* persuade, convince.

persuasion, *s. f.* persuasion, conviction.

perte, *s. f.* loss; ruin.

pertinent, *adj.* pertinent.

peser, *v. a.* weigh; ponder.

pessimiste, *s. m. f.* pessimist; — *adj.* pessimistic.

petit, *adj.* small, little.

petite-fille, *s.f.* granddaughter.

petit-fils, *s. m.* grandson.

pétition, *s.f.* petition, request.

petits-enfants, *pl.* grandchildren.

pétrole, *s.m.* petroleum.

peu, *adv. & s. m.* little, bit, few; ~ *a* ~ little by little, bit by bit; *un (petit)* ~ a (little) bit; *quelque* ~ somewhat; ~ *abondant* scanty; ~ *commun* unusual; ~ *confortable* uncomfortable; ~ *nécessaire* unnecessary.

peuple, *s. m.* people.
peur, *s. f.* fear; fright; *avoir ~ (de)* be afraid (of); *de ~ que* for fear that.
peut-être, *adv.* perhaps.
phare, *s. m.* lighthouse; headlight.
pharmacie, *s.f.* pharmacy, chemist's (shop).
pharmacien, -enne, *s. m. f.* chemist.
phase, *s. f.* phase.
phénomène, *s. m.* phenomenon.
philologie, *s. f.* philology.
philosophe, *s. m.* philosopher.
philosophie, *s. f.* philosophy.
philosophique, *adj.* philosophical.
phono(graphe), *s.m.* gramophone.
photo, *s. f.* photo, snap.
photographe, *s.m.* photographer.
photographie, *s. f.* photograph; photography.
photographier, *v. a.* photograph.
photographique, *adj.* photographic; *appareil ~* camera.
phrase, *s. f.* phrase; sentence.
phtisie, *s. f.* consumption.
physicien, -enne, *s. m. f.* physicist.
physique, *adj.* physical; — *s. f.* physics; *~ nucléaire* nuclear physics; — *s. m.* physique, constitution.
pianiste, *s. m. f.* pianist.
piano(forte), *s. m.* piano.
pièce, *s. f.* piece, part, bit, coin; play; room; joint.
pied, *s. m.* foot, leg; *a ~* on foot; *aller à ~* walk.
pierre, *s. f.* stone; rock.
piéton, *s. m.* pedestrian.

pieu, *s. m.* stake, post.
pieux, -euse, *adj.* pious.
pigeon, -onne, *s. m. f.* dove, pigeon.
pile, *s. f.* pile, heap; battery.
pilier, *s. m.* pillar, post, column.
piller, *v. a. & n.* pillage.
pilot, *s. m.* pile.
pilote, *s. m.* pilot.
piloter, *v.a.* pilot, guide.
pilule, *s. f.* pill.
pin, *s. m.* pine(-tree).
pince, *s. f.* pinch; pincers, pliers, tongs *(pl.)*.
pincer, *v. a.* pinch.
pipe, *s. f.* pipe.
piquant, *adj.* pungent, sharp; piquant.
pique, *s. f.* pike; *s. m. (cards)* spade.
pique-nique, *s. m.* picnic.
piquer, *v. a. & n.* prick, sting; lard; goad, spur.
piqûre, *s. f.* prick, sting; puncture; injection.
pirate, *s. m.* pirate.
pire, *adj.* worse.
pis, *adv.* worse.
piscine, *s. f.* swimming-pool.
piste, *s. f.* track; trace; runway.
pistolet, *s. m.* pistol.
pitié, *s.f.* pity.
placard, *s. m.* placard, poster; cupboard.
place, *s. f.* place; room; seat; square.
placement, *s. m.* placing; investment; *bureau de ~* labour-exchange.
placer, *v. a.* place, put, set; invest; sell.
plafond, *s. m.* ceiling.
plage, *s. f.* beach.
plaider, *v. a. & n.* plead.
plaindre, *v. a.* pity, feel compassion for; *se ~* complain.
plaine, *s. f.* plain.

plainte, *s. f.* complaint.

plaire*, *v. n.* please; *vous plaît-il de?* would you like to?; *s'il vous plaît* (if you) please; se ~ take pleasure, enjoy.

plaisant, *adj.* pleasant, pleasing.

plaisanterie, *s.f.* joke, jest; *par* ~ as a joke.

plaisir, *s. m.* pleasure.

plan, *s. m.* plan, design, plane.

planche, *s.f.* board, plank.

plancher, *s. m.* floor.

planer, *v. a.* plane.

plante, *s. f.* plant; sole.

planter, *v. a.* plant; set.

planteur, *s. m.* planter.

plaque, *s. f.* plate; slab; plaque; ~ *de police* number-plate.

plaquer, *v. a.* plate; lay on.

plastique, *adj.* plastic, — *s. f.* plastic art; figure; — *s. m.* plastics *pl.*

plastron, *s. m.* (shirt-) front; plastron; stiff shirt.

plat, *adj.* flat; plain; dull; — *s. m.* flat (part); blade.

plateau, *s.m.* tray; scale (of balance); plateau.

plate-bande, *s. f.* flower-bed.

plate-forme, *s.f.* platform.

plâtre, *s. m.* plaster.

plein, *adj.* full; filled; *en* ~ fully, entirely.

pleurer, *v. n.* cry, weep.

pleuvoir: *il pleut* it rains.

pli, *s. m.* fold, crease.

pliant, *adj.* flexible, pliant; folding.

plier, *v. a. & n.* fold (up), bend; se ~ submit *(à* to).

plisser, *v. a. & n.* plait, fold, tuck; wrinkle.

plomb, *s.m.* lead.

plombage, *s. m.* filling.

plombier, *s. m.* plumber.

plonger, *v. a. & n.* plunge, immerse, dip, dive.

pluie, *s. f.* rain.

plume, *s. f.* feather, plume, pen.

plupart, *s. f.* most, the greatest part, majority.

pluriel, *s. m.* plural.

plus, *adv.* more, most; further, longer; any more; *de* ~ *en* ~ more and more; *en* ~ *de* in addition to; *ne . . .* ~ no more, no longer.

plusieurs, *adj.* several, many, some, a few; — *pron.* several people.

plutôt, *adv.* rather, preferably.

pluvieux, -euse, *adj.* rainy, wet.

pneu(matique), *s. m.* tyre.

pneumonie, *s. f.* pneumonia.

poche, *s. f.* pocket; pouch.

poêle¹, *s. m.* stove.

poêle², *s. f.* frying pan.

poème, *s. m.* poem.

poésie, *s. f.* poetry; poesy.

poète, *s. m.* poet.

poétique, *adj.* poetic(al).

poids, *s. m.* weight.

poignant, *adj.* poignant.

poigne, *s. f.* grip, grasp.

poignée, *s. f.* handle; hilt; handful.

poignet, *s. m.* wrist; cuff.

poil, *s. m.* hair; bristle; coat.

poinçon, *s.m.* punch, bodkin.

poinçonner, *v. a.* punch, clip; stamp.

poing, *s.m.* fist.

point, *s. m.* point, dot; full stop; *deux* ~s colon; ~ *et virgule* semicolon; *à* ~ just in time; *être sur le* ~ *de* be about to; ~ *de vue* point of view.

pointe, *s. f.* point, head, tip.

pointer, *v. a. & n.* point.

pointu, *adj.* sharp, pointed.

poire, *s. f.* pear.

pois, *s. m.* pea.

poison, *s. m.* poison.

poisson, *s. m.* fish.

poissonnier, -ère, *s. m. f.* fishmonger.

poitrine, *s. f.* chest, breast.

poivre, *s. m.* pepper.

pôle, *s. m.* pole.

poli, *adj.* polished; polite.

police, *s. f.* police; policy; *agent de* ~ policeman.

policier, *s. m.* policeman.

policlinique, *s. f.* outpatients' department.

polir, *v. a.* polish, refine.

politesse, *s. f.* politeness.

politicien, -enne, *s. m. f.* politician.

politique, *s. f.* politics.

polonais, -e (P.), *adj.* Polish; — *s. m.* Pole; *s. f.* Polish woman; polonaise.

pomme, *s. f.* apple; ~ *de terre* potato.

pommier, *s. m.* apple tree.

pompe[1], *s. f.* pomp, ceremony.

pompe[2], *s. f.* pump; ~ *à incendie* fire-engine; ~ *à essence* petrol pump.

pompier, *s. m.* fireman; *les* ~*s* fire-brigade.

ponctuel, -elle, *adj.* punctual.

pont, *s. m.* bridge; deck; ~ *suspendu* suspension-bridge; ~ *inférieur* lower deck.

populaire, *adj.* popular; vulgar, common.

popularité, *s. f.* popularity.

population, *s. f.* popula-

tion.

populeux, -euse, *adj.* populous.

porc, *s. m.* pig, hog; pork.

porcelaine, *s. f.* porcelain, china(ware).

pore, *s. m.* pore.

poreux, -euse, *adj.* porous.

port[1], *s. m.* harbour (sea-)port; *arriver à bon* ~ arrive safely.

port[2], *s. m.* bearing, gait; carriage; postage; ~ *payé* postage paid.

portable, *adj.* portable.

porte, *s. f.* door(way), entrance; ~ *d'entrée* front-door.

porte-cigarettes, *s. m. pl.* cigarette-case.

portée, *s. f.* litter; range, scope; *à* ~ within reach.

portemanteau, *s. m.* coatstand; suit-case.

porter, *v. a. & n.* bear; carry; convey; wear, have on; hold; ~ *intérêt* yield interest; show interest; ~ *la santé de B* drink B's health; se ~ be worn, be carried; *comment vous portez-vous?* how are you?

porteur, *s. m.* porter, carrier; bearer.

portier, -ère, *s. m. f.* porter, door-keeper.

portière, *s. f.* door (on vehicle); (door-)curtain.

portion, *s. f.* portion, part, share; helping.

portrait, *s. m.* portrait.

portugais, -e (P.), *adj. & s. m. f.* Portuguese.

posemètre, *s. m.* lightmeter.

poser, *v. a. & n.* place, lay down, put; state.

positif, -ive, *adj. & s. m. f.* positive.

position, *s. f.* position, situation; attitude.

posséder, *v.a.* possess.
possession, *s.f.* possession; property.
possibilité, *s.f.* possibility.
possible, *adj.* possible; *faire tout son* ~ do one's best.
postal, *adj.* postal; post; *carte* ~e post-card.
poste[1], *s f.* post(-office), mail; *mettre à la* ~ post (a letter); *bureau de* ~ post-office; *timbre* ~ stamp; ~ *aérienne* air-mail.
poste[2], *s. m.* post, station, office; police-station; receiver, set; ~ *de* T. S. F. wireless-set.
postulant, -e, *s. m. f.* applicant, candidate.
pot, *s. m.* pot, can, jug, vessel, pitcher.
potager, *s.m.* kitchen garden.
poteau, *s. m.* post.
poterie, *s. f.* pottery.
potin, *s. m.* noise; (piece of) gossip.
poubelle, *s. f.* dustbin.
pouce, *s.m.* thumb.
pouding, *s. m.* pudding.
poudre, *s. f.* powder, dust.
poudrier, *s. m.* compact.
poule, *s.f.* hen; fowl.
poulet, *s.m.* chicken, fowl.
pouls, *s. m.* pulse.
poumon, *s. m.* lung(s).
poupée, *s. f.* doll.
pour, *prep.* for; ~ *cent* per cent; ~ *que* in order that.
pourboire, *s. m.* tip.
pourquoi, *conj. & adv.* why; what for; for what reason.
poursuite, *s. f.* pursuit, chase; ~s suit, action.
poursuivre, *v. a.* pursue, chase, prosecute.

pourtant, *adv.* however, still.
pourvoir, *v. n. & a.* provide (*à* for), supply, cater (*à* for).
pousser, *v. a. & n.* push; shove; urge; impel; grow; utter.
poussière, *s. f.* dust
poussiéreux, -euse *adj.* dusty.
pouvoir*, *v. a. & n.* be able, may; *se* ~ be possible; *cela se peut* that may be; — *s. m.* power.
pratique, *s. f.* practice, execution; experience; customers (*pl.*); — *adj.* practical, convenient.
pratiquer, *v. a.* practise, carry out; exercise.
préalable, *adj.* previous, *au* ~ first of all.
précédent, *adj.* precedent, previous; — *s. m.* precedent.
précéder, *v. a. & n.* precede; come before.
prêcher, *v. a. & n.* preach.
prêcheur, *s. m.* preacher.
précieux, -euse, *adj.* precious, valuable, costly.
précipice, *s. m.* precipice.
précipitation, *s.f.* precipitation, haste, hurry.
précipité, *adj.* hasty.
précipiter, *v.a.* precipitate; hasten, hurry.
précis, *adj.* exact, precise; — *s. m.* summary.
préciser, *v.a.* specify.
prédécesseur, *s. m.* predecessor.
prédire, *v.a.* foretell.
préfabriqué, *adj.* prefabricated.
préface, *s.f.* preface.
préférable, *adj.* preferable, better.
préférer, *v.a.* prefer; like

better.

préfet, *s.m.* prefect.

préjugé, *s. m.* prejudice, presumtion.

prélat, *s.m.* prelate.

préliminaire, *adj.* preliminary.

premier, -ère, *adj.* first, former; ~ *plan* foreground; close-up; *de* ~ *ordre* first-rate; ~ — *s. m.* first floor.

première, *s. f.* first night; first class (in a carriage).

prendre*, *v. a.* take, take up, seize; receive, accept; put on, wear; charge; catch; ~ *place* take a seat: *à tout* ~ on the whole; ~ *pour* mistake for; ~ *du corps* put on weight; ~ *l'air* take a walk; se ~ be taken, be caught.

prénom, *s. m.* Christian name.

préoccuper, *v. a.* preoccupy, engross; worry; se ~ trouble oneself.

préparatifs, *s.m.pl.* preparations.

préparation, *s. f.* preparation.

préparer, *v. a.* prepare, make ready; read for; se ~ prepare oneself, get ready.

préposition, *s. f.* preposition.

prérogative, *s. f.* prerogative, privilege.

près, *adv. & prep.* near, close by, close to; nearly; *a peu* ~ nearly (so); *de* ~ closely.

prescription, *s. f.* prescription.

prescrire*, *v. ι.* prescribe.

présence, *s. f.* presence, attendance; *en* ~ *de*

in the presence of.

présent[1], *s. m.* present, gift; *faire* ~ *de* give as a present.

présent[2], *s. m.* present (time); present tense; — *adj.* present, current *à* ~ at present; *jusqu'à* ~ till now, as yet; *pour le* ~ for the time being.

présentation, *s. f.* presentation, introduction.

présenter, *v. a.* present, offer; introduce; se ~ appear.

préserver, *v. a.* preserve.

président, *s. m.* president.

présomption, *s. f.* presumption; conceit.

presque, *adv.* almost.

pressant, *adj.* pressing.

presse, *s. f.* press; printing-press; haste; crowd.

pressé, *adj.* pressing; *être* ~ be in a hurry.

pressentiment, *s. m.* presentiment; misgiving.

pressentir, *v.a.* have a presentiment of.

presser, *v. a.* press, crush; hurry; *pressez-vous!* hurry up!; se ~ hurry (up).

pression, *s.f.* pressure.

pressurer, *v.a.* press, squeeze; oppress.

prestige, *s.m.* marvel; influence, prestige.

présumer, *v. a.* suppose, expect; presume.

prétendre, *v. a. & n.* pretend, claim; intend.

prétention, *s.f.* pretension, claim.

prêter, *v.a.* lend, attribute; se ~ lend oneself (à to).

prétexte, *s. m.* pretext.

prêtre, *s. m.* priest.

preuve, *s. f.* proof; *faire*

~ *de* show.

prévaloir, v.n. prevail.

prévenir, v. a. anticipate, inform, let know.

préventif, -ive, adj. preventive.

prévention, s.f. bias, prejudice.

prévision, s. f. prevision, anticipation; forecast.

prévoir, v.a. foresee, anticipate, forecast.

prévoyance, s. f. foresight.

prier, v. a. pray, beg; ask.

prière, s.f. prayer; request.

primaire, adj. primary.

prime, adj. first, early.

primer, v. a. surpass, excel; award a prize to.

primeur, s. f. early vegetables (pl.).

primitif, -ive, adj. primitive, original.

prince, s. m. prince.

princesse, s. f. princess.

principal, adj. principal.

principalement, adv. principally, mainly.

principe, s. m. principle.

printemps, s. m. spring-(time); au ~ in spring.

priorité, s.f. priority.

prise, s.f. taking; capture, catch; ~ de courant (electric) plug.

prisme, s. m. prism.

prison, s. f. prison.

prisonnier, -ère, s. m. f. prisoner.

privation, s. f. privation.

privé, adj. private.

priver, v. a. deprive.

privilège, s. m. privilege.

prix, s. m. price, cost, charge; prize; au ~ de at the cost of; ~ de la course fare; ~ par mille mileage; ~courant market-price; ~ fixe fixed price.

probabilité, s. f. probability.

probable, adj. probable.

probablement, adv. probably.

problématique, adj. problematic(al).

problème, s. m. problem.

procédé s. m. proceeding.

procéder, v. n. proceed.

procédure, s. f. procedure.

procès, s.m. (law-)suit, trial; faire un ~ u bring an action against.

procession, s.f. procession.

prochain, adj. near(est), next. — s. m. neighbour

prochainement, adv. shortly, soon.

proche, adj. near, neighbouring, close at hand.

proclamer, v. a. proclaim.

procurer, v. a. procure.

procureur, s. m. attorney.

prodigieux, -euse, adj. wonderful, prodigious.

producteur, -trice, s. m. f. producer; — adj. producing.

production, s. f. production.

produire*, v. a. produce, bring forth, yield.

produit, s. m. produce; product.

professer, v. a. & n. profess; teach.

professeur, s. m. teacher; professor; lecturer.

profession, s. f. profession.

professionnel, -elle, adj. & s. m. f. professional.

profil, s. m. profile.

profit, s. m. profit, gain.

profitable, adj. profitable.

profiter, v. n. profit (by).

profond, adj. deep, profound.

profondeur, *s. f.* depth; *dix pieds de* ~ ten feet deep.

programme, *s. m.* program(me); scheme.

progrès, *s. m.* progress, improvement; *faire des* ~ make progress.

prohiber, *v.a.* prohibit.

projecteur, *s. m.* headlight; searchlight; projector.

projectile, *s. m.* projectile, missile.

projection, *s. f.* projection.

projet, *s. m.* project, plan; scheme; ~ *de loi* bill.

projeter, *v.a.* project throw; scheme, plan.

prolonger, *v.a.* prolong.

promenade, *s.f.* walk; promenade.

promener: *se* ~ *go* for a walk; *se* ~ *en voiture* go for a drive.

promesse, *s. f.* promise.

promettre, *v. a.* promise.

promotion, *s. f.* promotion.

prompt, *adj.* prompt.

pronom, *s. m.* pronoun.

prononcer, *v.a. &n.* pronounce; utter; deliver.

prononciation, *s. f.* pronunciation; delivery.

propagande, *s. f.* propaganda.

propager, *v.a.* propagate.

prophète, *s.m.f.* prophet.

prophétie, *s. f.* prophecy.

proportion, *s. f.* proportion; ratio.

propos, *s. m.* talk, remark; *à* ~ in good time; by the way.

proposer, *v.a.* propose, offer.

proposition, *s. f.* proposal, proposition.

propre, *adj* own, peculiar; proper, fit.

propriétaire, *s.m.f.* owner, proprietor; landlord, landlady.

propriété, *s. f.* ownership; property.

propulsion, *s. f.* propulsion; ~ *à réaction* jet propulsion.

prosaïque, *adj.* prosaic.

proscrire*, *v. a.* proscribe.

prose, *s. f.* prose.

prospectus, *s.m.* prospectus.

prospère, *adj.* prosperous.

prospérer, *v. n.* prosper, get on (well).

prospérité, *s.f.* prosperity.

protecteur, *s. m.* protector, patron.

protection, *s.f.* protection, support.

protéger, *v.a.* protect; patronize.

protestant, -e, *s. m. f. & adj.* Protestant.

protestation, *s.f.* protest(ation).

protester, *v. n. & a.* protest.

prouver, *v.a.* prove.

provenir, *v.n.* come (from), issue, arise.

province, *s. f.* province, country, district.

provincial, *adj.* provincial, country.

provision, *s. f.* provision.

provisoire, *adj.* provisional, temporary.

provoquer, *v. a.* provoke; stir up.

proximité, *s.f.* proximity.

prudence, *s. f.* prudence, caution.

prudent, *adj.* prudent, cautious.

prune, *s. f.* plum.

pruneau, *s. m.* prune.

prunelle, *s. f.* pupil.

psaume, s. m. psalm.

psychologie, s. f. psychology.

psychologique, adj. psychological.

public, publique, adj. public, common; — s. m. public, audience.

publication, s.f. publication.

publicité, s. f. publicity.

publier, v. a. publish.

puce, s. f. flea.

puer, v. n. stink.

puéril, adj. childish.

puis, adv. then, after that.

puiser, v. a. draw up, fetch up.

puisque, conj. as, since.

puissance, s.f. power, might, force.

puissant, adj. powerful, strong; tout~ almighty.

puits, s. m. well; pit.

punaise, s. f. drawing-pin; bug.

punch, s.m. punch (drink).

punir, v. a. punish.

punition, s.f. punishment.

pupille, s.m.f. ward, pupil; — s. f. pupil (of the eye).

pupitre, s. m. desk.

pur, adj. pure, clean.

purée, s. f. mash, purée.

purement, adv. purely, merely.

pureté, s. f. purity.

purgatif, -ive, adj. & s. m. purgative.

purger, v. a. purge.

purifier, v.a. purify, cleanse.

puritain, -e, adj. & s. m. f. Puritan.

pyramide, s. f. pyramid.

Q

quai, s. m. quay; wharf; platform; billet de ~ platform ticket.

qualification, s. f. qualification.

qualifié, adj. qualified.

qualifier, v.a. qualify.

qualité, s.f. quality.

quand, adv. & conj. when; while; ~ même all the same.

quant à, prep. as for, with regard to.

quantité, s. f. quantity; amount; ~ de plenty of.

quarante, adj. & s. m. forty.

quart, s.m. quarter, fourth part; quart.

quartier, s. m. quarter; piece, slice; district; ~ général headquarters (pl.).

quatorze, adj. & s.m. fourteen.

quatre, adj. &s.m. four; fourth.

quatre-vingt-dix, adj. & s. m. ninety.

quatre-vingts, adj. & s. m. eighty.

quatrième, adj. & s. m. fourth; fourth floor; — s. f. third form.

quatuor, s. m. quartet(te).

que, qu', rel. pron. whom, which, that; of which, at which; — adv. how much, how many; — conj. that; than; as; if; as though.

quel, quelle, adj. what, which.

quelque, adj. some, any; a few; ~ chose something, anything; ~ part somewhere; ~ peu somewhat — adv. about, some.

quelquefois, adv. sometimes.

quelqu'un, -e, pron.

somebody; anybody.

querelle, s. f. quarrel.

quereller, v. a. & n. quarrel with.

question, s.f. question; point, matter, issue.

questionner, v.a. question, interrogate.

queue, s.f. tail; rear; queue; handle.

qui, rel. pron. who, whom; which; that; à ~ to whom.

quille, s. f. keel, skittle.

quincaillerie, s. f. hardware (shop).

quintal, s. m. hundredweight.

quinze, adj. & s. m. fifteen; fifteenth; ~ jours fortnight.

quittance, s. f. receipt.

quitte, adj. quit, free.

quitter, v. a. leave, give up, quit.

quoi, rel. pron. what, which; à propos de ~ what is it about?; ~ qu'il en soit at any rate.

quoique, conj. (al)though.

quotidien, -enne, adj. & s. m. daily.

R

rabais, s. m. reduction in price, rebate.

rabaisser, v. a. lower.

rabattre, v.a. beat down, pull down; reduce.

raccommoder, v. a. mend, repair.

raccourcir, v.a. & n. shorten, abridge.

raccrocher, v.a. hang up again.

race, s. f. race; stock; breed.

racine, s. f. root; prendre ~ take root.

raconter, v.a. tell, relate.

radar, s. m. radar.

radiateur, s. m. radiator.

radiation s. f. radiation.

radical, adj. radical.

radieux, -euse, adj. radiant, beaming.

radio, s. f. radio.

radio-actif, -ive, adj. radioactive.

radiodiffuser, v.a. broadcast.

radiodiffusion, s. f. broadcasting.

radiogramme, s. m. X-ray photograph; radiogram.

radiographie, s. f. X-ray photograph(y).

radioreportage, s. m. running commentary.

radioscopie, s. f. radioscopy.

radioscopique, adj. examen ~ X-ray examination.

radis, s.m. radish.

raffermir, v.a. strengthen, fortify.

raffinage, s.m. refining.

raffiné, adj. refined.

raffinement, s. m. refinement.

raffiner, v. a. refine.

rafraîchir, v. a. refresh, cool; se ~ cool down.

rafraîchissement, s.m. refreshment; ~s refreshments.

rage, s.f. rage, fury.

ragoût, s. m. ragout, stew.

raide, adj. stiff, rigid.

raidir, v. a. make stiff.

raifort, s.m. horse radish.

rail, s. m. rail.

railler, v.a. mock, rail at.

raillerie, s.f. raillery, mocking.

raisin, s. m. grape(s);

~ *sec* raisin.

raison, *s.f.* reason; judgement; *à ~ de* at the rate of; *avoir ~* be right.

raisonnable, *adj.* reasonable.

raisonnement, *s. m.* reasoning.

raisonner, *v. n.* & *a.* reason, argue.

ralentir, *v. a.* & *n.* slow down.

ramasser, *v.a.* gather up, pick up; take up.

rame, *s. f.* oar; prop.

ramener, *v.a.* bring back, take back.

ramer, *v. n.* row.

rampe, *s.f.* banister; footlights *(pl.).*

ramper, *v.n.* crawl, creep.

rance, *adj.* rancid.

rancune, *s.f.* spite, grudge.

randonneur, -euse, *s. m. f.* excursionist, hiker.

rang, *s.m.* row, line; rank.

rangé, *adj.* tidy.

rangée, *s.f.* row, line, range.

ranger, *v. a.* put in order; arrange; range; se ~ settle down; make room.

ranimer, *v.a.* revive, restore to life, refresh.

râpe, *s.f.* rasp, grater.

râpé, *adj.* shabby.

rapide, *adj.* rapid, fast; steep.

rapidité, *s.f.* rapidity, speed.

rappel, *s.m.* recall.

rappeler, *v. a.* recall, call back; bring back; se ~ remember.

rapport, *s.m.* product, yield; report, account; connection, relation; reference; *sous ce ~* in this respect.

rapporter, *v.a.* bring back; produce, yield; report, state; se ~ relate to, refer to.

rapprochement, *s. m.* drawing closer.

rapprocher, *v. a.* bring closer; se ~ draw nearer.

raquette, *s. f.* racket.

rare, *adj.* rare.

raser, *v. a.* shave, graze; pull down; bore; *v.n.* se ~ shave.

rasoir, *s. m.* razor; ~ *électrique* electric razor; ~ *de sûreté* safety razor.

rassembler, *v. a.* gather, assemble, collect.

rassis, *adj.* settled; stale.

rassurer, *v.a.* reassure, comfort.

rat, *s. m.* rat.

râteau, *s. m.* rake.

ratelier, *s. m.* rack; set of false teeth.

rater, *v. n.* & *a.* miss fire; fail.

ratification, *s. f.* ratification.

ration, *s. f.* ration.

rattacher, *v.a.* tie up again, join.

rattraper, *v.a.* catch again; catch up; overtake.

rauque, *adj.* hoarse.

ravager, *v. a.* ravage, lay waste.

ravir, *v. a.* delight.

ravissant, *adj.* ravishing, charming.

rayer, *v. a.* scratch (out); cross out.

rayon, *s.m.* ray, beam; spoke; radius; shelf.

rayonnement, *s. m.* radiation; radiance.

rayonner, *v.n.* radiate, shine.

razzia, s. f. raid.
réacteur, s.m. reactor.
réactoin, s.f. reaction.
réagir, v.n. react.
réalisation, s.f. realization; carrying out.
réaliser, v.a. realize.
réaliste, adj. realistic.
réalité, s. f. reality; en ~ in fact.
rebelle, adj. rebellious; — s. m. f. rebel.
rébellion, s. f., rebellion.
rebord, s.m. edge, brim.
rébus, s.m. riddle.
récemment, adv. recently, lately.
récent, adj. recent.
récepteur, s. m. receiver.
réception, s. f. reception, receipt; at-home.
recette, s.f. receipt; recipe.
receveur, s.m. receiver; conductor (bus).
recevoir*, v.n. receive; admit, take in; accept; v. n. entertain; aller ~ qn. à la gare meet s.o. at the station.
rechange, s. m. pièces de ~ spare parts.
recharge, s. f. refill.
réchaud, s.m. dish-warmer.
réchauffer, v. a. warm up again.
recherche, s.f. research; inquiry.
rechercher, v. a. look for, search for; research into.
récipé, s.m. recipe.
réciproque, adj. reciprocal, mutual.
récit, s. m. recital, account.
récital, s. m. recital.
récitation, s. f. recitation.
réciter, v.a. recite.
réclamation, s. f. claim, complaint.
réclame, s. f. advertisement; faire de la ~ (pour) advertise.
réclamer, v.a. demand, claim.
recommandation, s. f. recommendation.
recommander, v. a. recommend; introduce; request; register.
recommencer, v. a. & n. begin again.
récompense, s. f. reward.
récompenser, v. a. reward, repay.
réconcilier, v. a. reconcile.
reconnaissance, s. f. recognition, gratitude.
reconnaître, v. a. recognize, know; acknowledge; explore.
reconstruction, s. f. reconstruction.
reconstruire*, v.a. rebuild.
record, s.m. record (sport etc.).
recourir, v. n. ~ a have recourse to.
recouvrir, v.a. cover again, hide.
récréation, s. f. recreation, amusement, pastime.
recrue, s. f. recruit.
recteur, s.m. rector, chancellor.
rectifier, v.a. rectify, correct.
reçu, s. m. receipt; au ~ de on receipt of.
recueil, s. m. collection.
recueillir, v.a. collect; se ~ collect oneself.
reculer, v.a. put back; v. n. draw back, recoil.
rédacteur, -trice, s. m. f. editor; writer.
rédaction, s. f. drawing up; composition; editorial staff.

rédemption, s. f. redemp-
tion.

rédiger, v.a. draw up;
edit.

redingote, s.f. frock-
coat.

redire, v. a. repeat, say
again; trouver à ~ à
find fault with.

redoubler, v.a. redouble.

redoutable, adj. formi-
dable, dreaded.

redouter, v.a. dread, be
afraid of.

redresser, v. a. & se ~
straighten (up).

réduction, s. a. reduction,
cut.

réduire*, v. a. reduce, cut
down.

réduit, adj. reduced.

réel, réelle, adj. real,
actual.

réélection, s.f. re-elec-
tion.

réélire, v. a. re-elect.

refaire, v.a. do (over)
again.

réfectoire, s.m. refec-
tory, dining-hall.

référence, s. f. reference.

référer, v. a. refer; se ~ à
refer to; nous référant à
referring to.

réfléchir, v.a. reflect;
consider, think over.

réflecteur, s. m. reflector.

reflet, s. m. reflection.

refléter, v. a. reflect.

réflexe, adj. reflex.

réflexion, s. f. reflection,
consideration.

reflux, s. m. ebb.

réformation, s.f. refor-
mation.

réforme, s.f. reform,
improvement.

Réforme, s. f. Reforma-
tion.

réformer, v. a. reform.

refrain, s. m. refrain.

réfréner, v. a. bridle, curb.

réfrigérateur, s.m. re-
frigerator.

réfrigérer, v. a. refriger-
ate.

refroidir, v. a. chill, cool.

refuge, s. m. refuge; lay-
by.

réfugié, -e, s. m. f. re-
fugee.

réfugier: se ~ take shel-
ter, take refuge.

refus, s. m. refusal, de-
nial.

refuser, v. a. refuse, deny;
~ de connaître ignore;
être refusé fail.

regagner, v.a. regain,
recover; return to.

regard, s. m. look.

regarder, v. a. look at;
concern; regard.

régime, s. m. (form of)
government; diet.

régiment, s. m. regiment.

région, s. f. region, area.

régional, adj. local.

régir, v.a. rule, ad-
minister.

régisseur, s. m. steward;
stage-manager.

registre, s.m. register;
record.

règle, s. f. rule; ruler.

réglé, adj. regular; punctual; steady; ruled.

règlement, a.m. rule,
regulation.

régler, v. a. rule; regulate;
time; settle.

règne, s.m. reign.

régner, v.a. reign.

regret, s. m. regret.

regretter, v. a. regret, be
sorry for.

régulariser, v. a. regular-
ize.

régularité, s. f. regularity.

régulateur, s. m regulator.

régulier, -ière, adj. regular; correct.

rein, s.m. kidney.

reine, *s.f.* queen.
reine-claude, *s. f.* green-gage.
rejeter, *v. a.* reject, throw out.
rejoindre, *v.a.* rejoin; overtake, catch up; se ~ meet.
réjouir, *v. a.* give joy to, cheer up, delight; se ~ rejoice.
relâche, *s. f.* relaxation; respite.
relâcher, *v.a.* slacken, loosen; relax; se ~ relax.
relatif, -ive, *adj.* relative; ~ à relating to.
relation, *s.f.* relation, connection; report; *entrer en ~ avec* get in touch with.
relever, *v. a.* lift, take up, pick up; set off; *v. n.* recover.
relief, *s.m.* relief.
relier, *v. a.* bind (a book); hoop (casks).
religieux, -euse, *adj.* religious; — *s. m.* monk; *s. f.* nun.
religion, *s.f.* religion.
relique, *s.f.* relic.
relire, *v.a.* read (over) again.
remarquable, *adj.* remarkable, noticeable.
remarque, *s. f.* remark, observation, notice.
remarquer, *v. a.* remark, notice, observe; *faire ~* point out.
rembourser, *v.a.* repay, reimburse.
remède, *s.m.* remedy; medicine.
remerciement, *s.m.* thanks *(pl.)*.
remercier, *v.a.* thank *(de* for).
remettre, *v. a.* put back; put on again; post-

pone; se ~ recover (oneself).
remilitariser, *v. a.* rearm.
remise, *s. f.* remittance; delivery; allowance; revival, restoration.
remonter, *v. n. & a.* go up, remount; bring up again; set up again.
remords, *s. m.* remorse.
remorque, *s. f.* tow(ing), trailer.
remorqueur, *s. m. (bateau)* ~ tug-boat.
remous, *s. m.* eddy(-water), whirl.
remplacer, *v. a.* replace, substitute.
remplir, *v. a.* fill; fill up; fulfil; carry out.
remporter, *v.a.* take away, carry off; get, obtain.
remuer, *v. a. & n.* move, fidget about; se ~ be busy, move.
rémunération, *s. f.* remuneration.
renaissance, *s. f.* renascence; revival; *la Renaissance* the Renaissance.
renaître, *v.n.* be born again, revive.
renard, *s.m.* fox.
rencontre, *s. f.* meeting, encounter; collision.
rencontrer, *v.a.* meet, meet with; come across; run into; se ~ *avec* meet, be met with.
rendement, *s. m.* output.
rendez-vous, *s. m.* appointment, rendezvous.
rendormir: se ~ go to sleep again.
rendre, *v.a.* give back, return; yield; render; convey; ~ *un arrêt* issue a decree; ~ *compte* render an account, realize; ~ *visite*

pay a visit.

renfermer, *v. a.* lock up again, confine; contain, include.

renfler, *v.a.&n.* swell.

renforcer, *v. a.* strengthen, reinforce.

renfort, *s. m.* reinforcement; help.

renier, *v. a.* deny.

renom, *s.m.* reputation.

renommée, *s. f.* renown.

renoncer, *v.n.&a.* renounce, give up.

renouveler, *v.a.* renew, renovate.

renseignement, *s. m.* information; indication; *bureau des ~s* inquiry office.

renseigner, *v. a.* give information to; se ~ inquire, ask *(sur* about).

rente, *s. f.* income; rent.

rentrée, *s. f.* return; re-opening.

rentrer, *v. n.* reenter, go in; get back, return home.

renversé, *adj.* reversed, upset.

renverser, *v.a.* upset; overthrow; turn upside down; se ~ be upset, tip over.

renvoi, *s.m.* return; (cross-)reference.

renvoyer, *v.a.* return; dismiss; refer.

réorganiser, *v.a.* reorganize.

répandre, *v.a.* pour; spread, scatter, diffuse.

réparation, *s.f.* repair, amends.

réparer, *v. a.* repair, mend; make up for.

repartir*, *v.a.* answer.

repas, *s. m.* meal.

repasser, *v. n.* pass again.

répéter, *v. a.* repeat; say again; rehearse.

répétition, *s. f.* repetition; rehearsal.

réplique, *s. f.* retort, reply, answer.

répliquer, *v. a.* & *n.* reply, answer.

répondre, *v. a.* & *n.* answer, reply; respond to.

réponse *s.m.* answer; response; ~ *payée* reply paid.

reporter, *v. a.* carry back, take back.

repos, *s. m.* rest; *sans ~* restless.

reposer, *v. a.* lay again; *v. n.* rest, lie.

repoussant, *adj.* repulsive.

repousser, *v. a.* push back; repulse; drive back.

reprendre, *v.a.* & *n.* take back, get back; take up, go on; ~ *sa parole* go back on one's word.

représentant, -e, *s. m. f.* representative.

représentation, *s. f.* show, production; performance; display; representation.

représenter, *v. a.* represent; show, display.

reprise, *s.f.* renewal.

reproche, *s. m.* reproach, blame.

reprocher, *v. a.* reproach (with); blame for.

reproduction, *s.f.* reproduction.

reproduire*, *v. a.* reproduce.

républicain, -e, *adj.* & *s. m. f.* republican.

république, *s. f.* republic.

répulsion, *s.f.* repulsion.

réputation, *s. f.* reputation.

requête, *s.f.* request,

demand.

réserve, s.f. reserve; reservation; caution; de ~ spare; mettre en ~ lay by.

réserver, v. a. reserve, lay by; book (in advance).

réservoir, s.m. tank (petrol etc.)

résidence, s. f. residence, dwelling.

résident, s. m. resident.

résignation, s. f. resignation; submission.

résigner, v. a. resign; se ~ à resign oneself, make up one's mind.

résistance, s. f. resistance.

résister, v. n. resist.

résolu, adj. resolute.

résolution, s. f. resolution.

résonance, s. f. resonance.

résonner, v. n. resound, ring.

résoudre*, v.a. resolve; solve; settle; se ~ resolve, make up one's mind (to).

respect, s. m. respect.

respectable, adj. respectable, decent.

respecter v. a. respect.

respectif, -ive, adj. respective.

respectueux, -euse, adj. respectful.

respiration, s. f. respiration, breath(ing).

respirer, v. n. & a. breathe.

responsabilité, s. f. responsibility.

responsable, adj. responsible.

ressaisir, v. a. seize again.

ressemblance, s. f. resemblance, likeness.

ressemblant, adj. like, similar.

ressembler, v emble.

ressentiment, s. m. resentment, grudge.

ressentir, v.a. feel; resent; se ~ be hurt; feel still.

resserrer, v.a. tighten; bind.

ressort, s.m. spring; energy.

ressortir, v. n. come out again; stand out.

ressource, s. f. resource.

restaurant, s. m. restaurant; ~ à libre service self-service restaurant.

restaurateur, -trice, s. m. f. restorer; restaurant keeper.

restauration, s.f. restoration.

restaurer, v. a. restore.

reste, s. m. rest, remainder.

rester, v. n. remain, be left, keep; ~ en arrière, lag behind.

restituer, v. a. restore.

restreindre*, v. a. restrict.

restriction, s. f. restriction.

résultat, s.m. result, issue; avoir pour ~ result in.

résulter, v. n. result (de from).

résumé, s.m. summing up.

résumer, v.a. sum up.

rétablir, v.a. restore.

retard, s. m. delay; être en ~ be late; be overdue.

retarder, v.a. delay, retard.

retenir, v.a. keep back, hold back; hinder.

retirer, v.a. draw back, pull back; extract, get, derive; se ~ retire.

retomber, v. n. fall again, fall back; relapse.

retour, s. m. return; en ~ homeward bound; être

de ~ be back.

retourner, *v. n.* turn back; return, go back; se ~ turn round.

retracer, *v.a.* retrace; relate, tell.

retraite, *s.f.* retreat; retirement; *mettre à la* ~ superannuate.

retrancher, *v. a.* retrench.

rétrécir, *v.a.* contract; make narrower; shrink.

retrousser, *v. a.* turn up.

retrouver, *v. a.* find again, recover.

rétroviseur, *s. m.* (rear-vision) mirror.

réunion, *s.f.* reunion.

réunir, *v.a.* reunite; join again.

réussi, *adj.* successful.

réussir, *v. n.* succeed.

réussite, *s. f.* success.

revanche, *s. f.* revenge; return match; *en* ~ in return.

rêve, *s. m.* dream.

réveil, *s. m.* waking.

réveille-matin *s. m.* alarm-clock.

réveiller, *v.a.* & **se** ~ wake (up).

révéler, *v.a.* reveal; se ~ come to light.

revenir, *v. n.* return, come back; recur; cost.

revenu, *s. m.* income.

rêver, *v. n.* dream.

révérence, *s. f.* reverence; curtsey.

révérend, *adj.* reverend.

rêverie, *s.f.* reverie, fancy.

revers, *s. m.* back, reverse, wrong side.

revêtir, *v.a.* put on; clothe; cover.

révision, *s. f.* revision.

revivre, *v. n.* live again; *faire* ~ revive.

revoir, *v. a.* see again, look over; *au* ~ good-bye (for the present).

révolte, *s. f.* revolt.

révolter, *v. a.* revolt; se ~ revolt, rebel.

révolution, *s. f.* revolution; turn.

révolutionnaire, *adj.* & *s. m. f.* revolutionary.

revolver, *s. m.* revolver.

revue, *s. f.* review; magazine.

rez-de-chaussé, *s. m.* ground floor.

rhétorique, *s. f.* rhetoric.

rhum, *s. m.* rum.

rhumatisme, *s. m.* rheumatism.

rhume, *s. m.* cold (in the head).

ricaner, *v. n.* sneer, grin.

riche, *adj.* rich, well off.

richesse, *s.f.* wealth, riches *(pl.).*

ride, *s. f.* wrinkle.

rideau, *s. m.* curtain.

rider, *v. a.* wrinkle.

ridicule, *adj.* ridiculous; — *s. m.* ridicule.

rien, *pron.* nothing; not ... anything; trifle.

rigoureux, -euse, *adj.* rigorous, severe.

rigueur, *s. f.* rigour.

rime, *s. f.* rhyme.

rincer, *v. a.* rinse.

rire*, *v. n.* laugh; *pour* ~ for fun; — *s.m.* laugh(ing), laughter.

risque, *s. m.* risk.

risquer, *v.a.* risk, run the risk of.

rivage, *s. m.* beach, shore.

rival, -e, *adj.* & *s. m. f.* rival.

rivalité, *s. f.* rivalry.

rive, *s. f.* bank, shore, beach.

rivière, *s. f.* river, stream.

riz, *s. m.* rice.

robe, *s. f.* gown, dress,

frock; robe; ~ *de chambre* dressing-gown.

robinet, *s. m.* tap, cock.

robuste, *adj.* robust; strong, sturdy.

roc, *s. m.* rock.

roche, *s.f.* rock, boulder.

rocher, *s. m.* rock, crag.

roder, *v. a.* run in.

rôder, *v.n.* rove.

rogner, *v. a.* clip, pare.

rognon, *s. m.* kidney.

roi, *s. m.* king.

rôle, *s. m.* roll; part, rôle.

romain, -e (R.), *adj. & s. m. f.* Roman.

roman, *s. m.* novel; ~*s* fiction.

romançier, -ère, *s. m. f.* novelist.

romanesque, *adj.* romantic.

romantique, *s. m.* romantic.

romantisme, *s. m.* romanticism.

rompre, *v. a. & n.* break.

rond, *adj.* round; — *s. m.* round, circle.

ronde, *s. f.* round; patrol; *à la* ~ round about, around.

rondelle, *s. f.* ring, collar, washer.

ronfler, *v. n.* snore; roar.

ronger, *v.a.* gnaw, eat.

rose, *s. f.* rose; — *adj.* rosy, pink.

roseau, *s. m.* reed.

rosée, *s. f.* dew.

rosier, *s.m.* rose-tree, rose-bush.

rossignol, *s. m.* nightingale.

rôti, *s. m.* roast (meat).

rôtir, *v.a.* roast; toast; *faire* ~ roast, bake.

roucouler, *v. n.* coo.

roue, *s.f.* wheel; ~ *de secours* spare wheel; ~ *dentée* cog-wheel.

rouge, *adj.* red; — *s. m.* red (colour); *bâton de* ~ lipstick.

rougeur, *s.f.* redness, blush.

rougir, *v.n. & a.* turn red, make red; blush.

rouille, *s. f.* rust.

rouiller, *v. n. & a.* rust, get rusty.

roulage, *s.m.* rolling; carriage (of goods); haulage.

rouleau, *s.m.* roll; roller; scroll.

roulement, *s. m.* roll(ing), rotation; ~ *a billes* ball-bearings.

rouler, *v. a. & n.* roll; roll up, wind up; turn, revolve.

roulotte, *s.f.* ~ *(de camping)* caravan.

roumain, -e (R.), *adj. & s. m. f.* Rumanian.

route, *s. f.* road; highway; course; way; *en* ~ on the way; *en* ~ *pour* bound for; *code de la* ~ highway code.

routine, *s. f.* routine.

roux, rousse, *adj.* red-(dish).

royal, *adj.* royal.

royaliste, -e, *adj. & s. m. f.* royalist.

royaume, *s. m.* kingdom.

ruban, *s m.* ribbon; band.

rubis, *s m.* ruby.

ruche, *s. f.* hive.

rude, *adj.* rough, rude.

rue, *s. f.* street; ~ *barrée* no thoroughfare; ~ *de traverse* crossroad.

ruée, *s. f.* rush.

ruelle, *s. f.* lane.

ruer; se ~ rush, dash.

rugissement, *s. m.* roar.

ruine, *s. f.* ruin; wreck.

ruiner, *v.a.* ruin, destroy.

ruisseau, *s. m.* stream, brook; gutter.

ruisseler, *v.n.* stream, run, flow.

rumeur, *s. f.* noise; rumour.

ruminer, *v. a. & n.* ruminate, chew (the cud).

rupture, *s. f.* rupture.

ruse, *s. f.* craft, cunning.

rusé, *adj.* cunning, sly.

russe (R.), *adj. & s. m. f.* Russian.

russien, -enne (R.), *adj. & s. m. f.* Russian.

rustique, *adj.* rustic, rural.

rythme, *s. m.* rhythm.

rythmique, *adj.* rhytmical.

S

s' see **se.**

sa, *adj. poss.* his, her, its.

sable, *s. m.* sand.

sablonneux, -euse, *adj.* sandy.

sabre, *s. m.* sabre.

sac, *s. m.* bag, sack; ~ *a main* handbag; ~ *de couchage* sleeping-bag.

saccager, *v. a.* plunder.

sacré, *adj.* sacred, holy.

sacrement, *s. m.* sacrament.

sacrifice, *s.m.* sacrifice.

sacrifier, *v.a.* sacrifice.

sacristain, *s.m.* sexton.

sage, *adj.* wise, well-behaved.

sagesse, *s. f.* wisdom.

saignant, *adj.* bleeding; underdone.

saigner, *v. a. & n.* bleed.

saillant, *adj.* projecting.

saillir, *v. n.* stand out, project.

sain, *adj.* sound; ~ *et sauf* safe and sound.

saint, -e, *adj.* holy, sa-cred; — *s. m. f.* saint

saisir, *v.a.* seize.

saison, *s. f.* season.

salade, *s. f.* salad.

salaire, *s. m.* wages *(pl.)*, pay, salary.

sale, *adj.* dirty, filthy.

saler, *v. a.* salt.

saleté, *s. f.* dirt.

salière, *s. f.* salt-cellar.

salir, *v. a.* soil, dirty.

salle, *s. f.* hall; assembly room; house; ~ *d'attente* waiting-room; ~ *de classe* schoolroom; ~ *(de cours)* auditorium; ~ *familiale,* ~ *de séjour* living-room.

salon, *s. m.* drawing-room; saloon; *petit* ~ sitting-room.

saluer, *v. a. & n.* bow to; greet.

salut, *s. m.* salvation; bow, greeting.

samedi, *s. m.* Saturday.

sanatorium, *s. m.* sanatorium.

sanction, *s. f.* sanction.

sanctuaire, *s. m.* sanctuary.

sandale, *s. f.* sandal.

sang, *s. m.* blood.

sanglier, *s. m.* wild boar.

sanitaire, *adj.* sanitary.

sans, *prep.* without.

santé, *s. f* health.

sapin, *s. m.* fir(-tree).

sarcasme, *s. m.* sarcasm.

sarcastique, *adj.* sarcastic.

sardine, *s. f.* sardine.

satellite, *s. m.* satellite.

satire, *s. f.* satire.

satisfaction, *s. f.* satisfaction.

savoir*, *v. n.* know, be aware; be trained in; understand; be able to; — *s. m.* knowledge, learning.

savon, *s. m.* soap.

savourer, *v. a.* taste, relish.

savoureux, -euse, *adj.* savoury, tasty.

scandale, *s. m.* scandal.

scaphandre autonome, *s. m.* skin diver.

scaphandrier, *s. m.* diver.

scarabée, *s. m.* beetle.

sceau, *s. m.* seal.

sceller, *v. a.* seal; fix.

scénario, *s. m.* scenario.

scène, *s. f.* scène; scenery; *fig.* stage; *mettre en* ~ produce (a play).

sceptre, *s. m.* sceptre.

scie, *s. f.* saw.

satisfaire, *v. a. & n.* satisfy, please.

satisfaisant, *adj.* satisfactory.

satisfait, *adj.* satisfied.

sauce, *s. f.* sauce.

saucisse, *s. f.* sausage.

sauf, sauve, *adj.* safe; — *prep.* except, save.

saumon, *s. m.* salmon.

saut, *s.m.* jump, leap.

sauter, *v. n.* leap, jump; spring; *faire* ~ blow up.

sauvage, *adj.* savage, wild.

sauver, *v. a.* save, rescue; se ~ run away.

sauveur, *s. m.* Saviour.

savant, -e, *adj.* learned, clever; expert; — *s. m. f.* scholar.

saveur, *s. f.* savour, taste.

science, *s. f.* science, knowledge; *homme de* ~ scientist.

scientifique, *adj.* scientific.

scier, *v. a.* saw.

scolaire, *adj.* school; *année* ~ school year.

scooter, *s. m.* motor-scooter.

scrupule, *s. m.* scruple.

sculpter, *v. a.* carve, sculpture.

sculpteur, *s. m.* sculptor.

sculpture, *s. f.* sculpture.

se, s' *pron.* himself, herself, itself; each other.

séance, *s. f.* sitting, meeting.

seau, *s. m.* pail.

sec, sèche, *adj.* dry, dried up.

sécher, *v. a. & n.* dry (up).

sécheresse, *s. f.* dryness.

second, *adj.* second.

secondaire, *adj.* secondary.

seconde, *s. f.* second.

seconder, *v. a.* back.

secouer, *v. a.* shake.

secourir, *v. a.* help.

secours, *s. m.* help, succour, aid; *au* ~ help!

secousse, *s. f.* shake, jolt, jerk.

secret, -ète, *adj. & s. m.* secret.

secrétaire, *s. m. f.* secretary; — *s. m.* writing-desk.

secrétariat, *s. m.* secretariate.

secteur, *s. m.* sector, section; ~ *(de courant)* mains.

section, *s. f.* section

sécurité, *s. f.* security.

sédatif, -ive, *adj. & s.m.* sedative.

sédiment, *s. m.* sediment.

séduire, *v. a.* seduce.

seigle, *s. m.* rye.

seigneur, *s.m.* lord, squire.

seize, *adj. & s. m.* sixteen; sixteenth.

seizième, *adj.* sixteenth.

séjour, *s. m.* stay, visit; (place of) residence.

séjourner, *v.n.* stay, sojourn.

sel, *s. m.* salt.

selle, *s. f.* saddle.

selon, *prep.* according to; after.

semaine, *s. f.* week.

semblable, *adj.* (a)like.

semblant, *s. m.* semblance; appearance.

sembler, *v. n.* appear, look, seem.

semelle, *s. f.* sole *(footwear)*.

semer, *v. a.* sow.

semestre, *s. m.* half year; semester.

séminaire, *s. m.* seminary.

sénat, *s. m.* senate.

sénateur, *s. m.* senator.

sens, *s. m.* sense; judgement, opinion; direction.

sensation, *s. f.* feeling; sensation.

sensé, *adj.* sensible, reasonable.

sensibilité, *s. f.* sensibility, feeling.

sensible, *adj.* sensible, perceptible; sensitive.

sentence, *s. f.* sentence.

senteur, *s. f.* scent, smell.

sentier, *s. m.* path.

sentiment, *s. m.* feeling, sense, sentiment.

sentimental, *adj.* sentimental.

sentinelle, *s. f.* sentry, sentinel.

sentir*, *v. a.* feel, perceive; experience; smell; se ~ feel.

séparation, *s. f.* separation.

séparer, *v. a.* separate, divide; se ~ part.

sept, *adj. & s. m.* seven; seventh.

septembre, *s. m.* September.

septième, *adj.* seventh.

sérénade, *s. f.* serenade.

sérénité, *s. f.* serenity.

sergent, *s. m.* sergeant.

série, *s. f.* series.

sérieux, -euse, *adj.* grave, serious.

serin, -e, *s. m. f.* canary.

seringue, *s. f.* syringe.

serment, *s. m.* oath.

sermon, *s. m.* sermon.

serpent, *s. m.* snake, serpent.

serpenter, *v. n.* wind, meander.

serre, *s. f.* claw; hothouse.

serré, *adj.* tight, close, serried.

serrer, *v. a.* press, crush, jam, tighten.

serre-tête, *s. m.* crash-helmet, headband.

serrure, *s. f.* lock.

serrurier, *s. m.* locksmith.

servante, *s. f.* servant.

service, *s. m.* service, duty; favour; set; être de ~ be on duty; à votre ~ at your disposal.

serviette, *s. f.* napkin; towel; briefcase.

servir*, *v. a. & n.* serve; be in the service of; ~ à be used for; ne se ~ à rien be of no use; Mme est servie dinner is ready; se ~ use, make use of, help oneself.

serviteur, *s. m.* servant.

servitude, *s. f.* servitude.

ses, *adj. poss.* his, her, its; one's.

session, *s. f.* session.

seuil, *s. m.* threshold.

seul, *adj.* alone, single, sole, only.

sévère, *adj.* severe, hard.

sévir, *v. n.* punish; rage.

sexe, *s. m.* sex.

sexuel, -elle, *adj.* sexual.

shampooing, *s. m.* shampoo.

si, *conj.* if, whether; — *adv.* so, so much, such.

siècle, *s. m.* century.

siège, *s. m.* seat.

sien, -enne, *poss. adj.* his, hers; its; one's.

siffler, *v. n.* whistle, hiss.

sifflet, *s. m.* whistle.

signal, *s. m.* signal; ~ *d'alarme* communication-cord.

signaler, *v. a.* signal.

signalisation, *s. f.* signals *(pl.);* *feux de* ~ traffic-lights.

signature, *s. f.* signature.

signe, *s. m.* sign.

signer, *v. a. & n.* sign.

significatif, -ive, *adj.* significant.

signification, *s. f.* signification; meaning.

signifier, *v. a.* signify.

silence, *s. m.* silence.

silencieux, -euse, *adj.* silent.

silhouette, *s. f.* outline, silhouette.

sillon, *s. m.* furrow.

simple, *adj.* simple.

simplicité, *s. f.* simplicity.

simplifier, *v. a.* simplify.

simultané, *adj.* simultaneous.

sincère, *adj.* sincere.

sincérité, *s. f.* sincerity.

singe, *s. m.* monkey.

singulier, -ère, *adj.* singular, strange.

sinon, *conj.* (or) else, otherwise.

sire, *s. m.* sir, lord.

sirène, *s. f.* siren; hooter, fog-horn.

site, *s. m.* site, place.

sitôt, *adv.* as soon; ~ *que* as soon as; ~ ... ~ no sooner... than.

situation, *s. f.* situation; state; office, position.

situer, *v. a.* place, locate.

six, *adj. & s. m.* six; sixth.

sixième, *adj.* sixth.

ski, *s. m.* ski; *faire du* ~ ski.

skieur, *s. m.* skier, ski-runner.

smoking, *s. m.* dinner-jacket.

sobre, *adj.* sober.

social, *adj.* social.

socialisme, *s. m.* socialism.

socialiste, *adj. & s. m. f.* socialist.

société, *s. f.* society; company; ~ *anonyme* limited liability company.

sœur, *s. f.* sister.

soi, *pron.* oneself; himself, herself; itself.

soi-disant, *adj.* so-called.

soie, *s. f.* silk.

soif, *s. f.* thirst; *avoir* ~ be thirsty.

soigner, *v. a.* take care of, look after.

soigneux, -euse, *adj.* careful.

soin, *s. m.* care; *prendre* ~ *de* take care of; *aux bons* ~s *de* c/o.

soir, *s. m.* evening.

soirée, *s. f.* evening (party).

soit, *conj.* say; suppose; either ... or; ~ *que* whether.

soixante, *adj. & s. m.* sixty.

soixante-dix, *adj. & s. m.* seventy.

sol, *s. m.* soil; ground.

soldat, *s. m.* soldier.

soleil, *s. m.* sun; *il fait du* ~ the sun is shining.

solennel, -elle, *adj.* solemn.

solennité, *s. f.* solemnity.

solidarité, *s. f.* solidarity.

solide, *adj.* solid.
solidité, *s. f.* solidity.
solitaire, *adj.* solitary.
solitude, *s. f.* solitude.
solliciter, *v. a.* solicit, entreat.
sollicitude, *s. f.* care.
soluble, *adj.* soluble.
solution, *s. f.* solution.
sombre, *adj.* dark; dim.
sombrer, *v.n.* founder, sink.
sommaire, *adj. & s. m.* summary.
somme, *s. f.* sum, amount.
sommeil, *s. m.* sleep; *avoir ~* be sleepy.
sommeiller, *v. n.* slumber.
sommer, *v. a.* summon.-
sommet, *s. m.* top, summit.
sommier, *s. m.* spring mattress.
somnifère, *s. m.* sleeping-pill.
somnolent, *adj.* sleepy.
son¹, sa, *adj. poss. (pl. ses)* his, her, its; one's.
son², *s. m.* sound.
songe, *s. m.* dream.
songer, *v. n.* dream.
sonner, *v. a. & n.* ring, sound; *on sonne (à la porte)* there is a ring at the door.
sonnette, *s. f.* bell.
sonore, *adj.* sonorous.
sorcier, *s. m.* sorcerer, wizard.
sorcière, *s. f.* witch, sorceress.
sornette, *s. f.* nonsense.
sort, *s. m.* fate, lot.
sorte, *s. f.* sort, kind.
sortie, *s. f.* going out; way out, exit; *~ secours* emergency exit.
sortir*, *v. n.* go out, walk out, leave; *ne*

pas ~ keep indoors; *v.a.* take out, bring out.
sot, sotte, *adj.* foolish, silly.
sottise, *s. f.* foolishness, nonsense.
sou, *s. m.* sou, copper, penny.
souci, *s. m.* care, concern.
soucier: se *~ de* care for.
soucieux, -euse, *adj.* full of care, anxious.
soucoupe, *s. f.* saucer.
soudain, *adj.* sudden; — *adv.* suddenly.
soude, *s. f.* soda *(chemical)*.
souffle, *s. m.* breath.
souffler, *v.a. & n.* breathe; blow (out).
soufflet, *s. m.* box (on the ear); bellows *(pl.)*.
souffrance, *s. f.* pain, suffering.
souffrir*, *v. a. & n.* suffer, bear.
souhaiter, *v. a.* desire.
soulever, *v. a.* lift, raise; se *~* rise (in rebellion).
soulier, *s. m.* shoe.
souligner, *v. a.* underline.
soumettre, *v. a.* submit, subdue; se *~* submit.
soumission, *s. f.* submission.
soupçon, *s. m.* suspicion.
soupçonner, *v. a.* suspect.
soupe, *s. f.* soup.
souper, *s. m.* supper; — *v. n.* have supper.
soupir, *s. m.* sigh.
soupirer, *v. n.* sigh; *~ après* long for.
souple, *adj.* supple, flexible.
source, *s. f.* source, spring.
sourcil, *s. m.* eyebrow.
sourd, *adj.* deaf.
sourd-muet, sourde-muette, *adj. & s. m. f.* deaf and dumb (per-

son).

sourire, v. n. smile.

souris, s. f. mouse.

sous, prep. under; beneath; before.

souscripteur, s. m. subscriber.

souscription, s. f. subscription.

souscrire, v. a. & n. sign, subscribe (to).

sousdéveloppé, adj. under-developed.

sous-marin, s. m. submarine.

soussigné, -e, adj. & s. m. f. undersigned.

sous-sol, s. m. basement.

sous-titre, s. m. subtitle, caption.

soustraction, s. f. subtraction.

soustraire, v. a. take away; subtract.

soutenir, v. a. support, sustain, maintain.

souterrain, adj. underground; — s. m. subway.

soutien, s. m. support.

soutien-gorge, s. m. bra.

souvenir*, s. m. remembrance; souvenir; memory; — v. reflex. se ~ remember.

souvent, adv. often.

souverain, -e, s. m. f. sovereign.

spatial, adj. vaisseau ~, véhicule ~ space-craft, space-vehicle.

speaker, s. m. announcer.

speakerine, s. f. lady announcer.

spécial, adj. special.

spécialement, adv. specially, particularly.

spécialiser, v. a. specialize.

spécialiste, s. m. f. specialist.

spécialité, s. f. special(i)ty.

spécifier, v. a. specify.

spécifique, adj. specific.

spectacle, s. m. spectacle, sight.

spectateur, -trice, s. m. f. spectator, spectatress, onlooker; bystander.

spéculation, s. f. speculation.

spéculer, v. n. speculate.

sphère, s. f. sphere.

spirale, adj. spiral.

spirituel, -elle, adj. spiritual; witty.

splendeur, s. f. splendour.

splendide, adj. splendid.

spontané, adj. spontaneous.

sport, s. m. sport.

sportif, -ive, adj. sporting; sportsmanlike.

squelette, s. m. skeleton.

stade, s. m. stadium; fig. stage.

stalle, s. f. stall; box.

station, s. f. standing; stay; station, stop; ~ balnéaire watering-place, spa.

stationnement, s. m. stationing; parking; ~ interdit no parking.

stationner, v. n. stop: park.

station-service, s. f. service-station.

statistique, s. f. statistics; — adj. statistical.

statue, s. f. statue.

statut, s. m. statute.

sténographie, s. f. shorthand.

stérile, adj. sterile.

stimuler, v. a. stimulate.

stipuler, v. a. stipulate.

store, s. m. (Venetian) blind.

strabisme, s. m. squint-

(ing).

stratégie, s. f. strategy.

structure, s. f. structure.

studieux, -euse, adj. studious.

stupéfier, v. a. stupefy.

stupide, adj. stupid, dull.

stupidité, s. f. stupidity.

style, s. m. style.

stylo, s.m. ~ à bille ball(-point) pen,

stylo(graphe), s. m. fountain-pen.

suave, adj. soft, gentle.

subjonctif, s.m. subjunctive.

subjuguer, v.a. subjugate, overcome.

submerger, v. a. submerge, flood.

subordonné, adj. subordinate.

subordonner, v. a. subordinate.

subséquent, adj. subsequent.

subsistance, s. f. subsistence.

subsister, v. n. subsist.

substance, s. f. substance.

substantiel, -elle, adj. substantial.

substantif, s.m. substantive.

substituer, v.a. substitute.

substitution, s. f. substitution.

subtil, adj. subtle.

subvention, s. f. subvention, subsidy.

succéder, v. n. succeed (à to), follow; se ~ follow one another.

succès, s. m. success; result.

successif, -ive, adj. successive.

succession, s. f. succession.

sucer, v. a. suck (in).

sucre, s. m. sugar.

sucré, adj. sweet(ened).

sud, adj. & s. m. south; du ~ southern; au ~ southward.

sud-est, adj. & s. m. south-east.

sud-ouest, adj. & s. m. south-west.

suédois, -e, (S.), adj. Swedish; — s. m. f. Swede; Swedish (language).

suer, v. n. & a. sweat.

sueur, s. f. sweat.

suffire*, v.n. be sufficient, be enough.

suffisamment, adv. sufficiently, enough.

suffisant, adj. sufficient, enough; conceited.

suffoquer, v.a. & n. suffocate, choke.

suggérer, v.a. suggest, propose.

suggestion, s. f. suggestion, hint.

suicide, s. m. suicide.

suisse (S.), adj. & s. m. (f. Suissesse) Swiss.

suite, s. f. retinue; suite, sequence, result; a la ~ after; tout de ~ at once, directly; par ~ consequently; par ~ de due to.

suivant, adj. following, next; — prep. according to.

suivre*, v.a. & n. follow; comme suit as follows; ce qui suit the following.

sujet, -ette, s. m. f. subject; s. m. subject.

superficie, s. f. surface, area.

superficiel, -elle, adj. superficial.

superflu, adj. superfluous.

supérieur, adj. superior, upper.

supériorité, s. f. superiority.

supermarché, s. m. supermarket.

supersonique, adj. supersonic.

superstitieux, -euse, adj. superstitious.

superstition, s. f. superstition.

suppléer, v.a. supply; substitute, do duty for; v. n. make up for.

supplément, s. m. supplement; extra charge; excess.

supplémentaire, adj. supplementary, extra.

suppliant, -e, adj. suppliant; — s. m. f. supplicant.

supplier, v.a. beseech.

support, s.m. prop; support.

supporter, v.a. bear, support.

supposer, v. a. suppose.

supposition, s. f. supposition, conjecture.

suppression, s. f. suppression.

supprimer, v. a. suppress, abolish, do away with.

suprême, adj. supreme.

sur, prep. on; over; concerning.

sûr, adj. certain, sure; secure, safe; pour ~l to be sure!

surcharger, v.a. & n. overload; weigh down.

sûrement, adv. surely, certainly.

sûreté, s. f. safety; security.

surface, s.f. surface.

surgir, v. n. arise, spring up, emerge.

surmonter, v.a. surmount, overcome.

surnaturel, -elle, adj. supernatural.

surpasser, v. a. surpass, outdo.

surpeuplé, adj. overcrowded.

surplus, s.m. surplus, excess.

surprendre, v. a. surprise.

surprise, s.f. surprise.

surseoir*, v.n. & a. postpone, delay, put off.

surtaxe, s. f. surtax.

surtout, s. m. overcoat.

surveillance, s. f. supervision.

surveiller, v.a. supervise.

survenir, v. a. arrive unexpectedly; happen, occur.

survivant, -e, s.m.f. survivor.

survivre, v.n. survive, outlive.

susceptible, adj. susceptible.

suspect, adj. suspicious, suspect.

suspendre, v· a. hang up; suspend.

suspension, s. f. suspension.

svelte, adj. slender, slim.

syllabe, s. f. syllable.

symbole, s. m. symbol.

symétrie, s. f. symmetry.

symétrique, adj. symmetrical.

sympathie, s. f. sympathy.

symphonie, s.f. symphony.

symptome, s. m. symptom.

synagogue, s.f. synagogue.

syndical, adj. trade.

syndicat, s. m. syndicate; trade-union; ~d'initiative tourist information office.

synthétique, adj. synthetic(al).

systématique, adj. systematic.

système, *s. m.* system.

T

tabac, *s.m.* tobacco; *bureau de* ~ tobacconist's (shop).

table, *s. f.* table; board; food; ~ *des matières*, table of contents.

tableau, *s.m.* picture; scene; board, panel.

tablette, *s. f.* tablet.

tablier, *s.m.* apron; dash-board.

tabouret, *s. m.* stool.

tache, *s. f.* spot, stain; *sans* ~ spotless.

tâche, *s. f.* task, job.

tacher, *v.a.* spot, stain.

tâcher, *v.n.* try.

tact, *s. m.* touch.

tactique, *s.f.* tactics.

taille, *s.f.* cut; height, stature, size; waist.

tailler, *v.a.* hew, trim; cut.

tailleur, *s. m.* tailor.

taire*, *v.a.* be silent about, conceal; *se* ~ be quiet.

talent, *s. m.* talent, attainment(s).

talon, *s. m.* heel; counterfoil.

talus, *s. m.* slope, bank.

tambour, *s. m.* drum.

tamis, *s. m.* sieve.

tamiser, *v. a.* sift, sieve.

tampon, *s. m.* plug; tampon.

tamponner, *v. a.* plug.

tandis que, *conj.* whereas, while.

tangible, *adj.* tangible.

tant, *adv.* so much, so many, such, so.

tante, *s. f.* aunt.

tantôt, *adv.* shortly, by and by; ~ ... ~ now ... now.

tapage, *s. m.* noise, fuss.

taper, *v.a. & n.* tap, strike, knock; type.

tapis, *s. m.* carpet, rug.

tapisser, *v. a.* upholster.

tapisserie, *s. f.* tapestry.

tapissier, *s. m.* upholsterer.

tard, *adv.* late.

tarder, *v.n.* delay, put off; be long.

tardif, -ive, *adj.* late.

tarif, *s.m.* tariff, rate; price-list; fare.

tarte, *s. f.* tart.

tas, *s. m.* heap, pile; mass; crowd.

tasse, *s. f.* cup.

tâter, *v.a. & n.* feel, taste, handle.

tâtonner, *v.n.* grope.

taureau, *s.m.* bull.

taux, *s.m.* price, rate (of exchange); tax.

taverne, *s. f.* tavern.

taxe, *s. f.* tax.

taxer, *v. a.* tax, rate.

taxi, *s. m.* taxi; *station de* ~s taxi-rank.

tchèque (T.), *adj. & s. m. f.* Czech.

te, *pron.* you; to you.

technicien, -enne, *s. m. f.* technician.

technique, *adj.* technical; *s. f.* technique, technics.

technologie, *s. f.* technology.

teindre*, *v.a.* dye, stain.

teint, *s. m.* complexion; dye.

teinte, *s. f.* tint, shade.

teinter, *v. a.* tint.

teinture, *s. f.* dye; tincture.

teinturerie, *s.f.* dyeworks, dyer.

tel, telle, *adj.* such, like, similar.

télécommunication, s.f. telecommunication.

téléférique, s.m. ropeway.

télégramme, s.m. telegram, wire.

télégraphe, s.m. telegraph.

télégraphie, s.f. telegraphy.

télégraphier, v.a. & n. wire.

télégraphique, adj. telegraphic.

télémètre, s.m. rangefinder.

téléphone, s.m. telephone.

télescope, s. m. telescope.

téléspectateur, -trice, s. m. f. (tele)viewer.

téléviser, v. a. televise, telecast.

téléviseur, s.m. television-set.

télévison, s. f. television.

télex, s. m. telex.

tellement, adv. so (much).

témoigner, v.a. & n. testify; give evidence.

témoin, s.m. witness; testimony.

tempe, s.f. temple (forehead).

tempérament, s. m. temper(ament), constitution.

température, s.f. temperature.

tempête, s. f. storm.

temple, s. m. temple, church; chapel; lodge.

temporel, -elle, adj. temporal, transient.

temps¹, s. m. time; opportunity; à ~ in time; pendant ce ~ l in the meantime; en ~ voulu in due time; combien de ~? how long?; la plupart du ~ mostly; de ~ en ~ at times.

temps², s.m. weather; prévisions du ~ weather-forecast.

tenaille, s.f. pincers, pliers, tongs (pl.).

tendance, s. f . tendency, trend.

tendon, s.m. tendon, sinew.

tendre¹ ¹adj. tender, soft.

tendre², v.a. stretch; strain; bend; hang.

tendresse, s. f. tenderness.

tendu, adj. tense, taut.

ténébreux, -euse, adj. dark, gloomy, dismal.

tenir*, v. a. & n. hold; get hold of; hold on; take, contain; keep; se ~ stay, remain.

tennis, s. m. tennis.

tension, s.f. tension.

tentation, s. f. temptation.

tentative, s. f. attempt.

tente, s. f. tent.

tenter, v.a. attempt; try; tempt.

ténu, adj. thin, slender.

tenue, s. f. holding; session; behaviour.

terme, s. m. term; expression; goal, aim.

terminer, v. a. terminate, end, close; se ~ (come to an) end.

terminus, s. m. terminus.

terne, adj. dull, dim.

terrain, s. m. soil, earth; site; ground; ~ de jeux sports-ground.

terrasse, s.f. terrace.

terre, s.f. earth, land.

terreur, s.f. fear.

terrible, adj. terrible.

terrifier, v.a. terrify, frighten.

territoire, s. m. territory.

testament, s.m. will, testament.

tête, s. f. head.

têtu, *adj.* stubborn.

texte, *s.m.* text; type.

textile, *s.m.* textile.

textuel, -elle, *adj.* textual.

texture, *s. f.* texture.

thé, *s. m.* tea.

théâtral, *adj.* theatrical.

théâtre, *s.m.* theatre, stage; drama; *pièce de ~* play.

théière, *s. f.* tea-pot.

thème, *s. m.* theme, topic; prose.

théologie, *s. f.* theology.

théologique, *adj.* theological.

théorie, *s. f.* theory.

théorique, *adj.* theoretic, theoretical.

thermal, *adj.* thermal.

thermomètre, *s. m.* thermometer.

thermos, *s. f.* thermos.

thèse, *s. f.* thesis.

thon, *s. m.* tunny.

tien, -enne, *poss. adj.* yours.

tiers, tierce, *adj.* third; — *s.m.* third party.

tige, *s. f.* stem, stalk.

tigre, *s. m.* tiger.

tigresse, *s. f.* tigress.

timbre, *s. m.* bell; sound; (postage-)stamp.

timbre-poste, *s. m.* postage-stamp.

timide, *adj.* timid, shy.

timidité, *s. f.* timidity.

tir, *s.m.* shooting.

tirage, *s.f.* draught, pull(ing); impression; issue.

tire-bouchon *s. m.* corkscrew.

tirer, *v. a. & n.* draw, pull, drag; extract; derive; fire, shoot; print.

tiroir, *s.m.* drawer.

tison, *s.m.* brand.

tisonnier, *s.m.* poker.

tisser, *v.a.* weave.

tisserand, *s.m.* weaver.

tissu, *s. m.* texture, fabric; tissue.

titre, *s. m.* title; heading; right.

titrer, *v.a.* give a title to.

toast, *s. m.* toast.

toi, *pron.* you.

toile, *s. f.* linen; cloth.

toilette, *s.f.* dress, clothes *(pl.);* dressing-table; *faire sa ~* dress; *cabinet de ~* dressing-room.

toison, *s. f.* fleece.

toit, *s. m.* roof.

tolérance, *s. f.* tolerance, toleration.

tolérer, *v.a.* tolerate, bear.

tomate, *s.f.* tomato.

tombe, *s. f.* tomb, grave.

tombeau, *s. m.* tomb.

tombée, *s.f.* fall.

tomber, *v.n.* fall, fall down; tumble; decay; *~ sur* meet, run into; *faire ~* push down; *laisser ~* drop.

tome, *s. m.* volume.

ton[1], ta, *poss. adj. (pl.* tes) your.

ton[2], *s. m.* tone; colour; manner.

tondeuse, *s.f.* lawn-mower.

tondre, *v.a.* shear, clip, mow.

tonnage, *s. m.* tonnage.

tonne, *s. f.* barrel, tun; ton.

tonneau, *s.m.* barrel.

tonner, *v.n.* thunder.

tonnerre, *s.m.* thunder-(bolt).

toqué, *adj.* crazy.

torche, *s. f.* torch.

torcher, *v.a.* wipe, rub.

torchon, *s.m.* duster; dish-cloth.

tordre, *v. a.* twist, wring

(out).

torpille, s. f. torpedo.
torrent, s. m. torrent.
tort, s. m. wrong, harm, injury; *avoir* ~ be wrong.
tortue, s. f. tortoise.
torture, s. f. torture.
torturer, v. a. torture.
tôt, adv. soon, quickly; early.
total, adj. total, whole.
totalement, adv. totally, entirely.
touchant, prep. about.
touche, s. f. touch; key; hit.
toucher, v. n. & a. touch; feel; strike, hit; concern; — s. m. touch; feeling.
touffe, s. f. tuft.
toujours, adv. always, ever; still.
toupet, s. m. tuft, lock.
tour¹, s.f. tower.
tour², s.m. turn; tour, trip; feat, trick; (turning-)lathe; revolution; ~ ⊂ ~ in turns; ⊔ son ~ in turn; *faire le* ~ *de* go round.
tourelle, s. f. turret.
tourisme, s. m. tourism; touring; *faire du* ~ *à pied* hike.
touriste, s. m. f. tourist, hiker.
tourment, s. m. torment, torture.
tourmenter, v. a. torment; se ~ worry.
tournant, adj. turning; — s. m. turn(ing).
tourné, adj. turned; sour.
tournée, s. f. tour, walk; circuit.
tourner, v. a. turn, twist, wind; turn round; v. n. turn, revolve; turn out; turn sour.

tournevis, s.m. screwdriver.
tournoi, s.m. tournament.
tournure, s.f. shape, figure; turn; cast; appearance.
tous see **tout.**
tousser, v.n. cough.
tout, -e, adj. (pl. **tous, toutes**) all, every, any, whole, full; ~ *le monde* everybody; ~ *son possible* one's utmost; à ~e *force* at any cost; — adv. wholly, entirely; ~ *coup* suddenly; ~ *fait* thoroughly; ~ *de suite* directly; ~ à *l'heure* just now; ~ *au moins* at least; — pron. & s.m.everything, all; *pas du* ~ not at all.
toutefois, adv. yet, nevertheless, however.
tout-puissant, adj. almighty.
toux, s. f. cough.
tracas, s. m. bustle, stir; worry.
tracasser, v. n. & a. worry, bother; fuss; se ~ worry.
trace, s. f. trace, track; footprint.
tracer, v. a. trace, draw; lay out.
tracteur, s. m. tractor.
traction, s.f. traction, pull.
tradition, s. f. tradition.
traditionnel, -elle, adj. traditional.
traducteur, -trice, s. m. f. translator.
traduction, s. f. translation.
traduire*, v. a. translate.
trafic, s. m. traffic; trade, commerce.
trafiquer, v.n. traffic;

trade, deal.

tragédie, *s. f.* tragedy.

tragédien, -enne, *s. m. .f.* tragedien.

tragique, *adj.* tragic.

trahir, *v. a.* betray; deceive, mislead.

trahison, *s. f.* treason, treachery.

train, *s.m.* pace, rate; train; ∼ *couloir* corridor-train; ∼ *direct* through train; ∼ *de marchandises* goods train.

traîne, *s.f.* train (of a dress).

traîneau, *s. m.* sledge.

traîner, *v.a.* drag, draw; lead (to); delay; *v.n.* drag; lie about: lag behind.

train-poste, *s.m* mail-train.

traire*, *v.a.* milk.

trait, *s.m.* arrow; dart; flash; line; trait, feature.

traite, *s.f.* journey; stretch; export; draft, bill.

traité, *s. m.* treaty.

traitement, *s. m.* treatment; usage; reception; salary.

traiter, *v.a.* treat, use, deal with; call; entertain.

traître, *s. m.* traitor; — *adj.* treacherous.

trajet, *s.m.* passage, journey, course, crossing.

tram, *s.m.* tram(-car).

trammer, *v. a.* weave; plot; devise.

tramway, *s. m.* tram.

tranchant, *adj.* sharp, keen.

tranche, *s. f.* slice, chop, steak.

trancher, *v.a. & n.* cut; cut off; carve; break off.

tranquille, *adj.* quiet, calm; *soyez* ∼*!* don't worry!

tranquilliser, *v. a.* soothe, calm; se ∼ keep calm.

transaction, *s. f.* compromise, transaction.

transalpin, *adj.* transalpine.

transatlantique, *adj.* transatlantic; — *s. f.* deck-chair.

transfert, *s. m.* transfer.

transformation, *s. f.* transformation, change.

transformer, *v.a.* transform, convert.

transfusion, *s.f.* transfusion.

transistor, *s. m.* transistor.

transit, *s.m.* transit.

transition, *s.f.* transition.

transmettre, *v. a.* transmit; forward; pass on.

transmission, *s. f.* transmission.

transparent, *adj.* transparent.

transpiration, *s.f.* perspiration.

transpirer, *v. n.* perspire.

transport, *s. m.* transport, conveyance; *enterprise de* ∼ forwarding agency.

transporter, *v.a.* transport, convey; transfer; enrapture.

trappe, *s. f.* trap; trapdoor.

travail, *s. m. (pl. -aux)* work, job, employment; task; piece of work; workmanship; *petits travaux* odd jobs; *sans* ∼ unemployed.

travailler, *v.n. & a.* work, labour; take pains.

travailleur, -euse, *s. m. f.* worker, workman, workwoman.

travers, *s. m.* breadth; *à* ~ across, through; *au* ~ *de* through; *en* ~ across.

traverse, *s.f.* traverse; obstacle; crossing.

traversée, *s.f.* crossing, passage.

traverser, *v. a.* traverse, cross, go through; run through.

trayeuse, *s. f.* milking-machine.

trébucher, *v. n.* stumble; turn the scale.

tréfle, *s. m.* clover; club *(cards)*.

treille, *s. f.* vine arbour.

treize, *adj. & s.m.* thirteen!

tremblant, *adj.* tembling, shaky.

tremblement, *s. m.* trembling, shaking; ~ *de terre* earthquake.

trembler, *v. n.* tremble, shake.

tremper, *v. a.* soak, wet; dip; *il est tout trempé* he is wet through.

tremplin, *s.m.* springboard.

trentaine, *s.m.* thirty.

trente, *adj. & s. m.* thirty; thirtieth.

très, *adv.* very, most, very much; ~ *bien* very well; all right.

trésor, *s. m.* treasure.

trésorie, *s. f.* treasury.

trésorier, *s. m.* treasurer

tresse, *s. f.* plait, tress, braid.

trêve, *s. f.* truce, rest; *faire* ~ stop, cease.

triangle, *s. m.* triangle.

tribu, *s. f.* tribe.

tribunal, *s. m.* tribunal, law-court.

tribune, *s.f.* tribune, platform; grand-stand.

tributaire, *adj.* tributary.

tricher, *v. n. & a.* cheat; trick (s.o. out of).

tricot, *s.m.* (knitted) jersey.

tricoter, *v. a. & n.* knit.

triomphant, *adj.* triumphant.

triomphe, *s. m.* triumph.

triompher, *v. n.* triumph.

triple, *adj.* triple.

tripot, *s.m.* gambling-den.

triste, *adj.* sad.

tristesse, *s. f.* sadness.

trivial, *adj.* trivial.

trois, *adj. & s. m.* three; third.

troisième, *adj. & s. m.* third.

trolley, *s.m.* trolley (-pole).

trolleybus, *s. m.* trolleybus.

trompe, *s.f.* trumpet, horn.

tromper, *v. a.* deceive, cheat, take in; se ~ mistake, be mistaken; be wrong; *se ~ de train* take the wrong train.

trompette, *s. f.* trumpet; trumpeter.

tronc, *s. m.* trunk; stock; collecting box.

trône, *s.m.* throne.

trop, *adv.* too; too much.

trophée, *s. m.* trophy.

tropical, *adj.* tropical.

tropique, *s. m.* tropic.

trot, *s. m.* trot.

trotter, *v. n.* trot.

trottoir, *s. m.* pavement; footway.

trou, *s.m.* hole; gap; opening.

trouble, *s. m.* disorder; confusion; misunderstanding; dispute; — *adj.* troubled; muddy.

troubler, *v.a.* stir up,

disturb; make muddy;
muddle; confuse, per-
plex; upset; trouble.

troué, *s. f.* opening, gap.

trouer, *v. a.* make a hole
in; pierce; bore.

troupe, *s. f.* troop, band.

troupeau, *s.m.* herd,
drove; flock.

trouvaille, *s. f.* find(ing)

trouver, *v. a.* find, discover; find out; think;
contrive; se ~ be, be
found to be, prove;
turn out, happen; *je
me trouvais là* I hap-
pened to be there.

truite, *s. f.* trout.

trust, *s. m.* trust.

T.S.F., *s. f.* (=*télégraphie sans fil)* wireless
(set).

tu, toi, *pron.* you.

tube, *s. m.* tube; pipe; ~
de télévision TV tube.

tuberculose, *s. f.* tuber-
culosis.

tuer, *v. a.* kill; slay.

tuile, *s. f.* tile.

tumeur, *s. f.* tumour.

tunnel, *s. m.* tunnel.

turbine, *s. f.* turbine.

turbopropulseur, *s. m.*
turbo-prop aircraft.

turboréacteur, *s.m.* turbo-jet engine.

turc, turque (T.), *adj.* Turkish (language), Turk.

tuteur, -trice, *s.m.f.*
guardian, trustee.

tutoyer, *v. a.* to 'thee-and
thou' s. o.

tuyau, *s. m.* pipe, tube;
flue; ~ *d'échappement*
exhaust-pipe.

tympan, *s. m.* ear-drum.

type, *s. m.* type.

typique, *adj.* typical.

typographie, *s. f.* typo-
graphy; printing.

tyran, *s. m.* tyrant.

tyrannie, *s. f.* tyranny.

tyranniser, *v. a.* tyrannize
(over); oppress.

U

ulcère, *s. m.* ulcer.

ultérieur, *adj.* ulterior;
further.

ultime, *adj.* ultimate, last,
final.

ultra-violet-, -ette, *adj.*
ulra-violet.

un, une, *art. & pron.* a,
an; any, some; one;
l'~ ou l'autre either
one or the other; *ni
l'~ ni l'autre* neither
one; *l'~ et autre* both;
~*e fois* once; ~ *à* ~ one
by one.

unanime, *adj.* unanimous.

uni, *adj.* smooth, even,
level; united.

unification, *s. f.* unification.

unifier, *v. a.* unify; unite.

uniforme, *adj.* uniform.

union, *s. f.* union; agreement: match, marriage.

unique, *adj.* unique, sole,
only.

uniquement, *adv.* solely,
only.

unir, *v.a.* unite; level,
smooth; s'~ join.

unité, *s.f.* unity; unit.

univers, *s. m.* universe.

universel, -elle, *adj.* universal; world-wide.

universitaire, *adj.* academic, university.

université, *s.f.* university.

urbain, *adj.* urban.

urgence, *s.f.* urgency;
d'~ urgent; *en cas d'~*
in case of emergency.

urgent, *adj.* urgent, pressing.

uriner, *v. n. & a.* urinate.

urne, *s. f.* urn.

usage, *s. m.* use, custom;

habit, way; wear; *d'~* usual, habitual; *en ~* in use.

usé, *adj.* worn-out, shabby.

user, *v. n. & a.* use, make use of; wear out; use up; — *s.m.* wear, service, use; *être d'un bon ~* wear well.

usine, *s. f.* factory, works.

ustensile, *s. m.* utensil; implement, tool.

usuel, -elle, *adj.* usual, customary.

usure[1], *s. f.* usury.

usure[2], *s. f.* wear (and tear).

usurper, *v.a.* usurp.

utile, *adj.* useful, of use, profitable; *être ~ ( )* be of use.

utilisation, *s.f.* utilization.

utiliser, *v.a.* utilize.

utilité, *s. f.* utility, use.

V

va *int.* agreed!, indeed.

vacance, *s. f.* vacancy; *(pl.),* holiday(s), vacation; *être en ~s* be on holiday.

vacant, *adj.* vacant.

vacarme, *s.m.* noise, uproar.

vaccin, *s.m.* vaccine.

vacciner, *v. a.* vaccinate.

vache, *s.f.* cow.

vaciller, *v.n.* vacillate; reel; waver.

vacuum, *s. m.* vacuum.

vagabond, *s. m.* trampe.

vague[1], *adj.* vague.

vague[2], *s.f.* wave.

vaillant, *adj.* valiant.

vain, *adj.* vain; empty; *en ~* in vain.

vaincre*, *v. a. & n.* conquer, defeat.

vainqueur, *s.m.* conqueror, victor; — *adj.* conquering, victorious.

vaisseau, *s. m.* vessel; ship.

vaisselle, *s. f.* plates and dishes, table-service; *laver la ~* wash up the dishes; *lavage de ~* washing-up.

valet, *s. m.* valet; knave, jack.

valeur, *s. f.* value, worth; price; courage; *~s* securities.

valide, *adj.* valid; able-bodied.

validité, *s.f.* validity.

valise, *s. f.* valise, (travelling-)bag; suitcase; *~ diplomatique* dispatch-box, diplomatic bag.

vallée, *s. f.* valley.

valoir*, *v.n. & a.* be worth, be as good as; deserve; procure; yield.

valse, *s.f.* waltz.

vanille, *s.f.* vanilla.

vanité, *s.f.* vanity.

vaniteux, -euse, *adj.* vain, conceited.

vanter, *v. a.* extol, cry up; *se ~* boast.

vapeur[1], *s.f.* steam; vapour.

vapeur[2], *s.m.* steamer.

vaporeux, -euse, *adj.* vaporous.

vaquer, *v. n.* be vacant.

variable, *adj.* variable, changeable.

variante, *s.f.* variant.

variation, *s.f.* variation.

varier, *v. n. & a.* vary; *~ de ... a* range from ... to.

variété, *s. f.* variety.

vase, *s. m.* vase; vessel.

vaseline, *s. f.* vaseline.

vassal, *s. m.* vassal.

vaste, *adj.* vast; spacious.
vautour, *s. m.* vulture.
veau, *s. m.* veal; calf.
vedette, *s.f.* mounted sentinel; motor-boat; (film) star.
végétal, *s. m.* vegetable; plant.
végétation, *s. f.* vegetation.
végéter, *v. n.* vegetate.
véhémence, *s. f.* vehemence.
véhément, *adj.* vehement.
véhicule, *s. m.* vehicle.
véhiculer, *v. a.* transport.
veille, *s. f.* waking; vigil; eve.
veiller, *v. n.* sit up, keep watch; *v.a.* watch.
veine, *s. f.* vein; luck.
vélo, *s.m.* bike.
vélocité, *s.f.* velocity.
velours, *s.m.* velvet.
velouté, *adj.* velvety, soft.
velu, *adj.* hairy.
venaison, *s.f.* venison.
vendange, *s.f.* vintage, grape-harvest.
vendeur, -euse, *s. m. f.* salesman, shop assistant; saleswoman.
vendre, *v. a.* sell; *à ~* for sale.
vendredi, *s. m.* Friday; *le ~ saint* Good Friday.
vénéneux, -euse, *adj.* poisonous.
vénérable, *adj.* venerable.
vengeance, *s. f.* vengeance, revenge.
venger, *v.a.* avenge, revenge; *se ~* avenge oneself.
venin, *s.m.* poison.
venir*, *v. n.* come, arrive; grow; occur; arise; *~ de* come from; *~ à bout de* manage.
vent, *s. m.* wind; *grand ~* gale; *~ alizé* trade-wind.
vente, *s. f.* sale; auction; *en ~* for sale.
venteux, -euse, *adj.* windy.
ventilateur, *s. m.* ventilator.
ventilation, *s. f.* ventilation.
ventre, *s. m.* belly.
venue, *s.f.* coming, arrival.
ver, *s.m.* worm.
verbal, *adj.* verbal, oral.
verbe, *s.m.* verb.
verdeur, *s.f.* greenness; harshness.
verdict, *s.m.* verdict.
verdure, *s.f.* verdure; greenness.
verger, *s.m.* orchard.
vergue, *s.f.* yard.
vérification, *s.f.* verification; check(ing).
vérifier, *v.a.* verify; check; confirm.
vérité, *s.f.* truth.
vermicelle, *s.m.* vermicelli.
vernir, *v. a.* varnish; polish.
vernis, *s.m.* varnish; polish.
verre, *s.m.* glass.
verrou, *s.m.* bolt.
verrouiller, *v.a.* bolt.
vers[1], *s.m.* line; verse.
vers[2], *prep.* towards, to; about.
verser, *v. a.* pour (out) spill, upset; *v. n.* overturn.
version, *s. f.* translation; version.
vert, *adj.* green; hearty; sharp.
vertical, *adj.* vertical, upright.
vertige, *s. m.* dizziness.
vertu, *s.f.* virtue.
vessie, *s.f.* bladder.
veste, *s. f.* coat, jacket.
vestiaire, *s. m.* cloakroom.

vestibule, s.m. lobby, hall; grand ~ lounge.

veston, s. m. coat; complet ~ lounge-suit.

vêtement, s.m. clothes (pl.); ~s de dessous underwear, underclothes.

vétéran, s.m. veteran.

vétérinaire, s. m. veterinary surgeon, vet.

vêtir*, v. a. clothe, dress.

véto, s.m. veto.

veuf, s.m. widower.

veuve, s.f. widow.

vexer, v. a. vex, annoy.

via, prep. via.

viaduc, s. m. viaduct.

viande, s. m. meat; ~ réfrigérée chilled meat.

vibration, s. f. vibration.

vibrer, v. n. vibrate.

vicaire, s.m. curate.

vice, s.m. vice, evil.

vice-, prefix vice-

vicieux, -euse, adj. vicious; faulty.

vicomte, s. m. viscount.

victime, s.f. victim.

victoire, s.f. victory.

victorieux, -euse, adj. victorious.

victuailles, s. f. pl. victuals.

vide, adj. empty; void; vacant; — s.m. space.

vider, v. a. empty; drain.

vie, s.f. life.

vieillard, s.m. old man.

vieillesse, s.f. old age.

vieillir, v.n. grow old.

vierge, s. f. virgin, maid.

vieux, vieil, vieille, adj. old.

vif, vive, adj. live; quick; lively; full of life; bright, vivid; fiery, ardent.

vigilant, adj. watchful.

vigne, s.f. vine; vineyard.

vignoble, s.m. vineyard.

vigoureux, -euse, adj. vigorous.

vigueur, s.f. vigour force.

vilain, s. m. villain, cac

village, s.m. village.

ville, s. f. town, city; hôtel de ~ town hall.

vin, s. m. wine.

vinaigre, s. m. vinegar.

vingt, adj. & s.m. twenty; twentieth.

vingtième, adj. twentieth.

violation, s.f. violation.

violence, s.f. violence.

violent, adj. violent; excessive.

violer, v. a. violate, ravish.

violette, s.f. violet.

violon, s.m. violin.

violoncelle, s. m. (violon-) cello.

violoniste, s. m f. violinist.

vipère, s.f. viper.

virgule, s.f. comma; point et ~ semicolon.

virtuose, s. m. f. virtuoso.

vis, s. f. screw.

visa, s.m. visa, visé.

visage, s. m. face.

vis-à-vis, prep. opposite; facing.

viser, v.a. aim (at); aspire to.

viseur, s. m. view-finder.

visibilité, s. f. visibility.

visible, adj. visible.

vision, s.f. sight.

visite, s. f. visit; faire ~ à pay a visit to, call on.

visiter, v. a. visit; ~ les curiosités go sightseeing.

visiteur, -euse, s. m. f. visitor.

visser, v. a. screw (down, in).

visuel, -elle, adj. visual.

vital, adj. vital.

vitalité, s.f. vitality.

vitamine, s. f. vitamin.
vite, adj. fast; swift; — adv. fast, rapidly.
vitesse, s. f. speed; rate (of speed); gear; à toute ~ at top speed; boîte de ~ gear-box; ~ de croisière cruising speed.
vitrail s. m. church window.
vitre, s. f. pane.
vitrier, s.m. glazier.
vivant, adj. alive, living; full of life; de mon ~ in my lifetime.
vivement, adv. quickly, fast.
vivre*, v. n. live, be alive.
vocabulaire, s. m. vocabulary.
vocation, s.f. vocation, calling.
vœu, s. m. (pl. -x) wish, desire; vow.
vogue, s. f. vogue, fashion; avoir la ~ be in vogue.
voici, prep. here (is); le ~! here he is!
voie, s.f. way, road; route; line, track; means, channel.
voilà, prep. there (is).
voile¹, s.m. veil.
voile², s.f. sail.
voiler, v.a. veil, cover, hide.
voilier, s. m. sailing-ship.
voir*, v. a. see; look at; view; faire ~ show; ne pas ~ miss.
voire, adv. even.
voisin, adj. neighbouring, adjoining, next (door).
voisinage, s.m. neighbourhood.
voiture, s.f. vehicle, conveyance; carriage; car; coach; van; wagon; aller en ~ drive.
voiture-ambulance, s. f.

ambulance(-car).
voix, s. f. voice; sound; à haute ~ aloud.
vol¹, s. m. flying, flight.
vol², s. m. theft, robbery.
volaille, s.f. poultry, fowl.
volant, s.m. steering-wheel.
volcan, s.m. volcano.
volée, s.f. flight.
voler¹, v. n. fly; run at top speed.
voler², v. a. & n. steal, rob.
volet, s.m. shutter.
voleur, s. m. thief, robber.
volontaire, adj. voluntary; — s. m. f. volunteer.
volonté, s. f. will; à ~ at will.
volontiers, adv. willingly.
volt, s.m. volt.
voltiger, v.n. flutter about, fly about.
volume, s. m. volume; bulk.
voluptueux, -euse, adj. voluptuous.
vomir, v. a. & n. vomit, be sick.
vos, adj. poss. your.
vote, s. m. vote; voting.
voter, v. n. ~ & a. vote.
votre, adj. yours.
vouer, v. a. vow; dedicate.
vouloir*, v. a. want, require, demand; ~ bien be willing; je voudrais + inf. I should like to; comme vous voulez as you please.
vous, pron. you; to you.
vous-même, pron. yourself.
voûte, s.f. vault, arch.
voyage, s.m. journey; voyage; bon ~! a pleasant journey (to

you)!; *partir en* ~ set off on a journey; *faire un* ~ make a journey.

voyager, *v.n.* travel, make a trip.

voyageur, -euse, *s. m. f.* traveller, passenger.

voyelle, *s.f.* vowel.

voyou, *s.m.* hooligan.

vrai, *adj.* real, true, right; *être* ~ hold (good); — *s. m.* truth; *être dans le* ~ be right.

vraiment, *adv.* truly, really; indeed.

vraisemblable, *adj.* likely, credible, probable.

vu, *prep.* considering.

vue, *s. f.* sight; vision; view; *à* ~ at sight; *en* ~ *de* with a view to; *point de* ~ point of view; *avoir la* ~ *courte* be short-sighted; *être en* ~ be in the limelight.

vulgaire, *adj.* vulgar; common; coarse.

W

wagon, *s. m.* coach, carriage, car.

wagon-lit, *s. m.* sleeping-car.

wagonnet, *s.m.* tub; truck.

wagon-poste, *s. m.* mail-van.

wagon-restaurant, *s. m.* dining-car.

water-closet, *s. m.* W. C.

water-polo, *s. m.* water-polo.

wattman, *s.m.* tram-driver.

week-end, *s.m.* week-end.

whisky, *s.m.* whisky.

X

xérès, *s. m.* sherry.

xylographie, *s. f.* xylography.

xylophages, *s.m.* *pl.* xylophages.

Y

y, *adv.* here, there; *il* ~ *a* there is, there exists; *s'*~ *connaître* well informed.

vacht, *s. m.* yacht.

yeux *see* œil.

yogourt, yoghourt, *s. m.* yoghourt, yaourt.

yougoslave, *adj.* Yugoslav.

youyou, *s.m.* dinghy.

Z

zèbre, *s.m.* zebra.

zébrer, *v.a.* stripe.

zèle, *s.m.* zeal.

zélé, *adj.* zealous.

zénith, *s.m* zenith.

zéro, *s.m.* zero.

zézayer, *v.n.* lisp.

zigzag, *s.m.* zigzag.

zinc, *s.m.* zinc.

zone, *s.f.* zone, belt.

zoo, *s.m.* zoo.

zoologie, *s.f.* zoology.

zoologique, *adj.* zoological.

zut, *int.* ~*!* damn it!